LATIN

Story of a World Language

———◆———

JÜRGEN LEONHARDT

Translated by
Kenneth Kronenberg

THE BELKNAP PRESS OF
HARVARD UNIVERSITY PRESS
Cambridge, Massachusetts
London, England
2013

First published as *Latein: Geschichte einer Weltsprache,*
copyright © 2009 Verlag C. H. Beck oHG, Munich

The translation of this work was funded by Geisteswissenschaften
International—Translation Funding for Humanities and Social Sciences
from Germany, a joint initiative of the Fritz Thyssen Foundation,
the German Federal Foreign Office, the collecting society VG WORT,
and the Börsenverein des Deutschen Buchhandels
(German Publishers and Booksellers Association).

Library of Congress Cataloging-in-Publication Data

Leonhardt, Jürgen, 1957–
[Latein. English]
Latin : story of a world language / Jürgen Leonhardt ;
Translated by Kenneth Kronenberg.
pages cm
First published as Latein: Geschichte einer Weltsprache,
copyright © 2009 Verlag C.H. Beck oHG, Munich.
Includes bibliographical references and index.
ISBN 978-0-674-05807-1 (alk. paper)
1. Latin language—History. 2. Latin language—Study and teaching—History.
3. Latin language—Technical Latin—History. 4. Latin language,
Colloquial—History. 5. Latin language, Vulgar—History.
6. Latin literature—History. 7. Latin philology—History.
I. Kronenberg, Kenneth, 1946– translator.
PA2057.L4613 2013
470.9—dc23   2013010948

Contents

Preface to the German Edition

There are basically two ways to answer the question of whether Latin is a dead or a living language. It is certainly true that no community now exists in which Latin is the mother tongue, and in this respect Latin may be called a dead language. On the other hand, one is also justified in saying that Latin will be alive as long as there are people who speak and write it at all. The first answer reflects the perspective of linguistics, which does not view the Latin from the Middle Ages to the present as a normal language. The second answer is that of literary and cultural studies, which examines Europe's long-lasting Latin tradition.

The purpose of this book is to reconcile the contradiction between these two answers by melding linguistics and cultural history. As such, the book goes beyond the purely Latin because Latin culture in antiquity would have been inconceivable without Greek culture, and after the end of antiquity really cannot be examined without reference to the vernacular languages of Europe. We can come to grips with Europe's Latin cultural tradition only if we take into account the totality of the multilingual communications space in which it has always evolved.

In one way or another, I have been working on the topic of this book ever since I wrote my dissertation and for the first time engaged with Latin instruction as it was practiced during late antiquity. Among other things, I learned that our modern approach to learning and using a language does not reflect language-acquisition practices in premodern times. As a result of research on neo-Latin texts and a certain amount of practice in speaking Latin myself, I later came to the conclusion that we have no real concept of what it means to speak a "dead" language.

Without this practical experience with Latin as a world language, I could never have written this book.

I owe the fact that the book exists at all to my publisher, C. H. Beck, and in particular to my very able editor, Dr. Stefan von der Lahr, who was always willing to let me pursue my ideas and who pursued publication even after I switched from Marburg to Tübingen, taking on an array of new duties that kept delaying the book's completion. If I have succeeded in interesting my colleagues and a larger public in what I have to say, which is my great hope, I will have him to thank.

The interdisciplinary approach of this book could not have been undertaken without the support of many colleagues in different disciplines who were always willing to share with me the fruits of their research and to discuss unconventional questions. In particular, I wish to thank my former colleagues in Marburg, Michael Hahn, Erich Poppe, Elisabeth Rieken, Walter Sommerfeld, and Stefan Weninger, as well as my colleagues in Tübingen, Matthias Bauer, Tilman Berger, Max Grosse, Johannes Kabatek, Kurt Kohn, Christian Leitz, Mirella Lingorska, Maria Moog-Grünewald, Steffen Patzold, Franz Penzenstadler, Lutz Richter-Bernburg, Klaus Ridder, and Konrad Volk. I discussed two of the most important theses of this book a few years ago at a linguistics colloquium held at Marburg University. I am especially grateful to Peter Koch (Tübingen), with whom I discussed many of the questions that arise in Chapter 2 at a seminar that we held for students of Latin and Romance philology. He also subjected most of the manuscript to a close and critical reading, and he gave me valuable advice at a number of points. All of the remaining errors or imprecise formulations—which are probably unavoidable in a manuscript that has been looked at by colleagues in Egyptology and Slavic studies and all disciplines in between—are my own responsibility.

The following colleagues in Latin and classical studies read all or parts of the manuscript: Walther Ludwig (Hamburg), Eberhard Heck, Mischa Meier, Ernst August Schmidt (all Tübingen), as well as Johannes Göbel and Uwe Dietsche. I owe them an enormous debt of gratitude for their efforts on my behalf and for their many useful suggestions; I wish to thank Walther Ludwig also for our numerous discussions over the course of the past several years, which enabled me to profit from his incredible knowledge of the neo-Latin world. There were many other colleagues, unnamed here, from classical studies and other disciplines with whom I had brief discussions at conferences and other events, who freely gave me the benefit of their opinions about this or that detail or who otherwise offered valuable suggestions. My thanks to all of them.

Wolfram Böhm (Marburg), Verena Rube, and Christian Sigmund (both Tübingen) helped me to research individual questions. In addition, for the past three years Christian Sigmund made sure that I had access to all of the books I needed, even the most difficult ones to procure, helped me with all of the technical aspects of producing this manuscript, and made a first draft of the maps included in the book. I am in their debt.

I also wish to thank all of the people who were forced to take second place while I wrote this book: my wife in particular, my students at the philological seminar in Tübingen, and everyone else who was forced to deal with the fact that I was "doing something else." I especially want to thank my children, who touchingly gave me the space I needed and waited patiently and with such great understanding until "the book" was finished. It is dedicated to them.

JÜRGEN LEONHARDT

TÜBINGEN, OCTOBER 2010

Preface to the English Edition

In the foreword to the German edition, I noted that the ways in which Latin may be viewed as a "live" or a "dead" language would form the point of departure of this book. Since then, the notion that Latin remains a living language has received surprising confirmation: Google Translate, Google's online machine-translation service, now offers to translate out of and into Latin. True, the quality, which leaves something to be desired, lags far behind that currently achievable for other languages. As a result, Latin machine translations now guarantee little more than amusement. In addition, Google Translate still has trouble identifying a source text as Latin, doing so only after all other possibilities have been exhausted. Overall quality may increase in the future as the technology is further refined. Still, of all the great classical languages, Latin is the only one thus far to have kept its status as an actively used language in this technological venue.

This step toward automated language processing touches importantly on the history of Latin as a world language because, as I explain in this book, world language status is less a function of how many people actually speak a particular language. What matters is that a language dissolves its ties to a single group of native speakers and, supported by grammars and dictionaries, becomes a globally shared vehicle of communication. And this is occurring once again but now in a completely new way. The fixing of a language by means of a computerized dictionary and complex algorithms that capture syntax represents a new milestone in the history of language codification. What can be done with computers goes well beyond what is possible using conventional grammars and dictionaries, not only in terms of world languages, but all languages that are currently undergoing computer processing. At present, machine translation is used mainly by native speakers of one language seeking to understand or at least get the gist of texts in another. However, there is no reason that it cannot also be used to help nonnative speakers to learn foreign languages. Moreover, at this point translation programs and the language corpora on which they are based are in much the same place as literary canons and the defining of grammar rules two thousand years ago. Certainly, today's linguists prefer corpora based on oral communications to strictly literary models, and they believe that corpora should constantly be updated to reflect ongoing changes in a language. But who is responsible for ensuring that language corpora reflect the actual state of the language? Who determines that a usage has changed? And who has the authority to tell nonnative users (or even native users) of machine translation that their output should have no impact on their language as they speak it? It is perhaps too early to gauge the consequences of this linguistic development. Still, it brings us very close to the main issues of the history of Latin, which are discussed in this book. It may well be that in a few years this book will have to be expanded, with a new chapter on machine translation.

As it stands, the history of Latin as described here ends at the same place as in the German edition, that is, before the computer age. Nonetheless, the English edition has been thoroughly reworked. One goal of this revision was to remove details that would mainly have been of interest to German readers and to give the book a more international perspective. I also took advantage of an opportunity afforded by translation to tighten my argumentation, especially in Chapters 3, 4, and 5, and to elaborate on various points that were less fully treated in the German edition. In particular, I gave more room to the parallels between the development of Latin and the current development of English as a world language because these similarities will be of greater interest to readers of the English edition.

As part of the revision, it also seemed sensible to illustrate Latin's developmental stages with actual examples. This was quite a challenge because the book was also written to engage readers with no or at best only a passing knowledge of Latin. It is difficult for people with no grasp of a language to understand the significance of what may seem minute differences; thus, explanations and theoretical descriptions may seem overly abstract. Nonetheless, I did my best to highlight particular features of the language and its history that would be understandable to nonspecialists as well. This exercise was all the more gratifying because it afforded me a good opportunity to reexamine judgments that a Latinist like me takes for granted. I hope that I have succeeded in providing a narrative that offers something of value to both specialists and nonspecialists.

Unfortunately, work on the English edition was constantly disrupted because in October 2010 I was made dean of the newly established Faculty of Humanities at the University of Tübingen, and the hiring and disposition of faculty took more time and effort than I had expected or feared. On the other hand, constant conversation with faculty members in linguistics and literature gave me ample opportunity to think about the history of the Latin language in the context of their disciplines: classical studies, Oriental and Asian studies, history, and ethnology. Nonetheless, these professional duties meant that the revisions progressed in fits and starts. For much the same reason, new or secondary literature published since the first edition in 2009 has been only sporadically noted.

I wish to thank Geisteswissenschaften International—Translation Funding for Work in the Humanities and Social Sciences for its substantial financial support in making this English translation possible. I also thank Sharmila Sen at Harvard University Press for her interest in the translation and for her endless patience. Kenneth Kronenberg (a non-Latinist!) was much more than a translator. He and I together thought through many aspects of the translation, and his numerous queries and excellent suggestions have made parts of the English edition better than the German original. I thoroughly enjoyed our collaboration.

JÜRGEN LEONHARDT

TÜBINGEN, NOVEMBER 2011

Latin

1

Latin as a World Language

A Systematic Approach

O F ALL THE TRACES left by the Romans, the Latin language is probably the most ubiquitous. Latin continued to be the language of
record even as the last remnants of the Roman Empire dissolved into
new forms of statehood. In this respect it was as if nothing in Europe
had changed. Even when, during the early Middle Ages, the various
European vernaculars began replacing Latin, for a good thousand years
it would have been unthinkable to practice one of the higher professions
without a thorough grounding in Latin. In addition, Latin continued to
play a crucial role even after the vernacular languages had become well
established throughout Europe. Long after people no longer wrote or
spoke Latin as a matter of course, learning it was a must because, even
during the age of science, Latin continued to be a core subject not only
in the schools of central Europe but also in Russia, Scandinavia, North
and South America, and Australia. Although Latin ceased to be a core
subject in higher education during the twentieth century, it still had a
presence. And against all expectations, it has never become a merely
exotic subject but continues to be taught in many schools.

No other "dead" language continues to exert such influence throughout the world. Latin word stems form the basis of new scientific terminology. Some of the more sophisticated magazines still allow Latin
terms or brief quotations to appear on their pages untranslated. Surprisingly, the active use of Latin has even seen something of a resurgence recently. Latin circles have sprung up in Europe and the United
States, as have Latin journals and radio programs. When Finland held

the presidency of the Council of the European Union (in 1999 and 2006), it regularly published reports in the Latin language. In the fall of 2008, a German television station even broadcast a two-hour program about the Roman Empire in Latin, with German subtitles. In addition, in the Catholic Church, the Latin Mass, which had been banned after the Second Vatican Council (1962–1965), underwent a measured restoration. It seems that Latin is still different from other historical languages. So although ancient Babylonian is the province of Orientalists and hieroglyphics of Egyptologists, Latin remains what it has been for the past two thousand years: a world language.

What is key to understanding the history of Latin as a world language is that it was never restricted to the Latin classroom or to Cicero and classical literature. Rather, like English today, it was a globally accessible language that was required for communications and not merely for educational purposes. Nothing demonstrates the dimensions of this world language more clearly than the sheer quantity of writings in Latin. The mere fact that more Latin texts have been created and archived in libraries around the world since the end of the Roman Empire than were written in Roman antiquity is significant. But an extrapolation—which can be little more than an approximation, given the state of the sources— testifies to the continuing significance of Latin as a world language: the quantity of post-Roman texts is so extensive that it exceeds the total of all extant classical Latin texts by a factor of ten thousand.[1] This means that all of the writings that have come down to us from ancient Rome, including all inscriptions, constitute at most 0.01 percent of the total output. Of this miniscule percentage, Christian texts from late antiquity represent approximately 80 percent. What is generally known as *the* literature of the Romans, as it is taught in school, the works of authors like Plautus, Cicero, and Tacitus, forms little more than an infinitesimal point in the universe that is Latin, albeit one that shines brightly.

The sheer numbers must be illustrated to be fully appreciated. If we assume that the sum total of Latin texts from antiquity may be snugly accommodated in five hundred volumes running an estimated five hundred pages each, we would need about ten thousand times that number, that is, at least five million additional volumes of the same size, to house the total output in Latin texts. A brief overview of the use of Latin shows that our estimates are, if anything, on the conservative side.

Without a doubt, archived manuscripts and documents constitute the largest proportion of these texts. The documents of all cities and seats of government, residences of princes, and private archives throughout Europe were written in Latin well into the high or even late Middle Ages. In some cases, Latin continued to be used for official purposes much later, as in Hungary, where it remained the language of administration into the mid-nineteenth century. To this we must add the Latin documents of the Vatican and of all the dioceses and archdioceses throughout the world up to the present; international diplomatic correspondence into the early modern era (the documents of the 1648 Peace of Westphalia, for example, are in Latin); many of the minutes of European university administrations into the sixteenth and seventeenth centuries; as well as hundreds of thousands of inscriptions on buildings, paintings, and gravestones. The number of Latin certificates—certifications, doctorates, conferrals of title, and the like—stored in and out of archives is in the millions and continues to grow.

The second largest group involves expository or functional and scientific texts of all kinds. Until the end of the Middle Ages, almost all scholarly literature was written in Latin (the majority into the seventeenth century and a considerable proportion into the early nineteenth century). Theologians, jurists, and physicians used Latin exclusively in their communications; whether these involved the tracts of astronomers and philosophers or theoretical writings about music, rhetoric, and poetry, all were in Latin. We do not yet have a precise overview. Nonetheless, the raw numbers available for a few areas permit a rough estimate of the scope of its use. For example, an older and surely incomplete bibliography of modern astronomical literature contains several thousand Latin titles. An extrapolation from a collection of law dissertations housed in Frankfurt, which is assumed to contain only a small portion of the actual number of such dissertations, suggests that between 1650 and 1750 at least fifty thousand dissertations, perhaps as many as a hundred thousand, were written at universities in Germany and Austria, that is, in the "First German Reich," which came to an end in 1806. Even if each dissertation comprised about twenty-five pages, the total comes to well over one million text pages—and this, it should be noted, is counting only legal dissertations in the German-speaking world between 1650 and 1750, not other European countries. In some subjects,

Latin was a common scientific language into the nineteenth century, as is evident from philological and theological dissertations; so-called *Schulschriften,* academic annuals that were published by German high schools *(Gymnasien);* and scientific journals. Nonacademic expository and functional texts include hundreds of thousands of sermons from the Middle Ages, as well as speeches and poetry for all imaginable occasions such as weddings, baptisms, burials, conferrals of doctoral degrees, jubilee celebrations, which probably run into the millions. The quantity of letters written in Latin is also incalculable. The more than three thousand letters written by Erasmus of Rotterdam alone equal almost half of the total number of letters still extant from classical antiquity. Moreover, Erasmus was only one of several thousand persons from the Middle Ages and early modern period whose Latin letters we still have.

In comparison to Latin scientific and functional texts, which include a high proportion of works of great stylistic sophistication, the quantity of what might be termed "art literature" is surely much smaller. But even here, the preponderance of works written after the end of the Roman Imperium is considerable. It may come as a surprise, but a mere forty Latin dramas have come down to us from antiquity—the number of plays staged in Latin between the fifteenth and the eighteenth centuries is between five thousand and ten thousand. Only about a dozen Latin-language didactic poems have survived from antiquity; more than four hundred are known from the sixteenth to the eighteenth century. Even the number of medieval and modern epics exceeds the few classical representatives of that genre by more than a hundredfold. Only about a dozen dialogues, a genre invented by Plato, remain from Roman antiquity; the number of such works from the early modern period runs to four digits.

The public has little appreciation of either the history of Latin as a world language in the modern era or its omnipresence. When people think of Latin, they think of ancient Rome. The Latin taught at universities and in high schools that even have Latin programs deal generally, though not exclusively, with classical Latin literature from its beginnings around 250 BCE to late antiquity. True, people have some awareness that Latin was the sole means of communication for the church and in science in the western half of Europe during the Middle Ages and that it was very important in secular affairs. A solid grounding in Latin is an absolute necessity for any historian whose purview is the Middle Ages.

In reality, however, only the first half of the Middle Ages is ever really researched. For example, there has not been a complete accounting of Latin texts written in the High Middle Ages, and only the most important texts are available in copies or electronic form. Those researching the medieval Latin literature are all too often forced to travel to European libraries and read the actual medieval manuscripts. We have only an inadequate knowledge of Latin text production in the Late Middle Ages. There are relatively few professorships in medieval Latin. The discrepancy is even greater for the modern era. Here, attention is almost exclusively on the burgeoning literatures of modern European languages. All but forgotten is the fact that a considerable percentage of communications within Europe took place in Latin well into the eighteenth century and that most Latin texts stem from the modern era. In neither the nineteenth nor the twenty-first century has an academic discipline developed for Latin literature from this period. At best, with very few exceptions, these writings are the sidelines of specialists in the Germanic or Romance languages, classical philologists, philosophers, or students in other disciplines. Beyond that they might as well not exist.

Although a considerable upswing in neo-Latin studies has occurred in the past several decades, no real paradigm shift has taken place. Except for a few overviews of essay length and several regionally oriented works, no history of neo-Latin literature has as yet been written. What is more, even if some ambitious soul set out to write such a history, it would of necessity be the culmination of decades of preliminary research. Even then, the resulting work would hardly approach the level attained by studies of the European vernacular literatures. The smallest and most marginal European national literatures have been more thoroughly researched than the neo-Latin; this, even though up to 1600 and in some countries as late as 1700 and beyond, more literature was produced in Latin than in each of the national languages. In the Americas there was even a neo-Latin literature, which remains largely unplumbed. As a result, the views offered by literary and linguistic histories and, to a lesser extent by the histories of philosophy and the sciences and of European and premodern literature influenced by Europe, remain unbalanced because the Latin portion is either neglected or completely missing. The situation is paradoxical. Although Latin was part and parcel of a good education in the entire Western world well

into the twentieth century, Latin literature of the modern era is by far
the least known body of literature.

Europe's Disremembered Latin History

How is such collective amnesia possible? Superficially, the explanation
is rather simple. The exclusion of Latin does not relate to its entire history but rather to the centuries in which Latin was still used alongside
the newly developing written languages of Europe, that is, from the High
Middle Ages up to about 1800. This was when the newer languages for
the first time ceased to be merely marginal in the European written tradition. Although Latin still had a presence during this period, the future
belonged to the new national languages, and the proportion of Latin
texts went into steady decline. It is understandable that scholars would
be more interested in the waxing of literatures in the vernacular than
in the waning of Latin. The invention of the automobile in the late nineteenth century provides us with a similar development in that the horse
and buggy continued to play an important role alongside the car for more
than fifty years. Nonetheless, the wider public tends to be more interested in early cars than late horse-drawn carriages.

However, replacement alone cannot adequately explain the disappearance of neo-Latin literature from modern consciousness. Rather,
the neglect of Europe's Latin tradition is more the result of ideology.
After the Romans, Latin lived on mainly as a language taught in schools
according to the grammatical rules of an age long gone. It was no longer
the language of a people, and so it came to be viewed as a "dead" language. And dead languages can hardly be expected to give birth to anything live. Even today, they are viewed as something artificial, as a
learned cultural superstructure incapable of unfolding in real life.
Even Latin scholars, who should by all rights have been the champions
of Latin, adopted this prejudice and took a critical stance toward the
"dead" Latin of the post-Roman era. The view expressed a hundred years
ago about neo-Latin literature by the classical philologist Franz Skutsch
continues to be echoed by some of his colleagues today: "All of these
descendents of the Latin muse are of only secondary interest and will,
overall, attract only philologists and literary amateurs."[2]

The model undergirding this verdict is the notion of a "natural" language as one that develops randomly. Its core is not in the scholarly

literature but in orality: spontaneous usage unencumbered by schooling or even grammar. Modern linguistics as a whole, including comparative philology, which sprang up around 1800, and the subsequent "neogrammarian" school uncritically adopted the primacy of orality and passed it down. Spoken language was viewed, and to a certain extent still is, as the only legitimate object of linguistic analysis. Written norms and all forms of external influence on language were interpreted as cultural epiphenomena not to be identified with the essence of the language as such. As a result, languages like Latin, which are learned exclusively from books, are no longer a medium of exchange in the real world and are not viewed as languages in the strict sense of the word. Linguists were interested in Latin only insofar as it was a living language that was developing organically. As a result, they carefully studied the development of Latin as reflected in literary texts from its reconstructed Indo-European roots up to its grammatical calcification in the first century BCE. There was thereafter an almost seamless transition from "Vulgar Latin" to the study of the Romance languages. Virtually nothing is to be found in the linguistic literature about textual Latin after the first century CE. The field of sociolinguistics, which has come into prominence over the past several decades, might have been expected to have academic language standards in its sights. Unfortunately, it has to date barely engaged with the role of Latin in European history, in all probability because the field is almost exclusively oriented to the present, and the historical dimension is only now being discovered.

Beginning in the sixteenth century and then more intensively since the eighteenth, the primacy of "natural" language was joined by a second notion, namely, that one's individuality and one's inclusion in a national or social community *(Volksgemeinschaft)* can develop only from within the mother tongue and that the mother tongue alone enables individuals to express their deepest thoughts and yearnings. This basically Romantic notion of the vernacular as the soul of a people and the sole medium of artistic inspiration made Latin look like a stiff corset and the vernacular like a liberating return to nature. The notion of a national language, which developed out of this concept in the nineteenth century, combined an almost mystical primevalism with the modern political concept of the nation. In this view, the national language as mother tongue, safely unfolding from within its living source in the unfettered unconscious, yet secondarily cultivated by literary models and the act of communication, became the exclusive linguistic model for the development of personality. For the first time in European history, it was assumed that the language one had learned as a child would remain the most important. Although cultivated people were expected to master several languages, this in no way called into question the primacy of the mother tongue. Nonetheless, in the nationalistic nineteenth century, a person who could not be unambiguously assigned to a particular linguistic community became suspect. And because Latin was nobody's mother tongue, it was suspect for that reason alone.

Our alienation from Latin over the past two centuries increased further because of its lack of active use such that today it is encountered almost exclusively in works from the past. Latin is now viewed almost entirely as a historical language, whereas it was largely perceived as a timeless phenomenon during the eighteenth and early nineteenth centuries. Until very recently, the usual didactic methods of teaching Latin, which emphasized intellectual analysis of grammatical rules over actual language acquisition, drove home the final nail, relegating it to the status of a research tool for decoding historical texts or a sort of mental gymnastics. Teaching or learning Latin seems to be very different from teaching or learning modern languages. Latin, it seems, is not really a language at all but rather a piece of our cultural heritage. What is more, wherever things are inherited, as a rule death may be presumed.

The End of National Languages and the Rise of English as a World Language

This is where the present book commences. Its goal is not to recall the importance of Europe's Latin tradition or to review the treasures of classical, postclassical, and modern Latin literature. A whole series of books that do just that have been published quite recently. These include works by Joseph Farrell (*Latin Language and Latin Culture from Ancient to Modern Times*, 2001), Françoise Waquet (*Latin, or the Empire of a Sign*, 2001), Tore Janson (*A Natural History of Latin*, 2004), Nicholas Ostler (*Ad infinitum: A Biography of Latin*, 2007), and Wim Verbaal, Yanick Maes, and Jan Papy (*Latinitas perennis*, vol. 1, *The Continuity of Latin Literature*, 2007; vol. 2, *Appropriation and Latin Literature*, 2009). In Germany, Wilfried Stroh's *Latein ist tot, es lebe Latein!* (Latin is dead, long live Latin!) (2007) even became a bestseller in that country. Each of these books in its own way illuminates the history of the Latin language and culture in Europe and brings to the attention of specialists in other disciplines and to the broader public facts and understandings previously the province of Latin scholars alone. The success of these books heralds renewed interest in the overall history of the Latin language from its early beginnings to the present.

The subject of this book is different. Its brief is the status of Latin as a "dead" language. How did Latin become a language taught only in school? Why did Europe use this language for fifteen hundred years? And what exactly is a "dead" language, especially when it is still used as frequently as Latin? The conventional answers to these questions, that Latin became a world language because the Romans were a world power and that it remained a world language because Rome's cultural heritage and the Catholic Church of late antiquity influenced Europe's development, are simply inadequate and in some respects just plain wrong.

The goal of this book is to investigate the linguistic processes through which Latin developed into a world language—and a "dead" language—and to pay close attention to the principles that govern the development of other world languages throughout history and of languages that are conventionally viewed as "normal" living languages. My purpose is to rescue Latin from the status of "cultural heritage," and to demonstrate the extent to which Latin remained a living language like any other even after it had ceased to be spoken by particular peoples in the ancient world. Unlike some passionate defenders of the classical tradition, I do not adduce evidence by demonstrating how many people wrote or spoke in Latin into modern times or what they produced. There is no denying the difference between Latin and languages that have a living community of speakers. The question is, What do Latin and the "living" languages derived from it have in common? The differences between Latin and "living" languages, I intend to show, are gradual, not categorical.

Such an approach is much easier to take today than it was just a few years ago. The reasons for demoting Latin from the roster of active living languages over the past two centuries have become largely outdated. The exclusive concentration on spoken language in linguistics is giving way to questions about the relationship between culture and language. The questions so central to Latin, such as standardization of language, codification of written language, and the cultivation of language, are now being discovered by linguists as areas of legitimate research. They are no longer viewed as mere epiphenomena that are foreign to the organism of language as such. A reference work such as Nina Janich and Albrecht Greule's extremely informative and profitable *Sprachkulturen in Europa* (2002) (Language cultures in Europe) would have been unthinkable until recently. A major goal of my book is to show that the history of Latin should have been accorded a place within the tradition of "European language cultures" and should not have been slighted in Janich and Greule's book. In literature, a growing interest in the formation of culture and especially of literary canons, as well as the influence of cultural studies on literary and educational history, is paving the way for a new interpretation of the particularity of Latin.

One of the things that makes Latin especially interesting right now is globalization and the complex ties between different countries and cultures. The processes set in motion as a result, among them the rapid growth of English as the preeminent world language, have fundamentally shaken our notion that human beings develop language best by cultivating their "mother tongue." These processes also give us an opportunity to reflect in a novel way on exactly what transforms a "living" language into a "dead" one.

Let us turn for the moment to the question of mother tongues. Unlike the situation not too many decades ago, when in countries with strongly developed "national" languages only cultural and diplomatic elites faced the daunting prospect of learning several languages, large swaths of the world's population must now meet that challenge. In comparison to the nineteenth century, a much larger proportion of people around the world are forced by necessity to express complex ideas in a second language and to structure their "normal" lives in languages they did not learn at home as children. Multilingualism—and not merely the elementary ability to communicate but also written fluency and the capacity to negotiate in several languages—is the new ideal in the globalized world. It leads to fundamental shifts in the educational system, in which the mother tongue is supplemented and in some cases even supplanted by early bilingual education. Except in the case of English, the mother tongue has lost a piece of its absolute primacy, and English has become the essential global medium of exchange. It is currently the most important second language; so-called native speakers are now a clear minority. English, as we have understood for some time, is the successor to Latin. For the first time, an understanding of the achievement of Latin as a world language is at hand, independent of the apologetics of classical philologists. Moreover, the new role that English has assumed also raises many of the same questions that were once posed of Latin.

This is especially the case in those domains that for centuries had been the province of Latin: the sciences and scholarship, whether secular or religious. Here, the linguistic splitting caused by the various nationalisms in nineteenth-century Europe is striking. Within a small yet largely homogeneous geographical space, at least four languages of science of international significance—French, English, German, and Italian—blossomed, alongside several "smaller" European languages such as Finnish, Polish, and Norwegian, which became the bearers of their own scientific culture. However, when it came to publications meant for an international audience, practitioners all made use of the closest available "larger" language. This guaranteed the larger European countries that, as long as their inhabitants did not cross international boundaries, their mother tongue would suffice for all the usual domestic purposes. The well-schooled elites transcended international boundaries and made use of foreign languages as needed but tended to write in their own.

The establishment of English as the international language of science has fundamentally changed these well-established habits, perhaps most of all in Germany, where the national language developed into a scientific language much later than in most European countries and where the relationship between language and nation became especially problematic after the nationalist adventures that ended in catastrophe with the Third Reich. Alongside a resolute commitment to maintain German as a language of science at all cost, a countertrend demonstrates internationalism by the forced use of English. There are certainly numerous situations in Germany in which all of the participants of a discussion could speak German but prefer English out of the simple belief that it is integral to the enterprise of science. This means that, without knowing it, we now have the same relationship to English that the scientific community had to Latin in the eighteenth century. The question of what will happen with each of the national languages in literary and scientific endeavors has now become an issue that is being openly and publicly debated. In Germany, the former president of the Federal Constitutional Court, Jutta Limbach, even wrote a book about it in 2008.

Its translated title is ominous: *Does German Have a Future?* The large German scientific organizations have also become involved. After the initial euphoria about the internationalism of English, they are now attempting to take a more nuanced stance. Currently, the trend seems to be toward a blend, with much of the discussion centering on situations in which the international language of science or the mother tongue offers the most advantages. Essentially, this was the ongoing debate between Latin and the national languages between the sixteenth and the eighteenth century, and it is now to some extent being played out in reverse. Prior to 1800, the question was, How much should we entrust to national languages? Now the question is, How much of a role should they still be accorded?

The model of the mother tongue, which alone is capable of expressing what comes from the heart, which alone inspires poetry, which is available in every situation from everyday conversation to high literature and science, and which is fully developed, as linguists would say, is increasingly proving to be a peculiarly European path taken during the nationalistic nineteenth and twentieth centuries. Comparison with other cultural spaces and historical eras shows that ever since Latin ceased to be the common language of Europe, very few societies have been as consistently monolingual within large geographical territories such as the European nation-states. A glance at the countries of Africa and Asia and even at the United States makes it clear that the connection between ethnic or national identity and language in the large European nation-states is much more complex than has been the case until recently. The situation in premodern Europe, in which each region had its own language, while important areas such as religion, science, and supraregional communication were bound together by a single language (Latin), seems to have been more of a historical norm than an exception. And it appears that in terms of communication, Europe is now returning to its premodern self. In view of the challenges of the modern world, the categories of the linguistically foreign and the linguistically indigenous, which characterized discussions about language from the time of Pietro Bembo (1470–1547), who demonstrated a preference for Italian over Latin in his programmatic writings, have blurred.[3] The Roman poet Ennius (239–169 BCE) arrived in Rome from southern Italy, and although Latin was a language he had to learn, his contribution to Roman literature was great. He confessed to having three hearts: Roman, Oscan (the standard Italic language of southern Italy), and Greek. He did not even mention Messapian, the local dialect of his home region. That, in a nutshell, is the essence of multilingualism both in antiquity and in the modern world.

Of course, the hegemonic claims of national languages ended less because of a change in consciousness and more because the idea of the nation-state became increasingly untenable. The modern world not only is linguistically more complex but also has become economically and politically intertwined as never before. Interestingly, no sooner had the Cold War come to an end than a debate about empires developed. In the process, the historical model of the Imperium Romanum has gained unexpected salience in the political sciences. This model of empire entails linguistic organization, and not only for internal communication. Language pervades the cultural and political fabric of a society. The Romans themselves provide an example of how an empire may be multilingual. For long periods of time, Latin did not serve the function that national languages have in modern nation-states, as I show later. Rather, Greek and other cultural languages were allowed to flourish.

Today we see a tendency toward regionalization in almost all of the old nation-states, expressing a need to stake out a place for old regional languages in opposition to the dominant national language, which unites the citizens of a particular country. This is evidence that the national languages are not the "natural" languages of a particular nation but are cultural constructs imposed by intensive schooling and mandated commitments and obligations that, however, have never been completely able to displace loyalty to regional tongues. Examples include the reestablishment of Catalan and Galician, along with Castilian, as official languages in Spain; the linguistic reorganization in the newly independent states of the former Soviet Union, such as Lithuania and Georgia; the linguistic provisions regarding minorities in the Italian regions of Friuli and Sardinia; and last but not least the approval of regional variants in the classroom, even in a country as centralized as France. These trends are, in the final analysis, a recognition that premodern European realities were merely lying dormant as nation-states asserted themselves. They are now reawakening.

The exigencies of modern economics also require that languages be organized differently. Until the end of the twentieth century, trade and production were localized in a clear linguistic center even when a

company's reach was international—that is, a French company remained a French company no matter where it conducted its business.
Today this center has been replaced by a multiplicity of complex regional and national arrangements that are determined solely by the
technological possibilities. In this world, national boundaries constitute
little more than obstacles. On the one hand, business requires one or
several world languages to ensure communications; on the other hand
(and this much more so than in the sciences or politics), it requires connections with local cultures and languages. This is because a considerably larger proportion of society is engaged in economic, trade, and
production processes than in politics or science. These processes can no
longer be limited to a small elite group with a capacity to communicate
internationally.

Our interest in Latin as a historical world language will surely not
provide us with the key to solving modern issues. However, history
speaks to us more clearly when we understand where it anticipated our
problems, and conversely it sharpens historical distance and our view of
the present. Here, Latin has something to offer: a two-thousand-year-
old history that allows us to study the long-term development of particular constellations. Let me elaborate briefly on two understandings that
such a long-term perspective may bring.

First, world languages need not in any way reflect the linguistic application of political or economic power relationships. The enforced
spread of a language by a world power does not make it a world language;
as soon as that world power collapses, so does the language.[4] But Latin
continued even after the end of the Roman Empire. Latin even conquered northern Germany, Scandinavia, the northern parts of England,
and large territories in eastern Europe into Poland—regions that were
never under Roman sway. The vast majority of all Latin texts were written after the Roman Empire had ceased to exist. The example of Greek
is even more extreme. Ancient Greek was one of the most important
world languages for about a thousand years even though the political
might of Greece, if it ever really existed, reached its height during the
twelve-year reign of Alexander the Great. Sanskrit retained and even
expanded its importance as a common language in southern Asia long
after the political constellations from which it emerged had disappeared.
If one examines the matter closely, thousand-year-old empires are hard

to find. A generous view cedes to the Roman Empire only seven hundred years of hegemony. But as a world language, Latin has a history spanning more than twenty-three hundred years. Is English now a world language simply because the United States, Great Britain, and some other countries play a dominant global role in business and politics? Or does English now to some extent already exist in a space that is independent of nations? These questions provide a very interesting focus from which to make comparisons with Latin.

This leads to a second aspect of the particular connection between Latin and world languages in general. Historically, a very evident association exists between "world languages" and "dead" languages. A lifespan of two thousand or three thousand years means more than the mere continuity of a continually unfolding linguistic system as is the case with, say, German, from the first written evidence of Old High German in the eighth century up to the present. Such continuity is part and parcel of all languages, whether world languages or local dialects, and cannot be measured in terms of evolutionary processes over small time periods. It makes sense to speak of a language's lifespan only when describing periods in which the language remains sufficiently stable to give it a firm identity and an ability to facilitate communication over time. For modern Germans, Old High German is a totally different language, despite its name, because no one can now understand it.

As it began its ascent to the status of world language, Latin was already set in its essential characteristics, and this circumstance enabled people to read texts that were hundreds of years old. In fact, one of the major accomplishments of Latin is that it makes available to us not only relatively modern literature, science, and historiography but also writings in these areas that are thousands of years old. This is true of all historical languages that may be termed world languages: ancient Greek, the literary language of neo-Babylonian, Sanskrit, and the written form of classical Chinese. The world empires of language extend beyond space across vast stretches of time. This is perhaps less perceptible now because over the past two centuries most classical world languages have been superseded, and their modern successors—whether English or the modern standardized form of Chinese—are still much too recent to permit historical analysis. On the other hand, present-day High Arabic can still give us some idea of the long-term continuity of world languages.

Historical experience, however, shows that an actual world language comes into existence only when it really belongs to the world at large and is not just an expansion of one linguistic community at the expense of other linguistic communities. One of the core arguments of this book is that Latin, like all other world languages of premodern times, attained this status only after it had detached its standards from those of a concrete linguistic community and had to some extent become a "dead" language. The fact that historical languages then developed that hewed to the norms of bygone times was a secondary factor; anything that does not change and evolve over five hundred years or more becomes historical for that reason alone. This tells us nothing, however, about the future of today's languages. The actual development of languages around the world is not comparable to the history of Latin if only because modern global information networks and our greater capacity for mobility mean that the communications processes that impinge on language are completely different from those in previous millennia. Nevertheless, the histories of all world languages indicate that the origins of "dead" languages point to the problem of standardization, which exists in all languages up to the present but was especially prominent in all great world languages of the past. In this respect, as I explain later, the development of English under the conditions of its world-language status leads to interesting comparisons with the development of Latin, although premature parallels should be avoided.

The history of Latin, as I write it, is based on the connections between the daily realities of life in which a language was used in various epochs and which formed the foundation upon which the well-known milestones of Europe's Latin tradition were built: the writings of the "classic" Roman writers Cicero and Virgil, the medieval collection of poems known as the *Carmina Burana*, the works of Erasmus of Rotterdam, and finally the presence of Latin in modern times. In addition, I examine Latin's relationships with other languages, not only other historical world languages and English, its successor, but also modern European cultural languages, like German, French, and (British) English, which share a common history with Latin that extends over several hundred and in some cases thousands of years. Of course, such a description can make no claims to completeness. All of the observations and hypotheses advanced here require intensive examination and testing against source material. They must also be compared with the results of research in other disciplines. However, this initial view from a distance is useful and even necessary in spite of its provisional nature because such an overview can, by comparing epochs, allow particular features to come to the fore that might remain hidden if one simply examined the details.

Historical Culture Languages of the World

Extinct, Dead, Fixed: Conceptual Considerations

What we observe with Latin, that a language is handed down only through instruction in school, where, viewed quantitatively, most of the extant texts come from this "afterlife," is not unique. As indicated in the previous section, this is rather the norm than the exception for historical world languages. A review of older and more recent written cultures throughout the world indicates that this also holds true for many regionally more limited languages. In almost all regions of the world in which a written culture maintained itself for centuries, there is often a language that is learned in school and preserves this cultural tradition even after that region has experienced changes in population. Sumerian, classical Chinese, Old Church Slavonic, and Sanskrit are prominent examples.

The emphasis in linguistics on the processes of oral communication and the general lack of interest in historical linguistic research may be to blame for the lack of comparative studies of these languages to date. With the exception of the commendable work by the Romance specialist Helmut Lüdtke,[5] most studies have been content to discover that this or that language has certain similarities to Latin. Nor do I undertake such a comparative study in these pages but largely limit myself to Latin itself and bring in other languages as appropriate. Nonetheless, it seems useful at the outset to consider the basic terms used to describe the phenomenon of historical culture languages and to examine a few languages along with Latin that may contribute to a rudimentary typology.

When people say that Latin is a "dead" language, they usually mean one or several different things and tend not to discriminate. They may mean, that (1) Latin is no longer used as a means of communication (i.e., has become extinct); (2) Latin is no one's mother tongue; it must be learned in school; and/or (3) Latin is a language that has ceased to develop organically and has remained frozen in its classical form. But these are three very different phenomena. The turning point at which the developmental processes of the language came to a partial standstill occurred around the first century BCE (as Wilfried Stroh has recently stated), that is, at the time of the "classical" Roman authors like Cicero and Virgil. That is not to say, however, that Latin died out as the mother tongue of the Romans or that the language in any way became more limited in its scope of use. No one can doubt that Latin was the mother tongue of Tacitus and Pliny the Younger, who lived 150 years after that turning point. In addition, Latin continued in active use far beyond ancient times, when it had ceased to be anyone's mother tongue, and it has continued in use into the modern era and even into the present. When someone like Stroh declares that Latin "died" during the first century BCE and then claims that the end of Roman antiquity, the end of the Middle Ages, and the end of the eighteenth century should also be viewed as "deaths"—all of which Latin survived—this more than demonstrates the vitality of the language, which no one has yet managed to "kill off" definitively. However, as I demonstrate, these were not deaths but very different turning points in the history of the Latin language; moreover, Stroh has conflated phases of development that have nothing to do with each other.

Let us distinguish conceptually between these three outcomes, the first of which is designation as an "extinct" language. This really does not apply to Latin, which, unlike Etruscan or Hittite, continues to be used as a means of communication. The term *second language* covers the second outcome, that is, a language that is learned only later but is nonetheless indispensable in certain contexts. This correctly describes Latin, which was absolutely indispensable in certain situations during the Middle Ages and the early modern era in Europe. What is special about Latin is the fact that, during those times, it was no one's first language. I later discuss what it means for a language to be a "second language without a people."

But for Latin, the third outcome is the most important. We need to understand that, during most of its long history, the status of Latin corresponded neither to our concepts of a "natural language" nor to the current existence of Latin as a scholarly discipline. Although it is a second language that must be learned based on an immutable grammar, in practical use it is as alive as any other language. There is at present no generally accepted term to describe this linguistic circumstance, which, as I discuss in detail later, was the status of all premodern world and culture languages from Sanskrit to classical Greek to Arabic. I suggest the term *fixing* for this circumstance, which is used in both the German-language and English-language literature in a less specific sense but has not yet been clearly defined. By fixing, I mean a circumstance in which key features of the language cease to evolve. Fixing in this sense has much in common with the more common term *codification*, but with one important difference. In the usual understanding of the word, codification determines only a standard that all active users of the language agree to collectively. Codification undoubtedly has a very stabilizing effect on language, as is evident in the many countries that have language academies (the role of the French Académie française is preeminent in this regard). However, the intent is not to set a language for all time but to describe the state of the language at a particular time. English words like "thither" and "ere" are considered old fashioned today and are restricted to very particular usages; a hundred years ago they were still in common use. By contrast, certain basic patterns in Latin have not changed in two thousand years, and, if one decided to fiddle around with them, they would immediately trigger a sense that this is no longer "Latin." Virtually by definition, it is inconceivable that the genitive of *amor* should be something other than *amoris* or that the genitive case would be replaced by other constructions. The language in which this actually took place is no longer called Latin but French.

The term *fixed* is more precise in some important respects than the concept of *dead* language. Even more than the term *codification*, it leaves open what part of the language has become unchangeable. A fixed language is therefore not a language that is closed and can no longer develop but a language in which several core components remain unchangeable, while other parts continue to evolve as in any other normal language. Otherwise, Latin could never have continued to be used in active communication because a completely standardized language lacks the flexibility needed for the everyday purposes of speaking and writing. The standardization of Latin and other comparable languages affected mainly the forms and syntactic rules that are the framework of grammar. Still, wherever Latin was in active use, new words were constantly being coined, existing meanings changed, and the phrases and expressions typical of recurrent social relations reinvented. Accordingly, as long as it is a means of communication, a fixed language is simply a language with a fixed skeleton, within which dynamic linguistic processes may take place according to the same rules as in any other language. The Latin taught today in Latin classes throughout the world, which appears to be a completely standardized language, is merely the result of a rather strange perspective that does not take into account the active use of the language and views the translation of individual sentences or short texts as an exercise in scholarly construction. Wherever Latin is used as a means of communication, either oral or written, it immediately becomes clear that grammar alone is not enough. There is no such thing as completely standardized speech in any language.

Examples from Antiquity: Sumerian, Babylonian, Egyptian

Many ancient written cultures developed one or several standard languages that have clear similarities to Latin, and it is highly probable that this was true of all high cultures of antiquity. In many cases, we can only surmise the exact status of the language. For example, thousands of Mycenaean Greek tablets have survived from the second millennium BCE, but for only the past fifty years have we been able to decipher them. Mycenaean Greek had a largely unitary linguistic form over a very large territory, from which it is obvious that it must have been an administrative language. Similar assumptions can be made about Hittite, Etruscan, Punic, and many other ancient languages about which our knowledge is even sketchier. However, more than a few extinct-culture languages were of such importance and are so well documented that we know that they were not just fixed languages but, like Latin, continued to be used as standard languages even after they were nobody's mother tongue.

The development of the oldest documented written language in the world, Sumerian, is similar to that of Latin. Sumerian, which is attested by clay tablets back to approximately 2700 BCE, died as a "normal" vernacular language around 1800 BCE—the exact date and the precise circumstances are still a matter of debate—and was replaced by Babylonian.[6] However, because it continued to be taught in schools, Sumerian remained the language of religious rites and literature for more than fifteen hundred years—into the third century BCE. That is, the most recent known Sumerian texts were created at the same time as the Greek literature of the Hellenes. Interestingly, we can distinguish two phases. In the first phase, the Sumerian taught under the Babylonians apparently served the purpose of oral communication. They wrote instructional language manuals that bear an astonishing resemblance to the Latin dialogue books from the time of the European humanists. In the second phase, we see Sumerian only in inscriptions, which in all probability indicates that a few scribes (perhaps limited to a small number of cultural centers) were able to write such official texts. This parallels the situation of Latin today, when relatively few specialists are able to produce the small number of public documents in Latin still needed in today's world (e.g., Latin diplomas, official messages of congratulations at universities). Furthermore, the Sumerian instructional manuals have served as a model for millennia; glossaries and dictionaries effectively followed the Sumerian model to the end of the Babylonian period.

After the Sumerians, numerous written languages became widespread in the Mesopotamian region and the Near East. What is called the Standard or Babylonian literary language was especially important.[7] It came into being because a canon of writings developed during the last third of the second millennium BCE from the classical Babylonian works written around 1600. This canon came to represent the linguistic standard and continued to be used for more than a thousand years. The language in these texts became the literary and scholarly language of the Assyrians, and it continued to be used as such into the sixth century BCE, when the Babylonian Empire finally came to an end with the ascendancy of the Persians, who introduced Aramaic as the official language. Nonetheless, the Babylonian language continued to be taught in schools even after no one spoke it. We have some documents in this language from the Common Era. In terms of political and cultural importance, Babylonian literary language was the most important predecessor of Latin in the Near East.

In the Persian Empire, Aramaic, in the form that is known as Imperial Aramaic, became the lingua franca of an enormous territory that extended from Egypt to the Indus River. It showed a considerable level of standardization. Imperial Aramaic was undoubtedly a fixed language that, at least in this form, would not have been the vernacular language of a majority of the population. However, after the end of the Persian Empire, in the fourth century BCE, this linguistic form was no longer consistently nurtured under Alexander the Great. Nonetheless, Aramaic remained the most important language in the Near East and was, as we know, the language of Jesus and some biblical writings. However, it developed new forms and some written standards clearly distinguishable from Imperial Aramaic. The most important was Syriac, which came to assume special cultural importance for the Christian tradition.

The history of Egyptian is in some respects comparable to that of Latin.[8] Egyptian shows a continuous historical development from Old Egyptian (after the Old Kingdom, 2600 BCE), Middle Egyptian (after about 2200 BCE), Late Middle Egyptian (after about 2040 BCE), New Egyptian (after about 1400 BCE, in some cases even earlier), and Demotic (after about 700 BCE) to Coptic (after about the third century CE). Coptic was spoken into the sixteenth and seventeenth centuries, and continues to be used in the Coptic church. Neither New Egyptian nor Demotic Egyptian was ever used as a written language in high texts in Egyptian culture. That function was filled by Late Middle Egyptian until about 1200 BCE (Ramses II). After that, a form of Middle Egyptian has been attested that is known today as Neo-Middle Egyptian. This language was evidently propagated in school and was unalterable. It was based on Middle Egyptian, which was in some ways fundamentally different from the simultaneously attested forms of New Egyptian and later Demotic Egyptian. Over time, Neo-Middle Egyptian came to be used over a large territory that had previously been covered by Middle Egyptian, and it experienced a sort of renaissance, much as we see in the history of Latin. This language remained in use well into Roman times, that is, for more than thirteen hundred years. The Rosetta Stone, which Jean-François Champollion used to decipher Egyptian hieroglyphics, contained the same text in Greek, Demotic Egyptian, and Neo-Middle Egyptian. The fact that two different stages of Egyptian—the well-known Demotic form, which was similar to the long-understood Coptic, and Neo-Middle Egyptian, which was structurally more than a thousand years older—were chiseled into that stele greatly facilitated Champollion's task.

Fixed Languages and Ferguson's Model of Diglossia: Greek and Arabic

We now take a more detailed look at developments in the fixed languages that continued to be used into modern times. Here we see not only that a language is transformed into a fixed language after a certain period of time but also that we may describe in detail the particular

Figure 1. Inscription of King Nebuchadnezzar II of Babylonia (605–562 BCE) about building projects along the processional way in Babylon, which also included the Ishtar Gate (currently housed in Berlin). According to the Old Testament, the "Babylonian exile" of the Jews began under Nebuchadnezzar. This event is confirmed by preserved inscriptions. This particular building inscription is written in Babylonian literary language, which was consistently standardized in this form as early as the end of the second millennium BCE and continued to be used into the Hellenistic period. © The British Museum/The Trustees of the British Museum

historical progression of the fixing process and the communicative functions of the now fixed language in society. Two basic forms may be observed.

In one case, the language essentially remains firmly connected to a natural linguistic community even after it is fixed and is used as a supraregional language or even as a world language outside of its original linguistic territory. Within this linguistic community, it functions as an indispensable written language for all members of that community. Although the fundamentals of these fixed languages remain largely unchanged for many centuries and it is possible for a speaker to read texts that are a thousand years old (something that cannot be said of German or English), they are not "historical" languages because they are still currently indispensable. But because the actual language of the population continues to evolve, a split develops, usually after several centuries, between the high form of the language and the unregulated vernacular. Nonetheless, the speakers of this high language continue to be considered speakers of the mother tongue to the extent that they come from that specific linguistic territory because this fixed form of the high language is a constitutive element of that society. Two languages play an especially important role in the European context: Greek (at least until the early nineteenth century) and Arabic. As I explain later, Latin had this status into the final centuries of antiquity, when the written Latin language had already been fixed, while the vernacular language was evolving into the Romance languages.

In the second case, fixed languages are so embedded in a society that they are no longer the sole, binding written language; rather, they coexist with one or even several additional written languages that are closer to the vernacular language of the population. As a result, not all literate members of this society need to learn this language, which is reserved for specific purposes and contexts—and many members of the society are able to dispense with this language altogether. The most important historical languages of this type are Sanskrit and Latin, at least since the early Middle Ages, the latter maintaining its importance after other written languages, like Italian, began to evolve away from it. Historically, all of these second-case languages were once first-case languages. Only in their later stages (e.g., as happened when Italian and other Romance languages developed) did they give up their function as the sole written language. This is why I think of them as languages that, like people, are superseded by their offspring.

In order to classify the history of Latin as a typical case of a fixed culture language within a larger context, while at the same time keeping the particularities of Latin in mind, I first present an overview of developments in the Greek- and Arabic-speaking lands. This also makes sense because certain developmental steps are more clearly evident there and because the history of Greek had such an immediate influence on Latin.

The Greek language is first attested from the middle of the second millennium BCE in the form of Mycenaean clay tablets and then after a pause of several "dark" centuries again during the eighth century BCE with the written epics of Homer. The question still being discussed by specialists, about when Homer's epics were first written down, is not especially important in terms of linguistic history. This is because specialists are unanimous in the opinion that Homer's language was a special language that was never spoken by the population. Instead, it comprised a number of regional dialects—especially Ionian and Aeolian—and was the poetic language of itinerant bards, the so-called "rhapsodes," which preserved many of the archaic traits that had long passed out of the living language of the population. During recent debates on the historicity of Homeric Troy, the question has arisen (with serious and plausible arguments on both sides) about whether some few aspects of Homeric versification might not be traceable as far back as the Mycenaean period, which would speak for a continuity in the epic poetic tradition back to approximately 1300–1200 BCE. Although this cannot be proved, what Homeric poetic language makes clear is that the phenomenon of a historically preserved culture language need not be exclusively tied to a written culture but can also appear in oral poetry and literature.

Characteristic of the wave of literacy that swept Greece after Homer is its close connection to regional dialects: Aeolian in southern Asia Minor and adjacent islands, Ionian in northern Asia Minor, Dorian in the Peloponnesus, and Attic in Attica were the most important regional languages in which literature was written. Numerous other dialects are also attested in inscriptions. It should be noted that the population at the time would not have interpreted this multiplicity of linguistic forms as different languages but as mere variations on a single Greek language; the Greek word "hellenikos" was collective in this sense. That

being said, the situation in early Greece differed considerably from that
in Italy, where such a collective notion of an Italic culture or language
was unknown.

The fact that works of literature were created in most of the Greek
dialects, which were then received and appreciated throughout Greece
as models of literary genres, has led to a rather rare cultural phenomenon in which particular forms of dialect continued to be used for those
genres in other regions of Greece, albeit in altered or attenuated form.
For example, poets not within the Dorian dialect area continued to
write choral lyrical poetry in the tradition of the seventh-century Spar-
tan poet Alcman. This continued to be the case even after the establishment of Greek prose literature in the sixth century BCE, including
the works of the pre-Socratics or of the historian and geographer Heca-
taios. Of course, this implies that several forms of a literary koine (from
the Greek *koinos,* "common"), which was different from any spoken
language in any particular place, had already developed as a consequence of a few powerful literary works. Ionian was the most important literary language of the Greeks before the ascendancy of Athens
and, with it, of Attic Greek. Here we observe the development of a koine
even in inscriptions.

In the next step, regional literary languages were abandoned in favor of a uniform all-Greek language. Attic Greek was the big winner in
this process largely because of the political preeminence and cultural
importance of Athens during the fifth century BCE. Much of what we
view as typically Greek today either developed in Attica during this
period or was perfected there. We need think only of the Greek tragedies and comedies, the histories of Thucydides, the great Attic orators,
and Plato. The Athenian influence on the written language of Greece
can be found very early in Asia Minor. The victory of Attic Greek
would not, however, have been possible in this form without a second
political fact. The Macedonian royal court in northern Greece, which
until then had barely participated in the literary and cultural development of the Greeks, adopted Attic as its language in the fifth century.
This meant that Attic became the standard language within the empire
of Alexander the Great (356–323 BCE) and within the Greek world as a
whole. The Hellenistic koine that began here became the Attic literary
language, though it included a few Ionian elements. It remained the
language of Greece for at least three centuries.

To be more precise, Greek was the only common literary language of Greece. The actual linguistic situation on the ground was incomparably more complex. Within the Greek heartland, old dialects continued to be used for centuries (though increasingly influenced by the koine) and were also used in inscriptions. The literary language was, however, able to become independent of local Greek languages and form a sort of supraregional standard. Political developments also had a major effect on the Greek language. After the death of Alexander the Great, Athens continued to play a major role in the core Greek areas around 300 BCE under Demetrios Poliorcetes, the son of Alexander's most important general. However, the imperial centers of the Diadochi, into which Alexander's brief empire dissolved, lay outside the core Greek areas. Nevertheless, they had a greater interest in participating in Greece through literature. This applied all the more to the Ptolemaic court in Egyptian Alexandria. This city, where Greek was a completely new language introduced by a small class of rulers, managed to establish itself during the Hellenistic period as one of the most important literary centers. At times Alexandria outstripped even Athens in importance because it was where the Greek literary tradition was preserved. Alexandria played a central role in terms of textual continuity and the production of new literature.

This particular cultural and historical constellation, which resulted from Alexander's military campaign in Egypt and the founding of Alexandria, is quite remarkable. If we were to hazard an extrapolation from Alexander the Great to Napoleon, we might imagine the historical record to look as follows. Had Napoleon's campaign in Egypt been more successful than it actually was, he might have founded a city called Bonapartia. One of his generals would then have created a new French empire with no territorial connection to France and built the largest French library in the world, where well-trained scholars carefully pored over and critiqued texts and where the most important French literature was written. This extrapolation is not completely inapt because French, like the Greek of Alexander's time, was already a well-elaborated and codified literary language of supraregional importance. It was completely natural that within the isolation of the Egyptian exclave Greek could have defined itself only through the literary language; the same may be said, to only a somewhat lesser degree, of the other empires of the Diadochi, especially of the Attalid dynasty, in Pergamon. Instead of the literary language growing out of the oral tradition, as occurred in Greece, spoken Alexandrian Greek was actually the oral form of the literary language.

The connection between Greek literary language and what might be called the natural linguistic development of the nonliterate society was rent during this period at the latest. From this point onward, the Greek language, as evidenced by surviving texts, had become fixed. The external shape of the words and the key syntactic elements remained largely unchanged; at most, a few selective elements of the language continued to evolve. Up until then, for example, in addition to the indicative and the conjunctive modes, Greek had a third mode, the so-called optative (wish mode). Moreover, in addition to singular and plural they had a "dual" number, which identified the duality of things. These and similar grammatical peculiarities largely disappeared and made way for the linguistic structure that continues to form the basis of all European languages to the present. However, the vocabulary and typical phraseologies, among other things, continued to evolve.

For us, one of the most visible consequences of language fixing is that literary works for which no external evidence exists regarding provenance cannot be classified according to chronological or regional linguistic criteria. This is why the putative dates for certain works of literature may span several centuries. For example, the short but not unimportant tract *Peri hermenaias* (On Interpretation), which has been incorrectly attributed to the politician and philosopher Demetrios of Phaleron, is dated from the third to the first century BCE. The traces of organic linguistic development that enable us to say with certainty that the *Odyssey* represents a more recent linguistic stratum than the *Iliad* or that the tragic poet Aeschylus wrote before Euripides simply peter out in the context of Hellenistic literature.

The final step by which Greek became a historical language that had to be taught, however, is linked to what is known as *Atticism*.[9] After the first century BCE—in Rome earlier, it seems, than in Greece itself—a tendency developed to view the old "classical" literature of Attica, the works of historians like Thucydides and Xenophon; of orators like Demosthenes, Lysias, and Isocrates; of comic poets like Aristophanes; or of the philosopher Plato as the highest form of Greek and to imitate that form. But in view of the changes that Hellenistic Greek continued to permit, except for the strict culling of new words and expressions, this amounted to a reversion to a language that was already three hundred years old. As far as we can tell, this "repristinization" (a term coined by Albrecht Dihle) was the final act that decoupled the high form of the language from the everyday vernacular. This was possible only because the educational institutions that inculcated grammatical and literary standards functioned as well as they did. Increasingly, over the course of the first and particularly the second centuries CE, this language training became a marker of social prestige that extended well beyond the areas of literature and science. No person of ambition in the Greek world could any longer afford to speak the language that had been learned at home but was forced to learn the elevated Attic idiom. This was more or less true even for Athenians, whose spoken vernacular, four hundred years after the classical period, was no longer that of Aristophanes. From then on, Attic Greek was passed on from teacher to student, not from parent to child. Thus developed a rich array of Attic dictionaries and other language-training aids that ensured that the student would learn right from wrong, good form from bad.

In looking at this development, we have tended to emphasize that it enabled a social elite to split off from the people by identifying with the past and its literature. However, with regard to the function of Greek as an ancient world language, we should place more emphasis on the fact that, in this case, literature played a crucial role in creating a supraregional form of Greek that was understandable over a wide territory. We must ask how a standard supraregional language might otherwise have been established, given the technologies and means of communication in the ancient world. What is crucial is not the geographic distribution of the language but the fact that Greek had become a *pluricentric* language; that is, it no longer possessed a *central* speech community that might serve as a single standard for all. Even Athens was no longer such a center. There was, of course, a complete lack of media such as newspapers or other quickly reproducible writings having widespread distribution— not to mention electronic media, which in modern times have made it possible to spread linguistic standards and to disseminate linguistic innovations. The sole supraregional, nonlocal, and always available language authority was embodied in literature that could be archived in books and studied in school. The much-discussed intertextuality of Alexandrine literature is to some extent a consequence of this linguistic situation. This applies all the more to the renaissance of Attic Greek If we look past some extremely purist tendencies, which were the object of

derision even in the ancient world, Atticism provided a relatively uniform speech norm that could be learned at school regardless of one's
place of birth and early socialization. In later centuries, the Romans
would have taken a prime interest in communications with Greek cities
as well—and not merely as stuttering foreigners. Greek as a fixed language tethered to historical models enabled them to master the language almost as well as the Greeks themselves. Romans were able to use
this fixed language, Greek, to engage in intricate negotiations and to
describe complex objects and situations independently of place throughout the enormous Roman Empire—at least until the split between the
eastern and western halves of the empire and before Latin had acquired
all of the functions of Greek.

As has long been abundantly and painfully clear to classics scholars,
the linguistic significance of this development is evident in that the
transmission of Greek literature was closely tied to its function as a language model for the teaching of Greek in school. Over the centuries,
"classical" Greek texts—the Greek tragedies and comedies, the histories
of Thucydides and Xenophon, the speeches of Demosthenes and Isocrates,
even some of Plato's dialogues—were copied and recopied, thereby ensuring their survival. This was done primarily because that was how
Greek was learned. But this mechanism of transmission also meant that
important cultural achievements were written off simply because they
were not written in Attic Greek. As a result, preclassical and postclassical
literature has largely been lost, with the exception of the works of Homer,
which had a crystallizing effect on the development of Greek culture.
The entire output of lyrical, elegiac, and iambic poetry of the seventh
and sixth centuries has been lost, with the exception of Pindar's book
of *epinikia*. Archilochos, Simonides, Sappho, Anacreon, Bacchylides,
and Stesichoros survive only in fragments. The same holds true for the
Ionic prose of the sixth century, the most important losses from the perspective of European intellectual history having been the texts of the
pre-Socratic philosophers. Furthermore, almost all of Hellenistic literature has been completely lost, including key texts of Stoic and Epicurean philosophy, which were to have such an important overall influence on European intellectual life. We have Aristophanes's comedies
and probably also the classical Greek tragedies because the dialogues
within them served as models of Attic idiom. The even more important

comedies of Menander (which we now know would have added immeasurably to our understanding of Greek and Roman literature) were not passed on and are known to us only in part because, by pure happenstance, remnants of certain ancient papyrus rolls had evaded destruction.

But let us return to linguistic history. Since the ascent of Atticism at the latest, if not earlier, the Greek language had been characterized by a split that persisted throughout numerous historical stages almost to the present. Until 1977, the official standard written language of Greece was Katharevousa, a form of the language closely related to classical Greek, which had to be learned in school. Dimotiki, the vernacular language of the people, evolved increasingly away from this standard. In 1957, the Arabist and linguist Charles A. Ferguson described this state of affairs, which recurs many times in widely disparate cultures, coining the term *diglossia*.[10] Ferguson understood this term to mean a situation in which two strongly diverging variants of the same language coexist within the same society and are used according to certain internally defined rules. The particular case that engaged him was the division between high language and regional dialects, typical of all Arab countries. Ferguson drew parallels to the coexistence of High German and Schwyzerdütsch in Switzerland, of French and Creole in Haiti, and the then still official division between Katharevousa and Dimotiki in Greece. All of these cases involve variant pairs, one half of which (the "high" variant) requires academic training and serves as the language of literature, official business, and the like. It exhibits a strong degree of standardization and enjoys great prestige, whereas the other half (the "low" variant) is the spontaneous language of the population at large. It is primarily an oral language and is used neither in school nor in official communications. Its prestige is correspondingly low.

Unfortunately, Ferguson failed to consider that the evolutionary paths taken by the specific instances of diglossia that he described are completely different even though, as an Arabist, he should probably have noted this historical dimension. As a result, Ferguson's model must be further refined if we are to draw on it for our understanding of the development of historical culture languages.

The diglossia evident within Switzerland is a synchronous diglossia. It developed because, in relatively recent times, the written German language was introduced as a common high language in all German-speaking regions and in regions with completely different regional dialects. This resulted in the coexistence of a high language and a dialect centered on orality. The diglossia present in classical Greece, which continues in modern Greece but also characterizes the Arabic-speaking countries, is the result of language change. At some point in time the vernacular language of a particular population—in the Greek case in the Attic region—became the literary language. Then this original and fixed literary form continued to be used while the spontaneous, unregulated form of the language kept evolving. And this was precisely what happened in the case of post-Hellenistic classical Greek, in Arabic, and of course in Latin. This divergence occurred over time and became problematic only after several centuries.

Concretely, when we say that a diglossia consistent with Ferguson was present in Greece with the ascent of Atticism at the latest, we mean that the vernacular language of the Greek population had diverged from the established written form (in the direction of contemporary modern Greek) to such an extent that the difference was obvious and required special training at school. Of course, the regional interactions and overlays that determined Swiss diglossia also occurred in Greek. However, the growing gap between a literary language fixed at a particular historical stage and the unregulated vernacular language that continued to evolve was the reason that classical Greek became a historical language and representative of a past time.

Despite some changes, Greek diglossia has remained structurally consistent for the two thousand years following Atticism. Classical literary Greek, either in its stricter Attic form or in the somewhat more general Hellenistic koine, basically remained the high form of Greek into modern times. True, nonclassical strands of and influences from the evolving Greek vernacular may be found in profusion in late antiquity. In some cases, literature was written in a language approaching the vernacular. Nonetheless, at all times, ancient classical Greek remained the more or less implemented form of the language for more than fifteen hundred years, even under Turkish rule. The first Greeks who arrived in Italy in the fourteenth and fifteenth centuries and triggered a renaissance in Greek literature among the Italian humanists—writers like Constantinos Laskaris, Cardinal Bessarion, and Michael Marullus—wrote and taught classical Greek as "their own" language, not as a historical artifact.

Greek underwent a reorganization during the nineteenth century. Once Ottoman rule had been thrown off and the modern Greek state founded, the question arose about the proper language for the new state. Adopting classical Greek was one of the "strong" options under discussion. That would have been as if Latin had become Italy's official language after the reunification in the nineteenth century. As I discuss later, this comparison is not as far fetched as one might imagine, and if Italy had been reunited in the fifteenth century, this option might well have been chosen. But Greece chose a somewhat more moderate alternative: the written language of official business would be a reformed variant of classical Greek that had adopted a series of changes from the vernacular. Nonetheless, it was so close to the classical form that people with a humanistic education who had learned classical Greek in school had little trouble mastering it. This "pure" Katharevousa coexisted with the vernacular Dimotiki, which had diverged considerably from the classical language. The diglossia that had existed for eighteen hundred years was now codified in modified form. Still, this did not last, either, and the reason is probably that High Greek and the vernacular competed within the same space, and High Greek, which had to be carefully learned, came to have no real function in communications with other countries. This was different from the situation in Switzerland, where High German forms the basis for communications with Germany and Austria, or in the Islamic world, where High Arabic is the common language. This meant that now diglossia simply impeded communications within Greece. It was not surprising that the vernacular gained ground and in 1977 became the sole official language of Greece. Katharevousa is now used officially only in the Orthodox Church and in a few niche settings.

The history of Arabic diglossia is in many respects similar to that of Greek.[11] High Arabic is the common element connecting all Arab states (from the Arabian Peninsula, the Fertile Crescent, Iraq, and Palestine to North Africa, including Mauritania, Somalia, Egypt, and Morocco). However, it is not the actual language of the population in any of these countries and must be learned at school. The difficulties that Arab students have learning Arabic has been compared to Latin class in secondary schools in Europe. High Arabic is a historically fixed language. It largely retains the morphology and many of the syntactic features of classical Arabic as are found in the Koran and in the literature of the seventh to the tenth century. Since the nineteenth century, the vocabulary (both in terms of new words and the meanings given to old words) has changed to adapt to the requirements of the modern world. But as far as the core of the language is concerned, a person with a knowledge of present-day High Arabic can still understand twelve-hundred-year-old texts. The Koran, which was written in the seventh century, continues to be read unchanged. A number of regional languages have formed from High Arabic in the various regions of the Arabic world, including those spoken on the Arabian Peninsula in Saudi Arabia, or Iraq, or Syria and Palestine, or Egypt and Sudan, or in the Maghreb countries of northwest Africa. These "dialects" are so far removed from the high form of the language as to be virtually incomprehensible to nonlocal Arabic speakers. Much like the relationship between the Romance languages and Latin, these dialects evolved from old Arabic, and like the Romance languages they have a number of characteristics in common, though each dialect has its own peculiarities. High Arabic continues to be the language of choice for the news media, literature, and official pronouncements of all sorts, although local dialects have made some inroads in the past several decades. For feature films and other such popular productions, where the high form of the language would seem ridiculous, the Cairo dialect has achieved a recognized position as the spoken standard; it is also increasingly possible to publish literary works in the various regional languages. Nonetheless, this underlying diglossia and the art status of High Arabic are fundamental to the culture of the Arab world. It is as if all of the Romance countries of Europe used an updated form of Latin exclusively in written communications while the Romance languages themselves were relegated to the spoken word.

This diglossia extends back to the beginnings of Arabic literature. The question of whether its core may be traced back to an oral pre-Islamic poetic language, possibly an elevated form of the vernacular, is currently under discussion. If so, this poetic language would be comparable to the rhapsodic language of Homer. High Arabic became standardized and fixed very early. Beginning in the seventh century, the process was largely completed by the ninth. Numerous theoretical works, primarily of a lexicographic nature, attest to this process, and some of them remained in use until quite recently. This itself is evidence of an astonishing linguistic continuity. One of the achievements of this codification was that even early on those who were no longer native speakers of Arabic could continue to participate in Arabic written culture. The earliest Arabic grammar treatise was written by the Persian Sibawayh (d. 793 CE) and shows the important role that this standardization played in communications with other peoples.

The Arabic model of a language unchanging for centuries with a language community bound together by a high language based on literary norms, below which one or several oral vernaculars are in a constant state of evolution, is a model attested to in numerous societies. The development of Persian is quite similar. After the twelfth to fourteenth centuries, when the classics of Persian literature were written, it remained the virtually unchanged written language not only of Persia but also of other parts of Central Asia.

Pronounced diglossia may be found today in many Asian societies in which the literary language preserves an ancient linguistic tradition and must be taught in school. Sri Lanka is an extreme example. After the country gained its independence from England, Sinhalese, an Indo-European language whose written standards go back to the twelfth century, became the official language of state.[12] In terms of distance from the people, imagine for a moment that all official business in the United States had to be transacted in Chaucerian English and that bureaucrats and officials were forced to spend years acquiring the competence needed to perform their duties. At the same time, however, Tamil, which belongs to the Dravidian group of languages, is also spoken in southern India and Sri Lanka. It has been attested as a written language since the third century BCE, and it, too, exhibits pronounced diglossia between the spontaneously spoken vernacular and the historical written form.

Another excellent case of a historical culture language is classical Chinese. This form extends back, little changed, to the third century BCE. As a literary language, classical Chinese was in official use up to the beginning of the twentieth century and is still taught not only in China but also at Western universities, which (as with Sanskrit and Latin) have since the nineteenth century committed themselves to maintaining the classical literary traditions. However, the spoken language—or more precisely, the spoken languages—long ago diverged from this standard. Chinese diglossia differs from others in that Chinese writing consists of individual symbols for complete words, which means that, in contrast to other systems of writing, they can be read independently of the reader's own language or pronunciation. This special feature has influenced the use of classical Chinese both within the Chinese linguistic space and in other Asian countries. As a result, classical Chinese has, much more than other culture languages, always focused on written use.

Modern European languages also tend to preserve the historical written form, though to a lesser extent. French is the most profound instance of historical fixing in Europe since the seventeenth century. Official language policies ensure that its core elements remain stable. As a result of policies promulgated in Paris, French was the European language that most replaced Latin in the early modern period and was most subject to strict codification during the seventeenth century. The immutability of the codified rules—in other words, the fixing of the language—was not an unintentional side effect but an openly stated principle. It was not so much that the French wanted to supplant "dead" Latin with a living language; rather, the intent was to imbue the language of France with all of the qualities of Latin and in particular render it eternally immutable. One effect was that French became an important lingua franca in Europe during the seventeenth and eighteenth centuries, and it was routinely used by the educated classes and the nobility—even in Germany. But its norms were and continue to be enforced by strict oversight exerted by the Académie française. These norms, moreover, artificially sustained, permit not even the illusion that correct French describes a living vernacular. Compared with other European languages, French is closer to Latin in this respect.[13] Two hundred years ago, August Wilhelm Schlegel (1767–1845), who championed the vernacular in the spirit of German Romanticism, even called French a "dead" language.[14] The consequences of this strict codification of French, which remains official policy today, are easy to discern. Along with the rigorously controlled written language *(code écrit)*, a spoken language *(code parlé)* has developed so independently that linguists compare it to the divergence between the written norm and "vulgar Latin" in late antiquity. The question has even been raised whether France is not in fact heading toward diglossia of the Ferguson type.

Fixed Languages with Generational Supersession:
Latin and Sanskrit

Latin differs from the other languages discussed earlier in that it is not the exclusive written language of any particular population. The reason for this is not that Latin developed differently from Greek or Arabic. Rather, the vernaculars of the various populations diverged. The Greek spoken by the people and the regional dialects of Arabic were rarely committed to writing and as a result never created a fixed standard. By contrast, the various Romance languages that grew out of the regional variants of what is called Vulgar Latin themselves became literary languages and over the course of time became standardized. From then on, they replaced Latin as the means of communication. Diglossia resulted in genuine bilingualism.

This divergence of the Romance languages from Latin, and their scriptualization, has been a central focus of Romance studies for some two hundred years. But in view of the cultural and historical approach taken in this book, our view of the process will not be limited to the countries in which a Romance language is spoken. In fact, the same process took place even in the regions of Europe that were not Romanized but in which the population spoke a Germanic, Celtic, or Slavic language at home. The vernaculars were scriptualized, and over time they assumed the position that Latin had once occupied. One might perhaps say that the Romance languages are the daughters of Latin, while the other successor languages that did not emerge from Latin itself but converged with Latin as a result of secondary cultural and historical constellations may be viewed as Latin's adoptive daughters.

The development of Sanskrit probably has the most parallels with that of Latin. Sanskrit was originally the language of a small region in what is today northwestern India.[15] The Vedas have survived from the oldest times. Their language was already far removed from the vernacular of the population in 500 BCE, during the lifetime of the grammarian Panini. Panini's great achievement was to develop the grammatical foundations of the language, thereby fixing them permanently. Sanskrit subsequently became the culture language of the entire Indian subcontinent. However, other written languages also developed from the same Indo-European linguistic background, the most important of which was Prakrit or, more precisely, the various forms of Prakrit that were in use from about the fourth to the eleventh century (that is, when Sanskrit was no longer a "natural" language). Prakrit also became a historically fixed culture language, though over a considerably longer period of time than occurred in Romance Europe, and eventually gave way to Hindi, Bengali, and other languages. Much like Latin, which was used widely outside the Romanized regions, Sanskrit became the culture language in territories whose actual language was and remains very different. As with Latin, the literature that was created *after* fixing is immeasurably larger than the few works that have been passed on to us from ancient times. In a direct parallel to our distorted perception of the Latin tradition, this later literature has barely been acknowledged by modern Europeans—except where motivated by special interest, as typified by the *Kama Sutra,* which was written in the fourth century CE.

Hebrew in the early modern period is a special case of a culture language that existed in parallel with other written languages. As the common written language, it retained its historical form and connected Jewish populations throughout the Diaspora even as those populations adopted the local languages where they settled, including their written languages. Hebrew is the best-known case of a historical culture language brought back to life in modern times and given the status of an obligatory written and spoken language and of an official language of state.

All of these are clearly cases of a generational supersession because the fixed language was initially the sole obligatory written language in a specific linguistic area, which was later limited or even superseded by a more recent language—whether by a more recent stage of the language itself or by other languages. Of course, this did not take place all at once but over a long course of development in which the old culture language initially retained all of its functions. The history of Latin in Europe clearly fits into the conventional model of the Latin "mother tongue" and Romance derivative or "daughter" languages. In families, two generations live together for a time; likewise, the young Romance languages initially had little room to spread out and were dependent on Latin. Over time, they took on more and more functions until they either became independent or were suppressed by the language that gave them life. Only then, to stay with our metaphor, did Mother Latin really begin to be seen as an *old* language belonging to another generation just as our parents are by definition our elders, no matter what their actual age.

For our understanding of the phenomenon of fixed historical culture languages, it is important to understand that the acquisition and use of fixed languages does not differ in terms of generational change from languages that do not (yet) have successor languages. The fact that the spontaneous vernacular of a population could now be written and began to replace Latin did not, at first, change the old culture language. It would be incorrect to assume that languages like Arabic or Greek, which for a long time had no "daughter" or "adoptive daughter" languages, would as a result be less fixed in their underlying structure and be more open to change. Actually, the opposite is true. The official school Latin of late antiquity was certainly less open to change and linguistic inventiveness than were most forms of medieval Latin. The notion that Latin became a permanently "dead" language at the time of the scripturalization of French is an idea that took hold a thousand years after the fact but would not have been evident to Latin speakers at the time. It would have made no sense to people in ninth-century Gaul, tentatively attempting for the first time to commit the Romance vernacular to writing while at the same time being instructed in Latin grammar, to question whether their Romanized language was a variety of Latin or a completely new language. Awareness that Latin was a "dead" language was conceivable only once it was possible to dispense with Latin completely. But that occurred at the earliest during the sixteenth century. In addition, European linguistic history since the sixteenth century has been characterized by an "ideology" favoring a living vernacular learned at home and not at school, which has led to a deprecation of grammatically standardized languages. However, such devaluation of codified written languages is not a universal, cultural constant and is not present in like fashion in other cultures.

This becomes clear when we compare Latin and Sanskrit. Except in the Catholic Church, over the past hundred years real communication in Latin has been almost a taboo among Latin scholars. School Latin teachers thought it impossible to speak Latin in class, and writing in Latin was relegated to the status of grammar exercise. Among classical philologists, even "reading" Latin literature was sometimes viewed as a sign of superficiality: Latin was legitimate only in serious research into topics that warranted it. Only in the past few years has a modest revival in Latin communication occurred. The recent history of Sanskrit is different: whatever the status of Sanskrit in India may be today, a certain tradition of speaking or writing the language has always existed.[16] There are poetry contests, movies, and broadcast news programs in Sanskrit and in Latin—but a modest tradition lives on in India, while such manifestations in Latin are rare.

Nor can it be said that as a consequence of having undergone generational supersession, Latin has become a historically "more regressive" language than languages that did not produce offspring. The fixed core of word forms and basic syntactic structures in modern High Arabic do not differ significantly from those attested in ancient times. Knowledge of the modern high version of the language gains one entrée (with some effort) into thirteen-hundred-year-old Islamic texts. But the effort is much less forbidding than what an average American would face when trying to puzzle out *Beowulf* or some other Anglo-Saxon poem. This is why the Koran that is used today is linguistically the same as that of the seventh century. Let us imagine an Italian living at the time of Dante and Petrarch—in other words at a time when Latin and Italian were viewed as the *grammatica* and the *volgare,* respectively, of the same language. Such an Italian would have recognized the division between High Arabic and the regional dialects as being essentially the same as the relationship between Latin and Italian or between written Greek and the Greek vernacular.

By contrast, Latin has remained static as it is no longer subject to the challenges of the present. The real reason that Latin is viewed as a historical language today has more to do with its exclusion from the present than with any putative regression to speech norms of the past. Sanskrit, which retains its function as an actively used language, is much more open to influences from the modern world.

2

---◆---

The Language of the Empire

Latin from Its Beginnings to the End of Antiquity

I N TERMS OF the history of Latin, stating that the Roman Empire constituted an epoch all its own is more than to follow the usual land-
marks of historiography. This is because, viewed through the lens of
linguistic history, Roman power actually made itself felt at two significant points. First, as long as the Roman Empire existed, no new literary
language could develop despite the fact that many languages were spoken and written during that time. For more than seven hundred years
people made do with Latin, as well as the other languages that had existed before the Romans, namely Greek, Egyptian, Aramaic, Punic, Hebrew, and a few other languages. Over the course of a complex Latinization process that occurred between the second century BCE and the first
century CE, all languages other than Latin and Greek, that is, Etruscan
and all the other Italic languages disappeared on the peninsula. In the
provinces, especially in North Africa, Spain, and southern France, where
peoples speaking other languages lived, there was as far as we know no
serious attempt to develop an expanded written culture other than that
of Latin. But when the Roman Empire came to an end, the linguistic
situation, and with it literature, underwent a fundamental change.
One literary document written in a new language was the translation
of the Bible into Gothic in the fourth century, the Bible of Bishop Ulfilas;
however, we know almost nothing about the context in which it was
written. Soon after the end of the Roman Empire, in the seventh century, large numbers of texts began being written in Irish, along with
those in Latin, and as I discuss in greater detail later, this represented a

new chapter in the linguistic history of Europe. Second, Latin, originally the dialect of Rome, in the Latium region, was always the first language of the Roman rulers, initially of the consuls and then of the emperor. Latin was never the sole language of the Romans. But until the end, when Emperor Romulus Augustulus was deposed in 476, it was the language of those in power. After that, it was no longer. Although the rulers of the Goths, Lombards, Merovingians, and Franks may have used Latin as their official language in the way the Roman rulers had, it was nonetheless not their own language.

This does not mean that the Latin spoken during the time of the empire was the "vernacular" language of Rome or the mother tongue of the Romans. On the contrary, in describing the history of Latin over the seven hundred years of Roman rule, one could say that Latin had lost what is characteristic of vernacular languages. At the beginning, Latin was one of many regional dialects on the Italian peninsula. By the time the last emperor in the West had been deposed, Latin had basically become as far removed from the spontaneous vernacular of the population as it was during the Carolingian Renaissance, in the late eighth and ninth centuries.

Nor does the fact that Latin was the language of power in Rome mean that the Romans forced their language on the empire. The type of language imperialism practiced by modern national states, leading to the cultural conflicts that are all too well known to us, did not exist in the Roman Empire in this form. This is evident from the spread of the Latin language in Italy and then later in the relationship between Latin and other languages in the Roman world empire.

If we look at central Italy in the time between the sixth and the first century BCE—in other words, from when Roman power began to spread until the unification of central Italy as a Roman territory during the Roman Social War from 91 to 89 BCE—we find an extraordinarily complex situation.[1] Latin was the language of Latium, the small region around Rome, and as such it was only one of about two dozen Italic dialects, of which the most important were Faliscan, Umbrian, Oscan, Venetian, and Messapian. Celtic peoples lived in what is now northern Italy, north of the Po River, but nothing has survived of their language. The Italic dialects were so distinct from Latin that communication was virtually impossible. Compare, for example, a short line from the so-called Tabulae Iguvinae, a set of seven bronze tablets containing religious formulae, which are the most important extant documents in the Umbrian language (second to first century BCE; Latin translation below the Umbrian):

> pune publum aferum   heries avef anzeriatu   etu perniaf pustnaiaf
> cum   populum lustrare voles   aves observatum to   anticas posticas
> *(If you wish to perform a lustration of the people, observe the birds, those*
> *[coming] from in front and those from behind).*

This rather obscure observation had to do with birds as omens. In any case, seeing how different Umbrian and Latin were, it is not surprising that the notion of a common Italic language did not exist as it did among the Greeks despite all of the differences in their dialects. The term *Italic* was invented by modern philologists and had little to do with realities on the peninsula.

However, the linguistic situation in Italy was characterized by the existence of two large supraregional literary languages, neither of which was Italic. The first was Etruscan, in the north (which has still not been definitively classified), which with more than ten thousand inscriptions, few of which have as yet been satisfactorily deciphered, is still better documented than any of the Italic languages. Then in the south was Greek, which had arrived in the western Mediterranean as a result of the colonization of southern Italy and Sicily. In terms of culture and literature, the various Italian populations were forced to deal with foreign languages from the outset. The Romans, who were initially part of the Etruscan region of power (the legends of the Roman monarchy relate to this early phase of their history), learned much from the Etruscans, as the wealth of Etruscan traces in Latin makes abundantly clear. The Roman historian Livy (59 BCE–16 CE) reported that as late as the fourth century, noble Romans continued to be instructed in Etruscan (Livy 9.36.3). Later the Romans submitted to the Greeks to some extent, as I describe in greater detail later on.

Of course, once Rome became the sole real power in central Italy, after the fifth century, its language began to spread. This is not to say that the Latinization process transpired in parallel with the spread of Roman power. To the contrary, it is evident that the local dialects held out well into the first century BCE and in some cases even beyond. Oscan inscriptions that must have been inscribed not long before the eruption

Figure 2. Dispersion of the three main languages on the Italian peninsula prior to the spread of Latin (ca. fourth century BCE): Italic languages (Umbrian, Faliscan, Latin, Marsian, Oscan, Messapian, Volscian); Etruscan; Greek cities in southern Italy and Sicily. Punic was also spoken in Sicily.

of Vesuvius, in 79 CE, have been found in Pompeii. The documents that have survived give evidence of a complex linguistic situation in which the mutual influences exerted by bordering dialects are evident. The only direct evidence that we have about the process by which Latin spread in Italy is found in Livy, who states that upon being petitioned by the inhabitants of Cumae, the Romans permitted the use of the Latin language in official documents (Livy 40.32.1). We have no evidence that this was anything other than actual permission and not, as is so often the case with modern dictatorships, an iron decree justified to the outside world by a sham request for help.

Oscan, which with four hundred extant inscriptions that exhibit practically no regional differences, played a major role within the Italic languages.[2] Next to Latin, it is the best documented of all the Italic dialects. It is assumed that a supraregional linguistic form had developed here, an Oscan koine, and for the past hundred years scholars have even debated whether an Oscan literature might have existed, without coming to any well-grounded conclusion. This would be consistent with our understanding that the ancient term *Osci* did not describe an ethnicity but rather an association of various peoples united by language. Oscan influences have also played a role in Rome in historical times. We have evidence of the use of the Oscan language as a conscious demonstration of non-Roman identity on coins and inscriptions from the middle of the so-called Social War between Rome and the *socii*, that is, the confederate cities, which lasted from 91 to 89 BCE. After this bloody civil war came to an end and all of the inhabitants of central Italy were granted Roman citizenship, arguments arose about to whether Oscan should be the official language of the Latin confederation. By this time, Rome had long since become the most important Mediterranean power between Asia Minor and Spain. But at home, just a few miles from Rome, the political relationships between the Roman colonial cities, the cities of the Latin confederation, and the *socii* had become complex. At least in central Italy it would take a civil war to create a unified state organization. The variety of languages mirrors this political reality. It was almost as if arguments had broken out in England after the conquest of India over whether the inhabitants of Exeter were actually English citizens or whether Welsh should be given an official role in the political life of the country.

At the macro level, the linguistic arrangements of the Roman Empire may be gauged even after two thousand years by one rather astonishing fact. The Romans never suppressed a language if it already had an established written tradition when they arrived. In this, Roman expansionism differed markedly from that of Islam, which suppressed the old written languages of Syriac, Coptic, Greek, and, at least until the tenth century, Persian. The map of the current Romance-speaking areas of Europe—from Sicily through Italy to the Alps, the Iberian Peninsula, France, and parts of the Balkans—the areas where Latin became the language of the population, is largely congruent with that of areas that had no written culture prior to the Roman presence. The suppression of Etruscan and (partially) of Greek in southern Italy and Sicily is only an apparent exception. In fact, neither of these languages had been indigenous to Italy itself. Greek arrived with the wave of colonization after the eighth century, and in spite of the uncertain origins of the Etruscans and the still-contested classification of their language, it is clear that they came from elsewhere.

Wherever the languages of long-settled indigenous populations had been scriptualized and particularly where significant written cultures had developed, those languages continued in use even after conquest by Rome. This was true not only of Greek, which the Romans considered the preeminent language of culture, but also of Egyptian and many of the languages spoken in Palestine and Asia. The inscription above Jesus's cross was in Latin, Greek, and Hebrew—but none of these languages was the everyday language of the people of the area, who spoke primarily Aramaic. Furthermore, in western North Africa, where Latin continued to play a significant role as a literary language into late antiquity, the old Punic language was still in use at the time of Augustine of Hippo (354–430 CE). When Pliny the Elder in his *Natural History*[3] praised the Romans for having united so many barbarous peoples by giving them a common language, he was talking about the indigenous Celtic inhabitants of Gaul, not the Greeks, Egyptians, and other peoples with established written traditions.

But how is one to reconcile this with the notion that Latin was the "official" language of the Romans? It is clear that the Romans had no Latinization policy and that they forced students to speak only Latin in school (where these existed). They were not nationalists in the modern sense. Much closer to the truth is that the Roman Empire was a multi-lingual empire distinguished by three levels of language organization.

First, the natural language of any particular population. Latin was the natural language only in Rome and surrounding areas—at least at first. Later the language spread to other areas. But as we have seen, Latin displaced other languages only where Latin had specific basic advantages associated with trade and consumer goods, literacy, and intellectual culture. This was largely the case in what are today the Romance areas of Europe. Other than that, the inhabitants of each region continued to speak as they had previously.

Second, the level of military control and administration. Here, Latin was in fact indispensable as it was the language of the rulers. Soldiers were commanded in Latin; the taxation and the legal systems were administered in Latin. In addition, Latin was always the language of Roman officials; even during those times when all educated Romans spoke fluent Greek, only Latin was permitted in the Senate.

Third, the language of literature and of all more complex texts distributed in book form. In this regard, Latin differed significantly from most other ancient written cultures well into late antiquity. Here, the Romans really had nothing new to add. True, they were able to write early on, but in terms of their "higher" modes of culture, they were initially completely dependent on the older written cultures in their territories. This included first and foremost the Etruscan culture, which greatly influenced religious traditions and early theater, and then they came under the influence of the Greeks. In spite of the fact that this dependence was largely viewed as a sign of inferiority during the nineteenth century, the current, more balanced view focuses on the productivity and the cultural achievements that this association with Greece made possible. There is no denying that the Greeks deeply influenced Roman literature and language. The fact that ancient Greek is a prerequisite for scholarly research in ancient Latin literature shows just how important this relationship was.

Because of this, no linguistic history of the Roman Empire can neglect Greek. Not only was Greek culture older, but it also served as a model. Indeed, for many hundreds of years, the Roman Empire had a fundamentally Greco-Latin culture. This common history lasted as long as it did partly because, for many years, the languages were not on an equal footing. Their social and cultural functions differed markedly. During the second century BCE, when Rome assumed control of Greece and became a world power, Greek was already a world language, whereas Latin was little more than a local dialect. The long-term interaction between the languages that resulted shaped the Roman Empire for about six hundred years, and Latin continued to be entangled with Greek almost to the end of the Roman Empire.

The Adoption of Greek Literature

The year 240 BCE may be considered a watershed date in Latin literature. That was when, so we are told, the Greco-Roman dramatist and poet Livius Andronicus for the first time staged a drama in Rome that had been translated from the Greek, although we do not know whether his Latin version of Homer's *Odyssey* should be dated before or after this date. Latin literature as we know it, however, began with Livius Andronicus, and in its fundamentals this literature was a reshaping and an extension of Greek literature. It is not as though the Romans did not write before then. They certainly did, and they even wrote books. Toward the end of the fourth century BCE, the censor Appius Claudius Caecus (the builder of the Via Appia) published a collection of moral aphorisms and committed speeches to writing. After Livius Andronicus, the hallmark of Roman literature was that it derived from the Greek. With very few exceptions, among them satire, the first Roman literary works known to us were either translations or free adaptations from Greek works, and even later, authors continually drew on Greek sources. The genres of poetry, myth, philosophical and rhetorical systems, as well as many peculiarities of Roman historiography, are largely of Greek derivation.

Now it was quite common for ancient written cultures to adopt other literary traditions. Important Buddhist texts, which were originally written in Sanskrit, survive only in Tibetan translations, and the Japanese adopted texts wholesale from the Chinese, which was not especially difficult, given that they merely had to read the Chinese logograms in Japanese. The Arabs engaged deeply with the philosophical and scientific literature of the Greeks, and the Greeks themselves learned much from the great cultures of the ancient Orient. Nonetheless, how Roman written culture derived its forms from the Greek is unique.

Given the enormous presence of things Greek in Rome, it is astonishing that so little effort has been made to understand what drove the Romans to adopt Greek literary works and forms. It is simply assumed that, as they expanded their power during the third century and came into contact with the urban Greek cultures of southern Italy, they were so impressed by Greek cultural traditions that they decided to make them their own. In other words, up to now the adoption of Greek literature has been viewed solely as a bilateral affair between Romans and Greeks.[4]

However, the overall cultural situation in early Italy that I mentioned earlier makes a different explanation more plausible. In my opinion, the influence of Greek culture should be viewed as a pan-Italian phenomenon that affected more than just the Romans. After all, this culture was not limited to the Greek settlements; almost all intact Greek vases that have come down to us were found in Etruscan and Italic tombs. Greek gods were present in Etruria. The Etruscans apparently performed Greek tragedies in Etruscan translation,[5] and the tomb paintings in the southern Italian region of Lucania show that Greek prototypes were reworked in the local style.[6] This makes it quite improbable that the literary culture of Greece was completely isolated on Italic soil, where it was purportedly first discovered by the Romans. Rather, we need to recognize that the connection between Greek literature—or, more concretely, Greek theatrical practices and epics—and Italic forms of culture had already been introduced wherever the Greeks settled before the ascent of the Romans. In that sense, the innovation of the Romans consisted less of adopting Greek literature and more of adapting that literature to Italic forms that already existed in other regions, which they then aspired to in Latin.

The astonishing fact that none—not one—of the Roman poets before Lucilius (d. 103/2 BCE) came from Rome or spoke Latin as his mother tongue speaks for this sequence of events. Livius Andronicus was presumably a Greek slave. The next known writer, Naevius (third century BCE), came from Campania, an Oscan region. Ennius (239–169 BCE) came from Messapia (he also spoke Oscan), and his nephew Pacuvius from Brindisi, which was also Oscan-speaking territory. Plautus (ca. 250–ca. 184 BCE) came from Sarsin, in Umbria; the comedic poet Caecilius Statius (ca. 230/220–168 BCE) was probably a Celt from what is now northern Italy. Terence (185–159 BCE) appears to have been a special case: although he was born in Carthage, he may not have been Punic but a member of a completely different people. So why did the Romans allow their poetry to be written by foreigners? It is not enough to state what Cato and Cicero had already established, namely that poetry was not especially well received in early, moralistic Rome. There is another, more plausible explanation. The writers mentioned earlier were all grounded in Greek literature; otherwise, they would not have been able to make translations into Latin. Is it plausible that with their great poetic and theatrical know-how, although they may have learned Greek in their homelands, it took the Romans to get them to produce Greek plays for an Italic audience? As mentioned earlier, Ennius, the great epic poet and dramatist, said that he had three hearts, a Greek, an Oscan, and a Latin. Are we to assume that his political heart beat only in Greek and Latin and that before he came to Rome at the age of forty he used the Oscan language of his region of origin for prose works alone? The comedies of the Umbrian playwright Plautus apparently comprise a mixture of Greek theatrical texts and a non-Greek, probably Italic, improvisational theater, and the attempt to reconstruct the details has produced an entire scholarship of its own. Are we really to assume that Plautus first began to work on Greek texts only *after* he arrived in Rome? If he spoke Greek earlier, then it is highly probable that he had already worked on adapting Greek dramas, and if he had to learn Greek along with Latin *after* he came to Rome, the importation of culture from Umbria makes no sense. What is most likely is that practitioners of the theater had used Greek texts for dramas in their respective Italic mother tongues well before they arrived in Rome. If this is true, then the Romans did not actually imitate Greek literature directly but adopted from their neighbors the habit of translating Greek literature into an Italic language. The actual cultural transfer of literature, which has until now been ascribed exclusively to the Romans, had, in all probability, already been accomplished by other Italic peoples. We need to remember that although Latin may have been the most important Italic language by the end of the second century BCE, its status was not absolute. Other languages on the peninsula were not simply insignificant dialects in Latin's shadow. Oscan, for example, may well have been a southern Italian koine of equal or even greater supraregional significance than Latin during the third century BCE. It makes sense to view the adoption of Greek literature by the Romans as part and parcel of a more comprehensive process of Greek-Italic cultural exchange, which went far beyond the city of Rome and the region of Latium.

This assumes, of course, that an Oscan literature must have existed prior to the Romans. This question has been discussed for a good hundred years for other reasons, as mentioned earlier. Although we may never find actual evidence of this literature because it has not survived, we can nonetheless set forth a basic, useful methodological framework. The mere fact that the primary extant evidence, especially in the form of inscriptions, gives not the slightest hint of an Oscan or other literature is largely irrelevant because, in the absence of the direct transfer of Roman literature during the Middle Ages, we would be completely unable to infer the existence of classical Latin literature from surviving inscriptions. If we consider that the Romans reported next to nothing about their neighbors on the Italian peninsula, it should come as no surprise that classical authors knew nothing of such literature. If we were dependent on the Greeks for our knowledge of Roman literature, we would know very little even though contact between Greeks and Romans was intensive and of long duration. Furthermore, the question of whether such a "literature" even existed is much too literal minded. There was certainly no such thing as a recognizable book trade with a large reading public. Dramatic works and epics were the primary literary adoptees from the Greeks, and those are precisely the areas whose semiliterary character, retaining the traces of orality, is still evident in the Latin literature that survives. So, to imagine the reworking of Greek dramas it would be enough to assume the existence of dramatic texts solely for the purposes of performance without distribution in book form.

When imagining the Italic reworking of epic poetry, we also find it useful to think in terms of oral performance. However, epic texts based on Homer, along the lines of those used in Greek writing classes, may also have been used as school textbooks from the very beginning. We have good reasons to believe that Livius Andronicus's Latin translation of the *Odyssey*, the oldest Latin epic, from the middle of the third century BCE, may well fall into this category. Unfortunately, the evidence in all such cases is so scanty that we will probably never know for certain. Nonetheless, classification of the oldest Roman translations of Greek literature in the broader context of Italic-Greek cultural relations in the fourth and third centuries is a major prerequisite for understanding the origins of Latin literature.

Latin Takes Shape

From Its Beginnings to the Classical Period

The most important difference between Greek and Latin during this early period was not that the Greeks possessed a literature and the Romans did not. At issue is something far more fundamental: the Greeks possessed a written language that was standardized over a supraregional territory and could be learned in their academies based on an actual literary tradition. In addition, this language was already more or less linguistically fixed. The dramas of Euripides (480–406 BCE), which were performed in southern Italic theaters, were some two hundred years old by the time the Romans started translating them into Latin for their stage productions. How greatly the vernacular language of the Greek colonists in Taranto and Naples differed from that of the literary dramas can no longer be ascertained; what is certain is that such differences existed. Nonetheless, the written Greek language was already a world language with which people from far-distant regions could communicate. This is why the first Roman historian, Quintus Fabius Pictor, wrote his history in Greek toward the end of the third century BCE. In this sense, his reasons were not much different from those of Swedish or Japanese scientists who now publish their research in English. Even Cicero, in his defense of the Roman poet Archias, wrote that Roman literature was still read only in Rome, whereas Greek literature was read everywhere (*pro Archia* 23).

The consequences of this situation are clearly evident in the earliest Latin texts. The Latin found in early documents is always different, and we have enough evidence to say that the language changed rather quickly. The oldest Latin inscriptions are no longer even completely comprehensible. In the second century BCE, the Romans themselves had difficulty deciphering an agreement concluded with the Carthaginians in 509–508 (Polybius 3, 22, 3; compare also 7, 27, 2).

This is easily understandable when we look at the oldest Latin texts that have come down to us. One good example is the so-called Duenos inscription, a brief text written on a vase from the sixth century BCE. This text is difficult even for specialists to translate, and I am simplifying the spelling here because in the original the letters all run together; that is, there are no spaces between words. When we juxtapose the "classical" Latin forms of the words, it becomes clear how much the Latin language changed during the next few centuries.

IOVESAT DEIVOS QOI MED MITAT NEI TED ENDO COSMIS VIRCO SIED
iurat divos qui me donat ni in te comis virgo sit

ASTED NOISIOPETOITESIAE PACA RIVOIS DUENOS MED FECED EN
at te . . . paca rivis bonus me fecit in

MANOM EINOM DUENOI NEMED MALOS TATOD
manum . . . bono ne me malus clepito[7]

The only part of the text that is intelligible is *"duenos med feced." Duenos* was an older form of the word *bonus* (good), just as *duellum* (from which the modern word "duel" is derived) was another form of *bellum*. The word *med* is a well-known form of *me* that is found in Plautus, and *feced* is basically a variant spelling of the later *fecit*. Thus, this phrase means "A good man made me." As for the rest of the inscription, though many of the words seem almost intelligible, the sense of the whole eludes our understanding.

With the exception of the Law of the Twelve Tables, legislated in 451 BCE, no other text continued in general use for several centuries, so it would not have been necessary to understand a long-outdated form of the language. Even in the case of the Twelve Tables it is not clear whether the version of those laws that was widespread during the classical period, which is what has come down to us, was the original form or a later re-working that accommodated linguistic changes—or even a complete reformulation. Another extremely archaic text, the ritual song called the Carmen Arvale, which was in use through the centuries and survives in the form of an inscription from the third century CE, has very strange—indeed inexplicable—word forms. But in this case it seems very likely that the sounds of this text were simply passed down as a sort of liturgical formula without any attention to meaning. The Arval priests probably had as little understanding of the text of their own ritual song as do modern linguists.

In any case, the Latin language continued changing and developing up into the first century BCE. We can distinguish between older and more recent linguistic stages, and the language provides clear criteria for the dating of texts, though stylization played a role even early in the process. Even if we had no biographical information about the comedic poets Plautus and Terence, we would still be able to say that Terence must have been the later of the two, based solely on the linguistic structure of their work.

The process of linguistic standardization began with the adoption of Greek literature in Rome. Of course, it is possible that people involved in the theater at first wrote out versions of their dramas solely as performance aids without intending to create "literature." However, the fact remains that the continuity of texts in Latin begins with the first dramas and the translation of the *Odyssey* by Livius Andronicus. As mentioned earlier, it was probably unavoidable that the early Latin epic poems would have been used as a text for schoolboys who learned reading and writing with Livius Andronicus as Greek schoolboys did with Homer. Cicero and Horace were still familiar with this practice. For later works such as Ennius's epic poem, *Annales,* from the first half of the second century BCE, we must assume, however, that the original text was passed down and read unchanged. The creation of a literature that continued to circulate even decades later would have acted as a stabilizing force on a living and rapidly changing language. At the turn of the first century BCE, when Cicero was first learning to write, the Romans already had a sort of classical literature, with Ennius as the central author, along with a coterie of other illustrious comedic poets, tragedians, orators, and historiographers.

Nonetheless, even if the literary works of the second century BCE show a certain consolidation of the written language, no uniform standard had yet developed. Each work documents a different developmental stage of the language, especially in orthography. This is well demonstrated by a *senatus consultum* (decree of the Senate) from the year 186 that was aimed at suppressing the cult of Bacchus, which was associated with orgiastic debauchery. The story is told by Livy (39, 8–19). Purely by chance, a copy of this decree was preserved on a bronze tablet, which is housed in the Kunsthistorisches Museum, in Vienna. It begins as follows:

> De bacanalibus quei foideratei esent ita exdeicendum censuere neiquis eorum bacanal habuise uelet. sei ques esent quei sibei deicerent necesus ese bacanal habere eeis utei ad pr[aetorem] urbanum romam uenirent.[8]

> The following was decided regarding the Bacchanalias: Among the confederates, no one must have a desire for a place for Bacchanalias. If there be any who say that they need such a place for Bacchanalias, they should come to see the praetor in Rome.

This Latin is fairly close to the form of the language with which we are familiar. Where it differs is in the form *ques* for the nominative plural of the relative pronoun (*qui* in classical Latin) and the form *necessus,* encountered in Plautus but no longer used by Cicero. Although the form *uti* (instead of *ut,* "that") is seen later, it has an antiquarian feel. In the spelling that we are more familiar with the decree would read as follows:

> Qui foederati essent ita exdicendum censuere nequis eorum Bacchanal habuisse vellet. Si qui[s] essent qui sibi dicerent necesse esse Bacchanal habere iis uti ad praetorem urbanum Romam venirent.

Another reason that it is impossible to determine how "normal" Latin looked during the second century BCE is that all sorts of styles turned up in these early writings. We know today that works of Latin literature did not precisely mirror the actual vernacular of the population. This is true even of Plautus, whose comedic language used to be considered "vernacular Latin." (This fact notwithstanding, relatively speaking he continues to be our best source of information about the Latin vernacular of the time.) But we even find very early recourse to outdated speech forms in Latin literature to create an antiquarian feel; for example, the few extant fragments of Livius Andronicus's translation of the *Odyssey* (ca. 250 BCE) contain individual elements that, as far as we know, could not have been part of the living language of the middle of the third century. Of the two famous inscriptions on the tombs of members of the Scipio family, dating from the early second century BCE, the more recent inscription actually bears the more antiquated language. Textual language was always special but not primarily because (as in the bourgeois nineteenth century) literature was aimed at an educated class but rather because writing was per se something special, and no one expected a written text to reflect the spoken word. This also makes it easier to understand how plays achieved such success among the Romans even though their authors had grown up speaking other Italic languages or, as was the case with Terence, a completely different mother tongue. Tolerance for alien elements in works of poetry was undoubtedly high and should not be viewed in terms of romantic notions about the "soul of a people" expressing itself in poetry. On the other hand, political speeches required what might be termed "unaccented" Latin, and these were committed to writing very early as models for future public orators. Historiography, to the extent it served the elite's need for commemoration or self-justification, also required a more purified form of the language. It should therefore come as no great surprise that from the very beginning these two genres remained firmly the province of the urban Roman upper class. As far as these genres are concerned, we search in vain for authors from other regions of Italy—even though they dominated other areas of Roman poetry almost up to the time of Cicero. Unfortunately, we have only scattered fragments of early Roman speeches and historiography.

Even after the "invention" of literature in Rome there was no need for a really consistent standardization of written Latin because early Roman literature was largely confined to the city of Rome. Texts were written by their authors (Roman or from elsewhere on the peninsula) primarily for readers or listeners within the city itself. This does not rule out the possibility that Latin texts or Latin plays might have been received outside of Rome. However, this would have been a secondary effect that had no influence on their production. There was no supraregional distribution of literature along Greek lines; our modern-day contrast between "Romans" and "Greeks" results from the distorting perspective of modern nation building. This did not apply to Roman conditions, at least not until the classical era. Back then, "the" Romans were the inhabitants of the city of Rome and, outside of Rome, included the residents of individual colonies or even individual persons with Roman citizenship. And just as the Roman Empire retained the organization of a city-state into the first century BCE, so the Italic linguistic landscape continued to be a colorful patchwork for a long time.

Origins of Classical Literary Language: First Century BCE

The decades between approximately 80 BCE and the turn of the millennium are considered the golden age of Latin literature. The authors of this era constitute the canon of classical Latin literature. They include the orator, politician, philosopher, letter writer, rhetorician, and poet Cicero (106–43 BCE); prose writers like Caesar (100–44 BCE), Nepos (ca. 100–24 BCE), Sallust (ca. 86–34 BCE), and Livius (59 BCE-17 CE); and the poets Catullus (ca. 80–50 BCE), Lucretius (ca. 98–54 BCE), Virgil (70–19 BCE), Horace (65–8 BCE), Ovid (43 BCE-17 CE), Tibullus (ca. 60/50–18 BCE), and Propertius (ca. 50–15 BCE). All of these writers were born during the last decades of the five-hundred-year-old Roman Republic, and most of them saw not only its end but also the founding of a new form of government by Augustus. However momentous, this political revolution did not form a real break within the classical literature of the first century BCE. Almost certainly, all writers from the classical era, even those who wrote only as private persons, took part in the political and social life of the times, and the changing cultural and political conditions had an effect on their literary output. Nevertheless, in terms of the questions examined here, we may say that the final years of the Roman Republic and the first two decades of Augustinian rule may be viewed as a unit.[9]

During these decades the Latin language reached a developmental end stage and ceased to evolve. In other words, Latin became fixed.[10] Without a doubt, this end stage was initiated by the consolidation of the literary language of the second century BCE. Latin had already started to change less between the time of Plautus and the early days of Cicero, in other words, approximately between 200 and 100 BCE. The changes that did occur affected mainly details such as the final disappearance of certain archaic forms of inflection (such as the forms *ausim* ["I would dare"], *faxim* ["I would do"], and the remains of the third "optative" mode, which was, however, retained in Greek). In addition, the particular inflection to which a word belonged was more precisely defined. For example, in addition to *materia* (which belongs to the same declension as *causa* and forms the genitive, *materiae)*, ancient Latin also allowed for the alternative form *materies* (parallel to *res* or *dies,* with the genitive, *materiei),* which was later dropped from use. In addition, the famous (or notorious) subordinate clauses with *cum,* which have become a staple of the modern Latin class, with their various indicative and conjunctive constructions, were fixed in the form found in Latin grammars today only in the first century BCE. Some small changes like these continued to occur until the middle of the first century BCE, while we search largely in vain for even such minor alterations after the time of Cicero. The forms of declensions and conjugations are virtually unchanged since his time. Furthermore, the syntax found in Cicero and Caesar and in Virgil and Horace is still valid today. Even where later developments introduced new syntactic possibilities or new words, the old ones were never dropped. Just as the forms of Sanskrit grammar laid down by Panini remain eternally valid, the core of what we find in the Latin classics remains the foundation for anyone learning Latin in school today.

Why Latin became fixed during this particular period and at this stage is a serious question. We can find no compelling external development that might have mandated a new role for the Latin language within the Roman state, such as occurred in Greece as a result of the adoption of Attic as the language of the Macedonian court and the pluricentric organization of literature after Alexander the Great. True, the development of Latin in Rome, which was essentially that of a city-state, coincided with the transformation of the republican form of government into a systematically applied imperial administration under Augustus. The relationship of the center of the empire with its far-flung provinces was certainly changed, and the result was that the external parts of the empire played a new and more important role. Herfried Münkler has termed this particular step the "Augustan threshold," which in his view characterizes the development of empires generally, and he has applied the term to other empires as well. However, we do not know whether Augustus mandated the use of Imperial Latin or assigned to it a fundamentally new role. The standardization process, which Cicero had a considerable hand in, began earlier. The fact that Cicero was murdered in 43, with at least the consent of Octavian, the later Augustus, makes it clear that he cannot be considered part of the Augustan threshold. Developments under Augustus were only a part of the break that occurred in the language. We must also remember that a much greater separation existed between the language of administration and the language of literature and culture in the Roman Empire than is the case in the European nation-states that are familiar to us. What we do know is that the fixing of the Latin language proceeded from literature and not from administrative necessity.

Because no external reasons are evident, it is almost too easy, from our perspective, to ascribe the fixing of Latin to classical literature and its supreme artistic achievements. As a result, we tend to view the fixing of the Latin language in terms of a history of reception, and it appears to have been a by-product that the classical writers could never have intended. In the past few years, this particular viewpoint has been championed most vocally by Wilfried Stroh, who has even proposed a teleological threshold. According to Stroh, Cicero and his contemporaries had so perfected Latin that their enthusiastic successors deemed it definitive as a model and undertook no further changes. As Stroh put it, perhaps a little archly, Latin died of its own beauty.[11]

Such an exclusively reception-oriented view may satisfy humanists enthralled by the beauty of classical literature, but it mischaracterizes the nature of the process. Because even though there was no conscious language policy, we do discern a cultural dynamic that makes the fixing of the Latin language understandable and places it in an overarching cultural and historical framework. This in no way denigrates the aesthetic qualities of the classical authors. Without those qualities, the classical literary canon would never have survived for more than two thousand years. However, the causes that set this process in motion were of a different nature.

A linguistic analysis of the great turning point in this century must begin with an understanding of the ongoing debate at that time over which Latin was best. Many surviving documents show that the Romans themselves—naturally only a small culturally engaged group of upper-class Romans—spent much time and effort in an attempt to find ways to perfect and standardize their language. The creation of "classical" Latin was no unconscious act of genius on the part of Cicero, Caesar, Virgil, and a few others but was to some extent a declared goal at the time. The process was quite similar to public and written discussion of the *questione della lingua* (question of language) in the sixteenth century, from which the Italian literary language evolved.

We continually observe that processes of language clarification in society driven by public discussion are common during times in which large-scale political changes come to affect cultural consciousness permanently or in which new identities emerge. Moreover, such a break may be assumed to have occurred at the latest during the time of Sulla (138–78 BCE), which ended in dictatorship (82–78 BCE), and not during the civil wars that broke out after the assassination of Caesar in 44 BCE. The history of most modern European literary languages exhibits just such breaks associated with open discussions of language. And the *questione della lingua* mentioned earlier would have been unthinkable if not for the political circumstances around 1500 and the military superiority of France, which the Italians found so oppressive. It paved the intellectual way for a consciousness of Italian identity. A 1993 anthology dedicated to language-planning discussions in modern times—among them the Turkish-language reform associated with Kemal Ataturk's political reforms of 1930—bears the significant subtitle, the "First Congress" phenomenon.[12]

Without denying the uniqueness of each of these processes, the form of Latin literary language in the first century BCE fits nicely into this pattern, although no "first congress" took place in Rome. Interestingly, however, an upsurge in mentions of grammar studies occurred at that time. True, grammar in the Greek academic tradition of teaching right from wrong and explicating the poets had existed in Rome before Cicero as well. But the works about language of the first century BCE were quite different. For one thing, leading members of society were at the forefront of grammar reform. Cicero, for example, wrote about linguistic problems in the margins of his rhetorical writings. And Caesar also commented on the subject of grammar in *De analogia;* Antonius Gnipho, who taught both Cicero and Caesar, wrote a similar text, as did Staberius Eros, who taught Brutus and Cassius, Caesar's assassins. The historian Sisenna, whose historical work was later taken up by Sallust in his *Histories,* tried to make corrections to traditional Latin grammatical forms. Asinius Pollio, a confederate of Caesar and of Antonius, who was consul in the year 40 BCE and whom Virgil celebrated in his fourth eclogue, excelled in linguistic and stylistic criticism and may have written a grammar himself. His interest in the subject may be gauged by the fact that other authors dedicated their grammars to him. Varro Reatinus, an important figure, though not one of the leading ones in Rome during the first century BCE (a fine point of status that sometimes spared politicians their lives), wrote a work titled *De lingua Latina* in midcentury, a small part of which has survived. For a few other grammars all we have is the name of the author. Interestingly, Greek authors also wrote books about the Latin language in Greek.[13]

More important than the high social rank of the guild of grammarians, however, was the content of their work. As far as we can tell, they were less concerned with grammatical theory than with the proper form of good and correct Latin. This is most clearly demonstrated by Caesar's *De analogia,* which has unfortunately been lost, and Varro's *De lingua Latina.* Caesar was most concerned with irregularities of inflection in Latin, which, in his opinion, should be resolved by regularization, specifically by the principle of analogy. This preoccupation may well reflect the ordered mind of the master military strategist. It used to be thought that with this text, Caesar took his place within a long tradition of scholarly discourse, centered in Greek Alexandria, in which proponents of the analogy principle went head to head with other scholars who defended the irregularity, the "anomaly," of language, as it had evolved historically. More recent research, however, has made it more probable that this discussion was of great currency in Caesar's time. Some of the details of the text, which have come down to us by chance, show striking parallels to the recent German spelling reforms. For example, Caesar suggested that the genitive of Pompeius (Pompeiii) be written with three *i*s to distinguish it from the identically pronounced nominative plural (two *i*s) and vocative forms (one *i*).[14] In his work on the Latin language, Varro, too, discussed fine-tuning inflectional morphology; in contrast to Caesar, however, he had a more flexible attitude, recommending the principle of anomaly in some cases and of analogy in others. Unfortunately, we have no details about the works of other grammarians, although we know from titles like *De sermone Latino* (About the Latin Language) that they must have been about correct usage and norms. Titles like this are not found in later centuries; they seem to have been characteristic of the time.

The creation of literary languages often involves lexicography. For example, Arabic lexicography in the early Middle Ages was very important in the development of classical Arabic. Noah Webster's *American Dictionary of the English Language,* first published in 1828, established the parameters of American English by consciously distinguishing the English of the United States from that of the new country's former colonial rulers. In Rome during Augustinian times, Marcus Verrius Flaccus wrote the first comprehensive dictionary of the Latin language, titled *De significatu verborum* (On the Meaning of Words). This work was not a dictionary of standards for good Latin but presented the fruits of philological research on older words, many of which were no longer in use. However, because this dictionary gives evidence of the interest in documenting and researching the Roman tradition, it is very much a part of the "national" preoccupation with Roman culture that characterized the times.

The literature of the period also shows evidence of serious engagement with language. When Horace recommended that poets polish their works, he was doing more than exhorting them to order their thoughts. He was aiming at the means they used to express those thoughts. The way in which Cicero framed his words was not simply the fruit of unbridled genius; it points to conscious training. Some Augustan poets show clear and direct signs of theoretical study. Among other things, they used word etymologies that philological research had uncovered at the time as the basis for ingenious allusions in their poetry.[15]

The most notable feature of literary production during the time between about 60 and 10 BCE was, however, its curious relationship to Greek literature. Only during this period do we encounter writers who made a point of contrasting a work or genre of classical Greek literature with the corresponding Roman equivalent. This tendency probably began with Lucretius, whose didactic poem "De rerum natura" was, in terms of form, a Roman reworking of the didactic poem "Peri physeos" (About Nature), by Empedocles (ca. 494–434 BCE). Empedocles was a very widely read author. Cicero modeled his dialogues *De oratore, De re publica,* and *De legibus* on the tradition of Platonic dialogues and those of Aristotle. In his published speeches he apparently wished to become for Rome what the Greek orator Demosthenes (384–322 BCE) had been for Greece. Cicero even expressed his admiration by embedding quotations from Demosthenes's texts and imitating some of their structural peculiarities. The philosophical writings of his last years were less about introducing Greek philosophy to Rome (many had already read these in the original Greek); rather, he wanted to show that philosophical topics could be presented in Latin as well. Supported by thousands of structural and substantive references, Virgil's *Aeneid* was the *Iliad* and the *Odyssey* of Rome. His bucolic poems, called eclogues, were inspired by Theocrites (ca. 360–320 BCE); his pastoral didactic poem, the "Georgica," evoked in Roman readers Hesiod's "Works and Days" (first half of the seventh century BCE) and Hellenistic models that are unknown to us. The parallels between the historian Sallust and the Greek historian Thucydides (464–after 400 BCE) are obvious; Horace prided himself on having introduced to Rome the Aeolian song of Alcaeus of Mytilene and the poetry of Sappho (both ca. 600 BCE). He also compared his *Epodes* to the works of Archilochos (ca. 650 BCE) and Hipponax (ca. 540 BCE). Of the four books by Propertius, the last one, dedicated to the Roman foundation myths, picks up on the *Aetia* of Callimachos (305–240 BCE). To what extent the Roman love elegy, especially the first three books of Propertius and the *Corpus Tibullianum,* were modeled on Greek works or had Greek counterparts is currently unknown because of our fragmentary knowledge of Greek sources. Recent papyrus discoveries make it seem more likely that intertextual relationships to the older Greek elegy may have been closer than previously thought. Livius's relationship to the Greeks is looser; still, Quintilian (10.1.100) places him alongside Herodotus (490–ca. 420 BCE). Only the works of Ovid, virtually impossible to pigeonhole in any tradition, seem not to have had Greek counterparts. Moreover, Ovid, who was born in 43 BCE, is not representative of the authors we are examining.

When we examine this literary rivalry with the Greeks more closely, it becomes clearer that these authors did not in any way "transfer" a genre to Rome. Rather, they focused largely on individual works. Horace, as he himself stated (*carmen* III.30.13 and Epistles 1.19.25), not only *introduced* the Aeolian lyric and Archilochian iamb to Rome but was also their *last* practitioner. Sallust, often considered the originator of the historical monograph in Rome, died without a successor in that field. The love elegy, perhaps the most remarkable poetic genre of the Augustan age, ceased to be written long before Ovid's death in 16 CE. Even the philosophical works of Cicero, who is often cited as having introduced Greek philosophy into Roman literature, were individual efforts. Only centuries later do we find works that Cicero clearly influenced. The particular type of rivalry with Greek classical authors evident in the first century BCE was not a developmental stage in the course of culture transfer from Greece to Rome but rather a unique phenomenon limited to this epoch.

This rivalry was not, however, limited solely to classical Greek literature. Wherever we are able to examine the sources—too seldom with too many gaps, one should add—we find that the Latin classics of the first century BCE borrowed frequently from Hellenistic literature and from the Roman literature of the second century BCE. Virgil "reworked" Apollonios Rhodios and Ennius, and Horace emulated the satires of Lucilius. This trinity of cultural reference to ancient Greece, Hellenistic Greece, and ancient Rome applied mainly to the Augustan poets; older authors who were more influenced by the last phase of the Roman Republic, such as Lucretius, Catullus, and Cicero, were less apt to use ancient Roman literature as models. What we can say about the decades between approximately 80 and 10 BCE is that efforts were made to produce a classical Roman canon that was structurally similar to that of Greece. The evidence that has come down to us from Cicero (for example, in the preface to his philosophical writings), from Horace (*carmen* II.20; III.30), or from Ovid (*Metamorphoses* 15.871–879) make it clear that this was a conscious effort. These writers hoped to secure for themselves and their works a reputation on a par with that of the Greek classics. Decades ago, the Latinist Viktor Pöschl, an expert in Augustan literature, spoke about the "self-canonization" of the Roman writers.[16] As part of this self-anointment by leading cultural figures of their time, Cicero, Horace, and Virgil—and probably also Catullus and a few others— gave their works complex internal structures that can be detected only on close reading. The twelve books of Virgil's *Aeneid,* for example, which correspond to the twenty-four books of Homer's *Iliad* and *Odyssey,* can be divided into two units of six books each or into three units of four books, and this is only the most evident part of a far more complex composition. Not content with that, Augustan poets published carefully compiled "editions" of their own works during their lifetimes, in which they arranged the poems according to internal rules, so that philologists today must interpret not only the poems but also their place within the original compilation. Cicero went so far as to imitate the structure of two cycles of speeches by Demosthenes.[17] The fact that we call damning speeches philippics has to do with more than Demosthenes's series of speeches attacking Philip II of Macedon. Equally important are the fourteen speeches that Cicero gave in 44 and 43 BCE condemning Mark Antony, which he based on Demosthenes's speeches and actually called *Philippics.*

These efforts on behalf of the Latin language and literature were part of a more comprehensive self-reflection about Roman culture in those decades, most centrally about the role of Greek culture. It began, as the archaeologist Paul Zanker rightly pointed out in *The Power of Images in the Age of Augustus,* with the Hellenization of the Roman upper classes at the turn of the first century BCE and ended in the first decades of the rule of Augustus with the development of a new "language" of architecture and visual arts that linked Greece and Rome in a new way. Culturally, it is important to separate the fact that this process transpired from the hallmarks that came to characterize it in Augustan culture. If Caesar had not been murdered, if the Battle of Philippi (42 BCE) had never been waged against his murderers, or if the Battle of Actium against Antonius (31 BC) had turned out differently, there would never have been an Augustan culture. But Rome's new engagement with the Greeks had begun much earlier, and if Augustus had lost the civil war, others would have completed the process in their own way.

Figure 3. Marcus Tullius Cicero (106–43 BCE). Capitoline Museums. Cicero's speeches and letters and his theoretical writings on rhetoric and philosophy contributed greatly to the "classical" language of Latin prose. Up to the present day, his writings are among the most important models for all who write in Latin. Cicero was probably more responsible than any other single individual in history for the development of a world language. akg-images

That engagement was far more fundamental inasmuch as it shaped more than visual arts or language alone. Its most significant characteristic was a focus on Roman culture, including a sense of independence from what had been viewed as the more advanced Greeks. Whereas Livius Andronicus *translated* Homer's *Odyssey,* Virgil sought to *replace* it. This hewing to Greek models, as we see implemented in the texts, was not a sign of cultural dependence but a powerful attempt at Romanization. Cicero's rhetorical works were nothing less than an attempt to develop an independent Roman rhetoric that went beyond the mere adoption of Greek theoretical ballast. Not long after Cicero, Augustan poets began to reflect on their own poetry. Virgil and Ovid, for example, set down their reflections in allegorical form, often comprehensible only to the educated few, while Horace made his poetological questionings the subject of his own poetry. It is no accident that Horace's *Ars poetica,* next to Aristotle's poetics still the most important theoretical exposition on poetry that has come down to us from antiquity, was written at that time. The question of the form of the Roman state, the most important political issue of the middle of the first century, came under increased scrutiny as well.[18] Cicero set down his essentially conservative views on this controversy in *De re publica.* But evidence indicates that a certain Aurunculeius Cotta, who was an officer in Caesar's army in Gaul, also wrote on the subject, and we also have fragments of a theoretical tract about the state by the Greek philosopher Philodemos, dedicated to his landlord and benefactor, Calpurnius Piso, Caesar's father-in-law and consul for the year 58. This was the same Philodemos, by the way, who lived in Piso's magnificent villa in Herculaneum, which served as the model for the Getty Villa at the Paul Getty Museum, in California. We also have the title of a political pamphlet by Varro, the "Trikaranos" ("The Three-Headed"), which in all probability dealt with the establishment of the triumvirate.

These reflections on language and the language-clarification processes of the first century BCE should be placed within this larger context. But why exactly did the Latin language become fixed at that time in particular? One approach to this question has less to do with the reconstruction of historical processes than with systematic reflection on the conditions under which language was constituted in that society.

The goal of all of these efforts was never some sort of state-mandated standardization of the language. Nor do we have any reason to assume a direct connection between the discourse about a language and literature and the Roman military and civil administrations, the communications structures in the Roman Empire, or the rapidly advancing Romanization of the inhabitants of Italy, Spain, and southern France. The Roman *questione della lingua* related to the language of literature, and it was of concern mainly to the small, elite circle that valued subtleties of taste and the establishment of Latin as a literary language on a par with Greek. And this is precisely why it was more closely related to the Italian *questione della lingua* of the sixteenth century, which was also aimed at the literary language, than to the language-standardization processes initiated by the kings of Spain, France, and England in the sixteenth and seventeenth centuries, which were all about the exercise of political power.

At this point it seems useful to examine a Latin text in order to flesh out the process of creating a sophisticated literary language. This poses some difficulties because a high level of familiarity with the language is necessary to discern the expressive perfection that Latin authors were striving for. It would be useless to discuss stylistic features such as word placement (which is much freer in Latin than in less inflected languages) or the use of stylistic devices such as anaphora, chiasmus, metaphor, and paronomasia—that is, the entire repertoire of devices still provided to students in handbooks on the subject. Nor do the many ties to Greek literature define the essence of the classical literary language. We all know that an overexacting attention to syntax and style, especially when peppered with learned intertextual references, all too often results in tasteless or indigestible confections.

This is why I examine compositional and aesthetic qualities based on a sentence in which the stylistic devices of conventional literary rhetoric play only a minor role. Let us look at the beginning of Cicero's *De oratore*. We know from Cicero himself that he took great pains with the composition of this work.[19] As a result, we may expect the first sentence to have been honed to perfection. But at first glance, although it is well put together, the sentence itself seems rather pedestrian:

> Cogitanti mihi saepenumero et memoria vetera repetenti perbeati fuisse, Quinte frater, illi videri solent qui in optima re publica, cum et honoribus et rerum gestarum gloria florerent eum vitae cursum tenere potuerunt, ut vel in negotio sine periculo vel in otio cum dignitate esse possent.

> When, as often happens, brother Quintus, I think over and recall the
> days of old, those men always seem to me to have been singularly
> happy who, with the State at her best, and while enjoying high distinc-
> tions and the fame of their achievements, were able to maintain such a
> course of life that they could either engage in activity that involved no
> risk or enjoy a dignified repose.[20]

The sentence, like its unpretentious beginning, "when, as often
happens . . . I think over and recall," has more the quality of a prefa-
tory note for his brother, Quintus, than of the beginning of the book
itself. In fact, it contains a reference to Cicero's personal circumstances.
Cicero had had a triumphant career, rising from the middle class to the
highest public office, that of consul, and at the end of his first year in office (63 BCE), he thwarted the Catalinian revolution. Nonetheless, rather
than being rewarded for his services, he was attacked and sent into exile
for a year. This is what Cicero means when he muses about those who
were able to serve in their office without risk *(negotium sine periculo)* and
retire with dignity *(otium cum dignitate).* At the same time, this sentence
contains what amounts to a political program. We know, especially from
a lengthier passage in his speech "Pro Sestio" (§96–100), that Cicero
viewed this notion of *otium cum dignitate* very broadly as a principle of politics and policy. However, its use is allusive and not completely transparent. Thus, when Cicero uses this phrasing again here, he is also alluding
to an ideal state in which the ideal orator, whom Cicero describes in this
book, has an honored place. This phrasing alerts the reader that Cicero is
addressing not only Quintus but all Romans and beyond that anyone interested in states and their politics, including us. Cicero was a master of
this sort of polyvalence, seamlessly bridging the gap between what appears to be mere personal observation and what he believed to be more
generally applicable truths. Virgil was also a master of this technique, and
as a consequence his *Aeneid* is much more than just a heroic story.

Characteristically, the sentence makes use of duplication. By writing *cogitanti* and *memoria vetera repetenti,* Cicero divides his reflections
into pure thought and historical retrospection. By the same token, he
recalls the outstanding positions of earlier politicians, contrasting their
positions of honor *(honoribus)* such as aedile or consul with their actual
deeds *(rerum gestarum gloria).* By contrasting *negotio sine periculo* and *in
otio cum dignitate* the sentence ends with an antithesis in which each
part is itself divided into a two-part phrase.

Cicero's use of rhythm is also calculated. In Latin, each syllable is unalterably either long or short, and in Cicero's time (it was different some centuries later because the pronunciation of Latin changed) these prosodic qualities were more or less absorbed by all those who learned Latin as their mother tongue. This sense of how language sounded was not unique to the upper classes the way certain prosodic features of English were in the nineteenth and early twentieth centuries. This syllabication was the foundation on which verse was written, and because the syllables could be neither lengthened nor shortened, the rhythms that resulted were often complicated and asymmetrical and cannot be reduced to the triple and quadruple meters with which we are familiar. Furthermore, because syllable lengths were so characteristic of the language, people paid attention to the sequence of long and short syllables, especially at the ends of sentences, where the rhythm was often used for emphasis. The use of such cadences was drilled into all students as part of their lessons in rhetoric.

Examining the rhythmic pattern of the sentence as a whole, we find consciously selected regularities that are, however, so skillfully employed that the reader remains unaware of the scaffolding. Following the syntactic structure, I divide the sentence into six parts (colon, pl. cola, in the terminology of rhetoric):

Cogitanti mihi saepenumero et memoria vetera repetenti
– ˇ – | – ˇ – | – ˇ ˇ ˇ | – ˇ ˇˇ | – ˇ ˇ ˇ ˇ – –

perbeati fuisse, Quinte frater, illi videri solent
– ˇ – | – ˇ– | ˇ – ˇ | – ˇ – | – ˇ – | – ˇ –

qui in optima re publica,
ˇ? – ˇ – – – – ˇ–

cumet honoribus et rerum gestarum gloria florerent
ˇ? ˇ – ˇ ˇ – – – – – – ˇ– – – –

eum vitae cursum tenere potuerunt,
ˇ– – – – – ˇ | – ˇ ˇ ˇ– –

ut vel in negotio sine periculo vel in otio cum dignitate esse possent.
– ˇ – ˇ – ˇ– ˇ ˇ ˇ – ˇ – ˇ – ˇ– – – ˇ – – ˇ – –

The basic rhythmic element of the first two cola is the sequence ‾ ˇ ‾, a syllable sequence that in ancient Latin versification was given the name *creticus* (Cretan metrical foot). In his *Orator,* written in 46 BCE,

Cicero describes the significance of this sequence of syllables in prosaic texts (*Orator* §64). In Latin prose, the cadence called the double *creticus* (¯ ˘ ¯ ¯ ˘ ¯) later came to be used to end sentences on an especially strong note.

At the beginning of the sentence analyzed here we see two Cretan feet. Twice, a long syllable is followed by three short ones. This may be viewed as a rhythmic loosening, but also a variant *creticus,* in which one of the two long syllables is "dissolved" into two short ones. This interpretation, incidentally, is again reminiscent of the passage in *Orator* (§64), where Cicero discusses the syllabic sequence ¯ ˘ ˘ ˘ (called a *paeon* in ancient metrics) as a suitable variation on the *creticus.* Only at the end does this colon resolve into a freer rhythm by the introduction of even more short syllables.

The second colon also uses a *creticus* as a basic rhythmic element. Where Cicero addresses his brother by name, he introduces a syntactic break, and exactly at this point the rhythm, too, is interrupted; he then resumes in Cretan rhythm with the word *frater.* Overall, this slight interruption in syntax ensures that the colon as a whole does not feel rhythmically stiff. There is no sense of an artificial rhythmic uniformity.

In the third colon, it is unclear whether the first two syllables, *qui in,* are meant to be slurred together as was customary or, as I am more inclined to think, the relative pronoun is meant to stand alone as a single emphasized word, which would therefore be separated from the following word by a brief pause (hence the ?). In any case, this is not a Cretan rhythm but an iambic syllable sequence (i.e., alternating between long and short).

After an unclear beginning similar to that in the third colon, the fourth colon cannot really be interpreted rhythmically. At its center is a sequence of long syllables that are interrupted only sporadically by individual short ones. This is not rhythm in the musical sense but was apparently Cicero's tonal intention. The solemn words that he utters about politicians who are permitted to live out their lives in peace with their glorious offices and deeds behind them is matched beautifully by the heavy solemnity of the syllabic sequences. The end of this colon is formed using a so-called Cretan-trochaic cadence (¯ ˘ ˘ ˘ ¯ ¯), a rhythmic pattern that Cicero used so frequently at the ends of sentences (especially with the phrase *esse videatur*) that even in antiquity his many imitators made free use of this device (Quintilian X.2.18). The last colon, finally, exhibits a more alternating rhythm without being really regular, regardless of whether interpreted as iambic ($\smile$ $-$) or trochaic ($-$ $\smile$).

In addition to the rhythmic patterns, it pays to listen to the distribution of vowels. Whereas the vowel *i* predominates in the second colon, the solemn passage in the fourth colon is colored by darker *o* tones, which in the fifth colon give way to more *u* sounds. None of these analyses are adduced to prove that the author consciously employed these rhythmic or vocal devices. What is much more likely is that a man like Cicero, who spent his life engaging with the Latin language and who had years of experience formulating thoughts, simply drafted each text so that it met his aesthetic expectations. What was conscious, however, was the way in which he sought to fuse the perfect words with the perfect sonority.

After this detailed analysis, let us return to our more basic reflections. We need to remember that the elaborate and polished literary Latin seen in the works of the great writers of the first century BCE was not an artificial language. Unfortunately, modern descriptions of Latin, especially those not written by Latinists, often suggest that it was. This conception betrays the modern (since the nineteenth century) notion that the "real" language of a people can be only the unregulated language—and our historical experience that Latin is not a "natural" language. As far as the first century is concerned, this is definitely incorrect even though Roman poets sometimes indulged in esoteric flourishes. But the act of linguistic cultivation that Cicero and Caesar strove for should in no way be viewed as an act of segregation from the people. In fact, a Roman orator who sought to make his case before the Senate, the law courts, or the Plebeian Council would have been at a distinct disadvantage had he thrown up linguistic barriers to understanding. In his popular oratory, Cicero was no less "classical" than in his other writings.

But even if we assume that classical authorial Latin was a natural language to those who used it, the fixing of the language must have been the unintentional and so to speak involuntary result because the birth of a literature intended not only for Rome but also for the entire world and for the future was possible only if the Latin language was the same everywhere and for all times. In other words, any attempt to develop an authorial language on a par with Greek would inescapably have brought about a fixing of the language.

As discussed earlier, Greek had already become a largely fixed language with a number of literary centers several hundred years before Cicero. Unity was created within this large territory because the fundamental forms of the language that were set down in literature became established for all times in the academies. There would have been no other way, given the state of communications at the time, for a supraregional literary language to have established itself, let alone been passed down over the centuries. The move toward Atticism, which intensified during the first century BCE, led to an even more uniform and comprehensive standardization and further canonized the classical authors of the fifth and fourth centuries. The fact that Atticism appears to have originated in Rome raises the question, as yet not completely answered, of its relationship to classical Latin literary language.

In Rome, the claim that the Latin literary canon was on a footing equal to the Greek canon would automatically have implied that the relationship between language norm and literature could have and must have functioned precisely the same way in Latin as it already had in Greek. A classical literary work is a work that is read everywhere, even by people who speak another language, and which continues to be read for centuries even though the language of the population has evolved in the years since its writing. Furthermore, a classical work of literature is one from which students learn the written language in school. This had been the experience with the Greeks, and if the Romans intended to emulate them, fixing of the language was a more or less foregone conclusion. When Cicero wrote about the perfectibility of the Latin language, he meant—as demonstrated in many passages, especially in his most important work on rhetoric, *De oratore*—the living language as spoken by the Roman upper classes. But by his attempt to publicize his own speeches as models, patterning himself after Demosthenes, and to achieve in Rome the preeminence that Demosthenes had attained in Greece, Cicero set in motion a process in which, in the end, the Roman upper classes began to emulate the language of Cicero much as the Greeks had emulated Demosthenes and other Attic orators, cultivating not only their rhetoric but also their language. This defines the crucial turning point in the first century BCE. Whether the classical writers understood how this criterion for good Latin would affect literature is doubtful. Nonetheless, the fixing of the Latin language was the unavoidable result of the formation of a literary canon that was meant to replace the Greek.

If we compare the genesis of a fixed standard language in Greece and in Rome, the differences are now more clearly discernible. The classical Athenian writers of the fifth and fourth centuries never wrote with the intention of creating an ancient Greek linguistic standard that would stand for all time. Seen from the perspective of European intellectual history as a whole, the tragedies and comedies, the historical works, the orations and philosophical works were a miracle that could not have been anticipated. Their canonization and their function as language models belong to a later phase and were codetermined by political developments in Greece after Alexander the Great. The development of classical Roman literature, by contrast, was intentional from the very beginning. That intention was to repeat the Greek miracle and its subsequent canonization, and to claim coequality with their Greek model. The fact that the Romans succeeded so brilliantly that they have continued to influence Europe for two thousand years is attributable to the genius of their classical writers. Stroh's praise of the beauty of the classical language is fully justified. But their miracle was a result of their response to a question, a specifically Roman *questione della lingua.*

Latin as the Language of the Educated Classes and the Development of Romance Languages

What has come to be called the "classical period," the decades in the middle of the first century BCE, was felt to be a turning point in the cultural history of Rome immediately thereafter even though language instruction, as existed in Greece, did not really develop on a supraregional basis until the end of the third century. Latin was still the language of the city of Rome, and its inhabitants were aware that the Latin spoken on the Roman street was their language. Nonetheless, from that point forward, Latin was an essentially fixed language. The inflected forms and the basic syntax had, with minor fluctuations, reached the stage that continues to be taught in schools today. One result is that works written after the first century CE cannot be dated based on linguistic criteria. The dates of the historian Curtius Rufus, about whom very little is known, but who wrote a well-respected history of Alexander the Great, which continued to be a staple in schools well into the nineteenth century, has recently been moved from the first to the sixth century CE. Dating is no less an issue with the "Pervigilium Veneris," a very beautiful poem to the goddess Venus, which has survived in anthology with no known author, and scholars no longer even assign a century to the so-called *Declamationes maiores,* a collection of rhetorical exercises often attributed to Quintilian.

At the same time, we observe that literary activity and language instruction for the Roman upper classes increased markedly in the decades after Cicero. Of course, they had more time for such activities, given their relative political disempowerment by the new, quasi-monarchical state system. Be that as it may, formal rhetorical instruction, which Cicero had to justify in *De oratore,* now became a prerequisite for members of the upper classes. The formal exercises known as declamations came to play an important role in their education. The rhetorician and teacher Seneca the Elder (ca. 55 BCE–40 CE) left behind two collections of excerpts that give us insight into what rhetorical exercises must have looked like a few years after the death of Cicero and the ascent of Augustus. One hundred years later, the letters of Pliny the Younger (61/62–117 CE) give us a picture of a society in which rhetorical exercises and the writing of stylized letters had become a marker of class status. However, this evolution in cultural consciousness is especially evident at the end of the first century CE in the works of the rhetoric teacher Quintilian. His comprehensive *Institutio oratoria* is not only an instruction manual on rhetorical technique in the narrower sense but also a far-reaching plan for Greek-Latin bilingual language instruction. In his view, newborns were to be cared for only by wet nurses who spoke correctly. Later training involved the reading of model literary texts, with readings for boys selected by Quintilian. Then, in his tenth book, he presented the student a comprehensive overview of Greek and Latin literary history, in which the contents of the works selected were less important than their suitability to serve as models of good language.

That 140 years had passed between Cicero's death and the writing of the *Institutio oratoria* is of no importance in terms of the currency of Cicero's language. One need look back only 140 years from Cicero to the archaic literature of the third century to appreciate the historical importance of this fact. Quintilian held up Cicero as the quintessence of the Latin language—the gold standard. "Whoever loves Cicero should

Figure 4. Quintilian; choir stall in the Ulm Cathedral (Jörg Syrlin the Elder, 1469). Quintilian (second half of the first century CE) represented a linguistic culture in which language instruction based on the reading of classical Roman authors, especially Cicero, and constant training in cultivated usage had become extremely important to the Roman upper classes. He also promoted bilingual Greek-Latin education for Roman children. His importance to the linguistic culture of the Renaissance is exemplified by the Ulm choir stall, representative of the humanistic imagery of the late Middle Ages. akg-images

know that he has made a great advance."[21] Nonetheless, Quintilian persisted in the notion that language usage must be based in a living community of speakers; he even rejected emulation of the language of the past. But it is clear that he did not believe that current usage should derive from the average Roman population but rather from the *consensus eruditorum* of the educated class.[22] This consensus, however, was the result of literary and rhetorical training, which in turn was based on the texts of Cicero and Virgil. This represented a fundamental change in the relationship to language. In Cicero's time, an emphasis on cultivation might have offended more than a few distinguished Romans who had little feel for literature. A few generations later, the ability to express

oneself correctly in a language intimately tied to Latin literature became a mark of distinction acquired not through birth or social status
but through education. Language cultivated by intensive instruction
conferred social prestige. At its core, the Latin language granted a fundamental identity to the upper classes of the Roman Empire in late
antiquity. And the fact that Latin prose and oratory in particular were
now practiced by authors in far-distant outposts of the empire, not just
in Rome, shows that mastering Latin at the highest level was no longer
the province merely of native speakers in the capital. Like Quintilian,
Seneca, both father and son, came from Spain, while Pliny the Younger
and Elder were born in Como. Tacitus may have arrived in Rome from
northern Italy or even from Gaul.

One consequence of the establishment of a language of the educated
class was a widening gap with the vernacular of the population as a
whole. Of course, there have always been varieties of Latin, linguistic
differences between urban and rural areas, between different classes of
the population, between domestic and public communication, and the
like. The entire spectrum of fine sociolinguistic differentiation, which
is a hallmark of modern linguistics, was also present in ancient Rome,
and because neither the literary language nor the language of the elites
was identical to the language of the people, "Vulgar Latin" existed in
Rome from the very beginning. But now a new factor had emerged. For
the first time, an actual obstacle prevented linguistic changes that were
ongoing among the people from penetrating the language of the educated classes. The result was that the Romance languages came to evolve
away from the fixed Latin language.[23]

The stage of development that characterized the time of Quintilian
has its analogues in modern languages as well. France, the Czech Republic, Finland, and many other countries have elevated, literary forms
of language, which, at least in the twentieth century, were systematically transmitted in school to the more educated parts of the population. This form of the language is not determined mainly by the living
development of the language but by literary tradition and the prescriptive influence of language academies. In one form or another, teachers
have inculcated correct usage throughout the twentieth century in almost all countries. An example from the United States is writer and
literary critic Malcolm Cowley's complaint, in 1934, about how high
school English was taught in the early part of the century:

If we tried, notwithstanding, to write about more immediate subjects [i.e., not about the past], we were forced to use a language not properly our own. A definite effort was being made to destroy all trace of local idiom or pronunciation and to have us speak "correctly"—that is, in a standardized Amerenglish as colorless as Esperanto. Some of our instructors had themselves acquired this public-school dialect only by dint of practice, and now set forth its rules with an iron pedantry, as if they were teaching a dead language.[24]

It is unlikely that the standardized form of the language was quite as colorless as Cowley makes out because there was in the United States no academy capable of enforcing standardization. Nor does his critique necessarily shed light on the teaching of Latin in Rome. What we can say, however, is that although American English may be as aesthetically perfected as Cicero's Latin, standardization was necessary nonetheless because in the absence of mass media, divergent local developments would eventually have made communication all but impossible. And this was precisely the situation faced by Quintilian and his colleagues in schools of grammar and rhetoric in the first century CE.

The differences between the fixed form of a language and the language of less literate people were not all that large at first—probably not larger than the differences between the literary language and the vernacular spoken in France. But the gap continued to widen. The few surviving documents that give us insight into this vernacular language (used only in oral communication and never set down in literary form) lead us to conclude that this linguistic evolution toward Romance languages began quite early. The wall inscriptions in Pompeii, encased by the ashes of Vesuvius, which document the spontaneous expressions of less educated individuals from before 79 CE, exhibit features that foreshadow the Romance languages. For example, the preposition *cum*, which from the earliest times up to the classical period took only the ablative, is now found in accusative constructions (*cum iumentum, cum sodales*),[25] which points in the direction of the later collapse of the Latin case system. Or the spelling of the perfect tense *-curavit* as *-curaut*, which in the ancient pronunciation of *au* as *o* almost perfectly yields the later Italian form of the past tense *-ò* (as in *curò*, "he looked after").[26]

The development of the vernacular language that led to the Romance languages has been the province of Romance studies for well over a hundred years. But over the past several decades, sociolinguistic issues have taken their place alongside narrower historical linguistic analyses of matters such as the collapse of the case system and the development of the article. Josef Hermann, Michel Banniard, and Helmut Lüdtke, among others, are representative of this new trend. Unfortunately, we are not as yet able to reconcile this research with the findings of classical studies, which from its perspective covers the literary language and the educational culture of the first and second centuries CE. More interdisciplinary research is needed.

One especially important point needs to be addressed in this context. The form of the language that we observe in writers since the first century CE exhibits increasing individuality and demonstrates a conscious separation from everyday language. Kramer has talked about everyday language being "taboo."[27] This is not merely a question of word choice but points to a development that came to have fundamental importance for the later history of Latin. In the postclassical period, unforced communication in the vernacular was simply missing from Latin literature. It had previously been present in written material such that, despite their linguistic stylization, the comedies of Plautus and Terence from the first half of the second century BCE are an important source of everyday usages and the attitudes and gestures inherent in untutored, spontaneous conversation. Similarly, many passages from Cicero's letters give us a fairly good idea of how he and his closest friends probably spoke to each other; although somewhat more stylized, many sections of his philosophical dialogues nonetheless reproduce what must have been the then current tone of discourse. Finally, the letters and satires of Horace not only contain many colloquialisms but in general also show clear signs of having been influenced by the style and vocabulary of everyday language despite poetic reshaping. After Cicero, however, the vernacular disappeared from literature. As a result, all reconstructions rely either on texts up to the middle of the first century BCE or on inexpert scribes from later periods, who allowed the norms of their own vernacular to show through. One exception is a novel by Petronius, the *Satyricon* (better known in our time from Fellini's film), in which individual dialogues are written in an everyday style to flesh out particular characters.

This linguistic one-sidedness is not merely a question of word choice and style but also of the types of communications we find within Latin texts. When we examine Latin literature from this period more closely, we see that it contains almost no settings that would have encouraged the use of unforced, everyday language. Whereas the familiar German *du* would feel like an appropriate translation in many of Cicero's letters, in Pliny's letters, one gets the impression that the only proper form of address would have been the formal *Sie*. And this applies more or less to the entire later literary output. The dichotomy proposed by the Romanists Koch and Österreicher of linguistic distance (for communication with outsiders, officials, etc.) and immediacy (unforced communication with friends and family) is appropriate here.[28] The more Latin became the province of the educated and the more it became separated from natural language, even from that of the upper classes, the more associated it became with social representation and official communications— with the claim of being correct. The fear, so typical in the history of Latin, of embarrassing oneself by saying something incorrectly, began at this time. Grammatically correct Latin became a language of distance, the province of the educated elites both in written and in oral form.

The reduction of correct and sophisticated Latin to situations of communication requiring distance was one of the most consequential developments in the history of the Latin language. It is all the more remarkable because it was not a necessary development. It is certainly conceivable that the Roman upper classes, who spoke a cultivated Latin on official occasions, might also have evolved a looser but correct form for everyday conversation. This is precisely what happened with the high forms of European national languages later on. European elites bent on correctness in French, English, and German can still have fun, make love, and fight with each other without recourse to dialect or "vulgar" forms of the language. Of course, we do not really know how the Roman elites actually spoke. In any case, the language of proximity is completely absent in their literature. Interestingly, at the height of Atticism in Greece in the second century CE, we find among the writings of Lucian texts that successfully emulate communications entailing proximity. Even he, however, was not really writing down the spontaneous verbalizations of everyday people but showing virtuosity in the handling of scholarly language. Nonetheless, a separate register for everyday conversation in Greek remained. The severe reduction of the high form of the language to a language of distance seems to be a hallmark of Latin. It continued into late antiquity and even into the Middle Ages. With very few exceptions, orality was again taken up only in the "dialogue books" of the Renaissance and then again in the numerous Latin phrase books of the seventeenth and eighteenth centuries. It took Erasmus of Rotterdam (1466–1536) to perfect the urbane conversational tone of the ancient Latin comedies and of Cicero, as Lucian had done for Greek.

Greek-Latin Bilingualism from the First to the Third Century

An inventory of postclassical Latin literature, regardless of whether we limit ourselves to surviving texts or include lost works that we know only by reputation, yields a very curious result. This literature may be divided into two epochs that seem to be completely disconnected. The dense productivity of late Republican and early Augustan literature was followed between 50 and 120 CE by a second phase that included Seneca, Tacitus, Pliny, and Suetonius, as well as the poets Martial, Lucan, Persius, Statius, and Juvenal. Something of a break between these two high points appears to have occurred, during which fewer works of note were written. We do, however, have a few names and titles from this period, including a history by Velleius Paterculus and the already mentioned rhetorical excerpts by Seneca, the oration teacher, who was the father of Seneca the philosopher. But after Tacitus, works in Latin thin out. On the whole, very little poetry was written after the satirical poet Juvenal, around 100 CE; a few insignificant poets of the second century, known even then as the *poetae novelli* (approximately "new minor poets"), seem to have produced little more than artistic experiments in versification. As far as prose is concerned, only one genre was really alive between the second and the early third century: jurisprudence. Unfortunately, with the exception of *Institutiones,* by Gaius, no original texts have come down to us. But the most important collection of Roman law, the *Codex Iustinianus* (sixth century CE), makes frequent mention of works from the second and third centuries. As far as Latin prose of the second century is concerned, we know works by Florus, Gellius, Apuleius, and Fronto, who lived at the beginning or in the middle of the century. By the end of the second century, Latin literature appears to have come to a complete stop; the pamphlet *De die natali* (About Birthdays), by Censorinus, at the beginning of the third century, is a lonely straggler. From then on there is virtually no Latin literature through the entire middle years of the century up to the accession of Diocletian (284 CE). Christian literature alone seems to have thrived, with writings by Minucius Felix (probably the second century), Tertullian (about 200), and finally Cyprian (d. 256) and probably Commodian, although there is ongoing debate over whether he wrote during the third century. But—and this was completely new for Latin literature—most of these authors did not even live in Rome but rather resided in North Africa, the new center of Latin literary creativity. Fronto (ca. 100–ca. 176 CE) and Apuleius (born ca. 125 CE) were also North Africans.

This extraordinary discontinuity in Latin literature, which the Latinist and philologist Manfred Fuhrmann brought to public attention only a few decades ago, was brought about by the profound period of transition that the Roman Empire underwent during the third century.[29] It remains to be seen whether this time was one of actual "imperial crisis" or merely a difficult patch. Nonetheless, the fact remains that about two dozen emperors took their turns in power between 235 and 284—and most of them were murdered. In addition, the borders of the empire came under increasing attack, although these incursions never threatened its survival. For the early history of Germany, this decade saw the abandonment of the *limes* boundary and the end of Roman hegemony east of the Rhine and north of the Danube, which brought to an end three hundred years of rule by the Roman Empire.

It is clear that such periods of upheaval would not conduce to high literary and cultural achievement. But external history alone cannot provide us adequate explanations. This is because Latin literature began to ebb well before the crisis years of the third century, during the imperial rules of Hadrian (117–138 CE), Antoninus Pius (138–161 CE), and Marcus Aurelius (161–180 CE), in other words, during a time of economic prosperity and political stability. In addition, this loss of literary output did not affect Greek. The *Enneads* of Plotinus were written at just about the time (ca. 270) that Emperor Aurelian was building a wall around Rome to protect the city from the barbarian hordes (271–275). Plotinus's work opened a new chapter in the history of Platonism, and Greek historiography extended well into the third century with historians like Herodian.

As Fuhrmann noted, if only in passing, the peculiar development of Latin literature and language cannot be explained without reference to Greek.[30] However, we need to understand that the Roman Empire, which achieved its greatest territorial expansion during the second century, was organized rather idiosyncratically. Greek continued to be the first language in the eastern part of the empire. And although Latin was indispensable for administrative purposes, and many Greeks, among them Plutarch, learned Latin and read Latin literature, the vernacular and written language was and remained Greek. In the western part of the empire, on the other hand, the elites were fully bilingual. Educated Romans were even raised bilingually. In fact, Quintilian recommended that Greek, which was not the primary language spoken in Rome, should be the preferred language at school. Beginning in the middle of the first century, Rome's attitude toward Greece changed: whereas during the times of Cicero and Augustus the Romans, as we have seen, tried to place their culture on an equal footing with that of the Greeks, now they seem to have accepted the superiority of the Greeks, at least in philosophy and literature. Emperor Hadrian's friendliness toward the Greeks is notorious. In education, Greek and Latin culture formed a unity, at least in the west, and the two languages penetrated each other to such an extent that some modern researchers speak of a "Greek-Latin language league" *(Sprachbund).*[31] The classical philologist Albrecht Dihle wrote a monograph about "Greek and Latin literature during the Imperial Era" because he understood that there was no such thing as an independent Greek or Latin literature during that time. Important writers of the second century CE, such as Fronto or Apuleius, whom we know as Latin writers, wrote in Greek as well.

This is the cultural context needed to understand the disappearance of Latin literature after the second century CE. Obviously, the efforts of Cicero and his contemporaries to place Latin literature on a par with the Greek, thereby replacing it, did not succeed as hoped. Latin was able to displace Greek as a literary language only incompletely, and it appears that over the course of the first century, Greek actually gained ground. This is especially evident in philosophy, which had very strong links to Greece to begin with. The frequently voiced notion that Cicero had introduced Greek philosophy to Rome is not quite correct. Both during and after Cicero's prime, the polymath Varro, Brutus (Caesar's assassin), and the historian Livius also wrote philosophical works, about which we have only the most fragmentary knowledge. But then philosophy again became the province of the Greeks, even in Rome. In the middle of the first century CE, the Romans Musonius Rufus and Annaeus Cornutus, who taught philosophy to the satirical poet Persius, and the Phrygian-born Epictetus, who grew up in Rome and was a student of Musonius, wrote their philosophical works in Greek. And although the leading Greek philosophers tended to live in Rome, they also tended to avoid Latin. The philosophical works of Seneca, from the mid-first century CE were the exception; he wrote in Latin. The fact that Emperor Marcus Aurelius in the second century wrote his *Meditations* in Greek should not be taken as an expression of extraordinary reverence for the Greeks; it was simply common practice.[32]

Other literary genres flourished in Greek as well. Plutarch and Dion of Prusa (called Chrysostomos, or "golden mouthed" because of his skillful use of language) wrote around 100 CE. Lucian, Galen, Aelius Aristides, Appian, and Arrian wrote in the second century, and Athenaios, Philostratus, and Herodian in the third. These authors, whose output alone exceeds by several orders of magnitude the surviving literature from Homer to the end of the Hellenistic period, came to have a considerable influence on later European intellectual thought. Literary production in Greek was prolific, and Rome was increasingly at its center. A stay in Rome has been confirmed between the first and the third century for more than 40 percent of the more than 150 Greek writers whom we know by name, and many of them spent many productive years or even decades in that city. We know absolutely nothing about many of the writers with no known association with the city of Rome, and it may well be that a number of those did in fact work there. A few writings have survived from Greek writers who were not originally from Greece, such as the rhetorician Favorinus of Arles (second century CE). At least in terms of literature in the narrower sense, Greek, not Latin, was the world language of the Roman Empire.

There may well have been political and cultural reasons for this new Greek dominance, but those are not explored here. This dominance is, however, not comprehensible without an understanding of the status differential between Latin and Greek. In the first century CE and even more so in the second, the classical period of Atticism, Greek was a language with an established standard. Throughout the greater Roman Empire, grammar schools propagated this standard, which people learned by means of a standardized curriculum, at the center of which was classical Greek literature. This was as true in Rome as in numerous other cities. Native speakers of Attic Greek had long since died out, and Greek had become a historical culture language. Latin had not yet advanced to that level, although it was well on the way. Still, it was not yet a supraregional language since it was spoken mainly in Rome. Although many writers of the first and second centuries CE such as Seneca, Statius, Persius, Juvenal, Pliny, Tacitus, Suetonius, and others had not been born in Rome, they spent most of their productive years there. And even though Latin academies in all regions of the empire taught Latin, the language that students learned in Carthage or Milan was not necessarily the same as that in Rome, nor would their competence in the language have been equivalent. Only in the second century, with writers like Apuleius and Fronto, do we encounter the first authors no longer exclusively fixated on Rome.

In this sense, although Latin grammar and morphology were completely fixed by the first and second centuries CE, the canon of authors that would serve as the ineluctable model for students was not yet closed. The texts make this very clear. If the writers named earlier have anything in common, it is the diversity of their styles. With the later writers in particular—beginning with Tacitus and becoming even more pronounced with Fronto and Apuleius—we also observe linguistic contrivances in the form of bold neologisms and extreme artificial syntactic experiments (but without changing the rules of syntax). For prose writers, Cicero was not the only potential model; someone who modeled his writing on Cicero's letters was even referred to as a *simia Ciceronis,* Cicero's monkey.[33] In fact, during the second century, writers such as Fronto began to mine preclassical Latin literature, especially the prose of Cato the Elder (234–149 BCE), for choice words with a good ancient Roman sound to them. But these were used more as grace notes; they did not signal a thoroughgoing stylistic change. This is why the Latinist Eduard Norden's explanation that the "archaist writers" represented a return to an older language that was structurally comparable to the Atticism of the Greeks[34] is no longer given much credence.[35] Rather, the linguistic variety evident in this literature is more likely the result of Latin's having become "emancipated" from the vernacular of the population, with the result that Latin literature became ever more artificial. But it had not yet become a language completely independent of place and equipped with standards uniform throughout the empire. And although the relationship between Greek and Latin was no longer one of world language to local dialect, a difference in status still existed. Greece had a norm accepted throughout the empire; Latin had not yet achieved that standing. This was easier for the Romans to accept because they had easy access to Greek for that purpose.

However—and this is extremely important—this condition affected the literary language alone, for which questions of standardization and norms were of special significance because of the complexity of the texts and their great aesthetic sophistication. In other respects, Latin found its place as a world language at this time. We assume that the Romanization of populations in certain core regions of the Roman Empire was completed only after Cicero and that Latin was used extensively by the imperial military and civil administrations throughout the empire. This is demonstrated especially clearly by the fact that the second century, which saw a collapse of Latin literature and an almost complete halt to Latin historiography, rhetorical theory, and oratory, witnessed an upsurge in Roman jurisprudence. It seems that a functional division developed in the language, as often happens today. For example, the renowned law school in Berytos, now called Beirut, was something of an island where the Latin language thrived. Over the entirety of the Roman Empire, Latin was the language of administrative affairs, while Greek was the preferred medium for rhetorical training and literature.

The astonishing "gap" in Latin literature between the middle of the second and the end of the third century CE demonstrates that the effort to Romanize the culture, which had characterized the classical period between Cicero and Horace, had not met with the intended success. The attempt to create a Roman literary canon on a par with that of the Greeks had not really displaced Greek as the prime language of literature and philosophy even in the western parts of the empire.

But one part of the Roman Empire now sheared off in a direction all its own. Western North Africa—from Carthage to what is today Morocco—had since the late second century been the only other region of the empire in which Latin literature was produced. Africa was the home ground of writers like Apuleius, Fronto, and Gellius and later of the Christian writers Minucius Felix and, around 200, Tertullian. Finally, during the third century, as literary production ceased almost completely in the rest of the empire, Africa produced Cyprian, a Christian writer who died a martyr in 258, and (probably) Commodian. Even after the start of the imperial reforms under Diocletian (after 284), North Africa continued to play an outstanding role in Latin literary history. Both Lactantius (ca. 250–325) and Augustine (354–430) came from there; Augustine was eventually made bishop of Hippo, in what is present-day Algeria.

Literary historians and linguists have long examined the special position of Africa. Although the region is no longer considered to have had a specifically "African" Latinity of its own, during the period in question it was undoubtedly an economically and culturally vibrant province, and Emperor Septimius Severus (146–211), who founded the last great imperial dynasty before the crisis of the third century, was born there. The murderous intrigues in the Roman imperial houses and along the German *limes,* which were such a feature of the crisis-ridden third century, were foreign to Africa, and the notion that cultural life there may have been more stable is certainly justified.

If we now examine the history of Greek and Latin during that period, we can more precisely formulate the actual problem beyond these undoubtedly correct reasons. Whether the North Africans were more talented literary lights or whether their economic prosperity was more conducive to the production of literature is not really important. The real problem was linguistic. After the second century, Latin was used in literary texts more frequently in North Africa than on the Italian peninsula itself. Exactly why this was the case cannot be determined without considering the actual linguistic conditions in the region. In fact, this part of Africa had a very special position. With the exception of marginal areas, it was the only part of the later western Roman Empire in which, as far as we can tell, given the changes later set in motion by Islam, no thoroughgoing Romanization of the population occurred. The regional Punic language remained in use for written texts at least until the fourth century CE (the agricultural textbook by the Punic writer Mago, which comprises twenty-eight books, had even been translated into Latin). At the same time, there were no Greek colonial cities in the western part of North Africa; as a result no Greek-speaking population existed. Knowledge of Greek culture and language was gained solely by direct contact with Greece and the bilingual Greco-Roman school system. Even if we assume that Greek was a factor in the grammar schools in the larger cities, we can well imagine that Africa did not bring forth a bilingual Greek-Latin culture as occurred in Italy or Gaul.[36] Latin itself was therefore more important than in other parts of the empire for regional communication at all levels, and it successfully established itself as the second language of the overall population. By the second century CE, Latin had also become the language of the Christian church, while the Christians in Rome used Greek until the third century. The question of whether Carthage, the mighty power center re-founded and resettled by Caesar, established itself as a sort of artificially constructed second cultural center that played a role similar to that of Alexandria five centuries earlier is one that cannot as yet be answered. From a linguistic perspective at least this question deserves further study.

Late Antiquity

A New Epoch Begins: Latin Becomes a World Language

The reforms instituted by Emperor Diocletian after 284 CE ushered in a new epoch. The consensus among political and cultural historians is that late antiquity should not, however, be viewed simply as a less illustrious late phase of the Roman Empire but rather in its own terms. Although it seems to hearken back to a distant Roman past, Diocletian's reign gave birth to a culture that was new in many ways and anticipated later developments in Europe. In some ways, the adjective "late" in "late antiquity" has almost lost its meaning.

This is especially the case with the Latin language and literature. After a hiatus of more than a hundred years, Latin literature began once again to experience an upswing under Diocletian and the emperors who followed. Actually, it was more than an upswing: approximately 80 percent of all Latin texts that have survived from antiquity were written between the late third century and the middle of the sixth. This is why the current edition of the compendious *Handbuch der Altertumswissenschaften* set a precise date for the beginning of late antiquity: the year 284.

The literature of late antiquity differed in many crucial respects from everything that had come before. First, it exhibited a level of linguistic standardization that gave pride of place to a small classical canon of authors from the first century BCE, especially Cicero and Virgil, and secondarily Sallust, Horace, Livius, and (an exception from the second century BCE that is discussed later) Terence.[37] The Christian apologist Lactantius (ca. 300 CE) was so intent on emulating Cicero that he was later nicknamed *Cicero Christianus;* a few years later, the biblical poet Juvencus based his works on Virgil, among others. However, the Latin language now no longer exhibited the level of individual stylization that it had between Tacitus and Apuleius. At most, the great writers of late antiquity show some stylistic variation, but they do use the same form of the Latin language.

Second, the Latin language and culture were no longer concentrated in Rome but had become established across wide swaths of the empire. This was first of all a consequence of the growing political decentralization within the empire that occurred as Rome began to lose importance around 200. Diocletian introduced a separation of power based on four regents, the so-called tetrarchy, which in effect divided the empire into a western and an eastern part. As a result, the cities of Milan and Aquileia in northern Italy, Trier (in the Celtic region, now in the western part of Germany), and Nicomedia in the east became imperial seats along with Rome. In 330, Diocletian's successor, Constantine the Great (306–337), rededicated the Greek city of Byzantium on the Bosporus, renaming it Constantinople. He spent lavishly on public works to make it an imperial city worthy of the name, and for more than a thousand years it was the most important metropolis in the eastern Mediterranean and the center of the Eastern Roman Empire. Other cities like Carthage or Ravenna also experienced a cultural and an economic reawakening, and Gallic cities like Bordeaux (Burdigalum), where the poet Ausonius lived in the fourth century, Lyon (Lugdunum), and Autun (Augustodunum) became significant cultural centers. This was when Latin culture, which until then had been centered almost exclusively on Rome, really became pluricentric.

As had occurred centuries earlier with the Greek language, this was the step that turned Latin into a historical culture language that was completely independent of its living language community. This was where Latin first became a world language. The fact that Augustine could complete his training as a teacher of rhetoric in Carthage and then find an immediate position in Rome shows that the Romans themselves no longer had a lock on Latin. Even the French, who made such efforts during the seventeenth century to standardize their language, would never have invited a professor of literature or language trained in one of its colonies in North Africa to teach at a university in Paris during the nineteenth century.

To understand the uniqueness of this linguistic globalization process, it is useful to draw comparisons to two modern world languages, English and Spanish. Both of these were initially the languages of large empires, centered for several centuries in two cities: London and Madrid. Here they developed their own literary cultures with established language standards. Later, they, too, became pluricentric.

English, as the language of the British Empire, was already a language in worldwide use in the nineteenth century, and it was the first language in more or less the same countries in which it is used today. Even so, what constituted "good" English was never questioned—it was obviously the King's English. The fact that English was spoken in the United States, which did not belong to the empire, was not yet a relevant linguistic factor. For the British Empire, London played precisely the same role that Rome had for the Imperium Romanum into the second and third century. But with the dissolution of the British Empire and the ascent of the United States to world-power status, North America, Australia, New Zealand, and India eventually became linguistic regions on a par with England. In all of these countries, English is used independently as a first language without institutions such as a school system or media in common to coordinate the language with Greenwich Mean Time.

We see similar developments in the Spanish language, which as a result of colonization became the language of almost all of South and Central America, with the exception of Brazil, and of the Philippines. Although most of these countries gained their independence from Spain in the nineteenth century, peninsular Spanish remained the undisputed gold standard well into the twentieth century. In all probability, the Spanish Civil War (1936–1939) was the event that broke this dependence on Spain. All of the Spanish-speaking countries began asserting their cultural and linguistic independence, which enabled them to claim parity with their erstwhile colonial motherland.

The pluricentric evolution of Latin culture in late antiquity has much in common with the processes described earlier. Even though these processes brought about the individuation of entire nation-states in the Spanish and English worlds, whereas pluricentricity in late antiquity meant merely the cultural independence of cities (and most of them relatively close to each other, like Rome, Milan, and Ravenna), they are no less comparable. The unification of such a region into a single speech region, as we see in modern Italy, would not have been conceivable, given the communications and educational realities of the times. The process of creating a supraregional vernacular that shares a common standard crucially presupposes compulsory schooling and news media—especially television and radio—within the territorial reaches of the region. Given the realities of communications in late antiquity, Rome and Milan might as well have been as far apart as Spain and Argentina.

Observing the evolution of English and Spanish in the twentieth century, one realizes that cultural pluricentricity soon leads to divergence in a language. This process has resulted in regional forms that are no longer viewed as deficient variants. English has spawned a multiplicity of "Englishes," a paradoxical plural that has increasingly made its way into the technical literature. And the issue of the "ownership of English"—fundamentally, who gets to define what is "good" English—is an openly discussed question with real consequences in the classroom and beyond. In addition, the very evident differences between the Spanish spoken in Spain, Mexico, Argentina, and other countries poses a major challenge to global use of the language. For example, it is no longer acceptable to translate marketing or other materials for local consumption into a single "standard" Spanish. Such translations are "localized," and those destined for Mexico may be very different from those intended for use in most of the countries of the Southern Cone: Argentina, Uruguay, Paraguay, and Chile.

For English and Spanish, the question of whether there should be a global standard and, if so, in what form it should exist is an ongoing controversy. These two languages have dealt with this question very differently, and the dissimilarities reflect external circumstances. Two distinctions are of particular salience. The United States, which gained its independence from Great Britain and the British Empire in the eighteenth century, has become arguably the most important center in globally pluricentric modern English.

Spanish, on the other hand, is spoken almost entirely in countries that belonged to the Spanish Empire. In addition, the most important global function of English is as a second language and a lingua franca in communications involving *no* native speaker. Spanish, on the other hand, is primarily used for communications between Spanish-speaking countries and regions; it is rare for nonnative speakers to use Spanish as a lingua franca.

It is therefore not surprising that in spite of the coequality of the various national variants, there is more of a consciousness of what connects the Romance-speaking countries and more of a desire to emphasize and retain those linkages. Language academies play an important role in this respect. Originally, the Spanish standard was established by the Real Academia Española, which was founded in 1713 along the lines of the Académie française. Since the nineteenth century, academies have been founded in other Spanish-speaking countries, which assumed responsibility for observing and standardizing the language. In 1951, these academies founded the Asociación de Academias de la Lengua Española, which today comprises twenty-two national academies under the leadership of the Spanish Academy. Each of these academies closely follows the peculiarities of their specific variant of Spanish. Overall, however, they try to integrate these disparate variants into a more comprehensive basic standard, while retaining flexibility at the national level. In effect, this sort of pluricentric standard implies that a linguistic standard applicable to all regions is desirable in spite of regional variations.

In English, on the other hand, the regional variants continued to diverge. There is no concentrated effort to establish a supranational standard, and the use of English around the world evolves more or less at will. One exception is in pronunciation, where extreme divergence is already leading to considerable difficulties in communication, as a Bostonian vacationing on Jamaica might attest. One suggestion for dealing with this divergence is to establish a common minimum standard, a "core lingua franca" to ensure the viability of transnational communications.

Nonetheless, the question of whether there could, or even should, be a global standard for English is still not completely settled.[38] The English linguist David Crystal, who has written one of the most widely read books on the development of English as a world language, believes that a World Standard Spoken English (WSSE) will eventually develop.[39] In his view, it will neither derive from a single national variant nor attempt to harmonize different variants but will be its own transnationally defined and standardized variant that will differ from all national variants. This would precisely parallel what happened to Latin. In fact, Crystal himself notes the similarity and compares the differentiation of the various Englishes to the evolution of the Romance languages from Vulgar Latin, and he has compared the role of the transnational English standard with that of written Latin in late antiquity. He further believes that a diglossic relationship as described by Ferguson could eventually develop between the national forms of English and the emerging global form.

Whether this will be the future of English remains to be seen. Crystal's views have also sparked controversy, and of course the lightning communications and personal mobility that have become such a feature of modern life have created a set of circumstances completely unknown in the days of horse-drawn wagons and hand-lettered manuscripts.[40] Nonetheless, the parallels that Crystal reflects on are undoubtedly right. If we look at the specific political and cultural situation, in particular the development of a pluricentricity in which new centers come to enjoy parity with the old imperial centers and have in part even eclipsed them (the United States for English, Milan or Ravenna for Latin), and once we appreciate the crucial importance of English as a lingua franca, we realize that, of all the modern world languages, the position in which English finds itself is most comparable to that of Latin in late antiquity.

Given the long-term historical perspective afforded by Latin, two questions emerge more clearly than Crystal and others have formulated them. First, is it possible that English in its globalized form will lose all of its "native speakers" (who after all come from linguistic areas where regional forms of English are in constant flux) and therefore go the way of Latin, Greek, and Arabic, becoming in one way or another a language learned at school? And second, will the long-term existence of a globalized English automatically turn it into a fixed language because the elementary structure of English is laid down in grammar books, and no institution exists that has the power to mandate new rules to teachers around the world? Of course, global English will always invent new words and new ways of saying things, as did Latin. But the question of whether elementary features of global English morphology and syntax are fixed is not absurd. If we follow Crystal's approach to its logical conclusion, his diglossia model posits for English essentially what happened to Latin: not only will the regional varieties develop differently, as occurred with the Romance languages in late antiquity, but the global standard will also become in some way fixed. I should stress that these thoughts are in no way meant to predict a particular evolutionary path or outcome but rather to raise awareness of the basic conditions under which languages in pluricentric constellations develop, given our experience with five thousand years of written culture.

However, Latin in late antiquity developed differently from both English and Spanish in one particular respect. The development of pluricentricity today is quite transparent because we have access to the spoken language via modern media and because regional linguistic innovations are very quickly committed to writing. As a result, we can observe how the languages themselves become pluricentric; the (possible) development of a global standard above the written and spoken regional varieties is only a second step. Unlike English and Spanish, Latin became a pluricentric language not because its area of diffusion covered so many disparate political units but rather as a result of another, more pluralistic weighting of the centers within the still-existent Roman Empire, which had recently been reorganized by Diocletian and Constantine. So we would not expect that the written language would itself have developed regional peculiarities. Here, the fixing of a global standard was the first step. Regional divergences were restricted to the spoken word, and with very few exceptions nothing of that has survived. The Romance languages, however, evolved precisely from divergent trends at the level of everyday speech. Written Latin became a pluricentric language only in this respect, that grammar teachers in all cities had the same rights to discuss matters of correctness in speech. Latin became a language independent of place. In comparison to the time immediately before late antiquity, during which the core elements of Latin were already fixed, the changes were probably not all that great in practice. However, after a long developmental period, a more or less official threshold had been reached, after which correct Latin would be acquired in school by all inhabitants of the empire, including those of Rome.

Exactly what these evolutionary or developmental steps were remains largely opaque. For example, we do not know whether the new school standard was explicitly decreed by administrative or imperial fiat. We do know that both Diocletian and Constantine wanted to expand the use of Latin in the Greek-speaking areas of the East, and this could be an indication of some sort of overall plan. As in the first century BCE, the Roman Empire was now at a turning point that mandated an entirely new political self-understanding, and so it would have been quite normal for the language to reflect that. Unfortunately, we do not know the details.

The elaboration of a school standard during late antiquity had consequences for the relationship between Latin and Greek, which was different in the East and in the West. Before the advent of what we call late antiquity, Attic Greek was the standard language in the East, while

Latin was considerably less prevalent. But the elites in the West were raised bilingually, and Rome was probably the most important center for Greek writers. Latin, which was always the language of the imperial court, the military, and the judiciary, was seen as a literary language of relatively secondary importance; only in Rome was there a thriving Latin literature. The relative diffusion of the two languages changed with the final partition of the Roman Empire by Emperor Theodosius, in 395. Knowledge of Greek became much less common in the West. In the third century, the Christian church in the West, whose language had always been Greek, switched to Latin; in the fourth century, the church fathers Jerome and Rufinus of Aquileia began translating Greek works to make them known in the West. At the same time, Latin became the standard language of the West by the schooling process described earlier. Instead of a Greek-centered culture in the East and a bilingual culture in the West, by the end of the fourth century, two halves of the empire in which different historical culture languages predominated now confronted each other even though residues of the other language persisted. Greek literature was not immediately forgotten in the West, nor did Latin completely cease to be the language of the imperial court and of politics in the East. Nonetheless, the die had been cast, and the division into a Greek Eastern Roman and a Latin Western Roman Empire was now complete at the cultural level. The eventual loss of Greek in the West—an extraordinary development that marked the "Latin" Middle Ages and was not corrected until the Renaissance—cannot be explained merely by the overall loss of culture in a Western Empire increasingly subject to mass migration. Rather, it was more a function of the linguistic reorganization of the Roman Empire and the resurgence of Latin in late antiquity. The appellation *Latini* (Latin people) became an umbrella term for the people in the West. Whereas Romans wrote in Greek during the second century, we now for the first time find prominent Greek authors writing in Latin. These included the historian Ammianus Marcellinus (ca. 330–395) and the poet Claudian (ca. 400), whose Latin works are among the most important of late antiquity. Both came from Greek-speaking areas. Claudian, in fact, had begun as a Greek poet.

The linguistic partition of the empire also necessitates a reassessment of the contacts between Greek and Latin literature in late antiquity. To a much greater extent than earlier, the contacts between the

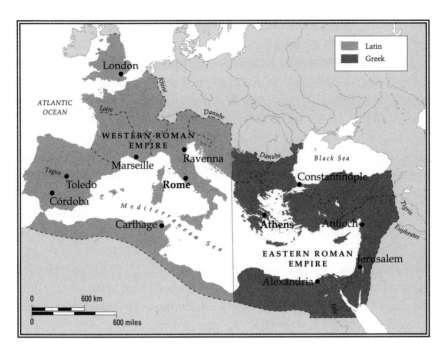

Figure 5. Latin and Greek in the Roman Empire of late antiquity. The border between the two halves of the empire also formed the linguistic border between Latin and Greek (with large areas of overlap in the Balkans).

two should be seen more in terms of a horizontal relationship between East and West than as the perpetuation of an old cultural unit. The fact that the grammarian Priscian, in Constantinople, for the first time translated the Greek grammarians Herodian and Apollonios Dyskolos into Latin in the sixth century and that Corippus composed Latin epics in Constantinople under the emperors Justinian (527–565) and Justin II (565–578) must be viewed in the context of efforts by Constantinople to unite the entire Roman Empire under a Latin imperial court. Justinian's compilation of the Roman legal tradition in his *Digesta*, which came to be of crucial importance in the history of law, was undoubtedly the result of the same effort even though the later *Novellae,* also known as Justinian's *Novels,* were written in Greek (the law school at Berytos eventually switched to Greek as well during late antiquity). From a linguistic perspective, it would be especially interesting to examine more closely the history of Neoplatonism, the most important school of philosophy to emerge in late antiquity. This has never been done before. The Neoplatonic school was founded in Rome by Plotinus (ca. 205–ca. 270 CE), who was probably born in the East, during the high point of the imperial crisis of the third century, which apparently did not have as deleterious an effect on Greek as on Latin literature. Plotinus's most important student, Porphyrios (d. 305), continued to live in Rome. After that, the history of Neoplatonism, and of philosophy as a whole, shows a clear split between a fairly large number of philosophers who lived in the East (in Athens, Asia Minor, Syria, and perhaps Alexandria) and wrote in Greek and those who lived in the West (Augustine Marius Victorinus, Macrobius, and Calcidius), who wrote in Latin. Numerous highly learned commentaries on Aristotelian and Platonic works were written in the East, and a sort of teaching curriculum for professional philosophers developed there. In Ravenna, at the beginning of the sixth century, Boethius conceived a plan to translate the works of Plato and Aristotle into Latin, write commentaries on Aristotle's treatises, and compose introductions to the so-called *artes liberales* (arithmetic, music, geometry) in emulation of Greek texts. This grand project, so consequential for the history of Western philosophy, was not, as is often stated, an attempt to preserve ancient culture from decay (which in this view was reanimated by Boethius) but rather a conscious attempt to transfer to the Latin West the way of teaching philosophy that had taken root in the East. This project even had a political thrust, given the situation in the early sixth century. As we know, Boethius was tried and executed by Theoderic, king of the Ostrogoths (d. 526), because he, along with the Roman senator Albinus, were accused of conspiring with Constantinople. The political side of this sad tale, to which the world owes the philosophical and literary masterwork known as the *Consolatio philosophiae*, which Boethius wrote as he resigned himself to death, is well known. Is it plausible that his focus on the Greek East had nothing to do with these political circumstances? Or did his Latin translations, in which he presented Neoplatonism in a fundamentally Greek manner, make Theodoric suspect him of being an "Eastern Roman," whatever the political facts might have been?

Teaching Grammar and the Linguistic Standard

In most cases, the history of grammar is a specialty of interest only to linguists. But things are different with historical culture languages. In some respects, such languages are even defined by grammar teaching because that is how the morphology and the elementary linguistic framework are codified.[41] Without Panini there would have been no Sanskrit as a historical culture language. In the case of Latin, the major light was Aelius Donatus, who during the fourth century was *grammaticus urbis Romae* (official grammar teacher of the city of Rome). In many ways he, much like Panini, represented a turning point in terms of ancient grammar, something that was not fully appreciated until recently. His work preserved the language at a time when transmission by natural means was no longer a certainty.

Of course, grammar, which was a Greek transplant, had become established in Rome fairly early. According to tradition, Crates of Mallos (end of second century BCE) was the first person to teach grammar in Rome. The usual, relatively uniform step in the Roman educational system, which was also borrowed from the Greeks, began with the primary-school teacher, who taught students to read and write.[42] The next step was the *grammaticus*. Although responsible for teaching "grammar," he also taught what was called *enarratio poetarum*, that is, the exegesis of "canonical" poetic writings. This feature of the system derived from the fact that the art of writing (and that is the literal meaning of the Greek term *grammatiké techne*) was learned by studying Homer and other poets, which meant that all theoretical questions were examined based on these texts.

In other words, the grammarians of late antiquity were part of a long tradition, and it has been demonstrated that the terminologies and grammatical systems that they developed were based directly on much earlier models. This is one reason that they have often been denigrated as derivative and mechanical compilers of older knowledge. It would be a mistake, however, to judge them too quickly. If we ask which ancient grammatical works have survived, we find something rather curious: whereas the works written up to the third century CE have all been lost and their authors are now known merely by name, the majority of Latin grammarians who wrote after the time of Diocletian were eagerly received and preserved during the following centuries. We have so many texts that their complete edition, published in the nineteenth century, comprises seven large volumes and many thousands of pages.[43] It is clear that for the European Latin tradition, the older works were dispensable, but those of late antiquity were not.

This is especially true of two authors who were for more than a thousand years among the most important writers in western Europe: Priscian and Donatus. The importance of Priscian, who lived in Constantinople during the sixth century, is that he dealt in detail with genus and the regular and irregular morphology of Latin words. Because these words could be looked up, given the systematic arrangement of his work as a whole, Priscian became an extraordinarily important source for the codification of Latin word forms. More than a thousand medieval manuscripts of his complete work or individual parts of it have survived.

However, Donatus, who functioned as *grammaticus urbis Romae* during the fourth century and as such taught Jerome, was even more important for the history of Latin.[44] In addition to a somewhat truncated commentary on Terence, he left behind a Latin grammar that came to be viewed for a thousand years as quite simply the perfect embodiment of grammar. By the early fifth century, its position of preeminence was such that Servius, who wrote commentaries on Virgil, also wrote a commentary on Donatus. Large numbers of other commentaries and editions followed. Pope Gregory (ca. 600) essentially equated Donatus with grammar when he excused grammatical errors by claiming that God's words could not be subjected to the rules of Donatus.[45]

Unfortunately, we are unable to compare these works with older grammars because, as noted earlier, they did not survive. Be that as it may, there are many indications that the later grammars were successful because they took into account the current state of the language, and at a time when the correct form of Latin was no longer transmitted by oral tradition, they assumed the role of arbiter. In other words, Latin grammar was on the cusp between its old role as a reflection of the vernacular for native speakers (with only a minor standardizing function) and a new role as a textbook for Latin as a second language.

This functional change remained hidden because we have almost no explicit evidence that these works of grammar were written for pupils who could no longer learn correct Latin from their mothers. The increasing gap between classical Latin and Vulgar Latin and the evolution of new vernaculars from Vulgar Latin were alluded to only very rarely in marginalia. Needless to say, Romance specialists have taken special interest in this evidence. Reactions to these changes in the language were noted implicitly through the rearrangement of traditional material and through brief asides that seemed rather innocuous at first.

We are still awaiting a systematic analysis; some examples demonstrate how we should read these texts.

Most of the grammars from late antiquity, whether by Charisius (fourth century), Diomedes (fourth century), or Priscian (sixth century), spend much time elucidating morphology. But when we come to Donatus[46] (although Plotius Sacerdos[47] took a similar approach at the end of the third century), this part did not take the form of a theoretical description but was reduced to inflection tables of the sort seen in all Latin grammars today. True, correct inflection had been part and parcel of the older grammars as well. But in Donatus, we see a new didactic desideratum. In his grammar, he placed the tables at the front. Before beginning the normal grammar curriculum, students, of course, had to learn the correct forms of endings, which were—anticipating the development of the Romance languages—at the very least garbled in the vernacular pronunciation, if not completely abandoned.[48] These tables, which came to be known as the *Ars minor* (approximately "small grammar"), took on a life of their own and in the original text and in its various reformulations had an illustrious career throughout the Middle Ages and into the fifteenth century.[49] The first printed book was not Gutenberg's famed forty-two-line Bible but rather Donatus's *Ars minor*, which Gutenberg, correctly sizing up the market, hoped to sell in class sets to schools. The grammarian Consentius (presumably fifth century) also demonstrates that inflected endings had become part of the curriculum. He tried to show how the forms of declension follow rules from which unknown forms may then be derived. For example, he wrote, "These are the differences in the singular declension that lead us methodically to the ablative, from which, in turn, we may determine the plural declension."[50] Interestingly, the goal of this method was often explicitly stated as *emendatio loquendi,* that is, Consentius was well aware that the Latin that was spoken was not correct and had to be "emended."

Inflection was not the only feature of Latin grammar that had become problematical. The evolution of the Romance languages brought with it increasing instability in noun gender and the principal forms of irregular verbs. A small grammatical tract, possibly written during the fifth century by a grammarian known only as Phocas, gives an excellent picture of the uncertainties faced by native speakers at the time.[51] Phocas provided a systematic overview of all of the types of noun endings with their declensions and genera and of the verb forms, including

cū docerēm docēmū docēret ꝶ prīto pfco cū doct⁹ sim l fueri
sis l suis sit l fuit ꝛ plr cū docti sim⁹ l suim⁹ sitis l fueri-
tis sit l fuerit ꝶ prīto plſꝗ pfco cū doct⁹ esse l fuisse ees vl
fuisses eet l fuis⁊ ꝛ plr cū docti eem⁹ l fuissem⁹ eetis l fuis-
etis eent l fuisser Futo cū doct⁹ ero l fueo eis l suis eit l fu
eit ꝛ plr cū docti eim⁹ l fueim⁹ eitis l fueitis erit vl fuerit
Infinito mo ſū nutis ꝛ psoīs tpe pūti ꝛ prīto ipfco docet
prīto pfco ꝛ plſꝗ pfco doctū ee l fuisse futo doctū iri Duo
ptidpia thūt a ūbo passiu prītū vt doct⁹ futur vt doced⁹
¶ Ego legis legit ꝛ plr legim⁹ legitis legūt ꝶ rīto iu
fco legebā legebas legebat ꝛ plr legebam⁹ legeba
tis legebāt ꝶ rīto pfco legi legisti legit ꝛ plr legim⁹ legiſ
tis legerūt vl legere ꝶ rīto plſꝗ pfco legerā legeras le ge
rat ꝛ plr legeam⁹ legeatis le gerāt Futūo legam leges le
get ꝛ plr legemus legetis legent Impatiuo modo tēpore
pſenti ad ſecundā ꝛ tercā psonam lege legat ꝛ plr legamus legite legant Futuro legito tu legito ille ꝛ plr lega
mus legitote legunto vl leguntote Optatiuo modo tē
pore pūti ꝛ prīto ipfco vt legerem legeres legeret et plr
vt legeremus legeretis legerent ꝶ Pretito pfco ꝛ plſꝗ pfco
vt legissem legisses legisset ꝛ plr vt legissemus legisseis
legissent Futūo vt legā legas legat ꝛ plr vt legamus le
gatis legant Coniūctiuo mo tēpe pūti cū legam legas
legat ꝛ plr cū legam⁹ legatis legant ꝶ Pretito ipfco cū le
gere legeres legeret ꝛ plr cū legeremus legeretis legerent
ꝶ Pretito pfco cū legerim legeris legerit ꝛ plr cū legerim⁹
legatis legerint ꝶ Preterito plusꝗꝟ pfco cum legissem

Figure 6. Donatus (fourth century CE), *Ars minor.* Mainz: Unknown printer of the thirty-six-line Bible, about 1453/1454. Paris, Bibliothèque Nationale. The correct declension and conjugation endings had to be practiced in school as early as the fourth century CE. The most famous grammar of late antiquity was that of Donatus, who placed morphology tables at the beginning of his book. This text continued to be used in Latin instruction well into the late Middle Ages. Johannes Gutenberg printed more than twenty editions; the first editions were printed even before his famous forty-two-line Bible. Approximately 350 printed editions of the text were published during the fifteenth century. None of them has survived complete because schoolbooks were not stored in libraries after use. This fragment contains the conjugation forms of the verb *legere* (to read), beginning with the large capital *L* about halfway down: Lego legis legit in plurali legimus legitis legunt Praeterito imperfecto legebam legebas legebat in plurali legebamus legebatis legebant . . . akg-images

the principal forms of all irregular verbs. His overview is essentially the same as in the detailed modern Latin grammars used in school. As Phocas made clear, this overview—which was of no use for native speakers—had a didactic purpose. For example, he introduced the section on verbs with the remark that all problems in this area may be resolved by recognizing the right conjugation and by knowing the correct form of the perfect tense. To what conjugation does a particular verb belong? What are the principal forms? These are the same questions that vex Latin students today.

In this context, we might wish to consider one small text that survived by chance in the form of a single manuscript from the eighth century and which is known today as the *Appendix Probi* because it was appended to the end of a grammar by a certain Probus. This text, like a dictionary, compares the Vulgar Latin forms of words with the correct written Latin forms. For example, we find *speculum non speclum* (compare Italian *spiecchio*, mirror) and *columna non colomna* (compare Italian *colonna*, column). Romance linguists have examined this text very closely because it is one of the very few surviving grammars from late antiquity that actually takes Vulgar Latin into account. But the truth of the matter is that the work of the grammarians of late antiquity was *largely* aimed at correcting the deviations introduced into pure Latin by the various vernaculars. These grammarians were attempting to preserve Latin as a historical culture language at a time when the language of the people had already moved on. By carefully examining the explicit fixing of word forms and by reading the texts carefully with this evolution in mind, we will, I believe, gain valuable insight into the linguistic situation in late antiquity.

Canonical Writings and the Faith in Language

But Latin could not be learned from grammarians alone. The things that they could not impart, including most of the syntax, definitions, and typical usages, was what the canon of classical authors was for. These authors were read at school as models to imitate, and so they had, without explicit language rules, the effect of an "implicit codification" of the language. But unlike in today's Latin classes, where students learn grammar and read authors, the population at the time actually spoke a living form of Latin that was not far removed from classical Latin. Because of this, the corrected form of Latin was to that extent a living language, although the final arbiters of correctness no longer resided among living speakers but among the dead. Cicero and Virgil were far and away the most prominent authorities, with Plautus, Terence, Horace, Sallust, and Livius of secondary importance. Unlike Greek, for which Alexandrian philologists formulated stringent lists of canonical literature, Latin followed a different path. Ovid, the love poets Propertius and Tibullus, and postclassical authors like Statius and Lucan continued to be read even though they played a much more subsidiary role in grammar instruction. Luckily, readers in late antiquity were interested in more than just language models, so some authors who were completely neglected in schools have survived. These included writers like Seneca, who could be read as a Christian author and who even in the fourth century was reputed to have corresponded with the apostle Paul, and the natural history of Pliny the Elder, which was indispensable if only for its factual information. But overall, it is clear that we would know virtually nothing about the classical literature of the Romans if that literature had not found its way into the body of language models that constituted a core component of language instruction in late antiquity.

Unfortunately, this same mechanism also led to the almost complete loss of preclassical Latin literature, including the epics of Ennius and the tragedies and comedies of the second century BCE. We would have a completely different picture of Roman literary and intellectual life if these and other preclassical works had survived. But as with Greek, the canon of classical literature that has come down to us resulted mainly from considerations of language. Writers whose language deviated from the standard of the first century BCE were simply no longer read in school. The fact that Terence and Plautus, two comedic poets of the preclassical language period, were included in the canon is only an apparent exception since both of them had in antiquity been considered models of Latin style.[52] It is conceivable that direct emulation of the Greek canon played a role in the inclusion of these comedic writers. After all, representatives of the "old comedy" of the fifth century BCE, especially Aristophanes, had been considered important models of pure Attic, especially of the vernacular—and this is the only reason that the comedies of Aristophanes have come down to us.

The special significance of the more exclusive canon is evidenced by the many commentaries written in antiquity on the works of the "received authors." It is unsurprising that poets led the way in this respect because, as mentioned earlier, one of the primary tasks of the grammarian was to explicate their works. It is difficult at this remove to tease out the details of this form of schooling because the purely normative and corrective functions of grammar instruction transitioned seamlessly into commentary and cannot be easily pulled apart. Even so, we have a very good idea of which poets were favored in grammar classes in late antiquity: first of all Virgil, followed by Terence and Horace. In fact, ancient commentaries on these writers have survived, in particular the monumental Virgil commentary by the grammarian Servius. Cicero, Livius, and Sallust and to a lesser extent Lucretius, Lucan, Persius, and Juvenal were all quoted by the ancient grammarians. The existence of copious explanatory marginalia, the so-called *scholia,* in medieval manuscripts of works by these authors leads us to conclude that they had probably already been commented on in antiquity and that some parts of these *scholia* may have derived from these ancient explications.

Classical Latin literature was quite simply central to intellectual life during late antiquity. What had begun in the first century CE with the Roman upper classes eventuated in the formalization of the language culture that took on the status of a cult, by which the Roman upper classes attempted to invoke the past glories of Rome. The Latin language was much more than a medium of communication: it was also part of Roman historical consciousness and national identity. And for the educated it was a status symbol with functional and aesthetic qualities. We see much the same use of language as a marker of social class today. There is, however, one essential difference: we would not give final authority over the use of language to authors who lived centuries ago.

For the Romans, Cicero, as the most important prose author, achieved canonical status of the sort not enjoyed by any individual in the Greek tradition. Quintilian's dictum that "Cicero is not the name of a person but of eloquence itself" (*non hominis, sed eloquentiae nomen,* Quintilian, *Institutio oratoria* 10.1.112) is no exaggeration, and at least in late antiquity Cicero was just that. It should be noted that eloquence in this sense did not simply imply clever wordplay and argumentation but had its core in the perfect mastery of classical Latin. Because of this, interest in Cicero was almost exclusively of a formal and linguistic sort. That his speeches and letters were unique historical documents and whether his

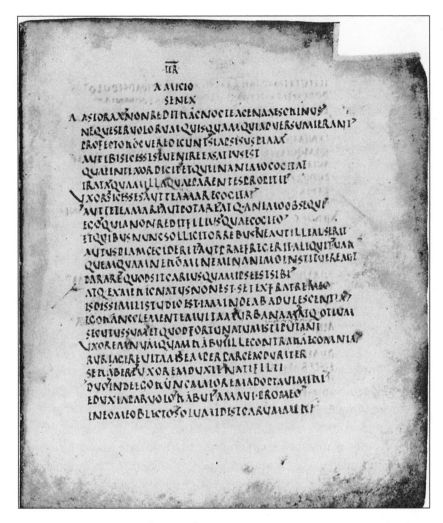

Figure 7. Terence, Comedies, Cod. Vaticanus Latinus 3226, manuscript from about 400 CE. In late antiquity, Terence was one of the "classics" used to teach Latin in school. The figure shows the beginning of his comedy *Adelphoe,* which is still taught. Micio, an older man, speaks to the servant, Storax: *Storax! Non redi[i]t hac nocte a cena Aeschinus . . .* ("Storax! Aeschinus has not yet returned from his dinner date this evening"). The script is the so-called *capitalis rustica,* which was the normal script used during the classical period. Other types of script were generally used in late antiquity; nonetheless, the old script was frequently retained for revered ancient classics, especially for poets. These editions, in other words, differ from "normal" books in their text layout. In the sixteenth century, this extremely rare manuscript belonged to Cardinal Pietro Bembo, one of the most important proponents of Latin "Ciceronianism" and a father of the Italian literary language. Biblioteca Apostolica Vaticana

philosophical works were intellectually important were not even considered issues worthy of discussion. Augustine, who was encouraged by Cicero's *Hortensius* to reflect on the meaning of life (*Confessiones* 3, 4), complained that the content of this work was neglected in favor of form in Latin classes.

But at the heart of the canon, even more so than Cicero, stood the work of Virgil. The fact that a "national" epic could reach beyond its mere literary function and serve as a key text for linguistic, rhetorical, philosophical, ethical, geographical, and other purposes was a legacy from the Greeks, for whom Homer played an almost biblical role. But if anything, Virgil's preeminent role in defining how Romans viewed themselves exceeded even that of its Greek model. The grammarians of late antiquity were inclined to demonstrate most grammatical phenomena with quotations from Virgil. It is quite probable that in certain circles a more or less rote mastery of the entire corpus of Virgil's writings would have been assumed. In any case, the *scholia* to Juvenal sometimes cite verses from Virgil not because his works help us to understand Juvenal but because the standard explication of the Virgil text (for us evidenced in Servius's commentary) contains helpful information for reading Juvenal. Apparently teachers could assume that their pupils had already learned the Virgil text together with the commentaries.[53] This means that, at a recitation, the many intertextual allusions in the learned poetry of late antiquity (e.g., Claudian) in all probability would have been recognized and savored not only by scholars but by educated listeners as well.

Virgil's works were not only model texts and grammatical exercises but also the personification of Roman culture. This is made very clear in a rather peculiar work, the *Saturnalia*, which presumably dates from the fifth century, by Macrobius, an author otherwise known as a Neoplatonic philosopher. At a Saturnalia in about 400—the pagan nature of this festival in a Rome already shaped by Christianity is itself a tip-off—Macrobius had prominent, educated Romans meet in scholarly conversation, among them Symmachus (a senator and classically oriented writer who only a few years earlier did battle with Ambrosius, the bishop of Milan, about the statue of the pagan goddess Victoria in the Roman Curia) and the Virgil commentator and grammarian Servius. The content of this rather expansive work consists almost entirely of an extensive discussion of Virgil and the technical knowledge that his works contain. Rhetoric, pontifical law, astronomy, philosophy, the relationship between Virgil and Greek literature, and a plethora of other details were meticulously worked through. Even though Macrobius included Euangelus, an opponent of Virgil's, the entire work is nothing other than a glorification of Virgil as the fulcrum of the intellectual world.

Virgil's preeminence may also be discerned from the manuscripts that have come down to us. That is because late antiquity saw the beginning of the transition to books; between the second and the fourth century CE, the fragile papyrus scrolls, which had up to then been the standard form for books, were replaced by the much more durable parchment codex. Naturally, Roman classics were sold in large editions, and because the texts were read during the Middle Ages, we have in some cases not only medieval copies but also manuscripts from antiquity either as fragments or (very rarely) in almost complete form, preserved by chance or as museum pieces in medieval libraries. The fact that no fewer than nine Virgil manuscripts are known from the fourth to the sixth century demonstrates the importance of his work in late antiquity (although only small fragments of five of these have survived). Among these are two extremely rare, almost complete illustrated codices (known as the *Vergilius Vaticanus* and the *Vergilius Romanus,* both of which are housed at the Vatican library). These manuscripts are among the most important artistic legacies of Roman antiquity. In terms of the number of fourth- and fifth-century manuscripts that have survived complete or as larger fragments, Virgil, with four codices, exceeds even the Latin Bible. Even in their external form, poetic manuscripts from late antiquity, again especially those of Virgil, are extraordinary. While the normal script used in manuscripts changed during the centuries after the birth of Christ, achieving the more rounded form that today is referred to as uncial, poetry, and in some cases biblical texts, continued to be written in the ancient Roman script used in Cicero's time, which we call *capitalis rustica* and which is very close to modern capital letters. Throughout antiquity, Virgil's texts, as far as we know, were written exclusively in the old *capitalis,* and there is not a single fragment in uncial or in any other script. Apparently, this script symbolized the extraordinary importance of canonical works. Poetry may well have been written in this script because it was felt to be integral to instruction in grammar, which was intimately connected with the cultivation and

Figure 8. Above, Biblioteca Apostolica Vaticana, Cod. lat. 3867, end of the fifth century *(Vergilius Romanus). At right,* Abbey of St. Peter in the Black Forest, Seminary Library, portrait of Mark the Evangelist (Trier, ca. 1000). This Virgil manuscript is a magnificent example of how a deluxe edition of the poet would have looked in late antiquity. The text is preceded by a portrait of Virgil. This type of author portrait was also common in Gospel manuscripts, which were the "classical texts" of the Christians. The depiction of Mark in the Trier manuscript continues to show the attributes of ancient portraiture of classical authors, including the scroll, which was how books were published in Roman times. Geistliches Zentrum der Erzdiozese Freiburg, St Peter auf dem Schwarzwald, RA 4 93/46

preservation of tradition. In the case of Virgil, people took it even a step further by creating an alphabet copied from stone inscriptions (which made them very cumbersome to write), the so-called *capitalis quadrata*. The complete lack of fragments in *capitalis quadrata* for other authors of antiquity makes it likely that this reverential treatment was limited to Virgil alone.

The classical culture of late antiquity, with Virgil at its center, shows clear signs of having been a book religion—in the sense that not a few teachers in the Renaissance and in the nineteenth century had greater faith in classical education than in God.[54] The quasi-canonical writings used in schools created a cultural identity and formed the most important basis for understanding the world and engaging culturally—and it was all drawn from books. The language of these texts was more than a mere medium; it was itself a cult object. In their constant references to texts by Virgil and other classical authors (learned by heart, much like the Bible), writers of late antiquity like Claudian and Symmachus behaved much like Christian authors, who to some extent used the text of the Bible as the bedrock upon which they built their ideas and arguments. Not only did the classics define Latin as a historical culture language; they were in fact fundamental to the life of the culture. Knowledge of these writings and their exegesis was how the world came to be understood. In this sense, the Roman culture of late antiquity and Christianity were completely different understandings—faith in the Roman past and its gods and philosophy versus faith in the Christian God as Creator. However, they also had one significant commonality; they were both centered in a historical canon. The Bible, like Virgil and Cicero, was a historical scripture requiring exegesis. They even evinced a certain equivalency in that they referenced events that occurred during the time of Emperor Augustus.

If we knew more about the layout and the illustrations in "classic editions" in relation to Bible design, we might have a better understanding of the Bible as a Christian "classic." There is no question that the layout of biblical manuscripts was based on pagan models, and the details of this emulation have long been the subject of study. Deserving of special mention is the fact that the type of author portrait found in numerous medieval Gospel manuscripts was undoubtedly copied from late antiquity and is virtually the same as the author portrait in the *Codex Romanus* described and shown earlier. We see the author sitting at a lectern with a book scroll in hand, his feet placed on a platform, next to him a container for other books. Another known pagan author portrait, that of Terence (in a Carolingian copy)[55] represents a very different type of iconography.[56] There is a question as to whether the Gospel portrait might not actually have a more specific relationship to the portraits of the classical pagan authors to the extent that, for example, Virgil and the Evangelists might be more closely related in this respect. While this deserves further attention, the surviving source material is simply too scant to permit us to draw any conclusions.

Jerome's Dream of a Double Latin Standard

To understand the history of Latin in late antiquity, we must not limit ourselves to the cult of the classics and the refinements of the rhetorical schools. The language of the Christians and the Latin Bible was very different in that it was both simpler and closer to the masses. It would be too simple to speak of a single Latinity of late antiquity, and hardly anyone currently believes that a specifically Christian form of the language existed.

In a letter (II.9), Sidonius Apollinaris, one of the most important writers of the fifth century, described his visits to two country estates. There was a library in one of them that he found especially praiseworthy, as it was divided into two sections. One section housed the "women's side," with works in the "religious style," the *stilus religiosus;* the other side, which was for the men, contained classical works. In his inimitable style, Apollinaris described these as *"cothurno Latialis eloquii nobilitantur"* (a rather flowery locution: those "who are raised to peerage with the cothurnus of words from Latium"). The author hastened to add that Christian writers, including Augustine and Prudentius, were also to be found there, and he explicitly defended the style of the Latin translation of Eusebius's church history.

Here, Sidonius touched on a problem that is of fundamental importance for the entire history of the Latin language and, beyond that, for the history of historical culture languages as a whole. Let us begin with the relationship between classical literature and Christianity.

Historical culture languages usually develop out of a literary corpus of canonical significance that contains myths and lore crucial to that particular cultural tradition. Sanskrit, for example, is firmly tied to Vedic literature, Egyptian hieroglyphics passed on ancient Egyptian ritual texts in fixed form, and classical Arabic would be unthinkable without the Koran and the Islamic tradition (even though these are only part of Islamic identity). But Greek, and especially Latin, developed very differently.

The point from which Latin developed into a historical culture language was the classical literature of the first century BCE. The aesthetic quality of this literature is an important characteristic. The nuances of word choice and sound, the rounded phrasings and prosody in prose, and rhythms in poetry—these were obviously the objects of intense authorial effort. In fact, classical authors brought forth works of world-class art. However, being pleasing was not the only goal of this cultivation of language. Rather, it was part of a more comprehensive culture centered on the human being. It had a humanistic thrust in that it viewed the cultivation of language and thought as integral; it was what made human beings human. In this sense, the cultural religion that was created was to some extent a religion of human self-development and unfolding. This aspect of what I wrote in the previous chapter about the sacralization of Roman literature has its roots in the first century BCE.

The role of language in Christian culture was very different. As a religion of humility, in which believers derived everything from the grace of God, Christians would have been repelled by the claim that the cultivation of language could lead to the perfection of humankind. And so, over the course of late antiquity, Christianity became engaged in an intense struggle with the ancient pagan culture of language. In the end, as we know, the pagan tradition became integrated into the Christian. Not only did church fathers like Augustine recognize that pagan philosophy could contain elements of eternal truth (Neoplatonism in particular made it easier to integrate philosophy and Christian theology), but its very language was also co-opted in Christian literature and sermons. Even though Augustine gave up his profession as a teacher of rhetoric when he converted to Christianity, the skills that he had perfected went into his great works. As Sidonius might have put it, even as a Christian he preferred the men's library. Without this integration, ancient literature may very well not have survived even to the extent that it has.

There was, however, never a complete integration. The fundamental problem may be summed up by the famous dream of Jerome (twenty-second letter), which had a powerful effect well into the early modern era. In his dream, Jerome was reading Cicero while fasting. He was so overcome by the smoothness of the prose that he no longer found pleasure in Christian writings with their clumsy language. Later, he became ill, and in his fevered nightmare he saw himself dragged before God's seat of judgment. Much like a catechist, God asked him who he was, and Jerome answered, *"Christianus sum"* (I am a Christian). But God replied, *"Ciceronianus es, non Christianus"* (You are a Ciceronian, not a Christian)—and Jerome was given a thorough beating. When he awoke, he realized that he had been dreaming—but the welts from his beating were all over his body. A taste for aesthetics in language was a form of sensuality and was damned as a sin. Christian truth was a simple truth that did not need the sheen of rhetoric, euphonious wordings, or ingenious phrasings. Not only was the uneducated language of the Latin Bible, the vitas and legends of the saints, and the church council acts and biblical commentaries to be tolerated, but that language was also to be elevated to an ascetic ideal.

Although the Romans came to be known more for their deeds than their literary aesthetic, this contradiction in Latin was more pronounced than in Greek, where a conceptual struggle such as was personified by Jerome's dream is much less documented. One reason may have been that the tension between sensuous rhetoric and stringent restraint in Latin predated its encounter with Christianity, which had its roots in ancient Rome. This may have been the case because the Romans, even more than the Greeks, had succumbed to the euphoniousness of language. Sound effects and extreme onomatopoeia were much more typical of ancient Roman poetry than of Greek. In addition, the classical poets, especially Virgil, Horace, and Tibullus, used consonants and vowels to create discreet but timelessly beautiful, musical works of art. One of the chief reasons that some passages in Cicero stymie attempts at translation is that reduplication, adjectives, or fillers have little to do with the content requirements of the sentence but are introduced solely for overall effect. On the other hand, the Romans were for many years very skeptical of the seductions of rhetorical culture. Cato's famous dictum, *rem tene, verba sequentur* (grasp the subject, and the words will follow), gives evidence of an ancient Roman simplicity that was viewed as a moral imperative. Not without reason did the Romans introduce the most extensive sumptuary laws in the ancient world. It is, perhaps, a specifically Roman irony that the complete victory of the language culture, which is mostly associated with the Roman classics, was again called into question by Christianity during late antiquity.

The synthesis of these two trends, which was brought about during Augustine's generation, did not, however, do away with the contradiction between the humanistic self-glorification of humankind and Christian humility. It was a latent subtext throughout the Middle Ages, though more in individual instances that are randomly grouped around a broad appreciation of Jerome's dream than in open controversies between different groups. However, with the Italian Renaissance, the classical tradition began to lead a life of its own once again. The renewed appreciation of the human being in Renaissance culture was also a renewed appreciation of human language and what it could do. But there— and this is an important difference from antiquity—it no longer contended with Christian humility in an absolute way. At no time did the humanistic ideal of language mesh more easily with Christian dogma than during the Renaissance. Astonishingly, this trend was seen across all confessions. Strictly humanistic training and the Latin exercises and readings in Jesuit schools differed almost not at all from the curriculum found in Protestant schools at the time. Only with the neohumanism of the eighteenth and nineteenth centuries did classical humanistic culture once again play the role of an ersatz pagan religion aimed against the Catholic Church. The founding of the Prussian humanistic secondary school *(Gymnasium)* during the nineteenth century and the development of a community of philologists that embodied this type of school symbolized the secularization of education.

After this overview of later centuries, we now return to late antiquity. The double standard of Christian and classical Latinity embodies not only an ethical side but a linguistic one as well. It, too, was of fundamental importance to Latin in late antiquity as a whole.

One way to approach the matter is to compare an average chronicle of martyrdom from late antiquity with a "classical" masterpiece of late antiquity.

Let us, for example, take a look at one of the best-known texts from the early Christian period, the so-called *Passio sanctarum Perpetuae et Felicitatis* (Passion of St. Perpetua and St. Felicity). Perpetua was a twenty-two-year-old woman born around 181 into a prosperous family. She had a small child and, along with her husband, was martyred in about

203 in Carthage. The story, which contains the saint's visions, was probably written by three different authors who lived in the third century. Here is an excerpt, a report on her interrogation (passio 6.1):

> Alio die cum pranderemus, subito rapti sumus ut audiremur. Et pervenimus ad forum. Rumor statim per vicinas fori partes cucurrit et factus est populus immensus. Ascendimus in catastam. Interrogati ceteri confessi sunt. Ventum est ad me. Et apparuit pater ilico cum filio meo, et extraxit me de gradu, dicens: Supplica; miserere infanti. Et Hilarianus procurator, qui tunc loco proconsulis Minuci Timiniani defuncti ius gladii acceperat: Parce, inquit, canis patris tui, parce infantiae pueri. Fac sacrum pro salute imperatorum.

> Another day as we were at meal we were suddenly snatched away to be tried; and we came to the forum. Quickly a report spread abroad through the parts near to the forum, and the crowd of spectators became immense. We went up to the tribunal. The others who were asked, confessed. So they came to me. And my father appeared at that moment with my son, and drew me from the step, saying: Perform the sacrifice; have mercy on the child. And Hilarian the procurator—he that after the death of Minucius Timinian the proconsul had received the right and power of the sword—said: Spare your father's grey hairs; spare the infancy of the boy. Make sacrifice for the Emperor's prosperity.[57]

Surely an extreme, though instructive, counterexample might be the beginning of Augustine's monumental *De civitate Dei* (Of the City of God). Augustine, the former rhetorician, had a command of the art of classical Latin that was probably unequaled in late antiquity. We owe the fact that the literary culture of Cicero found a legitimate place in the Christian tradition largely to Augustine.

> Gloriosissimam civitatem Dei sive in hoc temporum cursu, cum inter impios peregrinatur ex fide vivens, sive in illa stabilitate sedis aeternae, quam nunc expectat per patientiam [compare Rom. 8.25], quoadusque iustitia convertatur in iudicium, deinceps adeptura per excellentiam victoria ultima et pace perfecta, hoc opere instituto et mea ad te promissione debito defendere adversus eos, qui conditori eius deos suos praeferunt, fili carissime Marcelline, sucepi, magnum opus et arduum, sed Deus adiutor noster est.

> Most glorious is and will be the City of God, both in this fleeting age of ours, wherein she lives by faith, a stranger among infidels, and in the days when she shall be established in her eternal home. Now she waits for it with patience, "until righteousness returns to judgment" [Psalms

94:15]; then shall she possess it with preëminence in final victory and perfect peace. In this work, on which I embark in payment of my promise to you, O dearest son Marcellinus, it is my purpose to defend the City of God against those who esteem their own gods above her Founder. The work is great and difficult, but God is my helper.[58]

One does not have to have studied Latin to see that this is a single, long, and intricately constructed sentence that probably has little to do with how people normally spoke. Despite its complexity, the two parallel parts of it, which are introduced with the word *sive,* are readily understandable. English sentences written in this way tend to fall apart because English does not use cases but word position and punctuation to indicate the relationship between words. The English translation is broken into four sentences for precisely this reason.

The reference to no fewer than three Bible passages in a single sentence gives it additional scholarly heft by recalling the way in which poets of late antiquity constantly quoted Virgil and other classical authors. The rhythm is also notable, and all the more so since Latin pronunciation had changed considerably by late antiquity; Augustine himself remarked that his African contemporaries had lost all feeling for the use of long and short syllables (*de doctrina Christiana* 4.10.24). In other words, the rhythmic composition of the sentence was a piece of learned refinement and sophistication that very few would still have been able to appreciate. It may be completely coincidental that Augustine, like Cicero in the first sentence of *De oratore* (see earlier) used the *creticus* ($^-\smile{}^-$) as his basic rhythm. Although there is probably no connection with Cicero, we can, nonetheless, see by comparing the two that, if anything, Augustine dealt with rhythm much more strictly than Cicero; that is, Augustine's use of rhythm was much more intentionally sophisticated. The number of successive feet, without variation, is much larger than with Cicero, and only once does he make use of a "looser" variant in his paean ($|\ ^-\smile\smile\smile$).

Gloriosissimam civitatem Dei
$-\ \smile-|\ -\ \smile\ \ -\ |\ -\ \smile-|-\ \ \ \smile-$

sive in hoc temporum cursu . . .
$-\ \ \smile\ \ -|\ -\ \ \smile\ -\ |-\ \ -$

sive in illa stabilitate sedis aeternae, . . .
$-\ \ \smile\ -|-\ \ \smile\ \smile\smile|-\smile\ -|\smile\ \ -\ -\ \ -$

With regard to vocabulary, the chronicle of martyrdom is simpler; it is very sparing in terms of syntactic complexity, and its rhetoric is not shaped by the classics. In this sense, it is undoubtedly closer to the people (even though some minor literary stylization is evident). However—and this is crucial—the simpler text hews to exactly the same rules of grammar. The forms themselves and the syntactic connections are all correct. Even where (in other texts, but not in this one), as is inevitable in texts not written by masters schooled in grammar and rhetoric, elements of Vulgar Latin seeped into the narrative, this happened from a lack of knowledge and not with the goal of asserting a new standard for the language. Moreover, the deviant Latin in the Latin Bible (that of the oldest translations, even more than that of Jerome's much smoother and more professional Vulgate) was not actually Vulgar Latin even though less educated translators employed some elements of the vernacular. Textbooks for students of the history of Romance languages, which contain the earliest texts showing evidence of Romance development, rarely include the Latin Bible, and most of the "simple" Christian texts are almost completely missing. In short, the Latin of the Christians and the vernacular Latin of late antiquity were, like the classical Latin taught in rhetoric schools, manifestations of a fixed language with its sights set on the past. Instruction in grammar, correct word forms, and elementary syntax were not a matter of erudition or elegance but quite simply a prerequisite for reading and writing. Mixed written forms of "grammatical" and "Vulgar" standards, as were seen more frequently in Greek or Arabic in later centuries, were never recognized in Latin.

Nonetheless, there was a double standard comprising an elementary standard that preserved the external forms of the fixed language (and was in this respect different from the spontaneous language of illiterate people) but otherwise left room for the evolution of all other linguistic characteristics and a strictly classicist standard that continued to emulate the language of Cicero and other classical authors.

Of course, the field of literature was more complex because many writers wrote neither as simply as the authors of the *Passio Perpetuae* nor with the sophistication of Augustine in his great works. Augustine himself used a simpler form of Latin in his sermons, but Sidonius Apollinaris's story of the two libraries, the men's and the women's, marks a crucial point in the development of Latin in late antiquity. The difference between "maximal" fixing, which strictly follows a canon, and "minimal" fixing, which affects only the core of the language and leaves more room for improvisation, is important not only for late antiquity but continues to be an issue in Latin literature up to the present day.

The scholastic Latin of the late Middle Ages may be described as a Latin with minimal fixing, but so can the Latin of certificates, many medical tracts, and the scientific Latin of the seventeenth and eighteenth centuries. Wherever Latin is used actively, specification of a concrete language standard oscillates between these poles, which were so vividly depicted in Jerome's dream.

"Grammatical Latin" and the Language of the People

As we have seen, in late antiquity the language conditions in the Romanized part of the empire exhibited a split between a historically fixed "educated language" (which, as discussed earlier, included the "classical Latin" of the rhetoric school and the "simple Latin" of less educated, or consciously "ascetic" writers) and an unregulated "vernacular language," much as occurred with Greek with the ascendancy of Atticism and which is still the case with Arabic today. Because the later Romance languages essentially evolved from the vernacular language, research into these languages has exhaustively detailed the various developmental steps in the process to the extent that sources have survived. Over the past several decades, the linguistic interpretation of variances in the divergence of Latin and the vernacular has been increasingly important, and linguists have been especially interested in Ferguson's diglossia model. Unfortunately, Romance studies and classical studies have gone their divergent ways.

Controversy is ongoing about whether the interplay between the two forms of the language meets the conditions for which Ferguson coined the term *diglossia*. For one thing, the distance between the two forms of the language was not as great in late antiquity as was the case in modern Greece in the nineteenth and twentieth centuries or in the Arab world or in Switzerland. At least until approximately 600, even illiterate people seem to have understood unpretentious but grammatically correct Latin quite well. This was not, of course, the Latin found in Horace or Virgil but rather the "minimal standard." The form of Latin found there differed from the language of a simple Latin sermon about as much as the language of Auden or Eliot differs from that of a radio talk-show host.

Then again, two relatively established varieties exist in the cases that Ferguson described. Even if they are more or less variable in comparison to the written language, the regional Arabic languages and Schwyzerdütsch all exhibit a certain standard that is more or less stable over a large region. But this is precisely what could not have been the case in the vernacular language of the Romanized parts of the Imperium in late antiquity. It did not remain stable but changed drastically over the three to four centuries that are at issue here, evolving into the Romance languages. We do not, however, know whether that evolution was continuous or occurred in spurts. Regional shadings must also have developed along with the variants that eventually led to the divergent branches that we know as the Romance languages. Finally, the educational system of the grammar schools, which by themselves maintained the high form of the language, also changed over time and finally collapsed. If we look at Rome in the fourth century, we may imagine a language community in which a majority of the population were conversant with the written culture and the high form of the language was so omnipresent in everyday speech that it influenced the language of the entire society. If we turn to the Merovingian Empire of the seventh century, very few had active mastery of the high form of the language. About all we can really say is that a large gap existed between the educated and the vernacular forms of the language, which manifested in different ways.

When adjusted for historical conditions, Ferguson's model of diglossia still best describes the Latin of late antiquity; the high and low varieties that he described, for which Arabic was the model, apply to late antiquity as well. Latin, as the "high variety," was the written language; it had a fixed standard, was of high prestige, and was used in official communications. The "low variety" (in this case not an actual variety but more a system in motion) was associated with orality, was of low prestige, and was the language of everyday communication. But here we need to bear two basic facts in mind.

First, the contrast between Latin and the vernacular language was not the same as the contrast between the written and oral forms of the language. True, the vernacular language was not written. But correct school

Latin was also spoken by those who mastered it, just as High Arabic is spoken in some settings today. The question of whether the pronunciation followed evolutionary developments in the vernacular language (as in modern French, with its wide gap between spelling and actual pronunciation) can be answered both yes and no. We have good reasons to presume that speakers must have used some sort of classical pronunciation. For example, Augustine noted (*Confessiones* 1.29) that grammarians demanded that the word *homo* be pronounced with an aspirated *h*, which had long since disappeared from the vernacular and later from the Romance languages (as in the Italian *uomo* or the French *homme*).

Second, the contrast between Latin and the vernacular may not be reduced to a social contrast between the language of the educated and the uneducated. What is true is that the uneducated did not master correct Latin as an active language, but one must assume that educated people also knew how to use the vernacular where appropriate. The difference may best be described by saying that Latin was the "language of distance," the vernacular the "language of immediacy," to borrow from Koch and Österreicher. However, the rules governing which form of language was used when are no longer discernible. Although we may assume that correct Latin was spoken in the Roman Senate and in official discussions between members of the upper classes and that a conversation between two day laborers would have sounded very different, we do not know how two members of the upper classes spoke in intimate conversation. Was the average educated Roman practiced enough in the classical language to speak off the cuff for hours on end, or did he retreat to his own linguistic comfort zone after barely managing a few correct Latin sentences—as often happens in Arabic today? How did a master talk to his slaves? When making love, did educated couples engage in "pillow talk" in correct Latin? Or would that have sounded just too ridiculous? And to what extent did upper-class women need to master the high form of the language at all (a matter that Jerome touched on briefly)? We simply do not know the answers to these questions.

The answers are probably not of the either-or variety. Even the assumption that a people could have maintained a uniform high-language standard in long-distance communication is problematic not only because the written language itself was subject to the tension between the "maximal" and "minimal" forms of fixing, as discussed earlier. More important, experience with high language and dialect in German and Arabic shows that—at least in speech—uniform use of the written language or of the dialect is more of an exception, and that there is a linguistic continuum between the two. Individuals oscillate between these poles depending on their abilities and the situation in which they are communicating. An educated person will draw on dialect in many situations, and the uneducated will try to emulate "correct" speech when it seems appropriate or advantageous. The situation must certainly have been similar in late antiquity.

It should come as no surprise that these and other language arenas would have left no traces. For one thing, the pressure to limit such mixed forms to oral communication would have been considerable; otherwise, Latin would not have been the written language. It sometimes happens in modern Arabic that, say, a politician will express himself in dialect when speaking to the public, while the newspapers will then report a "corrected" version of his speech. Still, even if we assume that in late antiquity, when training in correct usage was not as consistent as it is now, less educated people actually wrote private notes or reminders, such documents have simply disappeared. The only evidence we have are texts set in stone, typically gravestones, or the very occasional text that has survived because it was of special interest. These texts, taken together, constitute our extremely sparse modern corpus of Vulgar Latin documents, and even these texts do not reflect the pure vernacular language but rather defects in the written language. They are therefore "mixed forms." If we could take a time machine back to late antiquity, we would find that the reality of the language spoken in Rome or Milan in the fourth and fifth centuries was extremely varied. If we were able to follow the young rhetoric professor named Augustine on his daily rounds in Milan (and perhaps even the following evening), we would undoubtedly come away with a far more complex understanding of language in late antiquity than the simplified distinction between a "literary Latin" and a "Vulgar Latin" would cause us to suspect.

3

Europe's Latin Millennium

From the Beginning of the Middle Ages to 1800

THE EDUCATIONAL REFORMS initiated or pursued by Charlemagne in his *Epistola de litteris colendis* (Letter on the Cultivation of the Sciences), promulgated in about 785, and the *Admonitio generalis* (General Admonition) of 789 proved a crucial turning point in the history of Latin. The reforms meant that the language, which had long depended on the teaching of grammar in schools, did not suffer the fate of literary Babylonian and die out but rather became the most important language in Western Europe for another thousand years. Examining the quantity of texts produced between the Carolingian literary renaissance and today, one is tempted to say that these were the real glory days of Latin. When Latin conquered Scandinavia and eastern Europe, it insinuated itself into regions that had never belonged to the Roman Empire proper and in which no one had ever spoken in Latin before. In the sixteenth and seventeenth centuries, Latin played an important role as a lingua franca in the east Asian mission of the Jesuits. In addition, students in North American universities from the seventeenth century until the first decades of the nineteenth were expected to master Latin much like their counterparts in Europe.

It is, of course, highly unlikely that Charlemagne took such a long view of things. Nonetheless, with his coronation as emperor on Christmas Day in the year 800, his empire became inextricably linked with the continuance of the Roman Empire and with Latin as the imperial language. Thus it is symbolically fortuitous that this state system came to a formal end in 1806, with the abdication of Francis II, the last emperor of the Holy Roman Empire of the German Nation, at approximately the same time that Latin lost its status as the language of communication, one that had united the disparate parts of Europe. For about a thousand years, Latin was the indispensable language of culture and science in Europe, and so it is no exaggeration to speak of Europe's Latin millennium.

What, however, justifies us in labeling this millennium as its own epoch, separate from Roman antiquity? It certainly cannot be that while Latin had been the natural language of the Romans in antiquity, this was no longer the case in the Carolingian era. On the following pages, I argue that what distinguished the Latin millennium from antiquity was not the new role of Latin, but the development of multilingualism in European culture. As described in the previous chapter, the Latin language had long been a scholarly language whose norms were determined by grammarians. In late antiquity, the vernacular spoken by the population in territories formerly controlled by the Roman Empire had, to the extent to which the people spoke Latin at all, evolved into variants that eventually solidified into the various Romance languages. This coexistence of spoken languages and written Latin did not change much as a result of the Carolingian reforms, except insofar as mastery of the largely superseded written language now required even more intensive study. In terms of the language itself, the educational reforms of the Carolingian period may well be seen less as a new era than as an attempt to reclaim the language as it was in late antiquity. It is even likely that Charlemagne viewed it as such: a return after the crises of the seventh and eighth centuries.

However, it is now generally agreed that Latin took on a new status during the Carolingian era, which, according to one frequently heard interpretation, was when Latin became a "dead" language. This interpretation is probably informed by twenty-twenty hindsight because we know that over the course of time Latin disappeared almost completely from the roll of actively used languages. It derives, in particular, from a Romance view of Latin, that is, a view that takes only the Romance portions of the Roman Empire into account. It is assumed that, in spite of the great distance between the spoken vernacular of the illiterate population and the written Latin language, a unity between these two forms of the language had nonetheless existed well into the "dark" centuries and that "vertical" communication had still been possible in late antiquity (which recent research has confirmed), that is, that the illiterate population was still capable of understanding the written form. At some point, however, the vernacular had evolved to such a degree that the differences were simply too great. In this interpretation, the Carolingian language reforms implied a final break because their strict reversion to the ancient form of the language amplified the distance from the actual language of the population. This—in this interpretation— was why the Romance vernaculars began to be written during the time of Charlemagne. Strictly speaking, the boundary between late antiquity and the Middle Ages marks a turning point after which the diglossia of the Romanized parts of the empire was transformed into genuine bilingualism, with Latin and the early forms of the Romance languages jockeying for position.

It seems to me that this perspective has some justification even though it is certainly difficult (and in the final analysis a matter of definition) to determine precisely when the Romance vernaculars actually became languages distinct from Latin. We must bear in mind that our first pieces of evidence of the use of "proto-Romance" languages, exemplified by a report about the Council of Tours in 813 and the Oaths of Strasbourg in 842, are random documents, and it is impossible to tell whether they represented a turning point or simply one step in a much longer development. In addition, it is clear that in Italy, the hub of the Latin language, even in the fifteenth century the coexistence of Latin and Italian had not advanced to the point of true bilingualism but was viewed as diglossia. As a result, it is advisable not to overstate the significance of the Carolingian language reforms for the end of diglossic status.

Multilingual Europe

Nonetheless, from the perspective of Latin as a world language, it does provide us an expanded model for describing the fundamental transformation between antiquity and "Europe's Latin millennium." What was truly new was not the distinction between the written Romance languages and Latin but rather the reestablishment of written languages per se in the regions in which Latin culture was a given. At the beginning of chapter 2, I stated that no new written language had developed from the vernaculars during the centuries when the Roman Empire existed. This does not rule out the possibility that Germans, Celts, or other peoples used their own alphabets or Greek or Latin letters. Germanic runes, for example, are attested into late antiquity. But as far as we know, no well-developed written language with literary pretensions arose to compete with Latin. Ulfilas's Bible translation into Gothic, from the fourth century, remains an exception, and we do not know whether it was one of a kind or a harbinger of later developments.

After the end of the Roman Empire, Europe began to reestablish its own written cultures, in many cases independent of the Carolingian Renaissance. The beginnings are seen in Ireland and southern England, where a very advanced, written Latin culture continued throughout the "dark" centuries that engulfed central Europe. Old Irish and Old English began to be written as early as the seventh century, if not before. The written Old Irish language, for which we have numerous documents from the eighth century, was so uniform that we must assume that standardization processes had taken hold much earlier. This is consistent with a small tract titled *Auraicept na n-Éces* (probably seventh century), in which the use of the vernacular was presented in programmatic form, even to the point of treating Irish grammar.[1] The written notations of Old Irish were not merely an aid for monks learning Latin or a means of saving vernacular poems, which had lived only in the oral tradition, but also the beginning of a complex written tradition that existed in parallel with Latin and integrated many of its cultural traditions. Old English, whose oldest written documents date from the eighth century, was used early on for literary purposes. For example, we know of works in Old English by the Venerable Bede, the Latin writer and scholar who died in 735. Old English was promoted during the time of Alfred the Great (847–899), something that did not occur anywhere else in the Latin linguistic space at this time. An entire array of works of ancient Latin literature was systematically translated into Anglo-Saxon. Whereas Old High German is attested in only sporadic regional language forms that developed into a more or less distinct written standard over time, Old English became a relatively uniform written language rather more quickly.[2] That written tradition survived the Norman Conquest, in 1066, extending into the twelfth century, well after the language of the people had evolved into something very different. Around 1000, the Latin scholar Aelfric wrote an Old English grammar that built on those of Donatus and Priscian. Its main point was to document that

Old English, too, was capable of a real grammar. As elsewhere, the writing of a grammar was an important step in the development of a written language, and we should compare Aelfric's work with textbooks such as Leon Battista Alberti's *Grammatica della lingua toscana* (ca. 1442) and Antonio Nebrija's *Gramática della lengua castellana* (1492). In fact, the systematic efforts of Alfred the Great meant that, compared with Old High German, Old English was a rather robust and stable language. The main reason that Alfred's reforms were later of such little consequence is that the Norman Conquest introduced the Romance language of the conquerors into England, which fundamentally changed the language. As we know, present-day English is not the continuance of an old Germanic form of English but a mixture of Germanic and Romance elements. Furthermore, there was never really a move in the England of Alfred the Great to anoint Old English as the sole language of the realm. Latin remained superordinate to Old English and remained in active and constant use as a literary language.

Written records in German also began to appear at the time of Charlemagne, in the eighth and ninth centuries. This was probably largely because, after years in which very little was written, the Carolingian reforms led to an expansion in literacy, which probably meant that the likelihood of finding written words in German also rose. Even early translations of Latin texts for church use give evidence of the promotion of German. Although the statement by Charlemagne's biographer Einhard that he was pursuing a grammar of the German language has not been confirmed by direct documentary evidence, it is thoroughly plausible.[3]

In this context, let us examine the first well-known documents relating to French. In 813, the Council of Tours decreed that the "peasant" form of the language, the *lingua romana rustica*, the precursor of French, should be used in sermons. The first written precursor of French, the Oaths of Strasbourg, which sealed the alliance between Charlemagne's nephews, Louis the German and Charles the Bald, against their brother, Lothar I, after the Carolingian Empire was divided, was recorded in 842. But this document does not yet qualify as written French, and we will see that, on the contrary, the new language finally emerged only in the eleventh century. Moreover, as we will discuss later, even the Italians of the fifteenth century saw Italian and Latin not as different languages but as two forms of the same language.

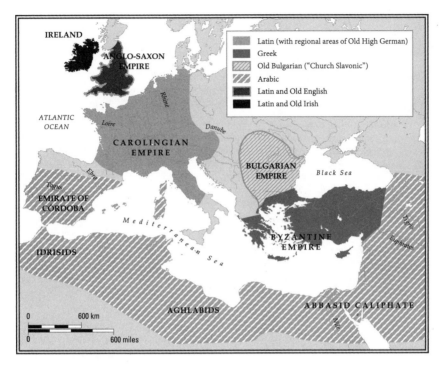

Figure 9. Europe during the second half of the ninth century.

As unassuming as these first traces of later European languages may have been, the course that they set was fundamental. One of the hallmarks of later Europe was its multilingualism. National languages and cultures blossomed in a territory characterized by a common religion, a common Roman tradition, and Latin as a common language. In addition to Irish, Old English, German, and French, we see the evolution of other Romance languages, including Castilian, Galician, Catalan, Portuguese, Italian, and, in the sixteenth century, Romanian. Polish, Czech and Slovak, Hungarian, and Croatian developed in the east, while Flemish evolved in central Europe. In the north, the Scandinavian and Baltic languages began to come into their own. One of the key characteristics of this multilingualism is that these languages coexisted within a primarily Latin culture. These were not different, isolated written cultures; rather, they were new written cultures that developed out of largely unwritten European vernaculars, all of which set their sights on Latin, with its stylistic possibilities, literary forms, and intellectual legacy.

lodharius me & hunc fratre meu post
obitu patris nri insectando usq; ad internet
ione delere conatus sit. Hostis cu aut
nec frat mea; nec xpianitas nec qd libe
ingeniu salua iusticia ut pax inte nosce
ad uiuare posset· eandem coacti rem ad
iudiciu omnipotentis di decliuimus· ut suo
nutu quid cuiq; deber& cont nti esse
mus· Inquo nos sco nostro p misericordiâ
di uictores existim· Is aut uic tus
una cu suis quo ualuit secessit· Hinc
uero fraterno amore correpti· nec non
& sup populu xpianu con passi· p sequi
atq; delere illos nolumus· Sedhac
tenus sicut & antea· ut saltem deinde
cuiq; sua iusticia cederetur· manda
uimus· At ille posthaec non cont
us iudicio diuino· sedhostili manu
iteru se me· & hunc fratrem meum·
p sequi non cessat· Insup & populu
nrm incendiis rapinis cedibusque
deuastat· Quâ obre· nunc necess
itate coacti con uenimus· Et quoniã
denria stabili fide ac firma fraternitate
dubitare credimus· hoc sacrntu inti nos
incons pectu uro· iurare decreuimus·

Non qualiba iniqua cupiditate illecti hoc
agimus· sed ut certiores sidi nobis uro
ad utrorio quietem dederit· decomu
ni profec tu sumus· Si aut qd abst
sacrntu qd fri meo iurauero uiola
re p sup sero· a subditione mea· nec
non & a iuramento qd mihi iurastis·

unu quêq; urm absoluo· Cuiq; karolus
haec eade uerba· romana lingua perorasse
Lodhuu ic eni maior natu ent· prior
haec deinde se seruaturu testatus e·

Pro do amur & pro xpian poblo & nro comun
saluament dist di en auant· inquant ds
sauir & podir me dunat· si saluarai eo·
cist meon fradre karlo· & in ad iudha·
& in cad huna cosa· si cum om per dreit son
fradra saluar dist· Ino quid il mi altre
si fazet· Et ab ludher nul plaid nuquã
prindrai· qui meon uol cist meon fradre
karle in damno sit· Quod cu lodhuuic
explesset· karolus teudisca lingua sic hec
eade uerba testatus est·

In godes minna ind in thes xpianes folches
ind unser bedhero gehaltnissi· fonthese
mo dage frammordes so fram so mir got
geuuizci indi madh furgibit· so haldih tesan
minan bruodher soso man mit rehtu
sinan bruher scal· in thiu thaz er mig
sosoma duo· indi mit ludheren in
noh heiniu thing ne gegango· the minan uuillon imo
ce scaden uuerhen·

Sacrntu aut qd utrorurq; populus
quiq; propria lingua testatus est·
Romana lingua sic se habebat· Si lodhu
uigs sagrament· que son fradre karlo
iurat conseruat· Et karlus meos sendra
de suo part lostanit· si io returnar non
lint pois· ne io ne neuls cui eo returnar
int pois· in nulla aiudha contra lodhu
uuig· nun li iuer· Teudisca aut lingua

Figure 10. Oaths of Strasbourg (842), Nithard, Historiarum libri, Paris, Biblio-thèque Nationale, Cod. lat. 9768, fol. 13r. This manuscript from the tenth century is the oldest text in a language that is demonstrably close to Old French. Written in Latin, with the oath texts in "proto-French" and in Old German, it is important documentation of the development of European multilingualism. The "proto-French" text begins on the fifth line of the right column:

> Pro Deo amur et pro christian poblo et nostro commun salvament . . .
> (For the love of God and for Christendom and our common
> salvation . . .)

The "correct" Latin and modern French spellings would be as follows:

> Pro Dei amore et pro christiano populo et nostro communi salvamento
> Pour l'amour de Dieu et pour le peuple chrétien et notre salut
> commun

The Latin declension endings (amor*e*, commun*i*, salvament*o*), which are missing in modern French, had already disappeared in the ninth century. This clearly demonstrates that the grammar of Donatus had a didactic function for speakers of "Vulgar Latin." © DeA Picture Library/Art Resource, NY

In essence, this was a repetition of the process of cultural transfer that had occurred a thousand years earlier in the constitution of Latin as a written language. Just as the written Latin culture was based on the Greek template, so the new, written European cultures absorbed much from Latin. In both cases, the first literary works were often translations or free adaptations of works from the older written culture. In both cases, the literate classes were bilingual for hundreds of years. Just as Roman writers mastered Greek well into the second century, so it would have been well-nigh unimaginable for a writer in a European vernacular to have had no contact whatsoever with the Latin world. And many of them mastered Latin as well as their vernacular language.

The Christian church (that is, the Roman Catholic Church up to the Anglican schism and the Protestant Reformation of the sixteenth century) stood at the center of this European cultural identity. The Latin Bible and liturgical texts were of crucial importance to Latin culture, especially in the early Middle Ages, as were the theological and historical writings of the ancient church fathers. The vernacular was also very important in church as the language of sermons—as prescribed by the Council of Tours. In addition, of course, Christian teachings were propagated in the vernacular among those untutored in Latin. One of the first great works of literature in Old High German was the *Heliand*, dating from the ninth century, which recounts the life of Jesus according to the four Gospels.

Nonetheless, the ancient pagan tradition clearly remained integral to European Latin culture. The modern notions that medieval culture was determined by the church and that only in the modern era did people rediscover the cultural values of antiquity do not hit the mark. Even in late antiquity, Christians were widely engaged with the traditions of pagan language and literature, and the intertwining of ancient Greek and Roman culture in the Christian tradition was accepted fact from the time of Saint Augustine at the very latest. During the Carolingian Renaissance, everything that remained of ancient literature was salvaged, not just those things that were "usable" by the church. If this had not been the case, then works like Lucretius's philosophical poem *De rerum natura* (On the Nature of Things), which laid out an Epicurean worldview so opposite to that of Christianity, could never have survived. The same may be said of the majority of Roman love poetry. The literature, philosophy, rhetoric, and poetics of ancient Rome formed a thread that was clearly visible throughout Europe's Latin millennium.

A third characteristic of this European multilingualism was that the roles of Latin and the vernacular languages were always changing; there was no prolonged period of internal stability. The thrust of the scriptualization of the vernaculars was not to displace Latin as the common language but to replace it while continuing the Latin tradition—but translated into the new languages.

But the history of Europe's Latin millennium describes more than a period during which Latin played an important role. It was also the period during which Latin was replaced by other languages. In this sense, the role of Latin paralleled the development of the empire founded by Charlemagne. During that millennium, the empire went from being the strongest political unit in central Europe to a stunted entity in form and ritual, the result of the growing significance of larger and smaller territorial powers and the political fracturing associated with it. Increasingly, it came to symbolize tradition and a residual sense of European identity. In much the same way, Latin was harried by the numerous European vernaculars, which eventually established themselves as national languages and pushed it aside. By the time the empire came to a formal end, in 1806, Latin was still imbued with the prestige of tradition, but its communicative functions had been superseded. The history of both the empire and of Latin after Charlemagne was from the beginning a history of internal dissolution and eventual replacement.

Latin Europe and Neighboring Regions

These peculiarities of Latin Europe come into clearer focus when we look at them in the context of neighboring states and not just in relationship to the old Roman Empire. This is because the empire of Charlemagne was not the only power that emerged during those centuries. A political reorganization took place over the entire territory of the former Imperium Romanum from the Mediterranean to Asia. And in contrast to the sometimes short-lived transitional empires that burst onto the scene after the collapse of the Western Roman Empire in 476 CE, these would have much greater staying power. One example was the Byzantine Empire, which had its center in Constantinople. Although formally the continuation of the Eastern Roman Empire, it had also undergone massive crises but achieved renewed political and cultural solidity during the ninth century. In addition, the Islamic Abbasid Caliphate, centered in Baghdad, experienced a glorious political and cultural expansion outside the borders of Europe. The Bulgarian Empire, which in 864 accepted Christianity under Boris I, also became an important factor in the ninth century. The development of these empires left traces in their languages.

The Byzantine Empire continued to use the ancient form of Greek as its standard language. As previously discussed, Greek had, at the latest since the Atticism of the first century BCE, become a language learned in school based on Greek "classics" (largely the same as those studied in classrooms today), from which the vernacular of the population had come to differ markedly over the course of time, resulting in diglossia. This meant that the language structure in the eastern half of the former Roman Empire was similar to that in the Romanized west, where a growing gap separated the vernaculars (often inadequately labeled Vulgar Latin) from the standardized Latin learned at school. To the extent that the Carolingians were even aware of what was going on in the east in the eighth century, they probably viewed their language reforms not only as a return to the Latin of late antiquity but also to the Greek East because there the literary culture and knowledge of the standardized language had not suffered the same collapse as occurred in the Latin West during the sixth and seventh centuries. The Photian Renaissance, in ninth-century Byzantium, named after its central figure, Patriarch Photios (ca. 810–893), during which ancient Greek and ancient literature were revived, may be viewed as a development parallel to the Carolingian educational reforms.

Arabic had been the main language in the Islamic sphere of control, which had been rapidly expanding since the seventh century. In the eighth century, the Islamic movement had already taken control of large tracts of the old Eastern Roman Empire—North Africa, Palestine, and parts of Asia Minor—and in Spain it had superseded the high culture of the Visigoths, which had been steeped in the Latin tradition. As different as developments in the Greek-Latin regions were from the Arabic, they had at least one commonality: a strongly codified language was required to secure interregional written communications under the rough conditions that existed at the time. This was especially true because the great powers, with the exception of Byzantium, had no real centers that were capable of setting the pace in cultural matters over a prolonged period. In the Islamic sphere of control, Medina, Damascus, Baghdad, and several other cities—Córdoba, in Spain, among them—continually jockeyed with each other for preeminence over a period of only a few centuries. Nor, by the same token, does the question of which city was the "capital" of the Frankish, Old Bulgarian, or English kingdoms give us any meaningful understanding of how power and culture were organized. In Charlemagne's case, even his most important imperial palace, in Aachen, was more a symbolic center than the actual heart and hub of an empire. The greater the forces of cultural pluricentricity, however, the more all of the parties involved felt the need for a common written language based on mutually accepted cultural norms.

In this potentially centrifugal situation, the Arabs responded with an intensive codification of the language that took place over two centuries.[4] Between the seventh and the ninth century, they developed what later came to be called "classical" Arabic literature, while at the same time thinking through and defining the basic theoretical properties of the Arabic language. They wrote dictionaries defining the basic meaning of words that, because of the way they were used in schools, were completely comparable to the Attic lexicons used in the standardization of Greek. By creating this framework, they quickly fixed the language, while retaining the morphological and syntactic features that still characterize High Arabic today. Although numerous other classical texts, especially the works of poets, were important in the formation of classical Arabic, the central position of the Koran, whose language has never been changed or adapted since it was written down in the seventh century, was crucial in fixing the high form of the language. But it was not the starting point of this development. It is even conceivable that a language based on orally transmitted poetry existed before Mohammed and enjoyed a supraregional status, much like that of the Homeric bards.

The indirect consequence of this codification was the development of the Arabic diglossia, which still exists today since the everyday language of the people continued to develop, thereby separating from the increasingly distant written language. It did not take long for writers who learned Arabic as a second language to begin to make a mark, which is a sign that the difference between native and nonnative speakers had disappeared. At this point, Arabic, like Latin and Greek before it, had become a language accessible only through the study of literature at school. It was the natural language neither of the caliphs nor of a small ruling class but rather the common language of the Islamic world as a whole. The difference between Arabic and Latin and Greek was essentially that the two languages of the Roman Empire had attained this status (and the appurtenant canonical literature) many centuries earlier, while Arabic, including its normative literary texts, was newly created. They were the result of conscious language policies not seen in the long history of the Roman Empire. The present spread of Arabic in parts of the former Roman Empire shows clearly just how effective Islam was in displacing the local culture languages. Whereas the Romans usually integrated older written cultures, Palestine, Syria, the Arabian Peninsula, and the North African states retained virtually no traces of either the Latin or the Greek tradition or of the languages that were indigenous to those areas at the time.

Another example of a reconstituted language that eventuated in a fixed literary language is the creation of Church Slavonic in the early Middle Ages in eastern Europe.[5] The political space in which this occurred was the First Bulgarian Empire, which formed the third great European power center between the Carolingian Empire and Byzantium. The first step toward developing a written Slavonic language was associated with the work of the brothers Methodius (born ca. 815) and Cyril (born ca. 826), who were called "apostles to the Slavs." Among other things, they created the Glagolithic alphabet, the forerunner of the Cyrillic alphabet, which was named after the younger brother. Their main goal was to create a liturgy in the Slavonic language. As early as 893, Church Slavonic was the quasi-official language of the Bulgarian Empire. Under Simeon the Great (ca. 865–927), large numbers of Greek texts, including nonliturgical ones, were translated into Slavonic. The fact that Church Slavonic was fixed and increasingly differed from the spoken Slavic vernaculars has long been viewed as a parallel with Latin. However, the development of Church Slavonic was somewhat different from that of Greek, Latin, or Arabic. For one thing, Church Slavonic was never really permanently standardized, nor did it have a uniform literary canon from which a standardized language could be taught. This means that Church Slavonic was characterized by a succession of ever-changing regional variants. In addition, it was cultivated outside the context of the church to a much lesser extent than was the case with Latin and Greek; thus, it came to function as a special form of communications in rather circumscribed situations. Nonetheless, what it had in common with Greek, Latin, and Arabic was that it largely hewed to past norms and made no claim to represent the spontaneous language of the population.

A comparison of the Latin cultural area with that of the other three discussed earlier makes it clear that by pinning his reforms to ancient Latin, Charlemagne not only revived the political and cultural traditions of the Roman Empire but also addressed the most elementary necessities of communications, which led to similar developments within the territories of each of the new political powers during those centuries. It is probably unimportant whether the initiators of the Carolingian language reforms modeled their efforts on the policies of Islamic rulers and were themselves a model for Byzantium and the Bulgarian Empire or whether all of these endeavors were more or less independent developments, the result of parallel necessities. What is clear is that a standardized language capable of dealing with written and oral communications in an early medieval empire would not have been possible without grammatical norms inculcated in schools just as had happened with Latin and Greek. The net effect was a supraregional written language that became fixed, while the vernaculars of the populations within the empire continued to change.

This comparison also makes it clear how the early multilingual written traditions of Latin Europe differed from those of its neighboring empires, which tended to be monolingual. Greek, that is, the "high form" of the language modeled on ancient Greek, remained the written standard in the Byzantine Empire up to the end of the fifteenth century. Literary forms such as the Byzantine novels, written in a "vulgar" form of Greek, blossomed over the course of the Middle Ages. However, this "vulgar" Greek never penetrated areas reserved for High Greek, such as the sciences or church texts. That any language other than Greek would have developed into a literary language would have been almost impossible because the Byzantine Empire was early on restricted to regions in which Greek or ancient Hellenized populations lived.

Nor did regional written languages emerge at first in the area in which Church Slavonic was used. Only much later, from the end of the

Middle Ages to the nineteenth century, as Slavic languages like Russian, Serbian, and Bulgarian began to congeal around a firm written standard, did use of the old, fixed Church Slavonic language become limited (primarily to the Orthodox Church), an evolution that mirrored developments in Romance Europe.

The sheer diversity within the Latin cultural area is clearest, however, when we compare Latin to Arabic, which became the sole written language binding together the entire Islamic world. A measure of linguistic diversity was returned to a portion of the Islamic world in the tenth century, with the emergence of Persian as a literary language, developed from earlier culture languages in that region. A second linguistic change resulted from the ascent of the Ottoman literary language in the Ottoman Empire after the fourteenth century. It, too, was a fixed language from which evolved modern Turkish, and it played an important role in the administration of the empire and in literature. However, Arabic largely remained the sole language for the sciences and for all matters relating to religion. Oral Arabic dialects, approximately comparable to "Vulgar Latin," were seldom written down, although some mixed forms found their way into the *Thousand and One Nights,* as will be discussed later. Until very recently, however, these dialects hardly made a dent in the hegemonic position of High Arabic as the official language for politics and literature.

Language and Power: The Special Position of Latin in Charlemagne's Empire

If Europe's Latin millennium was from the outset characterized by the dissolution of Latin, we have to ask ourselves why Charlemagne would have chosen Latin as the central written language of his empire. Why did he not choose his own Frankish mother tongue instead? Or would not a "reformed" variant of Latin closer to the vernacular *lingua romana rustica* perhaps have served better? Although it is certainly correct to state that Charlemagne viewed his empire as the successor to the Roman Empire, that answer is hardly sufficient. Charlemagne was not Roman; he spoke Frankish, a Germanic language that differed fundamentally from Latin despite their common Indo-European roots. In other words, the Carolingian language reforms, with their conscious mining of ancient culture, represented a unique situation. It was as if the Persians had recodified Arabic or the Slavs had pursued the reform of Greek. Nor is it sufficient to say that the Latin texts that had survived from Roman times were indispensable and that a policy of massive translation would have been inordinately costly (indeed, the rulers of the Bulgarian Empire and the English king Alfred had started such policies). Here I will show that the relationship between political power and language in Charlemagne's Europe was fundamentally different from that in any other power bloc in the early Middle Ages.

If we compare the Carolingian reforms of Latin with the other reconstituted or reformed languages of the ninth century, we find a very important difference. One of the special characteristics of Western Roman society during late antiquity was that members of other peoples with whom the Romans came into contact tended to be integrated into the Roman imperial administration and power apparatus. The most prominent early example was Arminius, the chieftain of the Germanic Cherusci and victor at the battle of the Teutoburg Forest, in 9 CE. Arminius had not started out as a Germanic freedom fighter; he had been socialized as a Roman and was the leader of an auxiliary Germanic troop before becoming a renegade. During late antiquity, many Germans, including Arbogast, Stilicho, and Aetius, had held high positions in the Roman military and imperial administration. After the last Western Roman emperor, Romulus Augustulus, was deposed in 476, by Odoacer, Italy was ruled by a king of Germanic origin. Later, the Ostrogoths set up their own state in northern Italy, as did the Visigoths in Spain, the Merovingians in Gaul, and the Lombards in northern Italy. In none of these cases was there a recognizable break in language or culture. On the contrary, the Ostrogoth court of Theodoric, in Ravenna, where Boethius and Cassiodor lived and worked, and the Visigoth Empire of seventh-century Spain under the influence of Bishop Isidore of Seville, became centers of culture where ancient Roman literature experienced a brief revival. The hegemony of the Germanic-speaking elites over Romanized populations, even in the core regions of the former empire, had for centuries been viewed as normal, as was the fact that these elites, even where they had not themselves become Romanized, nonetheless promoted Latin culture. As a result, they viewed themselves as legitimate heirs to the Rome of late antiquity—and they made no attempt to develop a literature in their own languages. The fourth-century translation of the Bible into Gothic, by Ulfilas, seems to have been made purely to facilitate religious services and did not lead to the elaboration of a broader Gothic written culture.

The conditions that resulted from the mass migrations of the period had, from the time of the Roman Empire, up to 476 and for a time thereafter, decoupled political power from the traditions of culture and language in a way that did not happen in any of the adjacent political spheres. This development gained steam over the next two hundred years, which were marked by the upheavals of the mass migrations, in part because the contributions of Rome and central Italy to Latin culture largely came to a halt. The city of Rome itself, which at one time had more than a million inhabitants, dropped to a fraction of that figure, and after 554 Rome formally belonged to the Eastern Roman Empire and was therefore more or less under the thumb of Constantinople. On the other side of the Roman world, the Latin cultural tradition in Visigoth Spain blossomed and would no doubt have continued if not for the Islamic conquest.

Among the most important centers of Latin culture during the period of the mass migrations were Ireland and England, that is, regions that had at most been only marginally subject to Roman power. Moreover, Ireland had never fallen under Roman sway. During the sixth and seventh centuries, this "insular" culture played a crucial role in maintaining the tradition of ancient Latin literature. But even more than that, it created a new basis for the transmission of ancient culture on the continent itself because of the missionary work of Columbanus and Boniface, among others. Almost all of the monastic centers in the Merovingian and Carolingian world owed their existence to this Irish influence. Fulda, Hersfeld, Saint Gallen, Reichenau, and many others were founded by Irish missionaries. What is more remarkable is that even in the core Romanized areas of the old empire, monasteries founded by the Irish—Luxeuil and Corbie in France and even Bobbio, south of Milan—became important cultural centers. By comparison, the old Roman centers—Rome, Milan, Ravenna, Pisa, and, north of the Alps, Trier, Mainz, and Lyon—played only secondary roles in maintaining the continuity of ancient culture in the Middle Ages. We know of many ancient Latin authors whose writings were salvaged only by the work done in the cultural centers of the north, such as Fulda; Tacitus was among the most important of these. We know of only a few whose works survived only in Italy.

The exclusive connection between the Latin language and the Roman power from which it emerged had been largely broken long before the beginning of the Carolingian Renaissance. Other peoples had shown that they were just as skilled at maintaining the cultural and linguistic traditions of the ancient empire as the Roman population had been.

This makes it clear that the Frankish king Charlemagne could make Latin the official language without being Romanized. On the other hand, it is understandable that Latin would not be the one and only language of this empire and that it would provide space for the development of the various vernacular languages into literary languages.

It is also important to recognize that the Carolingian Empire represented a displacement of power outside of the borders of the former Roman Empire. The most important imperial palace was at Aachen, and important cultural centers developed at the monasteries and bishoprics of Fulda, Hersfeld, Lorsch, Murbach, Saint Gallen, Reichenau, Salzburg, and Freising, as well as in Saint Riquier, in what is today France. All of these places were at the edge of or even outside the borders of the former Roman Empire. Because they were founded after the seventh century, they did not have the historical connection with antiquity either of the older centers in Rome, Milan, Tours, and Paris (which, though of continuing importance were not themselves determinative) or of the old Roman cities of Germany, such as Mainz, Trier, and Cologne. Nor did leading lights from the territories of the old empire play any particular role in the Carolingian reform efforts. The key people came from elsewhere: Alcuin came from York, Paul the Deacon was a Lombard (as in all probability was Peter of Pisa), and Theodulf, a Visigoth, came from Orléans. A similar imbalance is evident when we examine the literary tradition. While it cannot be said that no Carolingian culture existed in Italy or in what is today southern France, that is, regions of the Carolingian Empire that were also crucial parts of the Roman Empire, when we add up the works of poetry and the sciences, of the liberal arts and theology, we find that the cultural centers in the German-speaking countries exerted a certain dominance. Such a shift in the topography of power and culture never occurred in the Eastern Roman Empire. Constantinople, the center of the Byzantine Empire, had precisely the same function in antiquity. Charlemagne's empire and later the Holy Roman Empire of the German Nation, were not the "natural" successors to the Imperium Romanum; this claim was the

INITIUM ALIQUOD CREATU
RAE EIUS · SCITIS FRATRES
MEI DILECTI SIT AUTEM
OMNIS HOMO UELOX AD AU
DIENDUM · TARDUS AUTE
AD LOQUENDUM ET TARDUS
AD IRAM · IRA ENIM UIRI
IUSTITIAM DĪ NON OPERATUR
PROPTER QUOD ABICIENTES
OMNEM IMMUNDITIAM
ET ABUNDANTIAM MALITIAE
IN MANSUETUDINE SUSCI
PITE INSITUM UERBUM
QUOD POTEST SALUARE ANI
MAS UESTRAS · ESTO
TE AUTEM FACTORES UER
BI ET NON AUDITORES TAN
TUM FALLENTES UOSMET
IPSOS · QUIA SIQUIS AD AU
TORES UERBI ET NON FAC
TOR · HIC CONPARABITUR
UIRO CONSIDERANTI UUL
TUM NATIUITATIS SUAE
IN SPECULO · CONSIDE
RAUIT AUTEM SE ET ABIIT
ET STATIM OBLITUS EST
QUALIS FUERIT · QUI AU
TEM PERSPEXERIT IN LE
GE PERFECTA LIBERTATIS
ET PERMANSERIT · NON
AUDITOR OBLIUIOSUS FAC
TUS SED FACTOR OPERIS
HIC BEATUS IN FACTO SUO ERIT
SI QUIS AUTEM PUTAT SE
RELIGIOSUM ESSE ·

Figure 11. Kassel, Landesbibliothek, *Codex Bonifatianus* 1 (Victor Codex), sixth century, fol. 436v: Epistle of James. This manuscript, which contains Tatian's *Diatessaron,* or "harmony" of the four Gospels, along with several books of the New Testament, demonstrates the path taken by Latin culture from Italy to northern Europe. The *Diatessaron* was commissioned by Bishop Victor, who oversaw its completion in 546–547 in Capua. It was written in uncial script, the most widely used book face in late antiquity, which differs markedly from the book face used in ancient Rome, the *capitalis rustica* (see Figure 7).

The manuscript was in the possession of Boniface, who came from England, then, along with Ireland, one of the most important centers for Latin culture in Europe. It was brought to the monastery at Fulda, which was founded by one of Boniface's disciples in 744. Whether the manuscript, which now has an "insular" binding from the eighth century, was ever actually in England or was brought by Boniface to Germany directly from Rome is unclear. The marginal note (in somewhat darker script) was presumably written by Boniface himself: *per generationem creaturae eius id est ut praedicate evangelium omni creaturae . . .* (for the generation of his creature, that is, how you preach the Gospel to all creatures . . .). Hochschul- und Landesbibliothek Fulda

result of transposition. Part of this transposition was also the transposition of language.

Another reason that other languages succeeded in replacing Latin as the official language may have to do with the history of the Christian religion. Although Latin had been the language of the Catholic Church and has remained so, it had only secondarily become the language of the Roman Church. Historically, it had always been known that the books of the Old Testament were written in Hebrew, those of the New Testament in Greek. The Christian Church in Rome itself had long used Greek; the Latin translation of the Bible in western Europe, the so-called *Vetus Itala*, was made during the second century, and the later canonical form of the Latin Bible, the revised and corrected *Vulgate* of Jerome, dates to the fourth century. It would have been impossible to claim the same originality as the Arabic Koran, whose formulations are directly attributed to Muhammad and whose original form is essential to the authenticity of the religion itself. In Judaism, the original Hebrew text of the Bible was also much more closely connected with the religious tradition. Retranslation of the Bible, whose text was itself a translation, into Latin was therefore much less problematic. This may be one reason that Christianity made headway in Europe in many different languages and that the Bible and liturgical texts appeared in non-Latin form throughout the continent. Furthermore, this openness may have encouraged people to set down in writing the various European vernaculars in parallel with Latin.

Latin's New Status

The Family History of the Latin Language

Because of its peculiarities, European multilingualism, whose evolution I sketched out in the previous chapter, requires further elucidation to fully appreciate Latin's status in Europe. Simple models involving comparisons between "scholarly languages" and "vernacular languages" or between "dead languages" and "living languages" miss the main thrust of this process. It is my intention to show that neither the history of Latin nor the history of European vernacular languages can be fully understood unless they are examined in relation to each other.

One of the definitive criteria cited for the difference between "living" languages and "dead" ones is that the European vernacular languages continued to evolve over the centuries, whereas Latin remained static. But when looked at more closely, this turns out not to be a property of these languages per se but of their functions within a multilingual area of communications.

It is certainly true that the vernacular languages went through an astonishing development over the course of a thousand years. To convince ourselves, all we need to do is look at the differences between Anglo-Saxon, Chaucerian English, Shakespearean English, and the various Englishes spoken today. The same may be said of the evolution of German and French. We get the impression that these languages have always been "living"; their written forms simply took their cue from the state of the oral language at any particular time. But the truth is that this seeming aliveness was possible only within the protected space provided by Latin.

Let us assume for a moment that Charlemagne had actually tried to impose on his empire either the *lingua romana rustica,* that is, the precursor of the French spoken by the Romanized population, or his own Frankish, a Germanic language. It is virtually certain that this language would soon have become fixed and that diglossia of the Greek or Arabic type would have developed over time. Even though the language would have continued to evolve in ways that we cannot know, we can say with certainty that the high form of the language and the vernacular of the population would have diverged. News broadcasts, politics, and university classes would now be conducted all over Europe in some form of archaic *lingua romana rustica* or Frankish, while modern French, German, or even English would be restricted to daily business.

The written European languages that we know today could have developed only within a common framework that secured written communication. And this framework was created by Latin. Initially, the various vernacular languages were under no pressure from the need for supraregional communications; thus, it was immaterial whether the German spoken in Cologne was written differently from that spoken in Vienna. Nor was there any need for documents to be used over several centuries. Our modern view of German or French literary history and the "living" evolution of these languages over a millennium is the result of historical reconstruction during the nineteenth century. The accumulation of texts spanning all epochs makes it seem as if a continuity existed when in fact none did. A major epochal break in the European vernacular languages—the transition from Old High German to Middle High German and from there to New High German, as well as the transition from Old French to Middle French or from Old English to Middle English—were all more or less associated with the abandonment of all of the texts that had been written in the old forms of the language, which were then forgotten. The literary tradition represented by the Old High German *Lay of Hildebrand (Das Hildebrandslied),* the Middle High German *Song of the Nibelungen (Nibelungenlied),* and the poems of Walther von der Vogelweide, which lasted into the modern era, as well as the rich literatures of Old French, Provençal, and Old English, were relatively brief phases of the written culture that collapsed, thereby making way for new ones. If not for a few manuscripts of old texts that survived in libraries largely by chance, the history of the German language would begin more or less with Luther's Bible, and the French language with the poets of the sixteenth century. Only the history of Italian literature would extend back as far as Dante (1265–1321). For every text that needed to be accessible over the centuries—the Bible, liturgical texts, legal tracts, and scientific and literary texts—continuity was ensured by Latin alone.

Nevertheless, it would be incorrect to characterize Latin as changeless. Over the millennium that followed the reign of Charlemagne, Latin changed constantly, although these changes did not follow the developmental model delineated by modern linguistics. The history of Latin proper is probably the least researched area of European linguistics, not least because we completely lack the categories to describe the internal changes that take place in a historically fixed culture language within a multilingual cultural setting.

Latin and the other European languages have a common history not only politically but also with regard to internal communications. The revolution in literacy that occurred during the late Middle Ages, the invention of printing and new forms of media in the fifteenth century, and the growing interrelations between different parts of Europe as a result of trade and cultural exchange changed fundamentally what would be demanded of a written language. Latin was just as much subject to these changing conditions as the vernacular languages, and in the following chapters we will have ample opportunity to consider whether certain developmental steps followed by Latin and the vernacular languages did not in fact have common roots.

Besides this, there were other ways in which Latin and the vernacular languages were related to each other. The European written languages developed with the expressed goal of replacing Latin in all its functions. In this sense, German, English, and the Scandinavian languages are just as much daughter languages of Latin as the Romance languages, where the linguistic connections are much more direct. They, too, emerged out of a Latin language culture and replaced Latin in the territories under their control. They could perhaps be termed "adoptive daughter languages" of Latin, and their development described in terms of a family model. The first attested examples of French and German from the late eighth and ninth centuries are extremely sparse and even late into the Middle Ages are not directly reflective of the popular culture. They were written down by representatives of the Latin written culture within a Latin milieu, and the first German manuscripts completely lacking in Latin are from the eleventh or twelfth century.

Over the course of time, these new languages assumed more and more of the functions of the old mother tongue, and once they were finally able to do everything demanded of a language—the turning point occurred around 1800—it was time to emancipate themselves and send Latin into retirement. The various battles fought in modern times over the use of Latin and vernacular languages in politics, administration, science, and literature, which began in the sixteenth century and continued on into the nineteenth, might well be compared to the separation process experienced by adolescents and their parents. If we consider the relationships between Latin and the vernacular languages as a whole, it probably makes sense to speak of a "family history." Families involve more than the history of parents and their children. As long as a family continues to exert an existential bond, it, too, has a history independent of the individuals who are part of it. I focus on this family history in the next chapters.

Latin as a Second Language

In previous sections, I described the new status that Latin assumed at the end of late antiquity and the beginning of the Middle Ages. It was part of a multilingual system in which Latin was the fixed culture language and the other languages were relatively free to develop and evolve. Viewed linguistically, Latin essentially became Europe's second language. Fixed or not, as long as Latin was the sole, ineluctable high language of the Roman elites, it had a clear point of reference: it was the language taught and used by grammarians and literate Romans. To that extent, even the Latin of late antiquity may be accorded the status of mother tongue. However, as French, German, and the other European languages developed as written languages and languages of official communications, Latin eventually became a second language used only for certain purposes—or not at all.

We cannot define an exact moment at which this transition occurred. It makes little sense to ask whether Roman priests, who at the behest of Charlemagne sermonized in the "peasant" *lingua romana rustica,* understood Latin as the written form of their own language or as a foreign language. They probably did not. The fact that in fifteenth-century Italy, Latin and Italian were called *grammatica* and *volgare,* respectively, that is, two forms of the same language, would lead us to conclude that, at least in the Romance countries, there must have been a very long transition period between the diglossia of late antiquity and true bilingualism. In Germany, England, Scandinavia, and eastern Europe, where people spoke languages that were not direct "daughter languages" but more distantly related "adoptive daughter languages," this bilingualism would have developed completely differently.

In any case, European multilingualism meant that the vernacular languages became first languages not merely because they were learned at home but also because they developed their own culture and literature. This was how Latin became Europe's second language. The main point is that there were simply no more native speakers of Latin. The question of how Latin was to be defined and what criteria were to be used became a matter of definition at the latest during the Carolingian language reforms. The issue was at times very controversial even then, and battles over the definition of the Latin standard have continued up to the present day.

It is important to realize that, as long as it was in active use, this Latin "second language" remained a living language. Learning it was more like learning any "modern" foreign language, not at all like Latin classes today, which largely inculcate the rules of grammar. As long as Latin was in active use, no other way of teaching it would have made sense. The attempt to learn a language by the rules, by emulating the classical Romans, leads not to standardized language but to speechlessness. In a dialogue against the excesses of classical Latin learning written in 1528 and titled *Ciceronianus,* Erasmus made all of the telling points.[6] The main figure in this highly entertaining dialogue (still worth reading today), Nosoponos ("the sick man"), who suffers from morbid Cicero-mania, manages over the course of many days and nights of arduous labor to write a brief letter in Latin, using his enormous armamentarium of philological reference works; the poor fellow, however, avoids all conversation because he finds it impossible to speak Latin correctly without those works. His friend Bulephoros ("the advisor") tries to convince him that Cicero is not the sole epitome of good Latin and that in any case the slavish imitation of antiquity cannot possibly be our final goal. The point, of course, is that without an internalized competence in the language, neither writer nor speaker can develop an appropriate style. Furthermore, without that competence, no communication in Latin is possible.

The history of Latin teaching clearly demonstrates how this competence was achieved. Wherever Latin was actually used in communications, it was taught based on "real" situations, much like any modern foreign language today. Many of the rules of grammar that are typical of modern Latin classes were formulated by grammar teachers of the nineteenth century, when Latin was no longer taught for active use. Well into the nineteenth century, Latin grammars contained only form tables, the elementary categories of language analysis (e.g., types of words, word formation), and an introduction to the fundamentals of syntax. Very few consciously reflected on the fine points of Latin syntax. The few spectacular "discoveries," such as the correct use of the Latin relative pronoun, by the Italian humanist Lorenzo Valla in the mid-fifteenth century, obscure the fact that efforts to find fundamental rules of grammar were limited and that theory was placed in the service of actual language use.[7] The proportions of Latin grammar, readings, and conversation were just as much an issue well into the nineteenth century as they are now when teaching modern foreign languages, and the humanists in particular always favored minimizing the emphasis on grammar.[8] Whether a master of Latin prose and poetry like Petrarch (1304–1374) could have explained the use of the Latin gerund to the satisfaction of a twentieth-century Latin teacher is highly doubtful. As late as 1800, Friedrich August Wolf, one of the founders of Prussian

"Neuhumanismus," made the case that Latin should not be taught in terms of its grammar.[9] People learned from form tables and a few basic rules of word formation and elementary syntax, by reading texts, both ancient and more recent, and by communicating with other Latin speakers—who also happened to speak their own native languages. The only difference was that this communication began not at birth but later on at school, and conversation in Latin class was a given well into the nineteenth century. In other words, Latin was a completely normal second language, differing from other languages only in that it was no one's first language.

A second language can be acquired only from the "input" available to the learner, and where there are no native speakers, films, or recordings, the learner must make do with grammars, written texts, and communications with others who have also learned the language as a second language. The language that is learned in this manner is neither nonsense nor a confusion of deficient fragments but a real language. The term *learner language*, which has been used to describe the process of language acquisition, can certainly be applied to Latin. In linguistics, what this term conveys is the fact, confirmed by numerous studies, that, when beginning to learn a language, the learner's brain constructs its own language system from the available data. Of course, this language system differs from the actual norms of the target language, but it is a real system with its own internal logic and not a random groping for the norms of the language. When learning a "normal" language, such an internal learner language is an auxiliary construct. It is constantly subject to correction and, in the case of the native speaker, involves a clear goal: the ability to communicate with other native speakers. Of course, in the absence of Latin native speakers, the learner language took on an entirely new function in becoming the final arbiter of what was correct. It is probably not too much of an exaggeration to say that a Latin speaker's individual competence was much like a learner language with which the speaker simply had to make do. In fact, Latin speech and writing were highly individualized after the end of antiquity. How the language was used very much mirrored an individual's life history, and since there were no first speakers and no agreed-upon norm, a person's Latin was simply accepted. Who was to say the person was wrong? Petrarch's emulation of Cicero was a personal decision based on respect, and his works were very successful—

even though Pope Clement VI feared that his Latin, if he became papal secretary, would be incomprehensible to the average reader.[10]

This does not mean, however, that there was no Latin language community that, like any other, set standards and coined new usages. The same dynamic processes occur even in a community of people speaking Latin as a second language. A language continues to develop even within a fixed framework that has been established for it by cultural convention. The Latin language communities that existed in medieval monastic schools, in universities, or among jurists and physicians were genuine language communities that unconsciously developed their own standards. The process of elaborating new standards may be observed in "Latin-only days," which have become popular in the past few years (and which I have taken part in). Set speech patterns are quick to develop. These may be established by "model speakers"—often professional Latinists—but frequently a sense of the group determines greetings and farewells, various times of the day, meals, localities, and the like. While these linguistic arrangements generally hew to ancient norms, in more sophisticated groups, individuals frequently come up with words and phrases to fill gaps where no standard Latin words exist. If we were to record various groups at work, we would see very clear differences between them and be able to describe those differences precisely. The mechanisms at work in these fun get-togethers are exactly the same as occurred writ large in the history of Latin as a whole. The renewal of Latin in the Carolingian Renaissance and the introduction of Ciceronian standards within the humanism of the sixteenth century would never have been possible without the habits of language that developed over generations on a local and regional basis or in professional guilds or circles. In other words, the nonfixed parts of Latin continued to evolve throughout the Middle Ages and into the modern era. This applied not only to the forms of medieval Latin, which differed markedly from ancient custom, but even to the Latin of the humanists, to the extent that they followed the recommendations in Erasmus's *Ciceronianus*—except where they attempted to slavishly imitate an unachievable standard. And where those recommendations were observed, the new conventions that evolved are exemplars of Latin on a par with those of antiquity.

Any description of how competence in Latin was nurtured after the end of antiquity involves three parts: (1) the basic structures of the language, to the extent that they are set down in grammars, lexicons, and recognized model texts, must be fixed for all time; (2) a learner's language system must be constructed so that it is comparable to the formation of a learner language in the acquisition of a second language because it must replace the native speaker's language competence; and (3) dynamic processes of group communications, the engine of change in normal language, take place, but their effect is limited because the language is fixed and because the second language is limited to particular situations.

English as a World Language and Latin

The ascent of English to the status of world language, especially in the past twenty years, begs for comparison with Latin, not the type of Latin taught in school today but with Latin as a living world language as it was used in the Middle Ages and the early modern era. English is increasingly approaching the conditions that drove the development of Latin after antiquity because the relative importance of communications among native speakers is diminishing. It goes without saying that English is the first language in a great many countries. Despite the fact that Great Britain, the United States, Australia, and many other countries have developed their own forms of English, English has achieved its global preeminence primarily as a second language. It is estimated that, in the early 1990s, approximately 80 percent of global communications in which English was used as a second or third language, involved *no* native speakers whatsoever.[11] This means that, globally, people are no longer learning English primarily to communicate with the English-speaking world but to communicate with others whose native tongue is not English. The number of people who use English as their second or a foreign language now exceeds the number of native speakers by a factor of three.[12] No other language with world-language pretensions is in a similar position. Statistically, Chinese, Hindi, Arabic, Spanish and Portuguese, French, and German are used primarily to communicate within or with regions in which they are the official state and school language. More and more students are learning Chinese in Germany, but this is primarily because of China's increasing economic and political importance. No German would think of speaking Chinese to a prospective Japanese supplier or customer even if both had mastered that language. English, on the other hand, is a language comprehensible in all three nations. Thus they use English—but they use their own English without any native speakers exerting control. Whether the native speakers of a particular language have been dead for two thousand years or are separated geographically by two thousands miles is largely irrelevant, at least when it comes to using it as a second language.

The consequences of this situation are significant and are increasingly the subject of study and reflection in English-language studies. Viewed through the lens of Latin, changes have already occurred in English in the three criteria cited earlier for Latin as a second language: (1) the effect of dynamic linguistic processes in "secondary" language communities of nonnative speakers; (2) the replacement of a generally agreed-upon standard of the mother tongue by individually achieved language competences; and perhaps, (3) the importance of grammars and textbooks in fixing the language.

First, given the percentage of nonnative speakers using English in communications, it should not be surprising that influences on the English language that have their origin in language innovations by nonnative speakers have become a factor to be reckoned with.[13] When German, Finnish, or Japanese professors teach their own and foreign students in English, which they have learned as a second language, the effect is precisely the same as occurred in the Latin-only learning circles mentioned earlier, which develop their own conventions. And overall, the effect is very similar to what happened to Latin when it was the language of teaching at universities in the early modern era. Of course, it is unlikely that the innovations that such small groups invent will have a major effect on English as a whole. However, there must necessarily be consequences when communications among and with nonnative English speakers become the rule worldwide. The speech habits developed by hundreds of millions of people from Germany, Russia, Japan, Argentina, and all the other nations, which are then brought into international circulation, cannot simply be viewed as deficient variants of native English—especially since it is now impossible to determine which form of English is now the accepted standard. All of these variants exert their own gravity and bend the development of the language in the countries where English is the mother tongue.

Second, because English is a world language, people are less and less apt to conform to a native norm when learning it.[14] As a world language, English can function only if, heeding Erasmus, learners do not attempt to emulate an unachievable norm and those who actually use the language are accepted as authentic and accorded respect. The global reach of English leads to a situation in which, as with Latin in the Middle Ages, the language competence achieved through learning is no longer viewed in terms of an English-language standard but as an endpoint that is simply taken for granted. For the teaching of English, this means that the goal of imparting a native-English standard has become problematic and can at most be justified only in particular contexts.

But the consequences are even more far reaching. Within certain contexts, even the deficient language competence that individuals bring to communications based on their educational background must in day-to-day practice be accorded equal stature. There is no other way to ensure a language community among people who speak different native tongues and whose habits of language may differ markedly. At international conferences, it soon becomes clear whether someone speaks English fluently; however, in this context the fine points, the cues that tell us who is a native speaker and who is not, generally make no difference whatsoever because attendees are interested in the content. And in construction teams consisting of workers from around the world who use English as a lingua franca, we make do with an even lower level of language competence just so long as everyone on the team understands what needs to be done. Of course, this is how every lingua franca works. But what has become characteristic of English is that its use as a lingua franca has become the norm while native languages fade into the background. As this happens, the clear division between "native speakers" and "nonnative speakers" starts to disintegrate. Moreover, the problem of who "owns" English, an ongoing controversy, is no longer confined to the various countries that speak English as their main language; it has become an issue within that enormous global pool of speakers who use English as a second language. In this sense, English, more than any other language, is gradually coming to resemble Latin in the early modern era, which, though the most important language in Europe, had no community of speakers to whom it really "belonged."

Third, the question arises as to whether this shift toward use by nonnative speakers has not already contributed to fixing English in a manner that is as yet barely perceptible. A second language, after all, is learned, at least at the beginning, through instruction and suitable readings. But this presupposes valid descriptive norms; otherwise, learners would have no consistent way to approach vocabulary acquisition and the mastery of grammar, both of which are indispensable for older second-language learners. Now, if the number of people learning English from textbooks and readings far outstrips the number who imbibe the language with their mother's milk, then the function and role of these textbooks shift. Rather than being aids that describe the current state of the language, they take on a more prescriptive function. For a Korean learning English, the textbook does not impart the language habits of any particular country; it is "the" English language pure and simple. Given the totality of complex interrelations represented by all English instruction courses throughout the world, it is difficult to imagine a process whereby particular changes would be made uniformly in all teaching materials. This obviously suggests that the rapid spread of English as a second language will strengthen the trend toward fixing certain core elements of the language, which is the natural progression in any process of codification.

This suggestion is supported by further observations. We are already seeing that the changes that English is currently undergoing within the global context exhibit certain patterns that are similar to those observed in Latin after the end of antiquity. Both English and Latin share the relative stability of the external forms of words (inflection is rarely an issue in English), and the core components of syntax—that is, precisely the parts of the language that are codified in the dictionaries and grammars that learners study to acquire a second or foreign language. Neologisms and phraseology, on the other hand, are much more open to invention, and variant conventions can coexist in day-to-day communication without much difficulty. Preferences for one syntactic solution over another are also much more fluid.

But pronunciation is subject to the greatest divergences, both in Latin and in English. After the end of antiquity, writing was the only source of real continuity in Latin, while the words came to be pronounced differently, depending on where the speaker came from. In fact, the Romance linguist Helmut Lüdtke proposed this phenomenon as a criterion for the definitive "death" of a language.[15] This seems to me somewhat too sweeping a definition. However, if it has any merit, we will have to classify English as a dead language. After all, English, too, has evolved different pronunciations in the circle of countries that use it as the mother tongue and in those that use it as a second or foreign language. Russians, Japanese, Africans, and members of other language communities have brought the pronunciations characteristic of their own languages into English. As a result, they have created a multiplicity of variant pronunciations. But because mutual understanding is largely determined by pronunciation and because divergences have already become problematic for international communications, pronunciation is attracting more thought than any other area of language: discussion centers on what elementary characteristics of pronunciation are indispensable for mutual understanding and represent a common "lingua franca core," which will then be integrated into English teaching throughout the world.[16] These considerations are a first step toward standardizing grammars, much as occurred in Latin. Interestingly, no standard pronunciations were ever elaborated for the Latin of the Middle Ages and early modern era. The reason for this undoubtedly has to do with poor roads and conveyances. And, of course, there were no telephones or other electronic means of communication (which make it necessary for operators in Indian call centers to learn to speak with an American accent). Overall, it was rare for a Latin speaker in one country to need to talk to a "foreign" Latin speaker. But wherever unexpected encounters occurred (for example, when foreign legates read out Latin texts), complaints abounded about their unintelligibility.

The status of Latin in the Middle Ages as a second language without native speakers was not at all as different from the present circumstances as we might assume. Research into English and Latin that examines their use as a second and as a world language would be worth the effort and extend our understanding of the linguistic processes that are at work. But in the context of this book, the point has been to clarify the extent to which Latin could develop as a wholly normal language amid the multitude of European languages in the Middle Ages and the modern era.

Latin during the Middle Ages

The Second Birth of Latin

In the two preceding chapters, I located Latin within the overall context of "Europe's Latin millennium." I now turn my attention to some characteristics of the evolution of the language during particular epochs. I elaborate on a few points that are important for understanding the development of Latin within the system of European languages, the sorts of points that would be lost in a more literary or cultural examination that focused on historical details.

As I discussed earlier, despite its being fixed, the Latin of late antiquity functioned like any other language with a living language community. If that had not been the case, there would have been no European Latin millennium. The Carolingian reforms, which rescued Latin from the neglect of the Merovingian period, did more than reimpose grammatical correctness. On the whole, the period between the eighth and the twelfth century witnessed the reclamation of Latin and European literacy. This reclamation was not the work of scholastics per se; rather, it was possible only because a real language community developed for which Latin was a living *second* language.

The crisis in Latin culture from the mid-sixth to the mid-eighth century was radical. Except in Ireland and southern England, where language and literature continued to be cultivated, only traces of real Latin culture remained in central Europe. Knowledge and active use of Latin collapsed during the "Dark Ages," from about 550 to the end of the eighth century, much more thoroughly than was the case with Greek. Only meager remnants of a living scholastic tradition remained, including the grammars and literary texts that were preserved in libraries, the seed stock that provided the models for the renewal of Latin beginning in the late eighth century.

Because Latin was the only established written language, its disintegration was also a crisis of literacy. Western Europe, where nuanced written communications had for centuries come to be taken for granted, now once again faced the prospect of widespread illiteracy of a sort that had not existed for a thousand years. As early as late antiquity, the evolution of the vernaculars away from the fixed high form of Latin had created a situation in which it was more difficult to learn to write correctly than it had been when Latin literature was still in its archaic, rudimentary phase. In the third century BCE, learning to write required little more than mastering the alphabet; a thousand years later, learning to write proper Latin was tantamount to learning a new language. This increasingly required extensive study and the maintenance of a costly educational system, and where schools no longer existed, learning to write was transformed from broadly mastered cultural know-how into the province of specialists. The fact that the two centuries before Charlemagne have been called "dark" most assuredly does not mean that they produced no culture; rather, because contemporaries were no longer schooled in the art of writing, we have few written records from which to reconstruct whatever culture existed.

The "scholasticizing" of written culture had, of course, begun early in ancient Rome. One sign of this trend was that the profession of *grammaticus* became increasingly important. In Quintilian's time (first century CE), the grammar teacher taught mainly younger students; rhetoric was taught at a more advanced level. By the end of the third century or middle of the fourth, Plotius Sacerdos and Donatus were given the title *grammaticus urbis Romae*, indicating that they had achieved an official status as grammarians of the capital city. We learn little from the classical Latin authors, including Cicero, about whom we have the most biographical information, about grammar instruction, although Horace, in his discussion of the literary canon in *Epistle* II.1 70–71, mentions in passing his teacher Orbilius, whose pedagogy seems to have involved the judicious use of "strokes." But when we get to late antiquity, we increasingly read about who learned grammar from whom and which grammarian taught which renowned student. By analogy, today we often note whom an artist, a musician, or a surgeon trained or studied under. We know, for example, that Donatus taught Jerome, one of the fathers of the church, and that, in the fifth century, Felicianus instructed the poet Dracontius. The poet Corrippus (sixth century) was himself a grammarian. On the whole, a considerable proportion of Latin texts from the fifth and sixth centuries consists of writings about grammar, with very little about rhetoric. Grammar, in its literal meaning of "the art of writing," increasingly came to epitomize culture in late antiquity. It gave people access to the Roman past and at the same time access to literacy. As the school system disintegrated, even elementary matters such as the correct forms of inflection and Latin vocabulary came to assume something approaching cult status.

There is no other way to understand what is probably the most peculiar grammatical work that the Latin world had ever seen, one concocted by the grammarian Virgilius Maro, who probably lived during the seventh century, the cultural low point in Europe. We do not know whether that was his real name or an attempt at co-opting Virgil's cultural aura. In any case, Virgilius reported a number of strange "facts" such as that there were twelve types of Latin and that people had argued for fourteen days and nights over whether *ego* has a vocative case. He traced the genealogy of grammarians back to a certain Donatus, who lived in Troy and was said to have lived a thousand years. However we may try to explain such fantasies, they are evidence of a culture in which mastering the written language was an immense virtue, comparable to the deeds of great heroes of the past.

In the only two regions in which a relatively elaborated Latin culture continued to exist in the seventh century, the most important exponents of this culture wrote grammars, which indicates that grammar was more than a merely auxiliary discipline. In Visigoth Spain, which until its conquest by the Arabs was, along with Ireland, the most important standard bearer of ancient culture, Bishop Julian of Toledo (ca. 642–690) was the author of a grammar. Even more important was the *Etymologiae* by Bishop Isidore of Seville (ca. 560–634). This work was actually an encyclopedia of all disciplines, but because of its emphasis on word definitions and explanations, this work was also important in maintaining the Latin language. In terms of quantity, grammars took second place only to hagiography in the Irish culture of the seventh century, which retained the only genuine Latin culture during that period. The works of the "insular grammarians" form a significant group of texts linking antiquity and the early Middle Ages. The most important Latin authors of the Anglo-Saxons in the seventh and eighth centuries, Aldhelm of Malmesbury (ca. 640–709) and the Venerable Bede (ca. 673–735), wrote works on meter, which in antiquity had been an important part of grammar. In addition, Bede wrote a work on orthography that included information on the use of words. In the early eighth century, Boniface (ca. 680–754), who was probably the most important missionary working in Germany, wrote about meter and authored a grammar. Because the leaders of the church understood that only the art of reading and writing could ensure the spread of Christianity, grammar became a top priority during this period of cultural regression.

However, the growing importance of grammarians was not necessarily proportional to the actual mastery of Latin. The writings that have come down to us show this clearly, and even those may reflect not a contemporary standard but rather the peak achievements of individuals who modeled themselves on ancient texts.

Consider, for example, the much-cited story of the Bavarian priest who, when baptizing members of his congregation, incanted, *In nomine patria et filia et spiritus sancti* (In the name of the Fatherland, the Daughter, and the Holy Spirit). He should, of course, have said, *In nomine patris et filii et spiritus sancti* (In the name of the Father, the Son, and the Holy Spirit) (Boniface, letter 68). The pope wrote to Boniface, who had anxiously inquired, and assured him that these baptisms were indeed valid because the priest had performed them in good faith. But even more astonishing than the deficiencies of an individual cleric is the fact that, at least on the European mainland, real mastery of Latin is almost nowhere in evidence in extant texts from the seventh and early eighth centuries. The few writings that have come down to us from this time make it clear that their authors were struggling with the most rudimentary features of the language.

What is known as the *Chronicle of Fredegar,* a Merovingian history dating from the middle of the seventh century, shows this very clearly. One sentence should suffice to demonstrate the quality of the Latin. The author described the building of the Coliseum in Rome under Emperor Vespasian (69–79 BCE) as follows:

> Coloseos Romae erictus, habens altitudinem pedes cento septem, quem in nomen et laude victuriae suae, quae in Germania fecerat, erixit.

A translation into English of more or less equal quality might read as follows:

> At Rome the Coloseos was puilt, which was high hundr'seven feet and which he puilt to name and to prais his victoury, who he had made in Germania.

As is typical throughout the *Chronicle,* the sentence structure is extremely simple and contains little more than an enumeration of facts as a naive speaker might articulate them. The text also shows numerous errors of the sort that would have been characteristic of a speaker whose mother tongue was the Vulgar Latin that was already closer to the Romance languages. Mixing up *e* and *i* (*erictus* and *erixit* instead of *erectus* and *erexit*) and *u* and *o* (*Coloseos* instead of *Colosseus, victuriae* instead of *victoriae*), suppressing or mistakenly adding endings that, as in the French of today, were no longer pronounced with literal fidelity in Vulgar Latin (*cento* instead of *centum,* as in later Italian; *laude* instead of *laudem* and *quae* instead of *quam*). The writer's desperate desire to achieve competence is evidenced by numerous "hypercorrect" forms, that is, corrections that would frequently have been necessary given the pronunciation of Vulgar Latin but that were then transferred to cases where they were inappropriate. It would be as if a German learning English who had finally mastered the *th* (*thread* instead of *sread*) then extrapolated the sound to form *therial* and *thummer*. The peculiar form *victuriae* is an error of this sort because in fact the vowel "o" in *victor-* would have been correct in Latin as well, as it would in later Romance languages and English.

The *Vita of St. Corbinian,* who founded the bishopric of Freising in the seventh century (today the archdiocese of Munich-Freising), written by Bishop Arbeo of Freising (ca. 725–784), provides yet more evidence of the parlous state of Latin at the time. The actual biography begins as follows:

> Isdem venerandus vir Dei ex regione Militonense ortus fuit, ex vico qui nuncupatur Castrus, ex patre Waltekiso, genitrice Corbiniana; qui dum in utero conceptus fuisset, divina preveniente genitor eius evocatione languori correptus ex hac luce migravit.

An approximately equivalent translation might read as follows:

> Benamed reverend man of God came from the region by Melito, from a village which had been declared to have the name Castrus, from the father Waltekis and the female procreator Corbiniana. When he had been conceived in the uterus, intervened by divine recalling, his procreator, snatched away by weaknese, passed away from this light.

This text places enormous grammatical and stylistic demands on the reader that are simply not redeemed by the content. The elevated choice of words and nested constructions do not add up to a whole but simply make the text hard to understand. At the same time, the author violates Latin syntax (*dum . . . conceptus fuisset* instead of *dum conceptus esset*) and even elementary morphology (*Militonense* instead of *Militonensi*, *languori* instead of *languore*). The only errors missing in this text are those typical of Romance speakers because, although Arbeo probably had contact with Romanized circles in the Tyrol and in northern Italy, his mother tongue was a Germanic language.

These two texts are not exceptional; they are actually the norm, demonstrating how far practice had deviated from the ideal. Except in

Ireland and England, individuals with a (somewhat) better mastery of Latin were rarities, comparable to academics who learn cuneiform or hieroglyphics to decipher ancient texts. They were not representatives of an actual spoken culture. Even in the few centers where writing was cultivated, the grammar was usually rudimentary. Where more complexity was attempted, the writing all too often derailed.

Having said that, the extent to which ancient Latin norms were or were not mastered is probably the wrong question. We should be asking to what extent Latin was even used in general communications during the "Dark Ages." At the time of Augustine, mastery of Latin was a given, allowing entry into the collective discourse. Furthermore, although it was cultivated and strictly supervised by grammarians (something that Augustine complained about; compare *Confessiones* I.29), it was actively used by many people in both oral and written communications. Knowing Latin was nothing special. Although Latin skills were cultivated mainly in school, we may assume that, at least in higher circles of society, people could have conversed in school Latin or some form of it that differed markedly from the Vulgar Latin of the streets— just as in the nineteenth century some insisted on speaking High German as a matter of cultural or class identity in areas of Germany where a dialect was especially pronounced. But by the seventh century very little was left of this Latin competence.

Did a group of people exist in Merovingian Gaul who maintained the diglossia of late antiquity, insisting on speaking "Latin," however overgrown it may have been by the vernacular of the time? Or did knowledge of Latin imply a merely passive linguistic competence that, comparable to a modern student's knowledge of Latin, was just good enough to figure out more or less what was being conveyed in church? The latter is more probable, just as we may safely assume that Bishop Arbeo was likely the only person in his monastery or its surroundings who might even venture to write a more sophisticated text in Latin. Of course, no statistics were collected, but we are probably not far off the mark if we assume that at the time of Augustine more than a hundred thousand people in the Mediterranean basin and Europe had extensive schooling in Latin, whereas by the seventh century their number may have dwindled to a few hundred. These few educated individuals did not form a language community in the literal sense; they were the dispersed remnants of a once-vibrant culture, mastering as best they could an ancient cultural heritage through book learning. We may almost compare them to individual specimens of an endangered species on the verge of extinction, living a widely scattered existence but not forming an actual population.

Viewed from this perspective, the upswing in Latin skills triggered by the Carolingian Renaissance was more than a consolidation of ancient linguistic standards. In fact, over time it reanimated Latin as a language of both oral and written expression. The secondary evolution of this fixed-grammar language that occurred through the efforts of nonnative speakers, a process exemplified in the previous chapter by reference to modern Latin-only gatherings, took place throughout Europe as a collective effort over several centuries.

By the ninth century, Arbeo's clumsy vita of Saint Corbinian would no longer have been tolerated. Wherever such texts continued to be used, they were often heavily edited, and elementary grammatical errors and stylistic lapses corrected. In its ninth-century revision, the sentence cited earlier read as follows:

> Quoniam isdem venerandus Dei famulus Corbinianus ortus fuerat ex regione Militonensi, natus in vico qui dicitur Castrus, ex patre Waldekiso et ex matre Corbiniana; quo nondum nato genitor eius languore correptus rebus excessit humanis.

> The honorable servant of God came from the region around Milito. He was born in a village by the name of Castrus to his father Waldekis and mother Corbiniana. Prior to his birth, his father was snatched away by weakness and exited from this world.

It would be wrong to ascribe the "rescue" of Latin after the crises of the seventh and eighth centuries solely to the Carolingian Renaissance and to assume that Latin miraculously reappeared after Charlemagne. If we examine the burgeoning number of texts written in Latin in a growing number of centers, schools, and finally universities, it becomes clear that this process extended well into the High Middle Ages. By the eleventh and twelfth centuries, the high point of high medieval Latin culture, there were again hundreds of thousands of people in Europe who understood Latin and both wrote and spoke it fluently. While it continued to be the language of the liturgy, university lectures were now held almost exclusively in Latin, and a wide array of texts from the sciences to satirical and erotic literature was written in Latin as well.

In the process of this "natural" development, grammars and textbooks were no longer central to intellectual life and were again relegated mainly to the elementary schools. Of course, they continued to be in circulation, but leading intellectuals in the later Middle Ages no longer relied on them. As in any living language community, the daily practice of communicating in Latin was itself a large part of a person's education and was simply taken for granted.

This was a slow process that began only with Charlemagne's decrees. Grammars continued to predominate early on. Hardly any manuscripts of classical Roman authors have survived from the eighth century; numerous manuscripts with collections of grammatical texts, on the other hand, have. A few of these have become famous as singular testaments to a time when few writings survived at all. These include the Berlin manuscript (Staatsbibliothek Berlin, Diez B 66 Santen), written in about 790, which quite possibly originated in or around Charlemagne's court.[17] Manuscripts of works by Donatus, Priscian, and other grammarians of late antiquity have also come down to us from the period around 800. Surviving manuscripts of ancient classical texts such as those of Cicero, Horace, or Sallust, on the other hand, begin to appear in larger numbers only after the first third of the ninth century. Perhaps people felt the need to learn Latin correctly before grappling again with the more difficult Roman authors. But even in the ninth century, grammar continued to enjoy great stature. Erchanbert of Freising called grammar the "first of arts" in his commentary on Donatus, which dates from the first half of the ninth century. And Rabanus Maurus, one of the most important scholars of the Carolingian Renaissance, who after long service in the monastery in Fulda was made archbishop of Mainz in 847, wrote a grammatical work, in which he followed Priscian's grammar.

As the Middle Ages progressed, fewer and fewer grammatical works were written, and those that were tended not to be written by the leading intellectual lights of their time. Once again, grammar became the province of specialists, much as in antiquity. The authors of the most important grammatical texts in the High Middle Ages, Peter Helias (eleventh century), Eberhard of Béthune, and Alexander of Villedieu (twelfth century), were primarily grammarians. The works of the latter two, in particular the *Graecismus,* by Eberhard (ca. 1200) and the *Doctrinale puerorum* by Alexander (1199), which was used everywhere throughout the late Middle Ages, were didactic aids viewed as indispensable for teaching Latin to beginners. However, their role in the intellectual life of the times was negligible. Neither the great poets, theologians, and philosophers of the High Middle Ages nor the authors of worldly or spiritual poetry continued to write grammars. Although intensive efforts were made in the late Middle Ages to develop a philosophically based theory of language, which continues to be of interest to specialists today, these works were as little intended as aids in language acquisition as are most of the theoretical approaches taken by modern-day linguistics. It is notable that Thomas of Erfurt's tract *De modis significandi* (On the Various Types of Grammatical Meaning), one of the most important examples of this trend, written around 1300, was also widely known by the title *Grammatica speculativa.*

These documents demonstrate more than merely passing improvement in the understanding of grammar. The more that society used Latin as a second language in both written and oral communication, the more instruction in grammar again became a didactic exercise, as is unavoidable when learning a foreign or second language. Living communications became more important. It may well be that not all of those who lived during the Middle Ages could express their thoughts on a wide variety of conversational topics. But they did converse, and it was mainly in daily life, not on the school bench, that people learned how to engage in it. Correct morphology and elementary syntax were a given, enforced by the give-and-take of everyday communications just as in any other normal language.

Latin and the Scriptualization of the Vernacular Languages

The development of the vernaculars as written languages and their replacement of Latin would seem, from the perspective of posterity, to have been a continuous process. At the outset, Latin was everything, and the vernaculars were marginal phenomena. In the end, the vernaculars ruled the continent, and Latin disappeared almost completely, an increasingly bothersome relic of bygone times. It seems that the more the vernaculars came to the fore, the less space was left for Latin. In fact, such a zero-sum process actually occurred. For instance, when the French kings decreed, in 1539, that French would be the language of the courts throughout their domain, it was at the expense of Latin. When German became the literary language of the nation in the latter part of the eighteenth century and a supraregional German "classical" literature

legor scribor neutrum ut curro commune ut loquor
deponens ut loquor proficiscor .

Lego uerbum actiuum indicatiuo modo dictum tempore
praesenti numeri singularis figurae simplicis personae primae coniugationis testis correptae quod declinabi-
tur sic Lego legis legit & pluraliter legimus legitis legunt
Eodem modo tempore praeterito inperfecto legebam legebas
legebat & pluraliter legebamus legebatis legebant Eodem
modo tempore praeterito perfectum legi legisti legit & pluraliter
legimus legistis legerunt uel legere . Eodem modo tempore
praeterito plus quam perfecto legeram legeras legerat
& pluraliter legeramus legeratis legerant Eodem modo tempore
futuro legam leges leget & pluraliter legemus legetis legent
Imperatiuo modo tempore praesenti ad secundam & tertiam
personam lege legat & pluraliter legamus legite legant
Eodem modo tempore futuro legito uel legas legat & pluraliter
legitote uel legatis legant legunto uel leguntote Optatiuo
modo tempore praesenti & praeterito inperfecto Vtinam leg-
rem legeres legeret & pluraliter utinam legeremus legeretis
legerent . Eodem modo tempore praeterito perfecto & plus
quam perfecto . utinam legissem legisses legisset & plu-
utinam legissemus legissetis legissent . Eodem modo tempore
futuro utinam legam legas legat & pluraliter utinam legamus legatis legant . Coniunctiuo modo tempore praesenti
cum legam legas legat & pluraliter cum legamus legatis legant
Eodem modo tempore praeterito inperfecto . Cum legerem legeres
legeret & pluraliter cum legeremus legeretis legerent . eodem
modo tempore praeterito perfecto Cum legerim legeris legerit
& pluraliter cum legerimus legeritis legerint . Eodem modo tempore

Figure 12. Staatsbibliothek Berlin Cod. Diez B. Sant 66. This manuscript takes us directly to the center of Charlemagne's Latin reforms. Written around 790 at or near the school at Charlemagne's court, it contains a collection of Latin grammar texts, among them a work on the grammar of Donatus, revised by Peter of Pisa, one of the scholars whom Charlemagne summoned to his court. This page shows the conjugation of the verb *legere:*

> *Lego verbum activum indicativo modo dictum tempore praesenti numeri singularis figurae simplicis persone primae Coniugationis testis correptae quod declinabitur sic lego legis legit et pluraliter legimus legitis legunt. Eodem modo tempore praeterito imperfecto legebam legebas legebat . . .*

developed in Germany, this meant the displacement of Latin from many areas of cultural life and finally the end of neo-Latin literature.

But if we look at the relationship between Latin and the vernacular languages over the entire Latin millennium in Europe, we observe another process going on simultaneously. Although it is true that Latin eventually lost out to the vernacular languages, both profited during that period from the same cultural developments as well. We now follow this process, first in the early Middle Ages.

If we examine how and when the European vernaculars began to appear as written languages during the time of the Carolingian Empire, excluding developments in Ireland and England, we notice the following: the language with the most surviving texts after the late eighth century is Old High German. The large majority of these texts were written to help the inhabitants in Germanic areas gain access to the Latin world. What we find are translations of Latin texts or poetic adaptations of the Bible such as the *Heliand* and the Gospel harmony (a rhymed version of the Gospels) of Otfrid of Weissenburg, from the ninth century, and Old High German glosses in Latin manuscripts. The vernacular literature, that is, literature not derived from or referencing Latin models, such as the sixty-eight extant verses of the *Lay of Hildebrand*, a retelling of a Germanic legend, was marginal. The language that we encounter in these manuscripts testifies to the elaboration over time of firm habits of writing and of a supraregional standard but without the development of a real Old High German literary language. A new epoch in the language and literature of Middle High German begins after 1050. Not only do we find numerous great works of literature, such as *Parsifal*, the *Nibelungenlied*, and the songs of the minnesingers, which enjoyed a wider audience, but we also see that a literary language had begun to establish itself.

A precursor of French is mentioned in a report on the Council of Tours as *lingua romana rustica*, and a "Vulgar" version of the Oaths of Strasbourg has come down to us. However, in contrast to Old High German, these do not inaugurate a vernacular text tradition. Old French documents are extremely rare; in addition to the Oaths of Strasbourg we have the so-called Sequence (or Canticle) of Saint Eulalia, from the late ninth century, a poem about Eulalia of Mérida, a Christian martyred in about 300 in Spain. The French language begins asserting itself only toward the end of the tenth century, when it developed a rich Old

French literature over the course of the eleventh to the thirteenth centuries. More precisely, Old French and Provençal literature developed simultaneously because in the region that currently constitutes France, two equally important literary languages, French and Occitan, were used before the French kings decreed a single language in the late Middle Ages. Each language developed a relatively uniform written standard over a long period of time.

The other Romance languages appeared even later. The first written texts in Italian stem from the tenth century; however, Italian established itself as a written language only around 1200. Spanish became a written language after the Council of Burgos, in 1080, and Portuguese followed even later. Even though Spanish and Portuguese were scripualized later, it is only in the thirteenth century that they, much like Italian, are seen in large numbers of written documents.

It would seem at first glance relatively simple to explain this sequence of scriptualization. German appeared first because Latin really was a distant foreign language for the Germanic peoples. In the regions in which Old High German was spoken, Christian religious practice would have been impossible if the contents of the Bible or some central texts of the liturgy had not been translated into the vernacular language. Adaptations or translations of the Bible into French were made much later, undoubtedly because people could more or less understand the original Latin text. The sequence of the establishment of the Romance languages—first French, then Italian, Spanish, and Portuguese—seems to have been largely a function of the linguistic distance from ancient Latin. In Italy, the bridge to Latin would have been much easier for people to cross, thereby making a written vernacular less necessary; the opposite would have been the case in ninth-century Gaul, where Latin was completely unintelligible to the average person.

This sequence may actually have been the pattern in some areas of social communication. Sacred texts like the Bible are translated only in diglossic societies when the gap between the high form and the language of the people is so great that understanding is impossible. This principle is exemplified by events in Greece around 1900. When Queen Olga (1851–1926), the wife of King George I, commissioned a translation of the Bible into modern vernacular Greek, the "dimotiki," such a public outcry arose that the government collapsed. Even though the demotic version made the Bible more understandable, it was nonetheless perceived as a calamitous cultural loss. Furthermore, as is well known, the Koran is read in the same Arabic in which it was written in the seventh century, and it can be understood to some extent by those who are not trained in classical Arabic. We have no reason to expect that, in the ninth century, liturgical texts would have been translated into a proto-French that was still quite similar to Latin.

But this purely linguistic explanation of the sequence in which vernacular languages are committed to writing is not completely satisfactory. It would require us essentially to assume that the Romance populations of the Middle Ages simply held on to Latin longer, whereas the Germanic peoples, because their own languages were more removed from Latin, gravitated toward it more quickly. A look at the history of Latin literature from this perspective, something that has apparently never been done before, leads us to completely different conclusions. On the whole, vernacular literature flourished precisely where Latin culture flourished as well. This process began in the seventh and eighth centuries in Ireland and England, which were the most important centers of the ancient Latin tradition. Interestingly, these were the first regions in Europe to develop a written form of the vernacular.

The oldest vernacular texts in Europe are in Old Irish, and the Venerable Bede wrote texts in English as well. In the Carolingian period, up to the end of the ninth century, literature—understood generally as artful writing in a literary or poetic form—was not evenly distributed throughout Europe. Although authors all over the western and southern parts of Europe wrote in Latin up to the end of the Carolingian ninth century, their home regions and audiences tended to cluster in the German-speaking areas. Among the Germans, we might mention the polymath Rabanus Maurus (ca. 780–856) or the poet Walafrid Strabo (ca. 808–849), whereas in France the number of works is much smaller until the time of the Capetian kings, at the end of the tenth century. In the tenth century, we see a general decrease in Latin literature. The upswing that began in the eleventh century and continued into the thirteenth in France and Germany brought forth the rich Old French and Middle High German literature. But this was a golden age of medieval Latin literature as well. Until the eleventh century, we have little evidence of either Italian or Latin literature in Italy. Twelfth-century Spain shows obvious parallels between the writing of legal texts in Latin and Spanish.

Viewed from this perspective, it seems that Latin culture and vernacular culture were not engaged in a zero-sum game but appeared together. Wherever Latin culture flourished, which presumed experience in writing, there were also people who set about scriptualizing the still-unregulated vernaculars. Frequently, one and the same person was doing both.

Increasing Distance from Antiquity

One of the characteristics of medieval culture was that it was not as consistent in modeling itself on Roman antiquity as were the later humanists of the Renaissance. On the other hand, we now know that the blanket criticism that the Middle Ages neglected ancient literature is unjustified. After all, we know about the texts of Roman antiquity almost exclusively from medieval copies, that is, because there were people in the Middle Ages interested in keeping that culture alive. More to the point is that interest in the ancient traditions fluctuated during various phases of the Middle Ages. After a period of serious engagement with those traditions during the Carolingian phase, there followed a period of considerably less interest during the tenth and early eleventh centuries although, interestingly, this lack of engagement affected written culture as a whole. The "crisis of the tenth century" was real. But in the eleventh and then increasingly in the twelfth century, literature was produced in both Latin and the vernaculars, especially in France and Germany, and soon thereafter in Spain and Italy. Ancient authors also found a significantly larger audience. Interest in these authors, with the exception of Aristotle, waned during the late Middle Ages with the ascendancy of Scholasticism. The humanists who attacked the "darkness" of the Middle Ages mainly looked only at the two centuries that came before.

Nevertheless, the notion that classical antiquity was not as important for medieval culture as it was going to be for Renaissance humanism is not wrong. What this means becomes clearer when we look not only at the number of manuscripts of classical authors or at the role of classical literature as textbooks in schools but also at literary production in a broader sense. Here, the distance from classical antiquity became greater from century to century.

The Carolingian Renaissance was not a renaissance of antiquity per se but rather the recovery of a connection with the end of late antiquity,·

which had been severed by the cultural crisis of the seventh century. Emblematic of this are certain large buildings in which Carolingian architects consciously borrowed from individual buildings of late antiquity. The Palatine Chapel of Charlemagne, in Aachen, which was consecrated in 805, references both the Basilica of San Vitale, in Ravenna, completed in 546, and the Church of the Saints Sergius and Bacchus (now the Little Hagia Sophia), in Constantinople, which was completed in 536. The capitals and other architectural elements were imported directly from Ravenna, underscoring the spiritual connection. Another example is the Ratgar Basilica (no longer standing) at Fulda Abbey, one of the largest Carolingian churches, which was based on Constantine's Old St. Peter's Basilica in Rome, which was completed in 333. And the still extant Gate Hall of the Benedictine Lorsch Monastery was probably based on the narthex of Old St. Peter's as well.

As far as we can reconstruct, other churches built by members of Charlemagne's inner circle also borrowed from churches from late antiquity. These include Angilbert's church in St. Riquier and the Abbey Church of St. Denis in Paris. "Classical" antiquity, as typified by the arrangement of columns in classical temples or the Pantheon in Rome, played no major role in Carolingian architecture.

An equally tight continuity exists between the linguistic composition of Carolingian texts and those of late antiquity. As a result, study of the Latin literature in the Middle Ages requires a detailed understanding of the language and literature of late antiquity. This should not be surprising because, with Alcuin, Peter of Pisa, Paul the Deacon, and Theodulf of Orléans, Charlemagne was not convening in his court advocates of a new direction but rather the few outstanding representatives of the old Latin education still remaining among the Anglo-Saxons, Lombards, and Visigoths. Naturally, classical Roman authors like Virgil and Cicero continued to be important, but unlike in the Italian Renaissance, where they served as role models to be emulated, here they were relegated to a teaching function, as they had been in late antiquity. The few exceptions remained just that, including the renowned *Vita of Charlemagne*, by Einhard (ca. 775–840), which he modeled on the second-century imperial biographies of Suetonius. It should be noted, however, that Einhard evidently did not view the classical style employed in his vita as an absolute stylistic standard because he used a different form of Latin in other writings. Overall, one may say that the Carolingian Latin reforms did not impose new linguistic or stylistic standards but merely re-created an uninterrupted continuity with late antiquity.

An initial slump in Latin culture occurred during the tenth century, in terms of both the reception of ancient authors and the production of Latin texts. The eleventh to the thirteenth centuries, a time during which Latin literature blossomed in parallel with medieval vernacular literature in France and Germany, saw fundamental changes in the landscape of the Latin language and literature. Although classical forms were retained or reshaped, forms also began to emerge that are now viewed as typical of the Middle Ages. The Scholastic language typical of philosophy and theology emerged at this time. This language, which is associated with the high intellectual achievements of writers like Albertus Magnus (ca. 1200–1280) and Thomas of Aquinas, deviated considerably from the Ciceronian style, as evidenced by several decidedly unclassical linguistic idiosyncracies such as the construction of declarative sentences using *quod* instead of the accusative and infinitive. A brief section from Thomas's *Summa Theologica,* one of the most important works of scholastic theology, illustrates the point (*Summa* II.2, quaest. I, Art. 8:

> Videtur quod inconvenienter articuli fidei enumerentur. Ea enim quae possunt ratione demonstrativa sciri, non pertinent ad fidem, ut apud homines sint credibilia, sicut supra dictum est. Sed Deum esse unum potest esse scitum per demonstrationem; unde et Philosophus hoc probat, et multi philosophi ad hoc demonstrationes induxerunt. Ergo Deum esse unum non debet poni unus articulus fidei.

> It would seem that the articles of faith are unsuitably formulated. For those things which can be known by demonstration do not belong to faith in such a way as to be objects of belief among men, as was stated above. Now it can be known by demonstration that there is one God; and hence the Philosopher proves this, and many other philosophers demonstrated the same truth. Therefore that *there is one God* should not be set down as an article of faith.[18]

The diction in this sentence is rather far removed from Ciceronian Latin not only in the simple composition of the sentences but also in the individual technical formulations *(ratione demonstrativa, potest esse scitum)* and in unusual ancient word usages (*demonstrationes induxerunt; unus* used as an indefinite article before *articulus*). However, some of these features go back to the technical language found in Aristotelian treatises, which was often retained quite literally in Latin translations of Aristotelian texts (often stretching the linguistic possibilities of Latin beyond their limits).

After Albericus of Monte Cassino (ca. 1030–after 1105), new theoretical systems were developed for rhetoric and poetry based on ancient tradition although their refinement was largely independent. This included the models for prose texts, called *artes dictandi,* for the writing of letters and new poetry such as those of Geoffrey of Vinsauf (ca. 1200) and John of Garland (ca. 1190–1270). In Latin poetry, rhymes began to be added to the hexameter, which continued to be formed according to ancient rules of versification.

However, rhythmic poetry was the furthest removed from ancient traditions. In antiquity, Latin verses were composed according to the length, or "quantities" of the syllables that came to hand simply because of the nature of the language. However, as the Romance languages evolved during late antiquity, Latin increasingly lost this particular feature as well. The tradition of "metric" poetry measured by syllables was so entrenched that the syllable quantities, and with them the rules for constructing verses, continued to be taught and used in school as if people still pronounced their syllables in the manner of their ancient forebears. This tradition continued throughout the Middle Ages into modern times, and these rules continue to be taught in Latin classes just to enable students to read Virgil and Horace. Beginning in late antiquity, and especially in the eleventh and twelfth centuries, meters started to be constructed according to the regular sequence of word stresses and in some cases with end rhymes, just as we find in English or German today. These verses are easily heard and read as such even without having learned the rules of metrics.

These include the songs of the so-called goliards, the best known of whom is the "Archpoet" (ca. 1125–1135 to after 1165), whose real name is unknown. The most famous collection of such verses is found in the manuscript known as the *Carmina Burana,* a medieval song manuscript from the thirteenth century that was found in the Benedictine Benediktbeuren Monastery in Bavaria and was made famous by the twentieth-century settings composed by Carl Orff. Let us take a look at the opening stanza in Orff's iconic reworking (which was not, however, at the beginning in the original manuscript but ended up there as a result of a later rebinding):

Ó fortúna
Vélut lúna
Státu váriábilis
Sémper créscis
Aút decréscis
Víta détestábilis

O Fortune,
like the moon
you are changeable,
ever waxing
and waning;
Detestable in your ways

Although, as mentioned earlier, texts from Roman antiquity were read and reworked during the twelfth century, here, too, we see a certain independence of ancient standards. The Carolingian Renaissance largely adopted the literary canon and the preferred texts, and so it, too, placed Virgil at the apex. In addition, scholars of the day collected and copied all of the ancient literature that could be located. A work like the Epicurean treatise of Lucretius, with its mechanical-atomistic theory, which stood in glaring opposition to the Christian worldview, was nonetheless faithfully copied around 800 and has come down to us largely by luck. However, the High Middle Ages developed new criteria of its own for the selection of ancient literature, thereby creating its own image of antiquity. Ovid, who had been slighted during the Carolingian Renaissance, was brought to the fore in place of Virgil. Works by the epic poets Statius and Lucan also saw a revival. The love elegies of Propertius and the tragedies of Seneca, who were more or less marginalized in the early Middle Ages, have come down to us in manuscripts from the High Middle Ages but before the beginning of the Italian Renaissance. A similar pattern is seen with the love poetry of Catullus and Tibullus.

A comparison with the architectural forms of the Middle Ages already alluded to may be helpful in illustrating the increasing autonomy of cultural and historical processes from the grip of antiquity and in placing them in a larger context.[19] This is not to say, however, that some underlying connection exists between Latin and architecture. The parallels are much simpler than that: language and architecture were the two areas of ancient Roman culture that served as models, forming a real tradition with which to contend. This could not have happened

Regno.

regnabo

regnaui

sem sine regno.

F

d. CIII. Hefal ambulant paſſu fere pari. pro
digiuſ non redimit uitium auari. uirtuſ temparitia
quadam ſingulari debet medium ad utrumq; uitiū
caute contemplari. S i legiſſe memoraſ ethicam ca
toniſ. in qua ſcriptum legitur: ambula cum boniſ.
cū ad dandi gloriam animum diſponiſ. inter cete
ra hoc primum conſidera. quiſ ſit dignuſ doniſ. Dare

O fortuna uelud luna ſtatu uariabiliſ ſemp arceſ aut decreſcaſ uita de
teſtabiliſ nunc obdurat z tunc curat ludo mentiſ aciem et eſtatem poteſtace
diſſoluit ut glatiem. Sortl inmaniſ z inaniſ rota tu uolubiliſ ſt atu maliſ
uana ſaluſ ſemp diſſolubiliſ obumbratam z uelatam m quoq; miteriſ nūc pungo
dorſū nudum fero tui ſceleriſ. Sorſ ſalutiſ z uirtutiſ m nūc gaura e affecta et
defectuſ ſemp angaria hac i hora ſine mora cordis pulſu tangite q ꝑ ſortē ſternit fortē
mecū oē lugēte

Figure 13. Munich, Bavarian State Library, Codex latinus 4660/4660a *Carmina Burana.* The song manuscript found in the early nineteenth century in the library of the Benedictine Benediktbeuren Monastery contains more than a hundred poems from the twelfth and thirteenth centuries in Latin and Middle High German, as well as a few in Old French, some of them with medieval neumes. The collection itself dates from about 1230. Carl Orff popularized the *Carmina Burana* when he set a selection of texts to music in 1936. The Latin verses are almost all written in "rhythmic" meter, that is, with regular alternation of stressed and unstressed syllables and an end rhyme, as in German or English poetry. Orff opened his "scenic cantata" with the "Fortuna" poem. In fact, this poem originally appeared much later in the manuscript. At some unknown time, several pages of the manuscript were lost, and "Fortuna" was placed on top because of its beautiful illumination of the wheel of fortune. akg-images

with music or painting because the evidence did not survive. To the extent that European cultural history has always been a confrontation with ancient culture—whether embraced or rejected—it was only natural that the dynamics of this confrontation made themselves felt in Latin culture and in architecture. In any case, it is clear that the great turning points during which the relationship with antiquity changed are mirrored in these areas.

In terms of architecture, the Carolingian Renaissance saw the reaffirmation of architectural forms from late antiquity, especially in church construction (we know very little about secular structures, few of which have survived). After an undistinguished tenth century, Romanesque architecture from the eleventh century on elaborated a new style that, while borrowing from antiquity, had a specifically medieval look all its own. By comparison, the Gothic architecture that followed in the twelfth and thirteenth centuries and developed in parallel with the revival of medieval intellectualism, further distanced itself from ancient forms. It did so at a time when philosophy, theology, poetry, rhetoric, and poetics developed specifically medieval forms and when the Latin of Scholastic philosophy and medieval rhythmic poetry spread across Europe.

Another parallel between Gothic and Latin culture might be more obvious to a Latinist than to a literary scholar. The basic Latin grammars and lexicons of the twelfth and thirteenth centuries, such as the *Doctrinale puerorum* of Villedieu—who declared linguistic details to be standard that are found only in medieval texts—and the lexicon by John of Genoa, titled *Summa Grammaticalis* but better known as the *Catholicon* (1286), continued to be used unchanged until the time of the humanists. This means that in Italy they were used into the fifteenth century and in Germany as late as the sixteenth, which demonstrates clearly that people saw no need to revise or update the Latin in these very old works. Similarly, Gothic architecture characterized the Europe of the late Middle Ages for three hundred years in spite of a multitude of novel details. The next step is even clearer: while Renaissance architects were replacing Gothic architecture with models from the Roman Empire, the humanists were at the same time praising classical Latin as the best form of the language. In this sense famous architects like Filippo Brunelleschi (1377–1446) or Leon Battista Alberti (1402–1472) were acting on the same impulses as humanists like Valla or Barzizza.

However, the parallels go even further, though this is much less often appreciated because art historians rarely have a command of the history of Latin. When, during the late sixteenth and seventeenth centuries, architecture shed its strong emulation of Roman models and began to play with "baroque" elements, Latin largely began to relax its strong tendencies toward classicism and Ciceronianism in favor of a more complex and free use of ancient models. But while neoclassical architects were reverting to pure Roman forms in the period between about 1770 and 1840, neohumanists like Gesner and Ernesti were seeking to strengthen the role of Cicero and other classical authors in the school curriculum. Finally, the return to classic Latin literature in the eighteenth century was mirrored by the classicism of the architecture. Thus, with some justification, we may pursue this line of thought back into the Middle Ages and view the development of Romanesque and Gothic architecture as expressions of the distance from antiquity, which is also reflected in linguistic developments.

As far as the linguistic side of this process of increasing autonomy is concerned, one should note that the distance from antiquity achieved by Latin during the Middle Ages in no way influenced the way in which the core grammatical components of the ancient standard were fixed. At most, the deviations of medieval Latin involve the formation of new words and phrases, the definitions of individual words, style, and syntactic possibilities. Morphology and elementary syntax remained unchanged with the exception of a few minor details, and where changes appear to have occurred—as with the construction of declarative sentences using *quod* discussed earlier—we can usually find examples of this usage in late antiquity as well. The degree of aliveness of medieval Latin was limited to the fields that remained open to it in spite of how the language was fixed overall.

The morphological and syntactic stability of medieval Latin may become clearer if we compare it to Arabic. Middle Arabic, the form of the Arabic language typical of the period between classical Arabic and modern Arabic, appears to be linguistically parallel to medieval Latin. However, Middle Arabic differs from classical Arabic in that the grammatical standards were not strictly adhered to and took on many of the characteristics of the vernacular language. For the sake of simplicity, we might say that Middle Arabic texts have some structural linguistic similarities to the Vulgar Latin texts of late antiquity and the early Middle Ages in that the writer's lack of grammatical training left traces of the vernacular in the text. The most famous collection of texts of this type is today known as the *One Thousand and One Nights,* stories that were originally set down in a form of Middle Arabic and not in the classical form.[20] Interestingly, these tales were later published in classical reworkings; only recently has the collection again been published in its original form.

Medieval Latin, where it deviated from classical Latin, is something completely different. It did not draw from the vernacular but was an internal, autonomous progression of the Latin language that "surrounded" the fixed grammatical core that people learned in school. A comparison with written Modern Standard Arabic since the nineteenth century might be more to the point. There, too, the externalities of vocabulary, declensions and conjugations, and syntactic possibilities remained largely the same as those in classical Arabic. However, to keep up with the demands of modern life, new words were constantly coined, and the meanings of old words changed. In addition, the syntax continued to be reformed without, however, losing any of the syntactic possibilities that were adopted from classical Arabic. The development of medieval Latin may be viewed as just such a harmonization of a language having a fixed core while adapting to its new surroundings.

A World Language with No Standard?

The Latin of the Middle Ages differed from that of the late Renaissance not only in its relationship to antiquity but also in its internal diversity. The general tendency to emancipate itself from antiquity, as discussed in the previous chapter, does not mean that a new, comprehensive linguistic standard was created. The term *Middle Latin,* which has become a commonplace in Germany, suggests a uniformity that in fact never existed. While Latinist Peter Stotz's recently completed five-volume *Handbuch zur lateinischen Sprache des Mittelalters* (Guide to the Latin Language of the Middle Ages), the first real linguistic history of medieval Latin, shows many commonalities, his groundbreaking work confirms the sheer multiplicity that was medieval Latin. The clichéd notion of a medieval Latin dominated by the church, which neglected the ancient classical authors, and the notion that it was replete with Scholastic distortions and represented a return to barbarism may be traced back to the humanists of the fifteenth and sixteenth centuries, who aimed to usher in a new, more forward-looking future. But this characterization is largely false inasmuch as it applies—if at all—to brief phases or particular developments such as the philosophical terminology of the late Middle Ages. Even the famous "Epistolæ obscurorum virorum" ("Letters of Obscure Men"), in which an anonymous group of German humanists mocked certain positions and Latin usages of the medieval Scholastics at the beginning of the sixteenth century, have been shown to be a malicious distortion of reality. In fact, the High Middle Ages were a period of great diversity. In addition to literary and linguistic forms influenced by the classics, we also see new medieval trends that are instantly recognizable as such. This is especially true of poetry.

Today, our image is largely influenced by the poetry and songs of the goliards, itinerant scholars and singers (the fact that the realities were much more complicated is not relevant to our discussion here). The texts that have come down to us, among them those of the Archpoet, expound on love, wine, and other earthly pleasures and seem to be expressing a spontaneous joy in living. But this is misleading because most of these poems can be understood only if we recognize them as witty allusions to both spiritual and worldly literature. Ever since Carl Orff's setting of the *Carmina Burana,* these poems have achieved a much greater degree of recognition and are seen as representing a medieval love of life, which is largely a distortion. Some Latin works from this period are of an entirely different mold. Walter of Châtillon (ca. 1135–1204), who wrote rhythmic poetry in the style of the *Carmina Burana,* also wrote the "Alexandreid," an epic about Alexander the Great that evinced complete mastery of Virgil's epic language and ancient meter. The beginning of the first book hews closely to the subject matter of the ancient epics:

> Gesta ducis Macedonum totum digesta per orbem,
> quam large dispersit opes, quo milite Porum
> vicerit et Darium, quo principe Graecia victrix
> risit et a Persis rediere tribute Corintum,
> Musa refer . . .

> Sing, o muse, about the erstwhile deeds of Macedon's ruler
> around the world: how amply he dispatched warriors,
> how powerfully he forced Porus and Darius, and how under his
> leadership Greece exulted, and Corinth received back Persian
> > tribute . . .

Lyrical meters are occasionally found as well; in 1167, for example, Metellus of Tegernsee wrote poems to Saint Quirinus, the patron saint of the Tegernsee Abbey, in lyrical meter reminiscent of Horace.

A similar differentiation in style is found in prose, too. Literature in the strict sense, that is, historiography, letters, and official documents, continued in many cases to follow ancient language patterns. The Latin that Peter Abelard wrote to express his tragic love for his pupil Heloise in the middle of the twelfth century differs from ancient Latin only in a few inconsequential, novel phrasings. The narrative as a whole— except, perhaps, for the intrusive enumerations—exhibits the same sort of facility found in Cicero's letters:

> Quid plura? Primum domo una coniungimur, postmodum animo. Sub occasione itaque disciplinae amori penitus vacabamus, et secretos recessus, quos amor optabat, studium lectionis offerebat. Apertis itaque libris plura de amore quam de lectione verba se ingerebant, plura errant oscula quam sententiae, saepius ad sinus quam ad libros reducebantur manus, crebrius oculos amor in se reflectebat quam lectio in scripturam dirigebat. Quoque minus suspicionis haberemus, verbera quandoque dabat amor, non furor, gratia, non ira, quae omnium unguentorum suavitatem transcenderent. Quid denique? Nullus a cupidis intermissus est gradus amoris et, si quid insolitum amor excogitare potuit, est additum.

> Why should I say more? We were united first in the dwelling that sheltered our love, and then in the hearts that burned with it. Under the pretext of study we spent our hours in the happiness of love, and learning held out to us the secret opportunities that our passion craved. Our speech was more of love than of the books which lay open before us; our kisses far outnumbered our reasoned words. Our hands sought less the book than each other's bosoms—love drew our eyes together far more than the lesson drew them to the pages of our text. In order that there might be no suspicion, there were, indeed, sometimes blows, but love gave them, not anger; they were the marks, not of wrath but of a tenderness surpassing the most fragrant balm in sweetness. What followed? No degree in love's progress was left untried by our passion, and if love itself could imagine any wonder as yet unknown, we discovered it.[21]

Even some official papal letters from the High Middle Ages hearken back to the long periodic sentences characteristic of Cicero. The image that we have of medieval prose is much too one sided, influenced as it is by the philosophical language of the Scholastics as seen, for instance, in Thomas Aquinas's massive *Summa theologica* from the mid-thirteenth century or the language of medieval documents. Still, we need to be clear that these are primarily evidence of specialized languages that do not represent any sort of general standard. What conclusions would we draw if we took the tax code or mechanical patents as the standard by which English as a world language was to be evaluated?

When we compare conditions in the Middle Ages to those in late antiquity and modern times, a whole other way of grasping the multiplicity of medieval Latin comes into focus. It may well be that the single thread that weaves its way through the entire Middle Ages is the lack of controversy about what constitutes good Latin. Such discussion was virtually a constant throughout antiquity, from Caesar and Cicero to Quintilian to Augustine and Jerome. From the beginning of modern times and the first glimmers of Renaissance humanism in Italy, it has continued to be a lively topic up to the present day. We see concern for the language not only in reflections about correct standards but also in the profusion of style manuals and the like. Even today, correction guidelines for stylistic exercises involving translations into Latin at the university level are the subject of constant controversy. In the Middle Ages, note was taken here and there of the value (or lack thereof) of certain ancient authors, and there were rhetorical and poetic traditions and attempts at systematization. There was also a rich grammatical literature by which the rudiments of the language were passed down, and it was understood that Latin could be spoken more or less eloquently. The songs of the goliards also bespeak an acute linguistic artistry. However, what was lacking was an idea of what "good" Latin was and how one could achieve it.

There are reasons for this absence. For one thing, as we are increasingly coming to understand, during the Middle Ages, social or political norms in general were not systematically elaborated. This epoch, which was long believed to be uniform and unchanging, characterized by firm principles, turns out to have been exceedingly complex in terms of clearly enunciated ideas about political and social norms. The Middle Ages were the scene of endlessly convoluted power relationships, with barely any discussion of the forms that government might take. It was only with the reexamination of Roman law, which in many countries did not occur before the fifteenth century, that legal systems were worked out that went beyond an enumeration of customary rights. How a society was constituted, the rights and duties of princes and subjects, the organization of cities, the institution of schools, taxation—all of these were regulated somehow, sometimes even in written form. But there was no discussion of what sorts of arrangements were best and most universally valid, nor was there any systematic effort to enforce or implement these arrangements. Recently, the term *order configurations* has been used to describe the power relationships in medieval society, by which is meant a complex system of overlapping and interdigitated arrangements rather than a single order.[22]

By contrast, the modern era is characterized by an abundance of ideas about how states and relations should be ordered. The question of just how a government should be organized and how its functions arranged and delegated became central topics of concern in European societies only after the late Middle Ages, after about 1500. The organization of courts, schools, churches, and universities and rules of etiquette and medical practice are all characteristic of a modern mindset, and every effort is made to enforce these rules and organizational forms in daily life. The practice and theory of law were completely remade as a result of the reexamination of ancient Roman law and increasingly tied to the Roman language itself, more so than during the Middle Ages. Wherever ancient models were lacking, as in international law, we see the beginnings of systematization based on first principles; in the seventeenth century, Hugo Grotius even drafted regulations for traffic on the high seas, a sign of the new globalization. The background against which all of this occurred was the development of a new understanding of government that, far more than in the Middle Ages, began to deal in ideas that prefigured the modern territorial state and that in the nineteenth century eventuated in the organization of nation-states.

If we assume that public debate about language standards is less a linguistic than a social process, then the absence of medieval language standards must be viewed within this larger context. The ways in which medieval Latin was formed were complex. There was no real principle according to which several, sometimes inconsistent, standards could be reconciled; rather, what we find is a proliferation of individual standards and standards within small groups. Certain stylistic traditions continued to be propagated, such as the scientific Latin of the late Middle Ages or the usages unique to the papal curia; individual styles such as the lyrical Horace imitations of Metellus of Tegernsee were not uncommon, either. However, it would not have occurred to anyone to chide others on their "poor" Latin just as long as they used the vocabulary and elementary syntax correctly. And what we observe in Latin also applies to the European vernaculars. In practice, there were some attempts to elaborate a written standard, especially in Old French and Middle High German. However, no thought was given to how such a written standard should look or any dispute over who wrote better or worse German or French. For the European vernaculars, these discussions began only in modern times, spawning a lively tradition that most recently has included the German spelling reforms.

These considerations touch on a problem that is of fundamental importance for our understanding of Latin as a world language. It becomes clear that, even with a culture language as highly developed as Latin, it is not enough to look at its current standards. The key question now is whether it should have any standards at all. In any case, medieval Latin was less bound to a fixed standard than was the Latin of antiquity or the modern Latin of the humanists, and it could therefore do without arbiters of grammar and usage. In the Middle Ages, there was little room for passionate advocacy concerning language. When the humanists began their programmatic attack on medieval Latinity and especially on the use of Villedieu's *Doctrinale puerorum*, many Europeans simply continued to use it. However, no one would have thought to defend it because there was nothing programmatic to defend; medieval Latin was taught with no pretense of sophistication or cultivation—as is the case with many modern standard languages.

One way to illustrate the situation in which Latin found itself would be to compare it to the modern world language, English. Here, again, the parallels are obvious. Given how English is used globally today, it is possible to write in a variety of standards concurrently. A text written in sophisticated British literary English would in some respects be comparable to the medieval poetry written under the influence of the classical Roman poets. At the same time, however, a number of people are writing from a totally different literary tradition and for completely different purposes. Medieval philosophical, theological, and legalistic discourses have today given way to the specialized languages of economics, finance, natural sciences, medicine, and the law. As with medieval Latin, English today consists of a common core of rules; however, the precise location and parameters of this core are indeterminate. The question of whether a common English-language standard exists—or even should exist—is, as we have seen, an open question as well.

Latin in the Early Modern Era

The Reform of Latin and the Linguistic Reorganization of Europe

Imagining the span of time from the beginning of the Renaissance to about the turn of the nineteenth century as an epoch of its own—as we do here—may not, however, be totally justified. It seems almost obvious, at first glance, to view the Renaissance, a "rebirth of antiquity," as marking the end of the Middle Ages in a literal sense, especially since this "rebirth" was understood by humanists since Petrarch as the rebirth of the Latin language as well. Scholarship has, however, long shown that it is problematic at a minimum and probably impossible to draw a sharp boundary between the "Middle Ages" and the Renaissance. The "Renaissance" as an intellectual movement may be viewed from too many perspectives, the attempts to elucidate the forces that led to it are too manifold, and the continuities too various. Furthermore, some of these continuities extend from the Middle Ages far into modern times. The dividing line used here, on the other hand, 1800, cannot be thought of as definitive, either. The German historian Reinhart Kosellek viewed the hundred years from approximately 1750 to 1850 as a "saddle period" that fundamentally separated "premodernity" from "modernity." But like all of the other names of epochs like "the Enlightenment" and "the Romantic period," including terms used by the various disciplines such as baroque, classicism, or Biedermeier (from art history), they capture only parts of the reality and are often only conditionally applicable to developments that may occur at the same time. Even a term like *neohumanism*, which seems to be most closely connected with the Latin language, does not, as we will see, denote a sharp break in the history of Latin—even ignoring the fact that neohumanism *(Neuhumanismus)* remained a largely German phenomenon.

Our classification into eras of Latin language history is much more pragmatic and based largely on extrinsic considerations. The first attempts at grappling with a generally binding Latin norm are viewed as the beginning of the era. The end of that era is marked by the disappearance of Latin from active use in scholarship and the last niches of public administration, which occurred between 1750 and 1850. So the turn of the nineteenth century is generally regarded as the definitive end of Europe's Latin millennium.

In the chapters that follow, we will examine Latin in terms of the "family" of modern European national languages that emerged during this period, and we will make certain observations and advance certain hypotheses.

A first point to be made in relation to a larger European context has to do with what may be viewed as characteristic of Renaissance Latin, namely its orientation to the standards of classical Latin. The whole matter should be quite simple; that is, if the Renaissance is defined as a return to antiquity, Renaissance Latin should be simple classical Latin. It should mean renouncing the habits and proclivities of medieval Latin and returning to the standards of antiquity.

But, in fact, matters were much more complicated. Renaissance humanists had a rather difficult time defining what actually constituted classical Latin. This discussion, at times vociferous, lasted for more than two hundred years. As we pointed out earlier, Latin speakers in the Middle Ages were not obsessed with what constituted correct Latin. During the Renaissance, however, arguments over the best styles of written and spoken Latin were very much carried out in public.

Let us first look at the most salient facts. During the Renaissance, people generally agreed on one point. As discussed earlier, the Carolingian period of the ninth century sought continuity with late antiquity—including, of course, the classical authors who formed the school canon. However, the authors of late antiquity were no longer accepted as models of Latin writing during the Italian Renaissance, and what remained were the classical authors from Plautus to Suetonius. In effect, the literature of late antiquity, that is, the entire canon of Christian literature, including the church fathers Ambrose, Jerome, and Augustine, was dropped. Even the humanists in the church tended to agree. For example, Christian authors of antiquity played no role in Archbishop of Siponto Niccolò Perotti's (1429–1480) *Cornucopiae,* which was an important manual of correct Latin throughout Europe for several decades. Epitomizing this paradigm change is the fact that the largest ancient church, St. Peter's Basilica at Rome, which had been erected over the grave of the apostle by Constantine the Great during the fourth century, was torn down and replaced between 1506 and 1626 by the present structure, with its classical temple front. This astonishing concentration on pagan antiquity became so firmly anchored in the Renaissance that even the

Jesuits adopted it when teaching Latin—a fact that recent scholarship has brought to light. This is not to imply that the Jesuits in any way denigrated the church fathers or biblical Latin, but the Latin exercises that they gave to their ten-year-old pupils consisted primarily of Cicero's speeches and Virgil's *Aeneid*. But while there was general agreement on the importance of classical authors, the overall reformation of Latin remained the subject of intense debate for many years.

This process began with Petrarch, who, out of personal conviction, created his own Latin style during the mid-fourteenth century, basing it on the works of Cicero. Late in life he described his youthful enthusiasm for Cicero in a letter (*rerum senilium* 16.1). Rather than follow his father's instructions to study law, Petrarch immersed himself clandestinely in his beloved ancient classics, especially Cicero, the magic of whose language *(dulcedo sermonis)* especially pleased him. However, when young Francesco's father discovered what his son was really doing, he burned most of the manuscripts he found. This very modern conflict between father and son may be read as a sort of founding document of a new language consciousness based on aesthetic criteria just as Petrarch's account of his ascent of Mont Ventoux documents a new relationship between Renaissance man and nature. But as recent scholarship has shown, both documents are complex in that neither is a naïve, uniform expression of a new aesthetic or even of a "modern" consciousness. In any case, Petrarch's stylistic preferences were initially a matter of individual taste, and he was very much alone in his time.

It fell to a later generation of humanists such as Guarino da Verona (ca. 1370–1460), Gasparino Barzizza (ca. 1360–1431), and Vittorino da Feltre (1378–1446) to develop an educational program that aimed to spread classical Latin. And these people were less philologists and literary figures than language teachers who placed Cicero at the center of their educational efforts. A generation later, in 1435, Lorenzo Valla (ca. 1405–1457) created the first written codification of a new Latin standard, *Elegantiae linguae latinae* (Elegances of the Latin Language), a work that was influential well into the sixteenth century. At the same time, however, the reform of Latin was also the occasion of disputes among humanists. The expression "kitchen Latin," still heard today, goes back to a remark made by Valla about his colleague Poggio Bracciolini (1380–1459), who had certainly not learned his Latin from a cook.[23] He was just as much a proponent of ancient Latinity and one of the great scholars

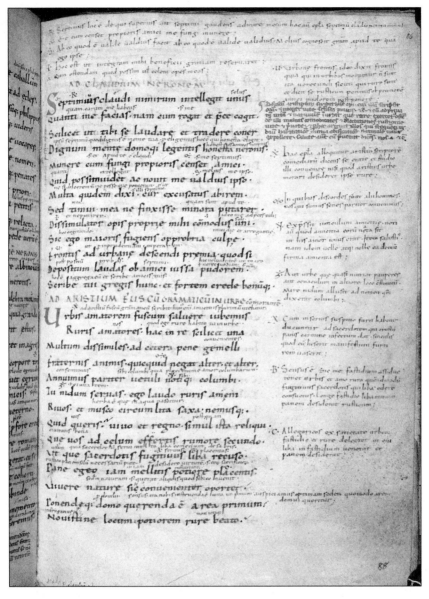

Figure 14. Florence, Biblioteca Medicea Laurenziana, Cod. plut. 34.1, fol. 88r, Horace, poems, tenth century. This manuscript was owned by Francesco Petrarca (Petrarch), who acquired it on November 28, 1347. Petrarch wrote numerous notes in it; this page, however, shows interlinear and marginal notes that were not written in his hand. They were the "basic commentary" that was included with the manuscript. Petrarch's Italian poems constitute only a small portion of his work, which was primarily written in Latin, including a Latin epic poem and two collections of letters of literary importance. akg-images

of his time. Later in the fifteenth century, humanists such as Giovanni Tortelli (1400–1466), Niccolò Perotti (1429–1480), Giovanni Sulpizio da Veroli (d. ca. 1490), and Angelo Poliziano (1454–1494) contributed to the reform of Latin with their textbooks and reference works. Facility in classical Latin prose eventually became something of a given in Italy. Ancient literary models, especially Cicero's speeches, became very popular as well. The beginning of a speech by the humanist Filippo Beroaldo, with which he prefaced a lecture on Cicero's speeches against Verres, is a good example of how the spirit of Cicero infused writing in the Renaissance:

> Vetus verbum est, viri praestantissimi, et instar proverbii apud eruditos celebratum, quod sic ait, leges bonae ex malis moribus procreantur: Etetnim nisi vitia agminatim erupissent, nisi mores mali velut herba irrigua (ut inquit Plautus) uberrime succrevissent, profecto leges supervacaneae fuissent, quae ad coercendas cupiditates vitiaque ex mortalibus tollenda latae sunt.

> It is an old saying, you brave men, and as well known as a proverb among scholars, that says, "Good laws have their origins in bad morals." Because if vices did not erupt in droves, if bad morals did not grow as profusely as well-watered weeds (to borrow from Plautus), then, in fact, the laws that have been instituted by men to place limits on desires and vices would have been superfluous.

But the generation after Valla began to ask whether "ancient" Latinity was not too broad a concept and whether Cicero should be the sole model. Of course, Cicero had always been the most important model for Latin prose, but around 1500, Cardinal Pietro Bembo (1470–1547), a humanist, and Christophe de Longueil (1490–1522), a Belgian who worked primarily in Paris and Italy, placed Cicero so exclusively at the core that he became the sole model, indispensable even down to minutiae of phraseology. The extremes to which this imitation of Cicero led becomes evident in a few of the speeches given by the French-Italian humanist Marcus Antonius Muretus. With his powerful opening sentences, Muretus attempted not only to ally himself with Cicero but also to trump him. Here is an example of the beginning of a speech—a single Latin sentence, mind you—about the connection between wisdom and eloquence (*De philosophiae et eloquentiae coniunctione*, Venice, 1557), which, among other things, hooks into the beginning of Cicero's speech *Pro Sexto Roscio Amerino:*

Si quis forte vestrum est, auditores, cui admirabile videatur, quod, cum ceteri ordinis mei homines in orationis fere alicuius et poematis explicatione versari soleant, eos sibi libros, quibus abditarum retrusarumque rerum ex uberrimis illis hausta philosophiae fontibus tractatio continetur, interpretandi quidem caussa vix esse attingendos putent, ego contra et altero abhinc anno quinque Ciceronis libros, quibus de summo bono in contrarias partes copiosissime disputatur, explicaverim et hoc tempore Tusculanas mihi potissimum disputationes, in quibus huius anni curriculum conficerem, elegerim: is, si mei consilii atque instituti caussam rationemque cognoverit, simul et id, quod facio, probabit et me, si aliter fecisssem, iustam doctorum et intellligentium reprehensionem nullo pacto effugere potuisse existimabit.

To those of you, [my] listeners, to whom it seems of import why, since most of the other men of my profession mainly engage in explication of a speech or a poem but do not consider it necessary to take to hand the books, the contents of which, drawn from the overabundant sources of philosophy, consist in the treatment of remote and arcane things, I, on the other hand, as early as the previous year last explicated the five books of Cicero, which discuss opinions, both for and against, about the highest good in the most eloquent manner, and I have now sought out the *Tusculanae disputationes*, in particular, in order to conclude with them the curriculum for this year: you will, once you have recognized the reasons and considerations of my plan and purpose, both approve that which I do and be of the opinion that I, had I acted differently, under no circumstances could have evaded the justifiable reproach of educated and reasonable men.

This exaggerated "Ciceronianism" was a force to be reckoned with for several decades; in 1559, the Italian humanist Marius Nizolius (1498–1566) published his *Thesaurus Ciceronianus*, which enjoyed a wide audience. In his 1528 dialogue "Ciceronianus," Erasmus criticized the excesses of Ciceronianism and demanded a freer stance toward ancient authors. At about the same time as Ciceronianism developed, however, Italy also produced Latin authors like Filippo Beroaldo, who valued the postclassical prose of Apuleius.

The German humanists who engaged in hefty debate in the second half of the fifteenth century were largely unaffected by strict Ciceronian impulses, and, like Erasmus, they were more generous in their assessment of "good" ancient authors. But they, too, expended considerable energy on language. They wrote numerous new Latin grammars, of which Philipp Melanchthon's (1497–1560) became the most popular, remaining in use into the eighteenth century. Humanists like the Alsa-tian Jakob Wimpfeling (1450–5028) and Heinrich Bebel (1472–1518), who taught at Tübingen, wrote manuals to help people write more ele-gantly. Paul Schneevogel (ca. 1460–1514), who wrote under the Latin name Niavis, and Laurentius Corvinus (ca. 1465–1527), a Pole, wrote "dialogue books" (i.e., short texts with models for everyday conversa-tion), the most successful of which was Erasmus's *Colloquia familiaria,* which was used and quoted throughout Europe for centuries. In the sixteenth century, Protestant school policies prescribed the teaching of a variety of Roman classics, and somewhat later this pattern was taken up almost unchanged by the Jesuit secondary schools, which began to open in midcentury. In 1599 they promulgated the *Ratio studiorum,* a Europe-wide language curriculum for Jesuit schools. Toward the end of the six-teenth century, however, stylistic rivals to Cicero began to find defend-ers. For example, the Dutch philosopher and philologist Justus Lipsius (1547–1606), one of the most influential thinkers of his time, advocated the Latinity of Seneca and Tacitus, whose styles differed markedly from that of Cicero. Only after about 1600 did the debate over style become somewhat less contentious. A new classicism then developed, Ciceronian at its core, with the other ancient authors forming a descending order of stylistic excellence. With some simplification (not to mention calcifica-tion), this order remained the standard for correcting style at German universities into the twentieth century. Styles too close to nonclassical authors like Tacitus and Suetonius were marked down half a grade; those that imitated the "church authors" of late antiquity, whose names teachers could barely bring themselves to enunciate, fared even worse.

At first glance, the debate over what constitutes the best Latin might seem to be a side issue, of interest mainly to Latin scholars. But if we take a closer look at Latin in the context of the "family history" of Eu-ropean languages, we see a number of very interesting phenomena. In fact, the search for a universal form of a language was not limited to Latin, and this return to ancient roots was not the beginning of a gen-eral re-Latinization of Europe. On the contrary, it was during the Re-naissance that the European vernaculars set off on their paths toward becoming modern literary languages.

An overview of the most important steps in this process may give us some idea of the fundamental changes experienced by European lan-guages at this time. These linguistic changes were most pronounced throughout Europe between about 1350 and 1650, that is, the decades that are today most generally understood to epitomize the Renaissance. This was especially true of countries like Italy, France, Spain, and England. In Germany and in the eastern European countries, this evolution was not really completed until the eighteenth century, but here, too, important steps had been made by the sixteenth century.

In France, Middle French, which was much closer to what we know as modern French, evolved from Old French after about 1350. In this form, French became the officially binding language throughout the kingdom in the sixteenth century and displaced Occitan, which was spoken in the south of the country, as the official literary language. This led to the transition to modern French in the sixteenth century, which in turn evolved into the language spoken today. This form of French was as much the result of extreme political measures as of literary efforts. The royal decree of 1539, which established French as the language of the courts, is an example of the former; poet Joachim du Bellay's 1549 statement of principles, the *Deffence et illustration de la langue françoyse* (Defense and Illustration of the French Language), an example of the latter. Bellay belonged to a loose group of seven poets known as La Pléiade, who believed that, with proper cultivation, French could become a real literary language, perhaps rivaling Latin.

We do encounter Italian in literary texts in the late twelfth century; however, the language developed slowly, and it was only in the fourteenth century that Dante, Petrarch, and Boccaccio established it as a literary language. The next important step in the history of Italian occurred at the beginning of the sixteenth century with the *questione della lingua*, which stimulated the development of modern literary Italian. One of the most prominent advocates of this new direction was Cardinal Pietro Bembo, the author of the 1525 treatise *Prose della volgar lingua* (Discussions of the Vernacular Language), which championed the language of Petrarch and Boccaccio as the model and standard for writing in Italian. In other words, following the Latin model, Bembo imbued older authors with authority; their works became the new canon. This should not be surprising because Bembo was, as previously discussed, among the most fervent advocates of a strict Ciceronian standard for Latin. In northern Italy, where French was a prestige language, Franco-Italian, an amalgam that was used only for literary purposes, developed between the thirteenth and the fifteenth century. For Italy, it was especially important in the transmission and reception of epics written in the French vernacular.

Early New High German developed in Germany beginning in the fourteenth century. By the sixteenth century at the latest, it had become a written language, with Luther's translation of the Bible (1522, 1534) furnishing the first canonical text. Whereas German texts written in 1300 in Middle High German are virtually unintelligible today unless one has linguistic training, the modern reader can comprehend those from about 1600 without much difficulty, though they may sound quaint.

In England, the linguistic landscape was largely shaped by the Norman invasion of 1066, which eventually led to the extinction of Old English. Since about the thirteenth century, much of the island population spoke what we now call Middle English, with an admixture of Norman French. The language of the court and upper classes, however, hewed to Anglo-Norman, which preserved the French of the continental conquerors. Over the course of the fourteenth century, Middle English slowly became the sole written language. It was standardized largely as a result of the most renowned work of the period, Geoffrey Chaucer's (1332–1400) *Canterbury Tales,* and then stabilized by the development of the printing press. Neither the Gaelic nor the Scots form of English ever became important literary languages; with the union of the kingdoms of Scotland and England in 1707, English became the sole official language.

Catalan, Castilian, and Galician were present as literary languages on the Iberian peninsula from the twelfth century at the latest (Basque was of no importance as a written language until well into the modern era). Here, too, the official displacement of Latin occurred very early; Castilian became the sole language of royal documents in the thirteenth century. With the unification of Aragon and Castile, Castilian became the official language of the entire region that is now Spain, without, however, actually displacing the other languages, as is evident today. Finally, Portuguese, which began to solidify in the twelfth century, had developed most of its modern features by the sixteenth century.

What we see with all of these languages is that the crucial steps toward becoming literary languages occurred between about 1350 and 1600. At the beginning of this period of transition, these languages were solidly rooted in the literary and linguistic traditions of the High Middle Ages. By the end, the medieval forms had been largely pushed aside, and their rich literatures languished, buried in the recesses of libraries.

Europe, however, now had approximately the same linguistic shape as it does today. Fundamental changes after 1600 occurred only in the Netherlands and at the edges of the continent, in Scandinavia, and (to some extent) in eastern Europe. In central Europe, the historical evolution of the various languages had largely come to an end; the forms taken by these languages at about or after 1600 were the basis for the standardization of the modern national languages in the seventeenth and eighteenth centuries.

By about 1600, the national languages had already displaced Latin in France, Spain, Italy, and England, at least outside the university and the church. Even the geographical range of French, Spanish, Portuguese, and English was about what it is today in Europe. Literary languages that had heretofore flourished and under other circumstances might have been culturally coequal with those languages either became extinct or continued to eke out a marginal existence as orally transmitted regional tongues.

Among the languages that were driven out of existence were Old Provençal, the language of the troubadours, which was widespread throughout France, and Franco-Italian, the literary language of northern Italy, which combined elements of both Italian and French. Literary languages that were demoted and marginalized included Catalan, Galician, and Irish. Numerous other languages that lacked an important literary tradition such as Breton, in France, and Scottish (Gaelic), in Britain, suffered the same fate and were forced to the margins by the insurgent national languages. The fact that most of these languages survived at least as spoken languages and that some, like Catalan and Irish, experienced a resurgence during the twentieth century and have undergone a real renaissance, both literary and in the schools, makes it clear that the fundamental changes that occurred at the time were forced by politics and not merely by natural developments. Europe underwent a real linguistic break with its past. Overall, the three centuries before 1350 (with the exception of the upheaval caused by the Norman conquest of England) and the three centuries after 1600 saw fewer changes in both the development and geographical spread of the European languages than did the 250 years of transition during the Renaissance.

In this context, efforts were made in both theory and practice to reestablish the best form of ancient Latin. In many cases, the same people were engaged in reforming both Latin and the vernacular languages.

Bembo, as we have seen, recommended Cicero as the model for Latin; he also championed Petrarch and Boccaccio for Italian. The Spanish humanist Antonio Nebrija (1444–1522) wrote the first Spanish grammar in 1492, but he also authored a Latin grammar. The poets of the Pléiade joined together in the mid-sixteenth century to advance French as the language of poetry; however, they wrote in both French and Latin. Robert Estienne, also known as Robertus Stephanus (ca. 1503–1559), for example, set standards for both Latin and French with his Latin-French dictionary (1539). Estienne also wrote a French grammar. Much like Nebrija in Spain, the French philosopher Pierre de la Ramée (Petrus Ramus, 1515–1572) authored both a Latin and a French grammar. Even in Germany, there are obvious similarities between the constitution of Latin and German literature. One example is Martin Opitz, whose 1624 "Buch von der deutschen Poeterey" (Book of German Poetry) was a milestone in the development of German as a literary language, was also one of the preeminent Latin poets of his time. It is interesting to note that Germany in particular, where public discussion about what constituted a German literary language had continued uninterrupted for almost two hundred years since the late sixteenth century, was also the European country in which arguments about what constituted good Latin were the most heated and varied. A few titles from the seventeenth century should give some sense of the intellectual ferment: *Observationes linguae latinae* (Observations on the Latin Language) by Rudolph Goclenius (1604); *Gazophylacium latinitatis* (Treasure Chest of Latin) by Georg Matthias König (1668); *Apparatus eruditionis* (Principles of Erudition) by Michael Pexenfelder (1670); and finally the widely known *Theatrum romano-teutonicum* (Roman-German Theater) by Andreas Reyher (1668).

The history of Latin gives us numerous instances in which theoretical considerations about Latin and the national literary languages tended to become intertwined, especially when one person focused on both processes. The fact that Bembo's Ciceronianism involved the same aesthetic and philological premises as his program to advance the Italian literary language in accordance with the *tre corone*, the three "classical" poets, Dante, Petrarch, and Boccaccio, is obvious. But the question of the relationship between Latin and the new national languages is much more fundamental. The conventional view is that debate over what constituted the great European national languages was an attempt to use Latin as a model for elevating the as yet unregularized vernaculars and to place them on an equal footing. That is almost assuredly what happened. However, once we recognize just how much debate was focused on Latin itself, a second point of view suggests itself. It would be too simple to say that Latin was the given language, which other languages had only to imitate. The need for a general, supraregional, aesthetically grounded linguistic norm applied to Latin as well. This was a high-level preoccupation for Latin writers during the Renaissance, and, viewed this way, Latin was less the "mother" of the European languages than just another language that needed to be brought up to date.

This perspective is also suggested by another line of reasoning. On closer examination, the search for a "classical" form of Latin, one of the preoccupations of the humanists, was in fact pointless because such a form never existed. A comparison with Greek will make this clearer. The "classical" form of Greek, largely the ideal that has come to be known as Atticism, is based on a series of authors who all lived and wrote in Athens between about 440 and 320 BCE: Plato; Thucydides; Xenophon; Attic orators like Isocrates, Demosthenes, and Lysias; the comic playwright Aristophanes; and finally the dialogue parts in the tragedies of Sophocles and Euripides, written in the Attic language. Only the tragedies of Aeschylus, who died in 456 BCE, fall outside this time frame, although no discernible linguistic differences are to be found. In other words, the standardization of classical, "Attic" Greek had a body of more or less homogeneous models to draw on that were created within a relatively short period of time in a single city. Lyric and epic texts that were not written in Attic Greek but in other dialects were excluded from this canon. So we have some historical justification for saying that the classical Greek taught in schools since antiquity was not a phantom but a real language, the Attic language of the fifth and fourth centuries.

But what is classical Latin? The authors known and read in modern times—from Plautus, who wrote around 200 BCE to Pliny the Younger, in the second century CE—offer us a profusion of different linguistic forms spanning about three hundred years, representing completely different genres written in different registers, and employing a variety of stylistic elements and techniques. Neither then nor now are deep linguistic studies needed to see these differences; all that is needed is an alert reader willing to commit to the texts. The few works of Julius Caesar and Cornelius Nepos that survived did not play much of a role as models either in antiquity or during the Renaissance. Be that as it may, how is one to distill a single standard from this disparate body of texts into something called "normal Latin"?

Should one—and this was an approach taken when teaching grammar during late antiquity—indiscriminately accept words and expressions found only in poets like Virgil and Horace as a model for prose even if they are to be understood poetically? Should Livy or even Tacitus occupy the same exalted ground as Cicero even though their language differed greatly from his? In short, what constitutes "classical" or even "good" Latin is a question that cannot be answered by reference to history.

This question of what is "standard" Latin still gives serious students of Latin a queasy feeling when they do style exercises. In 1999, it led the editors of Hermann Menge's nineteenth-century language textbook, which provided just such exercises, to exclaim in the preface that it is not possible to do more than describe the language usages of individual authors. The fact that such a thing as Ciceronianism developed in Latin but that no Demosthenism or anything similar developed in Greek (only Atticism) was not only a tribute to Cicero but also a way out of a historical dilemma.

The elaboration of a humanist Latin standard was no exercise in philological reconstruction but rather a creative process that continually required evaluative decisions. This underscores the notion that in some respects the reform of Latin was a development parallel to the establishment of the vernaculars as literary languages.

This coevolution of the European languages seems plausible at least to some extent, although simple explanations for complex phenomena are always dangerous and should be avoided. In a very general and nonspecific sense, one could, as Peter Burke has done, describe the elaboration of modern standardized languages, which includes the Latin reform that took place during the Renaissance, as part of an increasingly stringent and comprehensive process of civilization, something that sociologist Norbert Elias believed, in his magnum opus, *The Civilizing Process* (1939), characterized the development of European society. This perspective might well lead to a number of interesting observations.

One of the important reasons for developing clear rules was the rapid increase in literacy during the late Middle Ages, which did not begin with the invention of movable type by Gutenberg in the mid-fifteenth century but considerably earlier. In fact, in an attempt to satisfy the thirst for books, universities in the late Middle Ages developed commercial systems for the reproduction of text. As literacy spread through all areas of life, so did the demands for a supraregional language. Of course, Latin had already functioned as a medium of supraregional communication. However, the fundamental changes in communications since the late Middle Ages increased people's expectations of what a language should actually do. This should not be too difficult to imagine, given the rapid changes in global communications that we are experiencing today, which has made the issue of an international standard for English far more urgent than it was just twenty-five years ago.

Latin and the Formation of Modern Nation-States

These issues raise another point that is of cardinal importance to the history of Latin as a world language. At first glance, Latin would seem to differ from the newer European languages in that it was not the language of a particular people or region. It seems plausible that we would find a distribution of roles with French, Italian, Spanish, German, and other European languages occupying national territories, with Latin, much like English today, serving for international communications. However, the reality is more complex. It is true that Latin was absolutely indispensable in international politics into the seventeenth century, and in science up until about 1800. However, the attempt to model Latin on the spirit of antiquity and the notion advanced by the humanists—that writing and speaking beautiful Latin perfected the person—set up a peculiar interaction with the national consciousness that was emerging in the various European countries.

Italy, where the Renaissance originated, provides an ideal example of how this worked. But Italy's cultural characteristics differed so fundamentally from those in other European countries that a digression is necessary. Italy did not experience to such a great extent the sort of high medieval culture that developed in France and Germany between the eleventh century and the thirteenth. However, the Norman conquest of southern Italy and Sicily after about the second half of the eleventh century, as well as subsequent Hohenstaufen rule, had a significant influence. This may be seen today in the surviving Palatine Chapel in Palermo and in Emperor Frederick II's (1194–1250) Castel del Monte in Apulia. In Sicily, Frederick's rule saw the first Italian school of poetry, which was closely modeled on medieval Provençal poetry. This tradition, however, was short lived. Overall, Romance and Gothic architecture and the medieval literary forms that thrived in France and Germany were very sparse in Italy. Nor was there a Latin literature comparable to that in France or Germany. A new and very different urban cultural dynamic began thriving in northern Italy after the twelfth century in cities like Florence, Venice, Padua, Ferrara, and Urbino. The Renaissance developed out of this urban ferment. Another important influence was the law school in Bologna, which in the twelfth century became Europe's first university. A medieval written culture of greater range and complexity thus developed considerably later in Italy than in the north and became widespread only in the thirteenth century. Nonetheless, the works of Dante (1265–1321) appeared not that many decades after the beginnings of Italian literature, which date to about 1200.

Whereas Latin literature and the culture of the High Middle Ages north of the Alps saw a movement away from antiquity, Italy hewed much more to the ancient models and traditions. Perhaps this was true of the entire Middle Ages. But at least by the thirteenth century, we see evidence of a pre- or protohumanism, whose main proponents included the Paduan scholars Lovato Lovati (ca. 1240–1309) and Albertino Mussato (1261–1329), who engaged with the literature of antiquity, and especially with Latin tragedy, which had generally been neglected during the Middle Ages. Among other things, they produced critical philological examinations of texts. Recent scholarship has demonstrated that these two scholars were not simply isolated precursors but representatives of a broad cultural environment in the Italian thirteenth century, something that had not been recognized earlier because almost no research had been done on the Latin culture of this century.[24]

We should not be especially surprised that the connection with Roman culture was greater in Italy than in other European countries. After all, Rome was Italy's past; the ruins and remains of that past were visible everywhere, and place names and local histories attested to the connection with Roman antiquity. But what was even more important was that well into the early modern era, Italians considered Latin their "own" language. It only gradually became clear, and this much later than in other European countries, that Italian was an entirely new language that differed fundamentally from its Latin forebear.

One of the important documents of this change in the status of Italian as a literary language was Dante's *De vulgari eloquentia* (On Eloquence in the Vernacular). This essay did not differ greatly from others written in Italy up to the end of the fifteenth century in that Latin and Italian were viewed as two variants of the same language. These variants were identified as the *grammatica* (the language of those who had been taught grammar at school) and the *volgare* (the language of the people).[25] No one yet understood the process by which the language of Cicero and modern Italian took on such different forms; in the 1430s, however, the humanist and chancellor of Florence, Leonardo Bruni (ca. 1369–1444), came to believe that even in Cicero's time, *grammatica* was spoken only by the educated classes and that the uneducated people spoke Italian even then. Clearly, the coexistence of Italian and Latin in the fifteenth century was perceived as what we would now term *diglossia*. But after Dante, it was clear that *volgare* was also a written language, and so the term *extended diglossia* is perhaps apt when describing the way in which Italians perceived themselves. This self-perception was unique to Italy; it is not seen in any of the other Romance countries. In medieval France, for example, the language of the people had come to differ so greatly from Latin that it was completely evident that Latin and French were different languages. However, fifteenth-century Spanish and Portuguese did not differ from Latin any more than did Italian. The reasons that the diglossia of late antiquity continued only in Italy were less linguistic than a matter of self-perception.

To better understand the peculiar situation in fourteenth- and fifteenth-century Italy, one would do well to examine neighboring Greece. Until the conquest of Constantinople by the Ottoman army in 1453, an institutional continuity existed with the once-mighty Byzantine Empire. But by 1400, this empire had shrunk more or less to the city of Constantinople and a few residual areas in Greece and was constantly threatened by the ascendant Ottomans. Nonetheless, during the final centuries of its existence, Byzantium was a cultural presence in Europe. Under the last imperial dynasty of the Palaeologos family, that is, the speakers of the "old language" (by which was meant that after the end of rule by Rome, which lasted from 1204 to 1261, Greek once again became the language of the rulers), Byzantine culture flourished again. During this time, ancient culture once more played a major role, and it is today referred to as the Palaeologos Renaissance.[26] As commentators, philologists, and textual critics, Maximos Planudes (ca. 1255–1305), Manuel Moschopulos (ca. 1265–1316), Thomas Magistros (d. after 1346), and Demetrios Triklinios (ca. 1280–1340) all worked on ancient Greek literature, and their work continues to be of some linguistic and historical importance. In the small Peloponnesian city of Mistra, the Platonic philosopher Georgios Gemistos Plethon (ca. 1355–1452) established a program for the political revival of ancient pagan Greece. In addition, Maximos Planudes translated a number of Latin classics into Greek, among them Ovid's *Metamorphoses* and *Heroides,* Cicero's *Somnium Scipionis,* and Boethius's *Consolatio philosophiae.*

The relations between Byzantium and Italy during this period were so strong that the cultural activities discussed earlier were taken note of in the West. Petrarch wanted a Greek codex of Homer, which he was, unfortunately, able to read only haltingly. In Florence in the year 1361, Leontius Pilatus, a student of Barlaam of Seminara in Calabria (southern Italy), offered the first instruction in Greek. Of the first generation of Italian humanists, who date from a few decades after the Palaeologos Renaissance, some had lived in Byzantium for longer periods of time, including Francesco Filelfo (1398–1481), Ambrogio Traversari (1386–1439), Guarino da Verona, and Giovanni Aurispa (1376–1459). The latter brought a collection of more than two hundred manuscripts of Greek classics to Italy in 1423. A number of Greeks also made their way west, including Manuel Chrysoloras (1353–1417) and John Argyropulos (ca. 1415–1487), who taught the language to numerous Italian humanists, and Constantine Lascaris (1434–1501), who wrote the first printed Greek grammar. These contacts were encouraged by the union formed in Ferrara in 1439, which, under pressure from the Ottomans, once again united the Western and Eastern churches. The Greek philosopher Bessarion (1403–1472), a student of Plethon's, arrived in Italy as a result of these contacts between the churches. He stayed there, was elevated to cardinal in the Roman Church, wrote numerous works in Latin, and in 1468 bequeathed his precious collection of Greek manuscripts, among them many outstanding classics, to the Republic of Venice, where they are still housed in the National Library of Saint Mark, opposite the Doge's Palace.

These contacts between the remnants of the Byzantine Empire and Italy meant that the Italian Renaissance and the West rediscovered the Greek language and the classical authors of ancient Greece. It also meant an end to the purely Latin Middle Ages. Nonetheless, the emphasis on studying ancient literature after the thirteenth century also contributed to the revival of ancient Latin literature in Italy.

Even more important for the perception of Latin in Italy was the fact that in Byzantium the ancient diglossia of the Greek language remained almost unchanged into modern times. Ancient Greek, as it was taught in the schools, continued to be used as the written form, while the general population spoke a language that was already similar to the modern Greek spoken today. Italians who went to Byzantium would have noticed that certain works, such as novels, were written in a form of Greek that was close to the vernacular; that is, to some extent an extended diglossia existed in Greece as well. The parallels to the situation in Italy would have been obvious, and we must assume that Italians who had contact with Byzantium would have noted that the pairing of *grammatica* and *volgare* in Italy was analogous to the high form of Greek learned at school and the vernacular Greek of the streets.

The parallels to Greek would have seemed even more obvious if Italian travelers had peered out beyond their immediate geographical horizon. After all, a similar diglossia existed in the Arab world as well, where a grammatically regulated high form of the language existed alongside a number of vernaculars. Among the Arabs, too, were texts that were written in a language that was at the very least influenced by the vernacular—such as the *One Thousand and One Nights*. Dante, with whom theoretical reflection about *grammatica* and *volgare* began, may well have taken note even though it is no longer assumed that he used Arabic sources for his *Divine Comedy*. His teacher, Brunetto Latini, had been in Toledo, which at the time was a center for Arabic culture and a point of contact between the Christian and the Islamic worlds, and he surely reported on the complex linguistic mix that was to be found in this city. In addition, the Turks, with whom the Europeans had the most contact, though it was less than friendly, had a written and an administrative language that was enriched by numerous Arabic and Persian elements but was accessible only to the educated elite and unintelligible to the simple people. Finally, contacts with the Slavs would have turned up a similar constellation: the double existence of a fixed Church Slavonic and numerous living Slavic languages. In other words, the eastern Mediterranean was characterized by historically fixed high forms of the language in tandem with spontaneous languages that continued to develop. This was the context within which discussions about *grammatica* and *volgare* took place.

What is interesting about this constellation—and here we return to the main subject of this chapter—is not so much that people sought to reclaim Latin as a special form of their own language. In everyday practice there was little difference. This definition would not have spared an Italian schoolboy a single Latin class because it did not change the fact that Italian had by this time evolved to such an extent that Italians, too, were forced to learn Latin as a foreign language. However, the appropriation of Latin as a part of their own culture was a sign of a political consciousness and identity that sought continuity with the great traditions of the Roman past. Unlike in other parts of Europe that had also belonged to the Roman Empire, the ancient culture of Rome was not in the least foreign. The lamentable disunity of Italy, which included the papal schism of the fourteenth century, which lasted until 1417, provided fertile ground for just such a consciousness. The lonely attempt of Cola di Rienzi (1313–1354) to reestablish the Roman Republic should be seen in this light. Viewed this way, the reform of Latin during the Italian Renaissance also had a national facet. In Dante's *De vulgari eloquentia,* Latin, that is *grammatica,* was still the neutral and globally unchanged and indispensable conventional language of communication among scholars, whereas *volgare* was the actual mother tongue of Italians. For Petrarch, the rebirth of ancient Rome was a concrete idea. Over and above the personal honor, his crowning as poet laureate in 1341 (mainly for his Latin poetry; his renowned Italian poems had not yet been written) had symbolic value as well in that it recognized the greatness of Rome within the current cultural revitalization. In his *Elegantiae linguae latinae,* one of the most important texts of the humanist Latin reforms, Lorenzo Valla wrote that the Latin language was superior to all other languages in the world and that it had embodied the ancient Roman Empire. He directed a vivid appeal to his contemporaries to reestablish this ancient brilliance:

> Quare pro mea in patriam pietate, imo adeo in omnes homines, et pro rei magnitudine cunctos facundiae studiosos, velut ex superiore loco libet adhortari, evocareque et illis (ut aiunt) bellicum canere: Quosque tandem Quirites (literatos appello), et Romanae linguae cultores, qui et vere, et soli Quirites sunt, caeteri enim potius inquilini) quousque inquam Quirites urbem vestram, non dico domicilium imperii, sed par-

entem literarum a Gallis esse captam patiemini, id est, Latinitatem a
barbaris oppressam?

> Therefore, in my love for the fatherland and for all people and consistent
> with the significance of the matter, I wish to blow the horn to battle for
> all those who value eloquence and issue an urgent exhortation as from
> an elevated position: How much longer, quirites (by which I mean the
> educated) and admirers of the Latin language, who alone are the genu-
> ine quirites (the others are more like renters); how long, quirites, will
> you permit your city, I say not merely the capital of the empire but the
> source of literature and science, to be occupied by the Gauls, which
> means that Latinity will be suppressed by the barbarians?

Valla's appeal was written completely in the spirit of Cicero; not
only did he quote directly the *quousque tandem,* with which Cicero began his famous first Catiline Oration, but he also appropriated the end
of the sentence in which Valla reshapes a thought from *De provinciis
consularibus* (On the Consular Provinces §34). Superficially, the author
speaks specifically to the educated classes and evokes the image of the
conquest of Rome by the Gauls in 387 BCE. However, after Valla invokes
the ancient greatness of Rome, most of his contemporaries, upon hearing mention of the Gauls, might well have been reminded of the superiority of France and the powerlessness of Italy in their own time.

This understanding of Latin as the high form of their own language
and as a surrogate for the lost glories of the empire is also reflected in a
unique peculiarity of Italian literature. Poetry had been written in Italian since the thirteenth century. Dante, Petrarch, and Boccaccio were
bilingual authors, fluent in both Italian and Latin. In some way, Petrarch valued Latin above Italian because he wrote prose exclusively in
Latin. A certain shift in the structure of languages came about as a result of the pedagogical thrust of the humanists around 1400 and the
teachings of Guarino da Verona and Gasparino Barzizza. Though by no
means completely, Italian literature, and especially poetry, went into
decline, especially during the first half of the fifteenth century. The
great Italian humanists of the period after 1400, such as Coluccio Salu-
tati, Leonardo Bruni, Poggio, Lorenzo Valla, Giovanni Antonio Pontano, Francesco Beccadelli ("Panormita"), Enea Silvio Piccolomini
(later Pope Pius II), and Marsilio Ficino, all wrote exclusively in Latin.
In the fourteenth century, translation of literary works (from both
French and ancient Latin) into *volgare* was so widespread that the term

volgarizzamenti became commonplace in the book trade, and unlike the English equivalent, *vulgarization,* the connotations were much more positive. However, this trend declined around 1400, making way for a more wholehearted reception of ancient Latin texts in their original language. After about 1400, Latin gained ground at the expense of Italian and became the prestige language not only among the clergy but among the municipal elites as well.[27] But unlike in France or Germany, where Latin became the language of scholars and scholarship, in Italy it was the cultivated form of the language of the people.

It is against this background that the so-called *questione della lingua* of the early sixteenth century was settled by Bembo, who praised the Florentine writers Dante, Petrarch, and Boccaccio as models for the Italian language. Thereafter, Italian, "our language," as Bembo called it, gained the upper hand, and Italian spread throughout the country and all areas of life, except in the church and the university, where Latin continued to be the medium of exchange. Poetry continued to be written in both languages. In Latin, for example, brilliant works such as Marcus Hieronymus Vida's "Game of Chess" and the Latin poems of Pope Urban VIII, were written after 1500 and read throughout Europe. It would be wrong, however, to assume that Latin was simply displaced; the Latin and the Italian worlds now began to develop increasingly in parallel and independently of one another. The unity that had existed in Italy up to 1500 could not be reestablished.

In the western areas of the Mediterranean, developments were completely different from those in Italy.[28] In the ascendant centralized powers of France, Spain, and England (as well as in Portugal prior to the Portuguese succession crisis of 1580), the vernacular had been promoted much earlier by the rulers of those countries and placed in the service of governance. In the thirteenth century, French and Spanish became the official languages of documents, thereby displacing Latin in important administrative functions. The common written language of politically united regions became, so to speak, the regional form of the language of each of the power centers (Paris; Madrid, along with Castile; London). Moreover, this form of the language was elaborated into the literary language and was made compulsory as a written language for the general population, which tended to speak differently. In 1539, French became the official language of the court throughout France, and between 1536 and 1543, English Chancery Standard became the official language throughout England, including Wales, with Scotland following suit in 1603. In effect, while diglossia, the pattern in late antiquity, continued in Italy into the fourteenth and fifteenth centuries, the western kingdoms were by the sixteenth century well on their way toward establishing their vernaculars as national languages, with Latin continuing as the language of science and the church.

We might be tempted to assume that Latin was used in international communications, whereas national identities were forged by each particular national language. In a pragmatic sense this is, of course, correct. In the sixteenth century, Latin was still the language of choice for negotiating and settling matters throughout Europe. Only later did it begin to give way to French for these purposes. However, we find that the humanist movement in Europe was surprisingly national. This becomes clear when we examine the history of neo-Latin literature. This term does not describe the sum of all Latin texts but mainly fictional works—poetry, theater, and novels (in other words, those texts that today are found in "literary histories").[29] Specialized and scientific texts in Latin are often included to the extent to which they have literary merit, such as Erasmus of Rotterdam's *Enchiridion militis christiani* (Handbook of a Christian Knight) or his *Ciceronianus*. That a far larger proportion of texts in Latin was not literary—documents, legal and theological texts, and prose texts of all sorts—does not alter this fact. At the outset, we identified neo-Latin literature as the least known body of European literature. Even so, this body of literature contains numerous works whose authors are still famous. It began in fourteenth-century Italy with the Latin works of Petrarch and Boccaccio and continued in the fifteenth century with the works of humanists like Lorenzo Valla, Francesco Filelfo, Antonio Beccadelli, Giovanni Pontano, and many others. In Germany, neo-Latin literature in the narrower sense began with the "archhumanist" Konrad Celtis (1459–1508). Then followed a series of great Latin poets toward the end of the sixteenth century, among them Paul Schede (Melissus, 1539–1602), Petrus Lotichius Secundus (1528–1560), and the dramatist Nicodemus Frischlin (1547–1590). The shining light of the seventeenth century was the Jesuit Jacobus Balde (1604–1668). In Holland, Janus Secundus (1511–1536), whose *Liber basiorum* (Book of Kisses) was read and appreciated by Goethe, the English statesman and humanist Thomas More (1478–1535), and of course Erasmus wrote in Latin and they all had an international following.

From the perspective of today, neo-Latin literature in its totality seems to be a single, undifferentiated mass primarily because it has been so neglected, a literary tradition based on Latin as a world language that, for the last time, united Europe. But this is precisely where we need to distinguish more closely. Because if we look at the history of neo-Latin literature in relation to the development of the modern European national literary languages, it becomes clear that the development of humanist Latin literature cannot be separated from the first steps leading to the elaboration of national cultures. It is clear that neo-Latin literature flourished in all countries and coincided with the first blossoming of the various vernacular literatures both in terms of content and in many cases authors. For this reason, the neo-Latin literature of the Renaissance cannot in most cases be separated from its national context. What we saw in the previous chapter, namely that Latin and vernacular literatures flourished at the same time during the Middle Ages is here repeated in the context of individual European countries.

In Spain, neo-Latin literature, which arose during the second half of the sixteenth century, tended to exist in the shadow of Spanish. The most important Spanish proponent of Latin humanism, Juan Luis Vives (1492–1540), preceded the first blossoming of Spanish literature, but he is no real exception because he worked not in Spain but in France and England. Portugal, too, gave rise to very little Latin literature during the fifteenth century, and only in the sixteenth century did Latin and Portuguese literature develop in tandem.

Works of poetry were written in France during the second half of the fourteenth century, that is, during the time of Petrarch. However, after 1400, when Latin was on the upswing in Italy, poetry in France (where it existed at all) was produced primarily in French. Only in the sixteenth century, beginning with Salmonius Macrin (1490–1557), was there a first blossoming of neo-Latin poetry. Interestingly, this was more or less the time when Bellay wrote his *Deffence et illustration de la langue françoyse*, which, as was stated earlier, championed French as a literary language. Bellay was influenced by humanism, as were François Rabelais (ca. 1494–1553) and Clément Marot (ca. 1496–1544). Even Guillaume Budé (1468–1540), the greatest of the French humanists, wrote exclusively in Latin at this time. Humanism and the French language did not exist in opposition to each other but walked hand in hand. Moreover, as in Spain and Portugal, the development of a national literature in France that was heavily influenced by humanist thinking did not in any way spell the end of Latin literature. Large-scale and important works of Latin poetry were written well into the seventeenth and eighteenth centuries, including European classics such as René Rapin's *Hortorum libri* (Books of Gardens) (1665) and Cardinal Melchior de Polignac's *Anti-Lucretius* (1747).

In England, modern English established itself as the literary language in the sixteenth century—while Latin humanist literature was flourishing. The great dramas of English Renaissance theater were written at the same time as dramas in Latin. Other "classical" neo-Latin authors in England, such as Welshman John Owen (1564–1628) and Scotsman George Buchanan (1506–1582), wrote during this time, as did John Barclay (1582–1621).

In all of the countries discussed here, Latin and the vernaculars shared a common family history; the development of neo-Latin literature parallels that of vernacular poetry, which was written in the spirit of humanism.

Let us now turn to Germany. As we know, the process that resulted in a standard form of the vernacular throughout Germany was much slower and more halting than that in France, Italy, and England. No central political power was capable of decreeing that one particular form of a language would henceforth be the standard for administrative or literary purposes. Nor did the sixteenth century witness a cultural process comparable to the Italian *questione della lingua* that might have led in any programmatic sense to the elaboration of a common German literary language. There had, of course, been chancery standards, and Kaiser Maximilian I (1508–1519), among others, attempted to promote a uniform German orthography. In addition, Luther's translation of the Bible contributed considerably to regularizing the language. However, not until the first language societies of the seventeenth century, such as the "Fruitbearing Society," and the wide-ranging discussions about language during the eighteenth do we begin to see a process that would eventually lead to a uniform high form of German. In any case, this process had come to an end by the time Germany was united politically in 1871. In essence, the development of German was comparable to that of Italian—though two hundred years later.

Given this history, it should be obvious why Latin continued to be an important medium of exchange within Germany longer than it was in other countries. Although the differences between countries were not great in terms of the universities, where Latin remained the language of choice throughout Europe into the eighteenth century, the Reformation had introduced the vernacular into the liturgy in the Protestant parts of Germany, and here Germany led the way in replacing Latin. Overall, however, until the eighteenth century, the percentage of writings in Latin remained higher in Germany than in any other European country. Germans tended to use Latin even where it was not directly required by social convention.

This is evident, for example, in the great treatises on the modern state. Machiavelli wrote his *Dicorsi* (Discourses) and his most important work, *Il principe* (The Prince) at the beginning of the sixteenth century in Italian. Jean Bodin wrote his epochal treatise on the state, *Les six livres de la république,* in 1576 in French, although he authorized a Latin edition a few years later. Thomas Hobbes (1588–1672) wrote *The Elements of Law, Natural and Politic* in 1640 and *Leviathan* in 1651, while John Locke (1632–1704) published his *Two Treatises of Government* in 1689—all written in English. In Germany, these works were known and read only in Latin translation well into the eighteenth century, and German state and legal theoreticians like Hermann Conring (1606–1681) and Samuel Pufendorf (1632–1694) wrote exclusively in Latin. Interestingly, the treatise *De jure belli ac pacis* (On the Law of War and Peace) by the Dutch jurist Hugo Grotius (1583–1645), which is still cited in the development of modern international law, was published in Latin in 1625 and was translated into Dutch in 1626, into English in 1654, and into French in 1687–1688. A German-language edition was not published until 1707. One reason for this lag may have been that, in Germany, rulers preferred to leave potentially explosive material in Latin, where it would be less apt to incite the population. But the main reason was undoubtedly that for a long time German intellectuals simply viewed Latin as their natural and appropriate language.

This was not, however, only because no other language was available to them. Next to Italy, Germany was probably the country in which the acquisition of Latin humanist culture was most strongly propelled by a national consciousness.[30] Many factors that did not exist in other European countries may have been at work here. For one thing, the German humanists of the fifteenth century were in direct competition with the culture of Italy. Germany had for years been denigrated as a nation of uneducated barbarians, and Germans were at pains to prove that this was not only unjustified but also that they were a superior cultural force. The other factor was that ever since Charlemagne, Germany had seen itself as the continuation of the Roman Empire. The Holy Roman Empire of the German Nation, which was the name given to the political construct that existed from 1474 to 1806, transferred power from Italy to Germany, and with that transfer it conferred an imperial claim and a claim to Latin as Germany's proper and globally valid language.

Both of these factors are evident in the works of Konrad Celtis. When Kaiser Friedrich III crowned him poet laureate in 1486 in the Reichstag in Nuremberg, it was the first time that a German had received this honor. The ceremony was seen as symbolically re-creating the crowning of Petrarch in 1340 in the Roman capitol, and in this sense it revived in idealized form the ancient empire. With his *Four Books of "Odes,"* Celtis became the first German poet after Metellus of Tegernsee, in the eleventh century, to claim to be a successor to Horace, something that only Italian neo-Latin poets had presumed to do previously. His second lyric work, *Four Books of Love Poems,* rather esoteric poems despite their title, are a sort of erotic ramble through Germany. Celtis also planned an ambitious project titled *Germania illustrata,* an answer of sorts to the Italian humanist Flavio Biondo's (1392–1463) *Italia illustrata,* which was published posthumously in 1474. Early German humanism had a pronounced national component, as was evident from the reception in the fifteenth century of Tacitus's newly rediscovered *Germania,* which was touted as the early history of Germany. The German humanists, in particular the first generation around 1500, promoted the use of the vernacular, translated large quantities of ancient literature, and began thinking seriously about the value of the German language. Nonetheless, no real German literature developed at this time. Latin humanists like Celtis, Johannes Reuchlin, Willibald Pirckheimer, Sebastian Brant, Konrad Peutinger, Jacob Wimpheling, Heinrich Bebel, and finally Philipp Melanchthon set the tone as proponents of Latin humanist culture in Germany, and few if any German authors were pulling in a different direction. Among the German poets, the only one of note was Sebastian Brant, with his renowned satire, *Das Narrenschiff* (The Ship of Fools). Overall, one may say that in Germany the humanist reform of Latin served to some extent as a stand-in for the nonexistent debate over a national language, especially from the end of the fifteenth century to the second half of the sixteenth.

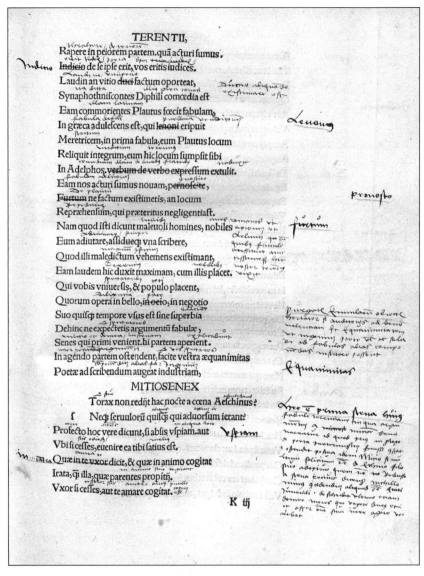

Figure 15. Terence, Comedies, Leipzig 1512 (Copy: Munich, Bayerische Staats-bibliothek 2 A.lat.b.141/1). This printed page has an especially wide margin and leading so that students could make notes. They did this either by taking dictation from their teachers or by copying other similarly annotated pages. As in Figure 7, eleven hundred years earlier, this page shows the beginning of the first scene of the comedy *Adelphoe*. As in late antiquity, people read Terence primarily to learn conversational Latin.

VIVENTIS·POTVIT·DVRERIVS·ORA·PHILIPPI
MENTEM·NON·POTVIT·PINGERE·DOCTA
MANVS

Figure 16. Philipp Melanchthon (1497–1560), engraving by Albrecht Dürer, 1526. Melanchthon was very important in the development of Protestant schools in Germany; he was later given the nickname "praeceptor Germaniae" (Germany's teacher). Melanchthon wrote numerous textbooks and rulebooks. Many of his students eventually taught at schools and universities and elaborated on the approaches that he initiated for creating an educational system. akg-images

Figure 17. Philipp Melanchthon, *Grammatica latina,* Leipzig 1672. Melanchthon's Latin grammar, which was first published in 1526, became the most important Latin textbook throughout the Protestant regions of Germany. Revised many times, more than 250 editions were printed into the eighteenth century. This particular edition, from 1672, is printed in only one language and contains not a single German word. This indicates the extent to which Latin classes were organized around Latin as a living language. Nonetheless, the seventeenth- or eighteenth-century student whose book this was wrote German translations next to the verb stems. With permission of the author.

Latin continued to be the most important language in Germany during the second half of the sixteenth century, all the more so because first the Protestant academies and then the Jesuit colleges succeeded in organizing and regularizing instruction in Latin on a hitherto unimaginable scale. The second half of the sixteenth century was a time when more than a few Germans viewed Latin as their mother tongue. This makes it even more regrettable that historians of German literature have so neglected the Latin literature that was written during the second half of the sixteenth century by authors like Jacobus Micyllus (1503–1558), Georg Fabricius (1516–1571), and Paulus Melissus (1539–1602). Only recently have they been accepted as part of German literary history. Only in the seventeenth century did German and Latin literature begin to develop in parallel, with the emphasis still on Latin. Martin Opitz (1597–1639) and Jacobus Balde (1604–1668) both wrote poetry in German and Latin, placing them in approximately the same position as Petrarch in Italy and the poets of the Pleiáde in France before them. The fact that Opitz has been celebrated as the founder of the "deutsche Poeterey," whereas the first critical edition of his Latin poetry was published only recently (i.e., in the twenty-first century) and that Balde, quite possibly the greatest poetic genius of seventeenth-century Germany, remained unknown because he wrote primarily in Latin is a clear sign that the reception and appreciation of Germany's own past has been distorted, primarily by the nationalism of literary historians in the nineteenth century.

Even the limited and selected details of the humanist Latin reforms in Italy, Spain, France, and Germany discussed here make one thing clear: there was little notion of Latin as a world language. In the fifteenth and sixteenth centuries Latin was the undisputed and exclusive language of the church (in Germany up to the Reformation), theology, including Protestant theology, and the sciences. It was also the language of international trade. However, all theoretical considerations of what constituted good Latin and all the efforts to produce a humanist Latin literature, that is, the conscious cultivation of a Latin "culture," took place primarily at the national level. Taking a closer look at the spread and reception of the writings of the Latin humanists in the individual countries, both the treatises on Latin usage and neo-Latin literature in a narrower sense, we quickly discern that, although the Italian humanism of the fifteenth century had a great effect on subsequent

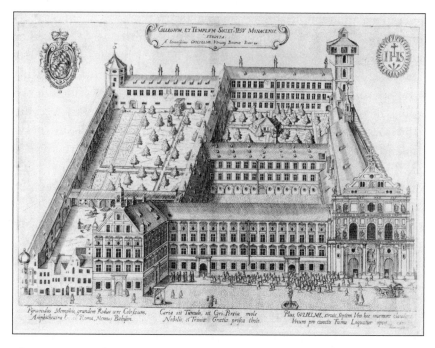

Figure 18. Munich, Jesuit College. The Jesuit schools developed in the mid-sixteenth century as a Catholic counterpart to the Protestant academies. With an ambitious teaching program whose humanist tendencies differed very little from those in the Protestant schools, they remained the most important transmitters of Latin education in the Catholic regions well into the eighteenth century. They especially emphasized the active mastering of Latin; among other things, they regularly staged Latin plays, which were generally written by the teachers and often portrayed current or historical events. Here, more than anywhere else, the goal was essentially to master Latin as one's mother tongue.

The Jesuit College in Munich, founded in 1559, was one of the most important in Germany. Magnificent new buildings were constructed between 1583 and 1597, among them St. Michael's Church, the most important Renaissance church still in existence in Germany. akg-images

humanist efforts in the other European countries, the points of contact among these other countries were rather more coincidental. The humanists tended to stay at home, and as a result very few scholars traveled or worked internationally even though they communicated by means of a language understood throughout Europe. The fraternity of those who traveled was vanishingly small and included the Spanish humanist Juan Luis Vives and above all Erasmus of Rotterdam, in many ways the quintessential European, who, though born in the Netherlands, worked freely in England, France, Italy, and Germany as if no borders existed. But almost all of the humanists mentioned in the last two chapters spent most of their lives in their countries of origin.

Still, none of this should be especially surprising. It has been replicated in the case of English. The global use of the language is not the same as a global culture. The relationship between language, literature, and regionality is the same for English as we have described for Latin. In every country in which English functions as a second language, the literature that is written in English tends to reflect that particular country. The Anglophone cultures outside of the primary English-speaking countries of Europe and North America, in particular those of India, New Zealand, and Africa, tend to focus on the culture of their own country. Of course, cultural exchange between English-speaking countries is facilitated because there are few language barriers, and individual works of literature achieve an international status that crosses all borders. This was precisely how the Latin linguistic community of Europe functioned in the early modern era. Seen as a whole, the unity of Europe under the umbrella of the Latin language and culture was not "antinational"; in fact, differentiation into nations took place not only in the vernacular but in Latin as well, or at least in Latin literature.

Let us now turn, finally, to the other European countries, including the Scandinavian and eastern European countries and the Netherlands. Here, too, we find that the periods in which vernacular culture gained momentum were precisely those during which Latin culture flourished. In Poland, this was epitomized by the Renaissance figure Jan Kochanowski (1530–1584), who wrote verse both in the local vernacular and in Latin—much like Petrarch in Italy, Bellay in France, and Opitz in Germany.

Nonetheless, the situation in these countries was a little different. Over time, the large language communities were able to develop

Feria 2ª. Sacru & concio more solito. sicut & Vespæ.

Feria 3ª. Sacru hora 7ª. Sodales aut ad Cœmeteriu egressi, q̃
5.º vel 6.º anno recurrit.

Junius.

In Vigilia SS. Trinitatis ab hora usq̃ ad 4.ᵃᵐ Schola

In Vigilia Corporis Christi à 1ª usq̃ ad 2ᵃᵐ Scholæ fuerunt. q̃a pridie
fuit p̃missa recreatio. alioq̃ nullæ afuere Scholæ.

Ipso festo mane hora 5ª lectum sacru in Aula. Vespæ hora 2ª.

Dñica infra Octauam Vespæ de more hora 5ª habitæ. ꝓ Suppli=
cationem Augustinianoꝝ.

In Octaua Corporis Christi sacrū hora 7ª in Aula lectum.
nullæ scholæ toto die.

Julius.

In Vigilia S. Joan. Baptistæ scholæ à 2ª usq̃ ad 4ᵃᵐ habitæ.

In Vigilia Aptoꝝ Petri & Pauli à prandio una hora scholæ.

In Vigilia dedicõis Templi S. Michaelis, à p̃ndio p hora~.

Ipso die nihil in Aula p̃ter Sacru hora 7ª lectu.

Ante Caniculares oẽs discipuli confessi.

In Vigilia S. Margaritæ hora 3ª dimissi discipuli ex Scholis.
Maior ipsis hoc anno potestas facta. nullo p̃scripto termino redit̃.
modo ad diem S. Laurenti adessent. Quod tamen plurimi non
fecerūt, maxᵉ nobiliores: causati ferè defectum equoꝝ, q̃ messem.

Deambulões in plateis post 1ᵐ signum ad Aulam dat̃, denuo
p̃hibitæ. aliqui ꝓ hoc noĩe puniti.

Figure 19. Munich, Bayerische Staatsbibliothek Cod. lat. 1550, fol. 70, *Diarium* of the Munich Jesuit College, 1595–1648. Even the daybook *(diarium)* of the Jesuit College was kept exclusively in Latin. This particular page contains a report on summer vacations in 1609:

> Ante caniculares omnes discipuli confessi.
> In Vigilia S. Margaritae hora 3.a dimissi discipuli ex scholis.
> Maior ipsis hoc anno potestats facta. Nullus praescriptus terminus reditus.
> Modo ad diem S. Laurentii adessent. Quod tamen plurimi non fecerunt, maxime nobiliores: causati fere defectum equorum, propter messem.

All of the students were exhausted by the dog days. On St. Margaret's Day (July 13) the students were dismissed from school after the third hour. This year they were given greater freedom; no date was set for their return; they were merely to be back by St. Lawrence's Day (August 10). Most of them were not, especially those from better families, and the reason they gave was that because of the harvest there were too few horses.

vernacular cultures that were more or less self-sufficient politically and culturally, which began to limit the need for Latin within the country. By contrast, small or marginal language communities had a much greater need to maintain and cultivate a language that allowed them access to their neighbors. For them, Latin remained important even after their national language developed. Bilingualism or multilingualism continue to be more common in countries like Finland, the Netherlands, and Sweden than in large, relatively homogeneous language communities. Generally speaking, large language communities, like those where English or French are spoken, tend to cling to their language.

In the case of Latin, its peculiar status as a "second language without a people" meant that one could not simply identify with a Latin culture but had to create it. This is at least part of the reason that the smaller European language communities not only became Latin speakers during the late modern era but also became important proponents of humanist culture.

As a case in point, in the late sixteenth and seventeenth centuries the Netherlands developed a Latin culture that spread throughout Europe. Works by the poets Johannes Secundus (1511–1536) and Cornelius Schonaeus (1541–1611), philologists Daniel Heinsius (1580–1655) and his son Nicolaus Heinsius (1620–1681), and philosophers and state theorists like Justus Lipsius (1547–1606) and Hugo Grotius, whose *De jure belli ac pacis* became one of the foundations of modern international law, were renowned throughout Europe. Of course, the economic prosperity and political successes of the Netherlands in the seventeenth century contributed to this culture, but this upswing occurred at precisely the time when the country was struggling to establish a standard for Dutch. However, if we examine the Latin culture of the Netherlands in relation to its own vernacular culture and to the Latin culture of other countries, the weighting is distributed differently. Latin was more important within the Netherlands itself than was the vernacular, and to a greater extent than elsewhere the works of the Dutch Latin culture were from the very beginning aimed at readers beyond its borders.

Latin was just as important to the Scandinavian countries as a bridge to the rest of Europe. In fact, the Latin tradition was especially significant in eastern Europe. In Poland and Hungary, for example, Latin was used as a politically neutral administrative language well into the nineteenth century and was the language of the social elites, who possessed a certain national consciousness into the eighteenth century. And knowledge of Latin continued to be more common there after World War II than in the rest of Europe.

Latin and the Elaboration of an Oral Standard

Collections of dialogues, which, for students, served as models of conversational Latin, were among the more interesting innovations of Renaissance pedagogy.[31] The best known of such works was Erasmus's *Colloquia familiaria* (Conversations among Familiars), or *Colloquies*, which for many years was part of the European literary canon. Among the dialogues we find a remarkable conversation between two wives. The newly married Xanthippe meets her friend Eulalia, who has been married for some time. They gossip about things like clothing, which provides an excuse to introduce some specialized Latin vocabulary from the textile industry. But soon the conversation turns to a description of Xanthippe's marital woes. Her husband, who had apparently been penniless before he got hold of her dowry, treats her badly at home. In addition, he is a shiftless good-for-nothing who consorts with other women. Things get unpleasant when he comes home drunk at night. After a brief discussion about the possibility of divorce (this may have been one of the reasons the Catholic Church placed the *Colloquies* on the Index of Prohibited Books), Eulalia describes her considerably more harmonious married life. Her marriage had known some turbulent times at the beginning as well, but the gentle Eulalia gave her husband no cause for irritation and—so it seemed at first—ensured the peace by her submissiveness. In fact, and this was the actual point of the exercise, Eulalia was giving her friend a model—the reverse of Shakespeare's *Taming of the Shrew*—by which women, with the means available to them, could get men to act less boorishly. The liveliness and light touch of the Latin dialogue are unsurpassed. The often snappy exchanges give us the flavor of the characters. Not only do the women know their way around fabrics and other commodities of the day, but they are sharp witted as well.

Whatever one thinks of the advice being dispensed, one has to admire Erasmus's way with words. However, one question remains: for what actual conversational encounter was it preparing students? The fact that two women were conversing is less than remarkable. Although higher education was not customary for women, it would never have occurred to anyone that a woman could not master Latin. Olympia Morata

(1526–1555), for example, was a Latin author of considerable attainment. What was far more exciting was that this was a chance conversation that emphasized the everyday and consciously avoided content having anything to do with academic Latin. Conversations like this had not existed in Latin literature for fifteen hundred years. The topics that Erasmus dealt with hearkened back to the comedies of Plautus and Terence and to Cicero's private letters.

Such texts once again gave Latin literature a sense of conversational intimacy, something that had disappeared from Latin once it began to be fixed in the first century CE. We also see this in the letters that Erasmus and other authors wrote, which no longer reflected rigid stylistic codes but give the reader a sense of an ongoing conversation. The same holds true of the Latin dramas of the Renaissance, in which (at least among the masters of the genre, especially the early Jesuit dramatists) the wordplay seems to have been lifted from everyday experience.

And here we get closer to the nub of the problem. Throughout late antiquity and the Middle Ages, Latin could undoubtedly be used among friends and family members to discuss everything from marital problems to what to wear and even much more banal matters of daily life. What was lacking was guidance and a generally accepted standard, and there was no literary genre in which such situations were set down in writing. There were rules about how to talk about God, Roman law, medical treatments, astronomy, and world history. There were rules about how to write an official letter, sermon, or speech. But when it came to everyday oral communication in and out of schools and universities, private letters not meant for third parties, or private conversations—all of the most important areas of private life—there were no rules and people could do as they liked.

In practice, we may assume that local and regional conventions were invented even though documentation is scarce. There were undoubtedly "secondary evolutions" of greater or lesser importance that would have been similar to the processes that take place in modern Latin circles. Where the words were lacking because they were not taught at school, people simply improvised. Words for going to the toilet were undoubtedly quite different in Leipzig (to the extent that toilets even existed) than in Paris. In any case, this was not something one wrote about, and people had to figure it out for themselves. In a more modern context, imagine an American banker having dinner with the

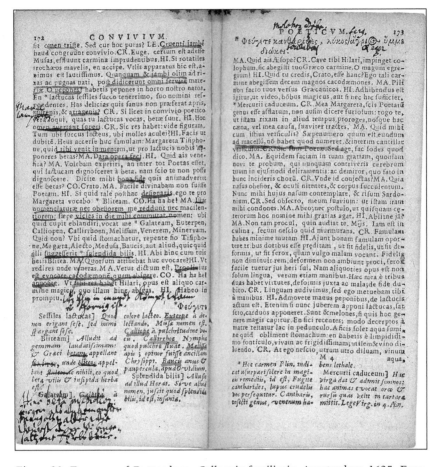

Figure 20. Erasmus of Rotterdam, *Colloquia familiaria*. Amsterdam 1635. Erasmus's (1466/1467–1536) collection of dialogues continued to be a standard work for teaching conversational Latin a hundred years after his death. The edition shown here (11×6 cm with 1.2 mm script) could be carried in one's pocket, providing instruction in proper conversation at any time. With permission from the author.

banker's Korean counterpart, whose command of English mainly encompasses finance. How do they talk to each other in private? They improvise.

We must assume a broad spectrum of possibilities and solutions for all of the everyday matters that were not covered in literary texts or in textbooks. The caricature of medieval Latin in the early sixteenth-century "Letters of Obscure Men" must not be taken as a true picture of the Latin of the day. Surely there was everyday conversation with which the humanists would not have found fault. We just do not know about it, and that is the issue. The significance of the collections of dialogues described earlier was that they provided models that simply had not existed before. Works of this sort began to appear only toward the end of the fifteenth century; in the Middle Ages, theoretical interest in the Latinity of everyday life is at best to be found in the few documents and remnants of exercise books that have come down to us by happenstance. Moreover, most of these come from the earlier Middle Ages.[32] In the late sixteenth and the seventeenth century, the new dialogue books were widely used in Latin class. In addition to Erasmus's *Colloquia familiaria*, the *Colloquia* of the French humanist Mathurin Cordier (1479–1564) and the *Progymnasmata Latinitatis* by the Jesuit teacher Jacobus Pontanus (1542–1626), also known as Jakob Spannmüller, remained standard works into the seventeenth and eighteenth centuries.

However, we can also see from other pedagogical practices how highly prized was the ability to communicate spontaneously in Latin. For example, school rules during the sixteenth century often stipulated that only Latin could be spoken during breaks. We have also found instances where parents, writing to their sons in boarding schools, wrote in Latin for the purpose of providing good practice.[33] The Latin school theaters, which the Protestants started in their Latin schools and which the Jesuits then turned into a model for all of Europe, were in essence language exercises. Most of the plays were freshly written for the purpose, not literary classics, and in addition to their moral and theological content, they gave the players a chance to practice their skills with a vocabulary spanning the most eloquent concepts of high tragedy and the most hackneyed usages from life on the street. Probably the most famous of the Jesuit dramas, Jakob Bidermann's *Cenodoxus*, exhibits the entire bandwidth of Latin communication styles to perfection. The piece begins with a comic bit of slapstick at the door of a great professor, who is in fact a charlatan and a fool, and it ends on a serious note with his eternal damnation. In short, Latin was taught as if it were a completely normal language and students were preparing to meet real Romans (of course, only classical Romans from Cicero's time), with whom they were expected to discuss the weather without an accent before coming to the business at hand. In the higher schools, not only was Latin taught, but the students' entire schooling was one long language exercise.

Again, what was new was not that Latin was used on a daily basis but that so much effort was expended on teaching everyday conversation to an established standard. To understand the humanist dimension of this practice, we need to turn our attention to antiquity. One of the interesting features of classical Greek and Roman literature is that it portrayed the entire breadth of conversation from elevated emotion to specialized technical language to banalities and witty repartee. It would (and I say this knowing that, given the number of historical culture languages, it is impossible for an individual to have a complete overview) be difficult to find other examples in the premodern era in which spontaneous expressions of everyday communication and loose, unforced conversation were reflected in writing as they were in the Greek comedies of Aristophanes, the Latin comedies of Plautus and Terence, and in Horace's satires, Plato's dialogues, and quite a few of Cicero's letters. It is as if the language of these texts were a tape recording of actual conversations—which does not mean that they lacked literary merit.

The liveliness of these texts was not the result of the constant use of well-worn expressions or colloquialisms (not to mention vulgarities) but of consistently selecting the right word tailored to each particular situation. This, as Jan Assmann has noted, is what distinguished Greco-Roman written culture from all other high cultures of antiquity.[34] In those cultures, writing was used primarily for administrative and religious purposes, and whatever literature was created was highly stylized. What the Greeks and their successors, the Romans, did was to allow a much freer and individual use of writing. By doing so, they paved the way for the depiction of conversational encounters. This was especially true of Athenian literature of the fifth and fourth centuries, Latin literature of the first century BCE, and particularly the somewhat older comedic authors Plautus and Terence—in other words, the group of classical authors who had such an immense influence on both languages. The classical epochs of Greek and Latin literature may be defined by their ability to transform the natural spoken conventions of their societies into literature.

In the early modern era, this peculiarity of the classical Latin literary canon made it possible to think about aligning everyday Latin conversation with ancient standards. The fact that this method of learning Latin was accorded such priority shows just how fundamentally it differed from modern Latin instruction, where training in grammar is the primary desideratum. Latin has come to epitomize a language of hard work, analysis, and logic. The humanists, by contrast, did everything they could to make Latin a living language learned primarily by hearing and speaking, like any other mother tongue. In their emphasis on using the language in life situations, the humanists came remarkably close to the practices used to teach foreign languages in the twentieth century: to the extent possible, learning a foreign language should replicate the way children learn their mother tongue in the first place. The notion that instruction in Latin should proceed along logical and analytical lines developed, as we discuss more thoroughly later, in the nineteenth century under the influence of new pedagogical approaches.

In addition, the focus on orality tied to a cultivated language norm further connects Latin with the development of other European languages. If we look at the evolution of the modern national languages from the sixteenth to the twentieth century, we see a very similar process unfolding in every country. They were initially written languages used for particular purposes, which, however, did not lay claim to being the language of the people, the majority of whom had to learn the literary forms of their language at school.[35] This was true in France, England, and Spain, where in each instance the national language emerged from the "normal" language of a particular region and then expanded its range as a result of having been adopted by the royal court. Eventually, the language became binding by governmental decree; in Italy and Germany, which had no central governmental authority, the elaboration of a language norm was, so to speak, outsourced to writers and intellectuals. The spread of such an elevated form of the language was a complex process in which the conversational practices of the court were key. Only after schooling became compulsory did the national languages spread slowly to the entire population.

In 1789, the French revolutionaries realized, to their chagrin, that only a tiny minority of their compatriots spoke French. Over the next several decades, they introduced educational policies that made French the official language and radically suppressed all competitors. A similar process took place in Germany, where between the late eighteenth and the nineteenth century, the German written language became the acknowledged language of the entire people, who had become literate as a result of compulsory education. In Italy, this process was not completed until the twentieth century.

The modern national languages not only developed horizontally, in the sense that a particular language was mandated within a defined territory, but vertically as well. By being inculcated in the schools, these languages, which were originally spoken by only a small portion of the entire population, now extended their range to all classes of society and for all manner of communication. The original "written language" then became a "high language" and finally the "language of the people." The fact that a man from Hamburg, in the north of Germany, can get together for lunch with a woman from Munich, in the south, and discuss any subject under the sun from the sciences to politics to personal issues to sports or art in a single German language is not the result of a natural process of linguistic evolution. If things had been left to nature, these persons would speak the dialect of their region or town, and in the case of Hamburg and Munich these dialects would for all intents and purposes be mutually unintelligible. A French man and an Italian woman would not face greater difficulties making themselves understood.

Germans understand each other because of a lengthy and systematically implemented educational process that began with their great-great-grandparents, who were made to go to school in the nineteenth century, and continues with the essays and other language exercises that are part and parcel of the school curriculum today. In addition, of course, in the past half century, radio and television have also tended to homogenize the language. A hundred and seventy years ago only very well-educated Germans from such vastly different regions would have been able to make themselves mutually understandable; 250 years ago, when social etiquette demanded perfected and stylized conversation, French would probably have been the language of choice—and 400 years ago, Latin. The production of linguistic uniformity was one of the crowning achievements of eighteenth- and nineteenth-century pedagogy in the service of nation building. Only after the process had run its course was it possible to say that German, English, or Italian were the "mother tongues" in their respective countries.

Let us return now to Latin. In hindsight, we see that the instruction in Latin that took place during the Renaissance was part of a common European development: each nation was to have its own language for literature and for spoken communications. But Latin was the first language with which this happened. Latin always possessed everything that might allow a language to evolve into the sole common language within a large territory. There was a community of Latin speakers who recruited from among the more educated. Its members were 100 percent literate and 100 percent school educated. Their education consisted not only in the acquisition of elementary reading and writing skills but also in learning how to express themselves in writing and in speech and to appreciate literary skills in others. Latin had everything needed to become a language of an entire society. Furthermore, because people educated in Latin were generally more socially mobile than the rest of the population and because communications in Latin crisscrossed Europe, these speakers realized that they possessed a supraregional language norm that went well beyond the limitations of mere technical vocabulary. They anticipated the process that would later be consummated in the eighteenth and nineteenth centuries by other languages. In this sense, Latin was the first modern European language.

In this context, we return to the question of the genesis of the new Latin written standard and of the written standards of the European national languages. Was Latin the model from which the other languages emerged? Or was it the other way around, that the formation of the modern nation-state, improved communications, and the increasing literacy of the population required greater complexity in all areas? Are the creation of language standards and the goal of a common language and educational system modern ideas? Or were they anticipated by Latin humanism, which looked upon the creation of a common language as an educational goal? Did the use of Latin as an elite culture language cement social differences, or did this Latin culture in fact contain elements that would allow class boundaries to be overcome because Latin was not a right acquired by birth (i.e., it simply distinguished between educated and uneducated people)?

I ask these questions in this context to show that the Latin contribution to the cultural history of modern Europe must be given much more thought than it has previously been given. Latin culture must be viewed as a dynamic one; it was not simply the continuance of an old scholarly tradition; rather, it was crucial to the major changes that occurred in Europe. The Latin conversational culture of the Renaissance that is discussed in this chapter was not a natural part of the Latin tradition. As I have outlined, it emerged from a very particular set of circumstances, and the following chapters will show that it then went into decline. Latin education that was aimed at making it the mother tongue of the people was not a timeless ideal; it was tied to very specific cultural conditions. I began this discussion with Erasmus's *Colloquia familiaria* and then considered the role of the Protestant and Catholic Latin schools in the sixteenth and seventeenth centuries. During the period thereafter the further development of the various national literary languages took Latin in a different direction.

Perfect Latin or Real-World Communications?

Although we have up to now stressed that Latin developed in parallel with the vernacular languages during the early modern era, an important difference nonetheless existed. Whereas the vernaculars actually succeeded in becoming national languages in the various language regions of Europe by the twentieth century as a result of a sophisticated school system that enforced these languages over entire territories, Latin eventually disappeared from the scene as an actively used language.[36]

For many years, this development was viewed as simply a matter of course because it seemed only natural that a "foreign" language would be replaced by a language "of our own." However, more recent experience has made it clear that world languages that function as a second language for many different peoples are indispensable, which raises the question of why Latin did not remain the lingua franca of Europe longer than it did.

One reason is obvious: the nationalism that developed during the early modern era also brought national languages, which were consciously elaborated and constructed between the fifteenth century and the nineteenth, to the fore. Wherever international trade was conducted from a national perspective and the world was divided into national spheres of influence, the idea of a lingua franca became increasingly less attractive. This held true not only within Europe but also for the imperialist division of the world. It would have made no sense for a language other than English to predominate within the British Empire. The same may be said of French. Wherever the Spanish and Portuguese conquered new lands, their languages conquered along with them. But wherever understanding between nations was necessary and desirable, a single, agreed-upon means of communication was required. Here, French, which the French kings had, from the sixteenth century on, promoted as a language of culture to rival Latin, came to play an extraordinarily important role in diplomacy. Of course, the European educated elites tended to be polyglot, especially during the nineteenth century. It goes without saying that they had learned Latin (and many of them Greek as well), but they also had a working knowledge of English, French, German, and Italian and were fluent in at least one of these languages, more often than not in French. In eastern European countries, fluency in French and German was (and in some cases continues to be) the norm in more educated circles. All in all, developments in Europe may perhaps be described as follows. Purely in terms of the demands placed on language in international communications, the decline of Latin as Europe's lingua franca made matters more complicated. Whereas a person could make do with only two languages during the Middle Ages, the speaker's regional language and Latin, international communications now required three or four. This multilingualism continues to haunt the European Union, and for internal communications it is highly unlikely that English will ever be the sole lingua franca.

Another important reason for the displacement of Latin from the roster of actively used languages is that only in the early modern era did people begin to view Latin as a "dead" language and therefore as being of less intrinsic value. This rejection of Latin became so widespread that in the end even classical philologists came to accept it as true. Eduard Norden's classic work on "the ancient art of prose," written around 1900, is a case in point. Norden claimed that in the final analysis the humanists had struck a crushing blow because they destroyed the relative vitality that medieval Latin still had by insisting on a strict—and therefore dead—standard based on classical Latin.[37] This thesis, controversial from the beginning, engendered vociferous debate. In fact, this position is hardly tenable, given that the vast majority of

Latin texts ever written were set to paper after the humanist reforms and that Latin continued to be the most important single language in Europe into the eighteenth century. As Wilfried Stroh notes, the humanists had actually saved Latin: "Those who blamed the humanists for the death of Latin stand history on its head, confuse the physician with the murderer."[38]

However, from the perspective of Latin as a world language, Norden's thesis deserves a second look because, it seems to me, it does contain a nugget of truth. The issue is not that Latin writers after the humanist reforms were forced to conform to words, phrases, and syntactic rules from antiquity and were therefore incapable of adjusting to the needs of a modernizing world. What was indeed harmful and even "deadly" in the true sense of the word was the phenomenon that Erasmus of Rotterdam had already taken up in his writings on Ciceronianism and that Stroh basically conceded: a strict classicism peering fearfully out from behind the barricades, making absolutely certain that each and every detail in a written work had a documented antecedent in the ancient texts. The moderate way of imitating the classics that Erasmus recommended would not only have retained Latin's openness to innovation but might very well have also become the basis for a wholly new European Latin standard. The future development of Latin as a world language in no way demanded that it hold fast to the scholastic philosophical Latin of a Thomas Aquinas or the language of the liturgy or even the corrupted versions of Latin that became widespread because people had not learned the language properly. It should have been possible to turn back the clock, so to speak, and to revitalize Latin on the basis of classical standards. This can be demonstrated even today: if it is permissible to introduce new words, Latin speakers or writers with aspirations to classical style can express themselves without the least sense of limitation in terms of register or subject matter.

The real problem that the humanist reforms created for Latin had to do with the completely different relationship that they created with the language. Whereas during the Middle Ages, Latin had an instrumental function in human communications and in people's understanding of the world, for the humanists, the act of mastering the language became a measure of human self-perfection. In the end, the most important difference between medieval and humanist Latin may well have been the time and effort required to learn it.

The crucial point was not that Latin was a foreign language in the modern era. Even in the time of Cicero, whose mother tongue in the modern sense was Latin, the Romans recognized that intensive language exercises and extensive reading were indispensable to making Latin coequal with Greek as a literary language. Cicero's ideal oratory as delineated in *De oratore* was an educational ideal that required much more than specific expertise; it also presupposed years of practice and literary study. Furthermore, in his letters on literature, Horace continually stressed the importance of carefully elaborated linguistic and stylistic form for all poets. A hundred years after Cicero, the educational trajectory described by Quintilian required many years of schooling and language exercises. Similarly, the humanist Latin reforms entailed a considerable increase in and intensification of language exercises. The extensive reading of Latin classics as a model for linguistic usage was something fundamentally new. In the Middle Ages, the reading of model authors was not considered all that important, but in the schools that were influenced by the humanists, these practices took up an inordinate amount of time.

When the European vernaculars themselves became literary languages, they eventually laid claim to an exclusivity that all but barred the coequal standing of other languages. In the long run, it was inevitable that the European vernaculars' claim to literary status—a claim that the early humanist prophets of the vernacular such as Bembo, the poets of the French Pleiáde, and Opitz in Germany had championed—would come into conflict with Latin. Cultivated competence in one's mother tongue—and that is what is at stake when people complain about the loss of national languages in the era of global multilingualism—requires long years of training, study, and practice. Those who now master one of the rich culture languages—whether English, French, Russian, German, Italian, Chinese, Japanese, or Arabic—have not done so thoughtlessly or automatically simply because they were born or grew up in that particular linguistic region. The type of arduous education described by Quintilian in his work on the training of orators as a prerequisite for the mastering of language is still required. Bilingualism that approaches complete mastery of both languages is possible only after years of concentrated foreign-language study (which very few have time for) or completely bilingual education, which is founded on a private life built on marriages in which both partners use both languages interchangeably. Accordingly, in order to remain in general use, Latin would either have had to achieve the status of sole language of culture while more or less becoming a mother tongue, with the vernacular languages assuming a subordinate status, or retain its function as a lingua franca and as the language of technical and scientific endeavors but with its role in private life and literature reduced. However, by attempting to follow both courses by making Latin the epitome of humanist education while imbuing the vernaculars with all the qualities and expressive possibilities of Latin, the European educated elites created an irresolvable contradiction—which is how I would reformulate Norden's thesis. European society simply could not sustain the effort needed to achieve this goal.

These issues are especially important when one looks at the history of Latin as a world language because a very similar conflict is currently taking place between English and the various national languages. The growing importance of English is viewed critically by those with an awareness of the literary sophistication of their own culture language. And even in the Anglophone countries, many who value the expressive complexity of English in literature decry the changes and simplifications that inevitably take place in English as a result of its function as a world language. These discussions are very similar to those that occurred during the Renaissance. The starting points, however, are different. In the Renaissance, Latin was the cultivated language, and the vernacular had to be refined according the model Latin provided. Now one of the refined vernaculars, English (and it makes no great difference which of the various "Englishes" of the world we examine) becomes a world language, and the unresolved question is, will this global English be a somewhat reduced form of lingua franca, while the national languages maintain their position? Or will global English damage the refined standards of the national languages because people have no time to master the subtleties of their own language? For the English-speaking world the question goes as follows: Will global English also have a strong influence on the various varieties of national English? Or will a new diglossia arise, as David Crystal supposes, with the national "Englishes" going their own separate ways?[39] Is it possible that the structure of this diglossia would be the opposite of the Ferguson model, the national or regional forms being the "high" variety, the global form being the reduced "low" standard?

The outcome of the current debate over the relationship among languages in our time is not the subject of this book. However, that debate may serve to sharpen our understanding of the problems created by the language culture of the humanists in the context of the rise of the vernaculars as culture languages. If we look back from today's perspective, we see that two lines of development set in relatively early and that they shaped the history of modern Latinity up to the present day.

First, there was a dichotomy between a humanist Latinity and a not so strictly regulated Latinity for technical and practical applications. The division into a classical and a nonclassical language, which Sidonius Apollinaris captured so nicely in late antiquity with his image of the "men's library" and the "women's library," reappeared in a new guise. Second, the defenders of a humanist Latinity increasingly downplayed the importance of the active use of the language because they understood that the ideal of a pure and elegant language was impossible in a world in which language was subject to the exigencies of efficient communication. The following chapters examine this dichotomy between Latin education and Latin communication more closely.

At first, it seemed that the humanist reforms would make Latin the cultivated mother tongue of all Europeans. Beginning in the fifteenth century, these reforms began to change the nature of schooling throughout Europe. The Protestant secondary schools, which came into prominence as a result of the Reformation in Germany, were among the first. Philipp Melanchthon, who, as stated earlier, wrote numerous rulebooks and popular textbooks, was certainly the defining figure, but others, like Johannes Sturm (1507–1589), who led the large supraregional gymnasium in the Alsatian city of Strasbourg, pursued the same goals. Latin instruction at the universities was also reformed to reflect humanist philosophy. The University of Rostock was one of the most impressive examples of how the activities of an entire university was reformed along humanist lines by a single outstanding figure. David Chytraeus (1530–1600), a student of Melanchthon, led that university from 1551 until his death. Even the Counterreformation was imbued with the spirit of humanism. The Jesuit order became a major force in the system of European schools. In terms of Latin instruction and language ideals, the Catholic and Protestant humanist schools differed very little. As recent research has increasingly shown, the educational ideals of the various European confessions were remarkably similar on the eve of the Thirty Years War (1618–1648). Furthermore, there has probably never been a time in the two-thousand-year-old history of Christianity when the ancient, pre-Christian tradition of classical culture and Christianity coexisted as harmoniously as they did during the century of the Renaissance.

In spite of the advances made by the vernaculars, these trends in the nature of schooling led to an increase rather than a decrease in the knowledge and use of Latin. Just as Latin eventually stabilized after the Carolingian reforms, a general, though lesser, stabilization occurred in competence in the language along humanist lines. The writings of the early humanists, in both Italy and Germany, sometimes show a certain awkwardness. For example, the Latin poems of Konrad Celtis, an early and vocal proponent of German humanism, are rather modest—which, it should be noted, does not make them less interesting to scholars. By the end of the century, however, because of the stress placed on schooling, mastery of elegant Latin that at first glance is hardly distinguishable from the Ciceronian model, was no longer anything out of the ordinary. In Germany in particular, where a national culture language developed later than in France, Spain, or England because of the country's fragmentation, Latin culture was all the more determinative during the period between late humanism and the Thirty Years War. At least within small, educated circles, Latin again became something like a mother tongue. This evolution was probably most pronounced in the Jesuit schools, where intensive language training, which involved stylistic exercises, mandatory readings from the canon, and especially the tradition of Latin school theater, which engaged the students, was the norm.

In the final analysis, however, this intensification of humanist Latin education in the sixteenth century was the first step toward making Latin a less than worldly language learned in the classroom. With the development of schools that emphasized humanistic Latin instruction, Latin was for the first time in European history taught without considering whether the students actually needed or had occasion to employ such a precise linguistic instrument in daily use. After all, both the Catholic and the Protestant secondary schools educated not only future theologians and doctors but increasingly also the sons of merchants, city patricians, and even craftsmen. Even the European nobility, which had usually been able to get along well enough without Latin during the Middle Ages, was forced to undergo training in Latin. Not all of the aristocracy went on to the university or took up a scholarly profession. Of course, knowledge of Latin would have been very helpful because, without it, people's occupational choices would have been severely limited, but they did not need the type of intensive training prescribed by the curriculum. The decoupling of the value of education from the needs of everyday life, which characterized the later history of Latin, began at the latest with the successful introduction of humanist methods throughout Europe in the sixteenth century.

The humanist reforms were limited in another sense as well. In spite of all efforts, Latin instruction along humanist lines never succeeded in completely transforming Latin usage. When we examine the great majority of extant Latin texts from the sixteenth century, it becomes obvious that very few of them achieved the fluency sought in the humanist schools and that the average Latin usage during the seventeenth and eighteenth centuries fell far shorter yet. One would not, however, assume this to have been the case from the printed textbooks and Latin dictionaries. By the mid-sixteenth century, the *Calepinus,* a dictionary first published in Italy by A. Calepino in 1502, which went on to become the most important Latin dictionary in the early modern era, especially in its German adaptations and expansions, and which was available in numerous editions, contained an almost exclusively ancient vocabulary. The same was true of Henri Estienne's *Thesaurus linguae Latinae* (last edited 1543), which was thought to be the "most perfect" scholarly dictionary of the early modern era; it continued to exert an influence on lexicography throughout the eighteenth century and even later. A "living" Latinity of the Renaissance, however, is nowhere to be found in this work; it documents only ancient usages, excluding even Christian late antiquity. New words to express things unknown in antiquity, such as *printing* or *pistol,* were not to be found in the humanist dictionaries; to the extent that particular words existed in antiquity, their meanings reflected ancient usages only. Latin dictionaries of the seventeenth century aimed at the layperson, not the scholar. Written with active Latin usage in mind, they consistently reminded the user that the dictionary in question aspired to improve current usage by returning it to the classical standard. These efforts to correct the language were not aimed at other textbooks that taught "bad" Latin but at the living oral tradition and at the jargons of specialists. There is no dearth of examples of usages criticized in the seventeenth century that were completely acceptable in the late Middle Ages but never found their way into the "official" post-Renaissance Latin textbooks.

In short, under the surface of increasingly enforced classical criteria taught in the humanist schools from the late sixteenth century on, we find in parallel less classical usages reflecting an oral tradition that sometimes represented a direct continuity with the late Middle Ages.

In the seventeenth and eighteenth centuries, the Latin discourses and traditions in the classic subjects of theology, medicine, and law continued to play an important role. This tendency was associated with an increasing split between Latin as the language of education and Latin as a world language. Wherever Latin really played an important role in communication between less educated people not really interested in literary perfection, it parted from the humanist ideals and contented itself with the expressive potential of jargon or of a lingua franca.[40] Even though the school standard continued to be an ideal that was realized by many, it was unsuccessful as a general language standard. The difference between English as a cultivated language of native speakers and English as the global language of business, finance, medicine, and the natural sciences finds parallels in the Latin of this period.

This is evident in the work of the philosopher Jan Amos Comenius (1592–1670), who was one of the most important theorists of language education of the early modern era. His *Janua linguarum* (Door of Languages) and *Orbis sensualium pictus* (The Visible World in Pictures), first published in 1658, introduced a groundbreaking fusion of image and word into the teaching of language and have become famous for that reason. But Comenius was also one of the very few, perhaps even the only theorist who not only recognized the discrepancy between the school ideal and real-world practice but actually accepted it as a given. In addition to his textbooks for beginners, the *Vestibulum latinitatis,* he also wrote the *Lexicon atriale,* a work that is virtually unknown today. Symbolically, the title relates the *Janua linguarum* and the *Vestibulum latinitatis.* Just as the "door to Latin" referred to the beginning stage of learning and the *Vestibulum* represented the antechamber of Latinity, so the atrium was the innermost part of the Roman house and therefore the place where one was most "at home" with the language. The goal of this dictionary was to replace the simple, practical Latin that students had learned in the *Janua* with an "even more Latin" *(latinius)* Latin, as Comenius put it.[41] As it happens, the words that Comenius presented as simple were not generally that un-Latin. On the other hand—and this is characteristic—they could usually be translated into modern foreign languages quite easily, whereas the "more Latin" phraseology often felt forced. For example, he used the word *computare* (to calculate) instead of *subducere numerum* (to place the number below) or *punire aliquem* (to punish someone) instead of the more elegant alternative *poenas ab aliquo petere* (to demand punishment of someone). Both of the latter usages are perfectly acceptable in Latin; however, they cannot be translated with any ease into English, German, or other European languages, and if they are used in, say, a German or Polish setting, they give the sentence a humanist patina for that reason alone.

A few examples should suffice to make even clearer the differences between a "humanist" and a "nonhumanist" way of expressing a thought in Latin.

The first example comes from a poem by the German Jesuit poet Jacobus Balde (1604–1668). Balde had been a professor of rhetoric at Ingolstadt from about 1635 and later at Munich and Neuburg. At the time he belonged to the Jesuit order, which, as discussed earlier, trained its students to achieve near-first-language competence in Latin. His own lyrical poetry, which Herder translated into German and even Goethe admired, was read throughout Europe, and he made a name for himself as the "German Horace." He may well have been the most gifted poet in Germany in the seventeenth century. Unfortunately, his poetry is too little known today—and remains almost entirely unanalyzed. But this may have to do with the fact that it is often difficult to perceive the charm of these poems if one has not learned Latin at a very high level.

In 1637, Balde wrote a tragedy titled *Jephthias* (The Tragedy of Jephthah) for the Jesuit theater in Ingolstadt. The story, a very popular one for operas and oratorios in the seventeenth century, is taken from the Old Testament (Judges 12:7). The Israelite general Jephthah, after defeating the Ammonites, vows to sacrifice the first living creature he meets upon returning home. This living creature, however, turns out to be his own daughter, who runs toward him, ecstatic at his safe return. In connection with the performance in Ingolstadt, Balde wrote a lengthy lyrical poem to the Jesuit scholar and historian Andreas Brunner (1589–1650) in which he described his motivation for writing the tragedy and the contents of the tragedy itself. Here are the first two strophes (Ode I, 33, V. 1–8):

> Jephthen daturo spiritus incidit,
> urgere scenam flebilibus modis,
>   Brunnere; qualem nostra suadent
>   tempora, deteriora priscis.

> Olim in theatrum sex modios salis
> Terentiani sparsimus; et molam
>   versare cum Plauto coacti,
>   movimus in podio cachinnos.

> Brunner, I, who am about to stage
> *Jephthah* in the theater, am overcome by
> the Spirit to beset the stage with unhappy strains
> —as is advisable in our times,
> which are worse than the old times.

> In the past, I strewed six bushels
> of Terentine salt on the theater,
> and forced to turn the mill with Plautus,
> I produced much laughter on the stage.

This text can be understood only by reference to the circumstances under which it was written and to the author himself. One needs to know that, in his earlier years, Balde had taught at a Jesuit secondary school and staged a number of comic plays with his students. But it also requires considerable skill in Latin. One has to know that "salt" can also mean "joke" in Latin to understand that Balde was saying that his jokes were in the manner of Terence. However, the well-versed reader will also take pleasure in the image that emerges from the literal meaning (I strewed six bushels), a concrete image of Balde and his sack of salt, which is absurd and funny and is meant to make his friend Brunner laugh as well. The reader must dispose over a very sophisticated knowledge of the language to appreciate such double entendres. The next sentence can be understood only if one knows that once, when the wolf was at the door, the comedic poet Plautus was said to have earned his living laboring in a mill, doing work that in ancient times was mostly done by slaves. Here, too, the reader's pleasure comes from the ambiguity. In a figurative sense, "turning the mill" means "producing comedies," but if one takes it literally, it might mean that Balde considered the comedic productions that were once part of his work to have been onerous. In addition, there are two direct references to the poetry of Horace: the second line, *urgere scenam flebilibus modis,* is taken almost verbatim from one of Horace's poems *(carmen* II.9.3), where, it should be noted, it appears in a completely different context and is therefore little more than a throwaway line that might tickle the cognoscente. More important is the expression *tempora nostra . . . deteriora priscis* (our times . . . worse than the old), which alludes to an equally pessimistic understanding of history in Horace *(carmen* III.6.45–46)—by which Balde probably meant that times were worse in the nineteenth year of the Thirty Years War than they had been earlier.

In the following verses, Balde essentially recounts the contents of his tragedy to Brunner. But rather than telling a simple narrative, he does so in the form of a vision in which the poet sees and takes part in the events of the tragedy in "real time." Let us look at a later passage, the high point of the action, when Jephthah's daughter runs toward her father (Ode I, 33, V. 41–46):

> Ah! in reversi, filia, filia,
> fatale patris laberis obvia
>   fatale votum! cur repente
>   castra fremunt ululata luctu?
>
> Vertuntur hastae: nulla sonat tuba:
> stat muta belli gloria . . .

> Ah! You, daughter, yes, o daughter,
> glide toward the fateful, fateful vow of your father
> who returns! Why does the camp
> suddenly howl with sorrow?
>
> The lances are lowered; not a trumpet to be heard.
> The glory of war stands silent and mute.

Grammatically, this passage is even simpler than the first and could probably be translated by any competent Latin student. Nonetheless, it is great poetry. First, the poet vividly portrays his horror at seeing the daughter running toward her father. The word repetitions *(filia, filia / fatale . . . fatale)* underscore his emotional involvement—a stylistic device frequently used in antiquity but one that a more modern reader will identify with immediately. The word *laberis* (you glide) is somewhat strange, however. Why does the daughter "glide"? We would expect her to run. And why does she glide not toward her father but toward the fateful vow? Perhaps this "gliding" best expresses the inexorability of the movement—as when in modern films, shocking sequences, like the protagonist jumping in front of a speeding car, are removed from "real time" and shown in slow motion. Or perhaps Balde associated her path with the silent movements of the stars and planets, which were customarily described with the word *labi* (to glide). In this interpretation, the daughter was inescapably drawn to her fate like the heavenly bodies in their astronomical constellations.

Surprisingly, the high point of the story, the actual meeting with her father and his immediate reaction, is totally absent. This, too, is reminiscent of film, where the director shows only the final moment before an accident or a murder and then cuts away from the actual event. The next scene depicts the overwhelming grief in the victorious army, which of course presupposes that the reader knows exactly what catastrophe actually took place. Balde underscores the fatedness of the daughter's sacrifice by describing visual and acoustic impressions, not the acts or affects of individuals, to indicate the changed situation. We hear the howling (ululation!), suggested by the cumulative onomatopoetic effect of the vowel *u* in *fremunt ululata luctu;* the lances are lowered *(vertuntur hastae*—a sign of grief in antiquity); the trumpets that customarily announce great victories are silenced *(nulla sonat tuba);* and "the glory of war stands silent." The poetic transfiguration occurs because "the glory of war" cannot literally "stand" either in English or in Latin. However, my real reason for presenting this example is to show that one really has to have mastered Latin very, very well to appreciate the aesthetic thrust of these lines. What is striking about this Latin is not that it conforms to the ancient standards (though it does) or that it is especially complicated. What is exquisite is the precision with which Balde freely wields the language, which can only be the result of his gifts as a poet *and* of his years of deep engagement with the ancient canon.

Let us now compare to Balde's poetry an example of a more pragmatic sort of Latin as epitomized by Isaac Newton's (1643–1726) *Philosophiae naturalis principia mathematica* (Mathematical Principles of Natural Philosophy), first published in 1687 and without a doubt one of the most influential works written in Latin in the seventeenth century. Here, Newton describes the laws of gravity and the principles of classical mechanics. Because mathematical concepts and operations make up so much of the book, I will select a brief passage from the preface, in which Newton describes his basic procedure:

Omnis enim Philosophiae difficultas   in eo versari videtur,
For all the difficulty of philosophy   seems to consist in this

ut a Phaenomenis motuum   investigemus   vires Naturae,
from the phenomena of   to investigate   the forces of nature
motions

deinde   ab his viribus   demonstremus   phaenomena
                                                     reliqua.
and then   from these forces   to demonstrate the other
                                                     phenomena

Et huc spectant   Propositiones generales
and to this are directed   the general propositions

quas Libro primo et secundo pertractavimus.
in the first and second book.

In Libro autem tertio   exemplum huius rei proposuimus
In the third book   we give an example of this

per *explicationem*   Systematis mundane.
in the explication   of the System of the World.

Ibi enim,   ex phaenomenis caelestibus,
In the third [we derive]   from the celestial phenomena

per Propositiones   in Libris prioribus Mathematice
                                      demonstratas,
by the propositions   mathematically demonstrated in
                                      the former books

derivantur   vires gravitatis
we derive   the forces of gravity

quibus corpora   ad Solem et Planetas singulos
                                      tendunt.
with which bodies   tend to the sun and the several
                                      planets.

The translation, by Andrew Motte (1729), has been adapted slightly to permit juxtaposition with the Latin text.

Just to be clear, this is in no way bad or somehow faulty Latin; in terms of syntax and vocabulary, these sentences could easily be found in the works of a Latin author of antiquity. On the whole, however, it is a text that can be translated into English without having to restate or recast the sentences. Newton thought in English and wrote in Latin. Latin as a world language, with its grammar and vocabulary intact, is made to be understandable by Latin speakers everywhere. But any hint of a specifically Latin aesthetic has been stripped away.

If we look at the actual social use of Latin in the early modern era, it is clear that such relatively less sophisticated, easy-to-learn Latin was much more prevalent than the stylistic perfection promoted by the humanists. In general, Latin held on longer where a lingua franca was required. Contrary to widespread belief, the sciences were by no means the first to give up on Latin. Scientists always desired international circulation of their findings (even if only in the form of secondary reading), as Newton's *Mathematical Principles* makes clear. This is why publications in the natural sciences continued to be written in Latin well into the eighteenth and even the early nineteenth century. One may say that the science of biology was founded with the Latin writings of the Swede Carl Linnaeus (1707–1778), and until recently Latin remained the "original" language for the description of plants and animals. Only in 2011 did it become possible to describe newly discovered plants in English as well.[42]

German historians, on the other hand, soon began to abandon Latin. After all, they cannot be faulted for wanting their histories of a particular locality or region to be read by a larger regional audience rather than by merely a small coterie of scholars. In addition, the percentage of philosophical works in the various national languages was high. Very important philosophical tracts were published in Spanish and French during the seventeenth century, such as René Descartes's *Discours de la méthode* (Discourse on the Method) (1637). Even in Germany, philosophical works were written in German as early as the first half of the eighteenth century; Christian Wolff (1679–1754) was an important figure in this trend. Moreover, the jurist Christian Thomasius (1655–1728), who is sometimes credited, with perhaps little justification, with having given the first lectures in German at a German university, was first and foremost a philosopher.

Like the natural scientists, physicians and lawyers also had practical reasons for retaining Latin. Physicians and pharmacists had a need for standardized terminology at a supraregional, even international level. Even today, although English has long supplanted Latin as the language of medicine, the generally agreed-upon Latin and Greek terms have only recently given way to those used in U.S. hospitals. In addition, their entire way of thinking about legal matters was bound to the system of Roman law. The fact that, by the eighteenth and nineteenth centuries, lawyers and physicians had turned these practical necessities into a professional culture that they used to distinguish themselves from (and sometimes even exploit) the rest of the population is another matter completely.

And what about the Catholic Church, which was connected to Latin in a very special way? The church, as is well known, continues to use Latin for certain official purposes; it is the language of papal encyclicals and canon law. Recently, it has to some extent reemerged as a language of the liturgy. Until a few decades ago, lectures in Latin were commonplace at the Pontificia Università Gregoriana, the papal university in Rome. In the public perception, by holding fast to Latin the church is signaling its focus on the past. This includes the obligatory Latin text of the Bible—which we know was not the original but a translation edited in late antiquity by Jerome. And then there is the philosophical tradition of the church, in particular the church fathers Thomas Aquinas and Bonaventure, the other great philosophers of the Middle Ages, and modern theologians, all of whom have left an indelible mark. Latin guarantees the historical continuity of the church—and the Catholic Church is the oldest institution with a formal structure in existence.

It is often forgotten that, into the seventeenth century, the role Latin played in the Catholic Church did not differ markedly from that in Protestantism and in the secular world. True, the Protestant churches introduced the various vernaculars into religious services, but this had as much to do with making it more accessible to the uneducated population as it did with creating clear national demarcations from Rome. Still, in terms of the education of church personnel and the use of Latin in theological discourse, the Catholic and Protestant churches differed not at all. As we have just seen, training in Latin at the Jesuit schools followed the humanist model just as it did at the Protestant ones.

At least since the late seventeenth century, however, Latin has in fact fulfilled a considerably more central function in the Catholic Church than in the regional Protestant churches. This is because the function of Latin as a world language was as important as its rootedness in the Latin tradition. In the seventeenth and eighteenth centuries, the Catholic Church was the only multinational organization in the European world. Latin was indispensable in religious services because it ensured the equality of all of its members regardless of their mother tongue. In many cases, it also spared communities discussions about which vernacular was most suitable for the liturgy, which would undoubtedly have caused splits. But in the Protestant churches, as we just noted, the introduction of German was also a way of distinguishing the German lands from Rome.

In terms of internal communications, especially with regard to theology, the training of church personnel, and dialogue with the "central authorities" in Rome, Latin had precisely the same function as English does today in an international corporation. Even today, no single language can replace Latin when it comes to publishing papal encyclicals, although it seems that these texts are now first written in Italian and then translated into Latin. Likewise, Latin has a function in church courts, which are still needed to annul marriages, for example. Overall, it is understandable that "Church Latin" came to epitomize a pragmatic form of Latin that did not hew to classic standards.

I have shown that the function of Latin as a world language existed within a dynamic environment, where it balanced the demands of humanism and those placed on it in day-to-day communications. This does not mean that all professors of rhetoric, Latin teachers, and poets wrote classical humanist Latin or that all scientists, jurists, and representatives of the Catholic Church used a kind of adulterated, pragmatic Latin. We are able to describe only broad trends. The reality was, of course, far more complex; there were always rhetoricians who never really mastered Latin and scientists who prided themselves on the precision of their language. And so I conclude this chapter with a poem by an author from whom one might not expect Latin poetry at all: the English astronomer Edmund Halley (1656–1742). Halley, who was the first to calculate the cyclical path of the comet that later came to bear his name, appended a poem to the first edition of Newton's *Principia mathematica*, in which he praised Newton's scientific work as the revelation of a new age:

> En tibi norma Poli, et divae libramina Molis
> computus atque Jovis; quas, dum primordia rerum
> pangeret, omniparens Leges violare Creator
> noluit, aeternique operis fundamina fixit.
> Intima panduntur victim penetralia caeli,
> nec latet extremos quae Vis circumrotat Orbes.
> . . . .

> Lo, for your gaze, the pattern of the skies!
> What balance of the mass, what reckonings
> Divine! Here ponder too the Laws which God,
> Framing the universe, set not aside
> But made the fixed foundations of his work.
> The inmost places of the heavens, now gained,
> Break into view, nor longer hidden is
> The force that turns the farthest orb.[43]

A strict classicist might criticize the fact that several words are not documented in classical antiquity *(libramen, computus)*. A theologian might find fault with the idea that the omnipotence of God is limited by Newton's laws of gravity and movement, as if these laws were somehow independent of the act of creation, but that God chose to include them. Be that as it may, literary historians will note that, without citing him directly, Halley was clearly referencing Lucretius (first half of the first century BCE), who, in his *De rerum natura* (On the Nature of Things), described the atom theory of the Greek philosopher Epicurus and, using this understanding of the physical causes of the world, attempted to free his readers from the fear of the Roman deities. Lucretius's poem (Book I, 62–79, and Book III, 1–30) contains a paean to Epicurus and his groundbreaking theories—and later in the poem Halley does much the same for Newton and the *Principia mathematica*. What Halley does quite nicely is mimic Lucretius's diction and some of his syntactic peculiarities, as anyone with a deep familiarity with Latin literature will appreciate immediately. The poem also provides evidence of how deeply rooted versification in Latin continued to be in the early modern era— especially in England, where the tradition continued well into the twentieth century. Overall, Halley's poem is a clean, stylistically skillful piece of work. However, a more detailed analysis, like the one of Balde's verses, would not make much sense here or give us a deeper understanding of the poem. In the end, this text, too, may serve as evidence that the struggle between Latin and the European vernaculars that took place between the seventeenth and nineteenth centuries had less to do with the choice of language per se and more to do with whether Latin or the vernaculars should be cultivated further. The humanist question was whether Latin would be the mother tongue of the educated populace or merely a useful world language.

4

---◆---

World Language without a World

Latin as the Language of Culture and
Education since 1800

T HE PROCESS by which Latin was finally retired as the indispensable
language of communications extended over several centuries. Nonetheless, that process may be said to have largely come to an end around
1800. In a more general sense, the years between 1760 and 1840 mark
the end of the Latin millennium in Europe, which had been inaugurated by Charlemagne between 800 and 814. It is more difficult, however, to delineate the individual steps in the retreat of Latin or to describe
any particular moment in the eighteenth century when the customs of
communication in Europe changed. One of the reasons is that far too
little is known about what Latin texts were published in the eighteenth
century. As a percentage of all published works in the eighteenth century, those in Latin generally accounted for something under 25 percent,
depending on country. Without a doubt, Latin was still a major cultural
factor, but by the middle of the nineteenth century, this was no longer
the case. A more precise picture would require detailed studies by country, region, and institution, bits and pieces of which already exist.

It is much more difficult, however, to establish the specific role and
relative weight of Latin during this late phase of its history. The reason
is that simply looking at publication statistics does not tell us much
about the actual use of Latin in communications. The reason for this is
that, over time, the divergence we described in the previous chapter between Latin education and Latin communication became ever greater.
Education in Latin, meaning the ability to understand Latin fluently

(passive mastery) and to use the language in daily life more or less correctly (active mastery) were still a given throughout the eighteenth century and remained so well into the nineteenth. But precisely because all educated people spoke or at least wrote Latin, it is not an easy matter to determine where Latin was used merely to satisfy tradition and where it was in fact indispensable for communication.

Statistics for Latin publications in the eighteenth century invariably show that even then they were concentrated in academic exercises within the university, in particular in academic rituals. During the eighteenth century, ceremonial speeches, academic certificates, and the like continued to be written in Latin. In all probability, the percentage of Latin lectures remained high. At the very least, doctoral dissertations continued to be common practice into the nineteenth century. In subjects like medicine and law, Latin was customary, even required, even though some candidates needed remedial help. In 1770, for example, Goethe submitted the Latin law dissertation that he wrote to the University of Strasbourg, although he had a more expert friend edit it for errors.[1] The faculty rejected his dissertation, but not because his Latin was deficient; what they found unacceptable was his free-thinking argumentation. In law, as in biology, medicine, and pharmacology, the need for precise terminology that could be understood in any country was probably more responsible for the persistence of Latin than any notion of tradition. Even today, international commissions that govern medical theory often continue to base their terminology on Latin and Greek, and, as mentioned in the previous chapter, it was only in 2011 that botanists were freed from the necessity of giving Latin names to newly discovered plants.

Poems for academic or even private occasions continued to be a widespread practice well into the nineteenth century. One sometimes encounters such academic rituals even today. Honorary degrees and official congratulations may still be written in Latin. Moreover, Latin boilerplate is customary when granting degrees at both European and U.S. universities. At the University of Oxford, Latin continues to be the language in which honorary degrees are conferred. In June 2012, for example, when the Burmese politician and Nobel Peace Prize laureate Aung San Suu Kyi was granted an honorary doctorate in law, Chris Patten (the last British governor of Hong Kong) gave the laudatory speech in Latin.

Nonetheless, we need more than a mere statistical analysis of Latin publications to understand the actual status of Latin as a language of communications. As noted earlier, Latin continued to play a major role in the Catholic Church in the late eighteenth century, both because it was used in the liturgy and because the church needed it to communicate across nations. Nevertheless, by about 1800 Latin played a negligible role in administrative and legal matters more generally—except in regions where peoples speaking different languages lived in proximity in complex political arrangements, where Latin continued to be a neutral language acceptable to all. For example, Latin was a useful compromise in the Hapsburg monarchy and the eastern regions of Prussia, which were populated by Poles and other Slavic peoples, well into the nineteenth century. Also, Latin continued to be the official administrative language of Hungary until 1848.

Even within the scholarly disciplines more broadly, the picture was somewhat more complex if we look beyond the universities. The varying rapidity with which the national written languages developed had an effect as well. To get an inkling of this complexity, let us return briefly to the sixteenth and seventeenth centuries and take a look at tracts regarding statecraft, which were generally written in an academic setting but whose influence was felt in the society as a whole. In Italy, Niccolò Machiavelli (1449–1527) wrote his seminal work, *Il principe* (The Prince) in Italian, as did Giovanni Botero (1544–1617), who in 1589 published *Della ragione di stato* (The Reason of State), one of the most important early treatises on the subject. Although the French state theorist Jean Bodin (1530–1596) also wrote in Latin, his most important work, *Les six livres de la république* (The Six Books of the Republic), was published in 1576, in French. Several years later, he also published a Latin edition. The English philosopher and state theorist Thomas Hobbes (1588–1679) published in both Latin and English, and his most important work, *Leviathan,* was written in English. Even John Locke (1632–1704), one of the most important theoreticians of the social contract in the early modern era, wrote in both Latin and English. By contrast, Latin remained the language of state theory in Germany and the Netherlands. Justus Lipsius's (1547–1606) influential *Politicorum libri sex* (Six Books of Politics), was published in Latin in 1589, as was Hugo Grotius's *De jure belli et pacis* (On the Law of War and Peace), published in 1625. On the other hand, the German jurist and human rights theorist Samuel Pufendorf (1632–1694) wrote in Latin and German. The fact that important texts written in the various national languages were regularly translated into Latin—and vice versa—ensured that their influence would be felt throughout Europe.

The history of the national academies may to some extent give us an overview of the language distribution in the eighteenth century. It goes without saying that the Accademia della Crusca for Italian (founded in 1583), the Académie française for French (1635), and the Real Academia Española for Spanish (1713), whose primary purpose, after all, was to cultivate and purify language, used the languages in question. But Latin had lost ground in the academies that were specifically established to cultivate the sciences as well. The first volume of the *Philosophical Transactions* of the Royal Society in London appeared in 1665 and was written in English. After the French-language *Journal des savants,* inaugurated only a few months earlier, it is the second oldest scientific journal in the world still in publication. It was also possible to publish in Latin, but this was mainly an exception for foreign scientists who did not speak English. The fact that Isaac Newton, who had been president of the Royal Society since 1703, published his *Principia mathematica* in Latin, though not at all unusual, in no way means that Latin was still the universal language of science in England at that time.

In Germany, on the other hand, Latin continued to be indispensable. Probably the most important German scientific journal of the eighteenth century was the *Acta eruditorum,* which had been published in Leipzig since 1682 and was renamed the *Nova acta eruditorum* in 1732. Until its demise in 1776, its treatises were in Latin, although an addendum was added in 1712, the *Deutsche acta eruditorum,* which was written in German and aimed at a broader public.

The academy founded in 1700 in Berlin known as the Kurfürstlich-Brandenburgische Societät der Wissenschaften (Society of Sciences of the Elector of Brandenburg), from which later emerged the Königlich-Preußische Akademie der Wissenschaften (Royal Prussian Academy of Sciences) (today known as the Berlin-Brandenburgische Akademie) published its series in Latin from 1710 to 1744.[2] However, in 1745 it began publishing the series in French.[3] This is not especially surprising since the academy was in Berlin, where Friedrich II of Prussia, whose German was notoriously inferior to his French, sat on the throne and where Voltaire was a frequent guest. In fact, French had become an important language throughout Europe; in the preface to the society's first French volume, the renunciation of Latin was said to be justified on the grounds that the Latin world was clearly shrinking, whereas French was now assuming the role that Greek had played in the time of Cicero.[4] But after 1804, the academy began publishing entirely in German.

The Königliche Gesellschaft der Wissenschaften (Royal Society of Sciences) in Göttingen (today the Göttinger Akademie der Wissenschaften), founded in 1751, stipulated that all treatises be published in Latin. However, again with an eye toward a larger public it also published a German-language review titled *Göttingische Anzeigen von gelehrten Sachen* (Göttingen Announcements of Scholarly Matters). But for the actual treatises, the society assumed that academy members could write Latin themselves, although they expressly permitted nonmembers whose scientific works were to be published by the academy to hire more expert assistants:

> Latina lingua in scribendis commentariis omnes utuntor: hac si quis in societatem non admissus minus utitur commode, velitque suos commentarios societati traditos actis societatis inseri, eos latine et vero pure verti, aut si latinis verbis concepti sunt, emendari curato, in eamque rem sumptus necessarios impendito.[5]

> All must avail themselves of the Latin language when writing treatises. When someone who is not a member of the society is not adequately versed therein such that he himself can write the treatises that he submits for publication in the Acts, he must ensure that they be translated into Latin (that is, into good Latin) or, if they are already written in Latin, that their language be corrected, he himself bearing the costs.

The Göttingen Academy never went through a French phase. Whether this had to do with the fact that the Hanoverian king George II, who founded the academy, was also the king of England is an open question.

During its first ten years, although the Kurfürstlich Mainzische Akademie Nützlicher Wissenschaften in Erfurt (Academy of Useful Sciences of the Elector of Mainz) (today the Akademie gemeinnütziger Wissenschaften zu Erfurt) allowed treatises to be published in volumes titled *Acta Academiae Electoralis Moguntinae scientiarum utilium quae Erfordiae est* (Acts of the Electoral Academy of Useful Sciences in Erfurt), the actual treatises were in both Latin and German. On the other hand, the Bayerische Akademie der Wissenschaften (Bavarian Academy of Sciences), founded in 1763, no longer bothered with Latin; it published treatises exclusively in German from the very beginning.

If we sample works in the natural sciences that did not emanate from the universities, we find a similar broad range. Until the nineteenth century, it was possible to write scientific treatises in Latin, but in the eighteenth century many such works were already being written in the various national languages. Of course, in the countries with well-developed literary languages, such as France and England, Latin played a much more subsidiary role. The three scientists for whom the currently used temperature scales are named are good examples. The German Daniel Gabriel Fahrenheit (1686–1736) wrote several articles in Latin that were published in the *Philosophical Transactions of the Royal Society*. The same was true of the Swedish astronomer and physicist Anders Celsius (1704–1744), who would not have been able to count on an international audience if he had written in his mother tongue. By contrast, René-Antoine Ferchault de Réamur wrote exclusively in his native French. Barely a hundred years later, Latin is hard to find in the natural sciences. The physicist and mathematician Georg Simon Ohm (1789–1854) wrote in German; Michael Faraday (1791–1867) in English. By contrast, the mathematician Carl Friedrich Gauss (1777–1855) continued to write in Latin. Several decades later, the mathematician Georg Cantor (1845–1918), following the academic custom, wrote his dissertation and habilitation thesis in Latin, although his published work was more often in German. Between 1823 and 1825, the jurist Christian Friedrich Mühlenbruch (1785–1843) published an influential three-volume legal textbook in Latin about the *Pandectae*, the digest of Roman law, which was translated into German in 1835.

These examples suffice to show that the decline was not a simple phenomenon. Outside the multinational Catholic Church, there were good reasons well into the nineteenth century to maintain Latin not merely as a necessary academic exercise but also as a real tool of communication. As these examples demonstrate, however, Latin ceased to be the necessary language of the sciences in spite of its omnipresence in the educational system.

Neohumanism, Latin, and Johann Sebastian Bach

The switch from Latin to the national language occurred much more quickly and radically in Germany than in any other country. In 1700, Germany was the most Latin of all central European countries; by 1850, active use of Latin had been pushed aside. Over the course of the eighteenth century, Germany was probably the country most heavily engaged in theoretical questions of Latin usage and Latin language instruction. This was probably because, in contrast to Italy, France, Spain, and England, where the transition to a common written language had for the most part already occurred, it was still a very lively topic in eighteenth-century Germany. It would be interesting to do a comparative study of critical writings on the German and Latin languages at that time.

In the eighteenth century, representatives of the educational reform movement known as "philanthropinism" such as Johann Bernhard Basedow (1724–1790) and Johann Heinrich Campe (1746–1818) played an important role in debates over how Latin was to be taught. Given the Greek word used to describe their movement, it might at first glance appear that they intended to purge the educational system of Latin altogether, replace it with a more "humane" education based on people's natural talents, and especially convey knowledge that gave people the practical skills needed to meet life's challenges. However, they had no intention of reshaping the human being by means of a thoroughgoing educational reform, and so the philanthropinists were not defenders of humanist culture. Still, since Latin was essential to people's daily lives, they were in no way opposed to it; what was important to them was that Latin instruction be more "humane," and they essentially took no position on where Latin should be used and where German.

This was in rather stark contrast to German neohumanism *(Neuhumanismus)*, which by 1800 was the leading educational reform movement in Germany. Neohumanism (the name distinguishes it from the Renaissance humanism of the fifteenth and sixteenth centuries) again looked back toward classical antiquity and placed ancient Greece at the center of its thought. Much like the Renaissance humanists, neohumanists believed that the person is shaped by the process of cultivating language. However, they no longer took it for granted that this schooling in language would eventuate in Latin fluency and use in daily life. Neohumanism played an important role in Germany in this split between Latin as the language of education and Latin as the language of communications. Both of the leading figures of the movement at the time (i.e., around 1800), Friedrich August Wolf (1759–1824), the founder of classical studies, and Wilhelm von Humboldt (1767–1835), the forefather of the German humanist secondary school (the *Gymnasium*) and

Figure 21. Johann Matthias
Gesner (1691–1761), rector of
the Thomasschule in Leipzig,
1730–1734. akg-images

the classical German university, wrote in German. Neither of them
defended either the use of Latin as a scientific or world language or the
reintroduction of Latin where it had already been superseded. The most
important effect of neohumanism was that it led to a rediscovery of Greek
literature, which had languished during the seventeenth and eighteenth
centuries in Germany, and to a renewed emphasis on the ancient classics
generally. But it did not entail any attempt to reintroduce a classically
enhanced Latin into daily life. German society generally, and especially
the increasing number of literate women, enjoyed the reintroduction
of the classics in the form of translations, such as those of Homer, by
Johann Heinrich Voss (1751–1826), which were published in great
numbers after the second half of the eighteenth century.

   This part of the story is well enough known. But beyond that, the
history of Latin and Latin education in the eighteenth century, in fact
of education as a whole at the time, has been inadequately studied. We
know more about the development of education in schools during the
Renaissance than during the eighteenth century.

   To get something of a picture of the status of Latin and how humanist interests increasingly came into conflict with the way in which Latin
was actually used, let us take a brief look at the Thomasschule in Leipzig

Figure 22. Johann August Ernesti (1707–1771), rector of the Thomasschule in Leipzig, 1734–1762. akg-images

between approximately 1720 and 1740. The reason for selecting this school is that, during this period, the school was directed by three especially gifted rectors. They were Johann Heinrich Ernesti (1652–1729), rector from 1684 until his death, and two scholars who are today generally viewed as forerunners of neohumanism, Johann Matthias Gesner (1691–1761), rector from 1730 to 1734, and Johann August Ernesti (1707–1781), rector from 1734 to 1762, who was a distant relative of Johann Heinrich.

Their fame, however, pales in comparison to that of their colleague, just below them in the school hierarchy, the cantor Johann Sebastian Bach (1685–1750). Bach is worth mentioning in this context because his appointment as cantor and his later work at the Thomasschule are far more closely connected to the history of Latin than might at first glance appear likely.

In 1723, when Bach applied to the school in Leipzig, its rector was Johann Heinrich Ernesti.[6] Ernesti was completely a man of the scholarly Latin culture of the seventeenth century. As a professor of poetry at the University of Leipzig—it was customary for rectors at the Thomasschule to have an appointment at the university as well—he wrote numerous occasional poems in Latin and other texts for all sorts of academic events. At the time, Latin instruction at the Thomasschule had a decidedly practical aim. The ancient classics played a far more subsidiary role in the curriculum than they had in the sixteenth century; the emphasis was much more on neo-Latin texts, which would have been of greater benefit to graduates in their later professions. This change was initiated by Jakob Thomasius (1622–1684), the father of philosopher Christian Thomasius, who had directed the school before Ernesti. Ernesti introduced a set of reforms at the school, one of which replaced Latin prayers with German ones. However, when the then cantor Johann Kuhnau died in 1722, the school was undergoing a period of instability primarily because Ernesti was old and sick and no longer had the strength to enforce discipline.

The official requirements of the newly appointed cantor included the ability to teach some scholarly subjects, and in Bach's case this meant teaching four hours of Latin and one hour of catechism per week. Latin instruction consisted of grammar and conversation, the so-called *colloquia;* the textbook used in Leipzig was the *Colloquia scholastica* by the French humanist Maturin Cordier, which was first published in 1561 but continued to be reprinted into the eighteenth century. In earlier times, the connection between Latin and music instruction had been unproblematic. Every cantor before Bach had attended the university and was undoubtedly qualified to teach the language. This had certainly been the case with Bach's immediate predecessor, Johann Kuhnau, who had even written his law dissertation in Latin. These were the sorts of scholars who taught the rudiments of Latin grammar and conversation to students at the Thomasschule.

Bach, on the other hand, never attended the university and as a result had never received formal training in Latin, although at the Michaelischule in Lüneburg he had received a good general education that emphasized Latin. The hiring process in Leipzig included an oral examination in Latin on the Lutheran faith, which he passed in March 1723. To the extent that one can reconstruct this examination, it tested not only his mastery of formulaic phrases but also his ability to speak Latin with some fluency. In other words, Bach's competence in Latin should not be underestimated, and it is not inconceivable that he was actually qualified to teach. In any case, at least on paper—and even then that was what counted in Germany—he had fewer credentials than the city council in Leipzig would have hoped for. According to the extant documents, the deliberations about whether to appoint him cantor revolved around precisely this question.

The first call went to Georg Philipp Telemann (1681–1767), who was the general music director of the city of Hamburg. Earlier in his professional life Telemann had spent time in Leipzig, and so he was a known quantity there both as a person and as a musician. He also knew Latin, having undergone a comprehensive humanist education. He even dabbled in Latin poetry. In 1721 he gave a speech in Latin on the occasion of becoming music director in Hamburg. In it he summarized his own relationship to the ancient languages in the following bit of verse from 1718:[7]

> Musik kann mit Latein sich wohl verknüpfen lassen,
> wie dies das Altertum vorlängst schon dargetan.
> Ein Kopf, der fähig ist, die Harmonie zu fassen,
> sieht auch den Cicero für keinen Kobold an.

> Music may well be linked with Latin
> as was done so long ago in antiquity.
> A mind capable of understanding harmony
> will not see in Cicero an imp.

Telemann must have looked like the ideal candidate to the authorities in Leipzig. However, he rejected their offer when Hamburg increased his salary to equal the Leipzig offer. In any case, he would have come to Leipzig only if someone else were found to teach Latin, but at his expense, so that he would have been free to pursue his music.

The next candidate called by the council was the court kapellmeister in Darmstadt, Christoph Graupner (1683–1760). Graupner had studied law in Leipzig, so he would necessarily have had the requisite knowledge of Latin for the position. However, Graupner's employer, the landgrave Ernst Ludwig of Hessen-Darmstadt, refused to release him. But never fear: as a result of the attention, Graupner, too, received a raise. It was unclear whether the rest of the candidates could have taught Latin—or "inform," as it was called at the time.

On April 9, 1723, the mayor of Leipzig, Gottfried Lange, who was one of Bach's supporters, updated the city council on the status of the search:[8] "The one we were considering for the position of cantor, Graupner, was unable to resign because the landgrave of Hessen-Darmstadt would not release him. Other than that, the suggestion has been made to send for Bach, the kapellmeister in Cöthen, Kauffmann in Merseburg, and

Schotte; however, all three will not be able to inform at the same time; in the case of Telemann we have already considered division."

At this point, the council minutes contain the following notorious remark by the judge in the Leipzig district court, Plaz: "He finds considerable cause to deem the latter questionable because if we cannot get the best, we would have to accept the mediocre." This was not a judgment about Bach the musician but about his overall qualifications, which did not meet the requirements for the position as a whole. The Leipzig city council was split, and since the council also oversaw the schools, it is not surprising that in naming a cantor it would also want a competent Latin instructor. In the end, on April 22, 1723, the city council of Leipzig voted unanimously to offer the position to Bach. The council even permitted him to hire another Latin teacher at his own expense. This session of the council is documented in two records, which are largely in agreement. They show that although the assumption was that, at least officially, Bach would take on the role of "informer," they had serious doubts about whether he was up to the task. Court councilor Kregel expressed himself as follows: "And he would not evade the information; however, if he could not carry this out, he could have it done by another."

The option of having another teacher take his place in Latin class seems to have been not only an accommodation to a candidate who wished to concentrate on his music but also an actual fallback in case Bach was unable to pull his weight. Even Councilor Plaz agreed to this solution: "Bach is in good standing and his person agreeable, especially since he declares his intention not only to inform the boys in music but to do so otherwise in the prescribed manner in school. We will see whether he can achieve the latter, but he should ensure that he may resign in Cöthen."

If I interpret these statements correctly, the city council voted on Bach—almost certainly at the urging of Mayor Lange—in spite of the fact that a considerable number of the councilors doubted his ability to "inform" in Latin. On the other hand, the council would not have wanted to admit that it had failed in its search for a qualified Latin teacher. That is why they were content when Bach agreed to teach, which spared them an uncomfortable debate about the duties of that position. In addition, the council had a fallback in case difficulties arose, one that had been offered to Telemann and would therefore not have attracted attention. In all probability, the councilors never really anticipated that Bach would teach Latin himself. Even so, the decision to allow Bach to find someone to teach in his stead caused other problems because the city had neglected to consult church authorities. The Lutheran superintendent, Salomo Deyling, felt so insulted that he boycotted Bach's installation. Bach immediately reached an agreement with Carl Friedrich Pezold, the tertius, that is, the third individual in the Thomasschule hierarchy after the rector and the cantor, whereby he would teach Bach's Latin classes for fifty thaler a year—about 8 percent of his salary.

The process described here has been documented in detail by Bach researchers. However, until now it has been interpreted exclusively from the perspective of music and its culture, that is, whether Bach's position in Leipzig was that of a traditional municipal cantor or of some new type of court kapellmeister. In this context, it is important to note that Bach's installation was advanced by Mayor Lange, who, on the Leipzig city council, favored the interests of the Saxon elector. However, the significance for the history of culture as a whole would be incomplete if the narrower educational aspect were not taken into account. To date this has not been done—which brings us back to how things stood with Latin at the time.

The first thing to understand is that at the beginning of the eighteenth century it could no longer be taken for granted that a cantor at the Thomasschule would be able to teach Latin. It is no coincidence that at least half of the applicants for the position were unable to "inform" at all. However, in addition—and this really was a historical coincidence—during the first years of Bach's tenure, the Thomasschule was one of the most important centers in Germany for deliberations on the future role of Latin in Europe. For this reason alone, it is worth taking a closer look at Bach's appointment in this larger context.

Carl Friedrich Pezold (1675–1731), the teacher who substituted for Bach, was not simply a Latin teacher but also an important member of the scholarly community of Leipzig. More than a hundred years ago, his contributions in this area were deemed important enough to merit an entry of his own in the *Allgemeine deutsche Biographie,* the German national biography. Pezold was a member of the philosophical faculty at the university and a senior member of the scientific society called the Collegium anthologicum. Beginning in 1717, he published a Latin journal titled *Miscellanea Lipsiensia: ad incrementum rei litterariae edita* (approximately,

Leipzig Miscellany for the Advancement of Literature and Science); by 1723, twelve volumes comprising several thousand pages had appeared. The journal was dedicated to the advancement of knowledge in a wide array of historical, philological, literary, and scientific fields; essentially, the range of topics mirrored those taught at the universities of the time by the "faculty of arts." All of the articles were written in Latin. Now in Germany at the time, German was rapidly replacing Latin as the language of science. Since 1712 one of the great scientific journals of the eighteenth century, the *Deutsche acta eruditorum*, was also published in Leipzig in the German language. Pezold, however, was clearly an advocate of the retention of Latin as the language of science. He was in some ways a forerunner of the *Societas latina*, which was founded in Jena in 1734 to promote the use of Latin. But the undertaking was privately financed, and as the forewords to numerous issues make clear, it quickly ran into financial difficulties. After about 1720, the issues contain overly effusive dedications and thanks to patrons, most of whom were members of the Leipzig city council. A number of the councilors who in April 1723 decided on Bach's appointment were also evidently sponsors of Pezold's Latin journal that year or in previous years. We can only speculate about whether Pezold's reputation as an advocate of Latin influenced the council's decision; ironically, a few years later complaints were voiced that he was neglectful if not remiss in his teaching.

In 1723, at almost exactly the same time as Bach's appointment, a detailed article exceeding a hundred pages appeared in Pezold's *Miscellanea Lipsiensia*, written by the Lutheran theologian Michael Heinrich Reinhard (1676–1732) and titled *De officiis scholarum adversus impietatem seculi* (On the Duties of School Personnel against the Godlessness of the Times). In this treatise, Reinhard addressed, among other topics, the importance of instruction in the Latin language, giving voice to educational theories that were completely out of step with the times and conceivable only before the advent of German neohumanism.

On the one hand, Reinhard protested against an exaggerated humanist view of Latin studies: "We read the ancient writers in order to school ourselves in the language or to acquire knowledge of history or, finally, to plumb their wisdom. Learning languages correctly is not education in and of itself but rather a necessary and extremely useful educational instrument."[9] He voiced concerns about teachers who spend too much time with their students on pagan eloquence or poetry, justifying his perspective by referencing Melanchthon, who also decried the overemphasis on ancient poetry. On the other hand, Reinhard was absolutely adamant that Latin was the only acceptable international language of science, and he rejected all attempts to accord the modern European languages any greater importance. He was especially incensed at philosophers who were now writing in German. According to Reinhard, while Greek and Hebrew were still considered indispensable for the interpretation of the Bible, Latin was held in contempt. "Are they in such manner able to encompass the entirety of wisdom and science in the German tongue alone? And are we thus to be locked within our borders, refrain from exchange with other nations, or because we are tired of it replace the single language that has up to the present been the common language of scholars and learn ten others?"[10] In particular, he noted that French and Italian speakers would never even consider learning German, while only Germans derived a perverse pleasure from admitting the superiority of foreign languages. Apparently, even then Germans derived cultural self-affirmation from learning the prestige languages of others while neglecting their own.

This article appeared in the final issue of *Miscellanea Lipsiensia*. After Bach was appointed, the journal ceased publication. It is unclear whether Pezold simply could no longer find time, given his Latin duties, or whether the fifty thaler that he received from Bach had something to do with it.

Johann Heinrich Ernesti died in 1729, and his successor, Johann Matthias Gesner, took the reins in 1730. As a result, the Thomasschule was led for several years by a man who, like few others, had paved the way for German neohumanism. Gesner was one of the important philologists and educational theorists of the eighteenth century. His knowledge of Latin and Greek was seemingly inexhaustible. In addition to revising Basilius Fabri's *Thesaurus eruditionis*, a Latin dictionary that had already been revised numerous times, he also revised Henri Estienne's *Thesaurus linguae latinae*, the greatest Latin dictionary of the Renaissance, which had last been revised in four volumes in 1573. His ambition was to capture and define the vocabulary of the ancient authors correctly but not to give instruction on how to speak or write Latin. As one of the founders and first professors of the University of Göttingen in 1734 and as founder of the Göttingen Philological Seminar, he is rightly viewed as one of the precursors of modern classical philology. When teaching Latin, he encouraged the reading of classical authors and even compiled a Latin reader, the *Chrestomathia ciceroniana*, which was reprinted numerous times and contained selected readings from the works of Cicero.

It is not, however, a simple matter to assess Gesner's place in the history of education and in particular in the history of Latin language practices because he combined elements of traditionalism, neohumanism, and philanthropinism. His theoretical work on education started in 1715 with a treatise titled *Institutiones rei scholasticae* (Institution of Schools). If we compare Gesner's statements in that treatise about the position of Latin with those of Michael Reinhard, we see some rather interesting differences. Gesner placed a great deal of emphasis on the reading of classical writers. In particular, he was against spontaneously spoken Latin; thus he was critical of school rules, common since the Renaissance, that required students to speak Latin during breaks.[11] Clearly, classical correctness was more important to Gesner than fluency. At the same time, he wrote favorably about modern languages, recommending that people cultivate the German language and learn French and Italian as well.[12] Aside from Latin, those were the two foreign languages that mattered in Germany at the time and the ones that Bach dealt with the most: French was the language of the nobility and the courts, while even then Italian was the world language of music.

Even in his later treatise *Primae lineae isagoges in eruditionem universalem* (Foundations of an Introduction to General Education), which was published in 1756, Gesner appears to have placed little value on the actual speaking of Latin. In it, he described how, earlier, he had been of the opinion that students, who, after all, needed Latin only to read legal, theological, or other scientific texts, should not read the ancient classics but should be instructed using textbooks that prepared them for real life. This approach had already been introduced at the Thomasschule by Thomasius, and his successor, Ernesti, had retained it.[13] But then Gesner did an about-face, making the case for the formative power of the classical authors. He pondered, somewhat surprisingly, given what he had written before, whether the active use of Latin might not serve a positive function, namely, in the treatment of scientific topics that were best kept from the broad mass of people. Examples included historical topics, especially the history of antiquity, philosophy, and law, as well as metaphysics and disputations about epistemology and the truth of the Christian religion. These are the sorts of topics from which he wanted to exclude those who were not educated in Latin. After all, if simpler minds were to hear that even scholars disagreed about such important questions, might they not fall prey to nihilism?[14]

In other words, there were at least times during which Gesner stood in the tradition of Latin as a medium of exchange in the sciences, though perhaps for not completely laudable reasons. While he was rector of the Thomasschule, he reintroduced the Latin school prayer, which his predecessor, Ernesti, had replaced with a German one because otherwise "rudité and ignorance would gain the upper hand."[15] In this vein, Gesner also undertook to revise Johann Gottlieb Heineccius's (1681–1741) *Fundamenta stili cultioris* (Foundations of Good Style), published in 1719 and one of the most important stylistic manuals of the time, which had primarily been written for jurists, who needed to write and speak Latin fluently.

Above all, however, Gesner's partial adherence to the old humanist tradition of Latin speech sheds light on one of the most famous documents concerning Bach's life. In 1738 he wrote a detailed description of Bach's virtuosity as a conductor in his first book of commentaries on Quintilian, specifically where Quintilian says that a musician must have the ability to perform many fingerings simultaneously (1.12). Here Gesner makes the point that Bach stands head and shoulders above the ancient musicians. In its clarity, it is not only one of the most important contemporary documents about Bach, about whom we otherwise know very little, but also one of the most important musical documents of the early eighteenth century. Bach researchers have naturally gravitated to it, but they have never questioned the context in which it was written. What, after all, is such a contemporary observation doing in a commentary on an ancient author? Still, a reading of Gesner's book shows that it was not merely a scholarly commentary, even though the usual philological details—textual criticism, parallel passages, explications of difficult passages—make up most of the body of the text. Rather, in passages in which important questions are addressed, Gesner presented his author as an authority on modern life. For example, in the famous passage in which Quintilian rejects corporal punishment (I.3.14), he writes very personal comments in which he differs with Quintilian about the efficacy of beatings but recommends them only to punish lack of discipline. In this commentary, Gesner shows that in the final analysis he stood by the old humanist tradition, which viewed the ability to speak Latin and the mastery of rhetoric as educational ideals and identified closely with the doctrines of the ancient authors.

Gesner's successor at the Thomasschule, Johann August Ernesti, was known as a philologist, primarily because of his editions of classical authors; among others, he edited the works of Homer, Xenophon, Polybius, Cicero, Suetonius, and Tacitus. In 1742 he was made professor of eloquence at the University of Leipzig, to which he added a professorship in theology in 1759, focusing on biblical hermeneutics. What is known about Ernesti's relationship with Bach is that, though harmonious at the beginning, it turned acrimonious after 1736 because of a dispute over who was competent to appoint a choir prefect, a quarrel that was never resolved. The last years of Bach's life and the tenor of his compositional work, which were increasingly separated from the life of the Thomasschule, were affected in no small way by this dispute. Ernesti was, much more clearly than Gesner, of the opinion that Latin no longer had a role to play in everyday life and that it was better to write good German than bad Latin. Although his philosophical textbook, *Initia doctrinae solidioris,* which was written in 1734 at the Thomasschule and was widely distributed in the eighteenth century, was written in Latin, its foreword is explicit in its position on language. Ernesti wrote that everyone prefers a well-written German text to a poorly written Latin one. As evidence he adduced the works of Christian Thomasius, whose German books found great favor because of the elegance of their prose, while his Latin volumes found few readers and were completely forgotten after his death.[16] Ernesti championed the ancient classics even more resolutely than Gesner, and he favored Cicero's philosophical works in particular. His interest in the ancient classics primarily had to do with their content, which he detailed in his *Prolusio de intereuntium humaniorum literarum caussis* (Prologue concerning the Reasons for the Decline in Humanist Education), which he published on April 19, 1736, as an invitation and introduction to a series of Latin declamations held by students graduating from the Thomasschule.

Among the speakers at this school event was Krause, the choir prefect over whom Ernesti and Bach would soon lock horns. Based on a contemporary note, the consequences of the dispute had been interpreted as indicating that Bach later came to view the humanities, the *humaniora,* less favorably and that Ernesti came to despise music. The personal side of this dispute surely bears scrutiny, especially since neither Bach nor Ernesti were conflict averse. However, if we note that Ernesti consistently promoted the reform of classical studies during public events at the Thomasschule, which he, as director, had to open, we begin to suspect that the conflict may have been driven by the neohumanist Ernesti's growing demands on his students.[17] For them, reading classical authors and practicing style in the manner of Cicero probably took a good deal more time and effort than practicing the conversational Latin needed in the professions, which the elder Ernesti had demanded of them. Furthermore, an abyss began to open between music and Latin that was structurally comparable to that between the arts and the sciences in the later secondary schools. By hiring Bach in 1723, the Leipzig city council essentially set a precedent. The future of Latin consisted in exercises centered around the classical authors. In many areas, Latin was no longer indispensable; thus music and Latin were no longer as "linked" as Telemann had believed in 1718. Even taking into account the personal nature of the dispute between Bach and Ernesti, it also signaled that an era had come to an end.

Classicism, Neohumanism, and Latin Instruction in the Nineteenth Century

The most remarkable aspect of the change in the fortunes of Latin and its culture between 1750 and 1850 was not that it lost its status as an active language but rather that this loss had no effect on Latin instruction in the schools. On the contrary, Latin experienced a new upsurge as a language of the educated classes, but one without any practical application. As a consequence, students in a German secondary school in 1850 spent approximately as much time learning Latin as they would have a hundred years earlier—and matters were not much different in other European countries and even in the United States. Paradoxically, this continuity in the curriculum represented a paradigm shift in ideas about education that could hardly have been more radical.

During the years in which Latin was losing its practical value, knowledge of Latin actually became even more widespread among the educated. This was because Latin began to be taught wherever the European tradition of humanist education was valued. Naturally, Latin was taught in schools throughout the European colonies, but this represented little more than an expansion of the national school systems of the colonizing nations. What is more interesting is that the classical tradition also found favor in Russia, a country that had previously been shaped by Greek Orthodoxy and Slavic language traditions. The reforms initiated by Peter the Great (1672–1725) created a linguistic opening toward the West, which necessarily required Russia to confront Latin. The reason that the Saint Petersburg Academy of Sciences, founded in 1724, began publishing its treatises exclusively in Latin in 1728 and continued to cling more stubbornly to the practice than many academies in the central European countries may well be that Russian treatises simply would not otherwise have been read in other countries.[18] In general, however, by the end of the eighteenth century French had displaced Latin in Russia as the preeminent language of science. Nonetheless, Latin retained its place in the educational system into the twentieth century.

Finally, the history of Latin instruction in the United States is noteworthy. In contrast to the Russian experience, the need to make oneself understood probably played a much lesser role; we know of no Latin scientific publications that were meant to be read in Europe. In the United States, too, Latin and Greek were a regular feature in schools from the very beginning. Instruction in reading and writing Latin, including writing Latin verses, was highly valued. One example should suffice. In 1800 a certain Samuel Wilson (about whom little more is known than that he wrote several schoolbooks that were printed in Lexington around 1800) wrote a poem based on the *Carmen saeculare* of Horace to commemorate the Fourth of July, the last three verses of which are quoted here. The author draws a direct parallel between the founding of the Roman Republic after the kings were expelled and the founding of the American republic after its war of independence from the English monarchy. Interestingly, Wilson tied this political new beginning to a new beginning in classical education:

> En superbis regibus et fugata
> cara Libertas oriente ab ora
> advenit exul, simul inferensque
>   Palladis artis.

Sacra nunc Phoebo melicisque Musis
templa fundantur: nucibus relictis
imbibunt haustus dociles alumni ex
    fonte perenni.

Floreas longum, America o beata,
libera et felix vigeas in aevum
filii juncti et maneant Columbi
    unanimesque.[19]

Look! Even freedom that was
driven out by proud kings
returns from exile, bringing with it
the arts of Pallas Athena.

Now temples will be built to Phoebus and the
musical muses: after they have left the nutshells,
inquisitive students will draw deep draughts
from the eternal source.

Long may you blossom, o happy free America,
and may you survive the times happy and strong,
and may the sons of Columbus remain united
and harmonious.

The stubbornness with which Latin clung to its position as a language of the educated population all over the world while its importance as a world language dwindled is astonishing. One would not, of course, have expected such an old and exalted tradition simply to have disappeared; the cultural identification with Latin and its connection with humanist notions of education was strong enough to overcome the new social realities, at least in the schools. Such stubborn survivals are seen in other areas of life as well. For example, riding and fencing continued to be important markers of class and caste long after they had ceased to be relevant in war. And in the case of Latin, passive knowledge was necessary at a minimum to read the scientific literature well into the twentieth century. For all of these reasons, one would not have expected schools simply to abandon their Latin requirements, but the fact that nothing whatsoever changed is unusual.

Ferreting out the reasons is not easy. As already discussed in the previous chapter, research on Latin instruction in the eighteenth and early nineteenth centuries is unsatisfactory, and in fact considerably more is known about the Renaissance humanist tradition of teaching in the sixteenth century. But one reason is clear. The end of the Latin millennium did not entail rejecting antiquity. On the contrary, it coincided with a new fascination with Greece and Rome that was felt even in the United States. The century of classicism had begun.

The term *classicism* is generally applied only to architecture, which further underscores the lack of serious research on the history of education. In architecture, it is clear that, after a few precursors that at least in France extended into the seventeenth century, architects revisited the formal language of Greek and Roman antiquity but in a new light. The fact that in England and the United States—less so in Germany and France—this also entailed engagement with the formal "classical" language of the Italian Renaissance, particularly the works of Andrea Palladio, does not negate this focus on antiquity. Well-known examples of classical architecture include the Brandenburg Gate in Berlin (1817) and the Capitol in Washington, D.C. (begun in 1790).

However, classicism as an educational movement in Europe has hardly been examined. In Germany, the classical movement is now known as German neohumanism (*Neuhumanismus*), whose early proponents included Johann Matthias Gesner and Johann August Ernesti, as detailed earlier in the present chapter. Initially, neohumanism was concentrated in the Protestant parts of Germany, although the movement had an effect in Catholic areas as well. Neohumanism became the leading educational reform movement in German schools because Wilhelm von Humboldt, who had since 1809 been the Prussian minister of education, grounded the recently created Prussian secondary school system in neohumanist ideals. The tradition of the German humanist secondary school that he bequeathed lasted almost to the present day.

The basic idea of this new movement was that education in languages was quite simply the path to cultivating the whole person, and this was especially true for the ancient languages, which were esteemed as models. In this sense, neohumanism was a secular movement, a revolt against the Christian tradition of education—although no open conflict between the two ever broke out. To the outside world, the neohumanists presented their movement as being within the European Christian tradition. As a practical matter, however, institution of the humanist secondary schools meant that philologists replaced theologians as the main conduits to the ancient traditions. For more than a century it was customary for classical philologists to head the secondary schools in Germany. During the late eighteenth and the nineteenth centuries "philological seminars" turned out teachers trained in modern methods at universities throughout Germany.

In other respects, however, neohumanism differed markedly from Renaissance humanism. Although the Renaissance rediscovered the Greeks, this reengagement did not entail a devaluation of Latin culture, and Latin continued to be at the center of educational practices. The proponents of neohumanism, on the other hand, tended to view Greek as the "original" and the Latin culture of the Romans as a mere copy. As a result, they accorded Greek art, language, and literature pride of place. In Germany in particular, philhellenism was so pronounced that at times contempt for Roman literature and culture were more or less out in the open. We will return to this phenomenon later.

Probably the most important difference between Renaissance humanism and the classicist project of the eighteenth century was that none of the neohumanists made any effort to promote the ancient languages as vehicles of communication. As we saw earlier in this chapter, Ernesti believed that it was more important to write well than to write in Latin. Nonetheless, the ancient Latin, and especially the ancient Greek language and literature, continued to be viewed as exemplary. They made up the illustrative material used in exercises to help students achieve mastery. In Germany, Greece was more important than Rome in this respect. August Wilhelm Schlegel (1767–1849), Friedrich August Wolf (1759–1824), and Wilhelm von Humboldt (1767–1835) transformed the concept of humanism: while Cicero, Petrarch, and the humanists of the Renaissance sought to cultivate their practical Latin skills, Humboldt and Schlegel aimed at a better understanding of Latin. Renewed interest in the scientific study of languages—and here Humboldt and Schlegel were situated at the beginning of modern linguistic research, Wolf at the beginning of classical studies—was combined with the idea that pure study, not study directed at a profession, should be at the heart of education. This meant that it was good to study Latin—and especially Greek—even though these languages were not needed in daily life. In fact, the very nonutility of classical education ensured its educational value. Humboldt believed that, because Latin and Greek were fully developed and their evolution complete, they were especially well suited to contribute to the elevation of the human spirit by affording us insight into the nature of language.

A somewhat different version of this concept, the theory of "formal education," was developed by educator and secondary-school director Friedrich Gedicke (1754–1803) in Berlin. Rather than their nonutility, Gedicke emphasized the indirect benefits of ancient languages and their abstract educational value. Learning these languages could help people to acquire skills that would be useful in practical daily life even though they never actually used the language they had learned. Compared to those of Humboldt and Schlegel, Gedicke's contributions to education in the nineteenth century have been largely forgotten, but the fact is that his influence is felt even today.

German classicism and neohumanism were primarily a matter of intellectual reflection and educational theorizing. The intensity with which these matters were contemplated may be one of the reasons that Germany in the nineteenth century became such a center of the classical tradition and classical studies. The classical tradition could not have had nationalist significance in Germany because, until 1871, Germany consisted of a multitude of states that did not yet constitute a nation. At most, one might claim that discussions about antiquity were a proxy for discussions about nation in a political sense. The situation was different in other countries. There, great national events were perceived in relation to ancient models. The rise of the British Empire was equated with that of the Imperium Romanum. And in France, precedents in antiquity were constantly sought for the French Revolution and the rise of Napoleon; the same was true in America for the Declaration of Independence and the first decades of the republic.[20] In both cases, the founding of a republic, that is, a nonmonarchical, free association of all citizens, harkened back to the democracy of the Athenians and the republic of the Romans. This was not, however, a matter of wishing to repeat ancient history. If we trace the development of these political ideas, it is clear that they were new and that the imprimatur of antiquity was more or less tacked on.[21] Nonetheless, the crucial point in terms of classical studies was the enthusiasm with which people viewed the ancient parallels, regardless of whether they were warranted. The leaders of the American Revolution did not limit their enthusiasm for the ancient world to symbolism, although they did not shy away from such connections, as the choice of the word "Capitol" demonstrates. They considered it far more important to study the ancient classics—in the original language—in order to meet the political challenges of creating a new country.

The Rediscovery of the Historic

However, classicism in its various guises around 1800 cannot alone explain Latin's ongoing dominance in the educational system, especially since its actual influence in society had largely waned by midcentury. Apart from this renaissance of interest in antiquity, history itself was being subjected to reevaluation, and the "old" languages benefited from this renewed attention. This particular development is of interest with regard to Latin because the parallels with changes in other languages become clear in this context.

At about the time when Latin was concluding its transformation from a language in normal use into an exemplary model not taught for its practicality, the study of historical literatures and languages was coming into vogue in Europe for the first time. Very few in premodern Europe had paid much attention to the non-Latin literatures of the past. On the contrary, because Latin was viewed as timeless and because it enabled effective communication over the centuries, the products of other written cultures were simply neglected and forgotten. In the early eighteenth century, philologists had only the most rudimentary understanding of the languages common in Europe in the Middle Ages or on other continents. The gradual codification of the modern European languages and the development of the literary works that still form the basis of our literary canon created the conditions under which texts remained before the public eye over longer periods of time. In effect, the literature that has *never* been forgotten emerged in fourteenth-century Italy with Dante, Petrarch, and Boccaccio; in the first half of the sixteenth century in France with Rabelais and later with the French "classics"; in the second half of the sixteenth century in Spain with Cervantes and Lope de Vega; in England in 1600 with Shakespeare; and in the eighteenth century in Germany with Weimar classicism. But the linguistic steps that led to these literary achievements and the literature of earlier times had vanished from consciousness.

This is exactly what changed in the second half of the eighteenth century. Throughout Europe, historians and philologists began to examine the still extant textual evidence and the historical stages that eventuated in the modern national languages. In 1753, Johann Jacob Bodmer for the first time edited Wolfram von Eschenbach's *Parzival;* Thomas Percy's *Reliques of Ancient English Poetry* was published in 1765; and the first edition of the *Song of the Nibelungs* appeared in 1782. The nineteenth century saw the systematic recovery of virtually the entire corpus of forgotten medieval literature. Critical editions were published, and the buried medieval precursors of modern German, French, and English were reconstructed.

The period around 1800 also saw the rediscovery of historical texts and languages outside of Europe. At the beginning of the nineteenth century, Jean-François Champollion deciphered the Egyptian hieroglyphics, thereby opening up an ancient written tradition that had lain dormant since late antiquity. Cuneiform was deciphered at about the same time by Georg Friedrich Grotefend, who also attempted to reconstruct the ancient Italic languages of Oscan and Umbrian.

Finally, the early 1800s also saw a reconnection to historical languages in other parts of the world that, like Latin and Greek, had a living tradition. Of these, the most important were Sanskrit and the "classical" Indian literature created in it. Schlegel and Humboldt took an intense interest in this literature, and out of this preoccupation developed the academic disciplines of classical Indology and Indo-European studies. Although Persian was known in Europe in the early modern era, interest in the language deepened at the end of the eighteenth century, and translations were made into a number of languages. Goethe's *West-östlicher Divan* (West-East Divan) was inspired by the poems of the Persian lyric poet Hafez (fourteenth century), which were translated into German in 1812 by the Orientalist Josef von Hammer.

Overall, the decades between 1770 and 1840 were marked by a broad interest—unique in European history up to then—in historical languages and literatures. This was also the time when Latin finally lost its status as a language in active use. But because Latin was also an old language, it, too, became an object of historical interest. In effect, it ceded its status as lingua franca—and was rediscovered as the most important European historical language. The continuing role of Latin and Greek as educational keystones in Germany would be unthinkable if they were not embedded in this new historical understanding.

This turn toward historical languages around 1800 should not be mistaken for traditionalism. Many of the languages and literatures that caught people's attention at the time had been completely unknown before. This meant that their study was actually progressive in the sense that it opened up wholly new fields of exploration even though the basic interest lay in the past and not in the future. It represented a modern, questioning type of history, well before historicism became the driving force in historical thought during the first third of the nineteenth century. In contrast to historicism, however, for which, to quote Leopold von Ranke (1795–1886), each epoch was "immediate to God" and had its own intrinsic value, these investigations of the past were, in the case of Latin and Greek, focused not on all epochs but specifically on antiquity and the first centuries of the Middle Ages. The loss of so much late sixteenth- and seventeenth-century neo-Latin literature from the cultural memory of our own epoch is largely the result of this blocking in the nineteenth century.

Latin and the Natural Sciences

The discovery of the historical languages was not just a question of expanding knowledge but also one of historical methodology. Over the course of those decades, various procedures were established that were "scientific" in a sense that is still recognized today. The discovery of Sanskrit was very much bound up with the emergence of historical linguistics. By the same token, classical philology was given a new foundation as a method-based science. As the spirit of historicism came into its own over the course of the nineteenth century, classical antiquity began to be studied along scientific lines, not just as a model to be emulated. Although the beginning of this movement goes back to the eighteenth century, the middle of the nineteenth century was a turning point in this sense.[22]

This turn of events was extraordinarily significant for the teaching of Latin and the presence of the language in society. It was when Latin came to be viewed as an essential tool for training students in grammar and logic; it was also used to separate the good students from the bad.

This trend was probably most extreme in Germany. Otherwise, it is hard to understand the peculiar schizophrenia that characterized classical studies in Germany, at least during the second half of the nineteenth century. On the one hand, instruction in Latin as a formal exercise continued to be absolutely central to the school experience; at the same time, Greek literature was extolled, whereas Latin literature was denigrated. Let us leave aside the well-known gibe by historian Theodor Mommsen that Cicero was a "bungler," a "journalist's nature in the worst sense" because he was not comparing Cicero unfavorably to the Greeks but to Caesar. A more pertinent example would be the first sentence of the history of Roman literature (1870) by the Latinist Sigmund Teuffel (1820–1878), probably the most important such work written in the nineteenth century. "The Romans lacked the versatility, many-sidedness, and imaginative power of the Greeks; their eminent qualities are sober and acute thought, and firmness and perseverance of will." And these characteristics, Teuffel continued, virtually disparaging his own undertaking, were "decidedly unfavorable to art and literature."[23] Reading this, we should bear in mind that German secondary schools dedicated approximately half the school day to such a language and such a literature.

But in fairness, Teuffel did not completely denigrate the Romans. Although he doubted their ability to produce art and literature of high quality, at least he had no doubts about the sobriety and sharpness of their thinking. Here we see the labeling that still dogs Latin and its virtues. Latin is a logical language; therefore, mastering it fosters logical thinking. This line of argument first appeared in the nineteenth century; the (much) earlier tradition emphasized its very praiseworthy elegance, typified by the title of Lorenzo Valla's famous *Elegantiae linguae latinae* (The Elegances of the Latin Language), written in 1444.

Latin philology followed along in this turn toward academic exercise. A coherent theory of Latin syntax was first formulated in the mid-nineteenth century; this was also when questions of syntax for the first time became central to Latin instruction. The humanists of the Renaissance had railed against the overuse of textbooks; instead, they placed great emphasis on reading the classics and on conversation. The neohumanism of the eighteenth century did much the same; in fact, the neohumanist reformers made every effort to ensure that where Latin instruction had degenerated into the mechanical acquisition of phrases and forms, the classics would be introduced, thereby giving students suitable models to emulate. Not one of the elite neohumanist founders of classical studies ever wrote a book on Latin grammar: not Ernesti or Gesner, not Friedrich August Wolf or the philologist Friedrich Thiersch, not Gesner's successor, Gottlob Heyne, or Friedrich Creutzer, the founder of the Heidelberg Philological Seminar. No one did.

Nonetheless, in the decades between 1820 and 1880, a cornucopia of grammars was published in quick succession. Some of them are in use to this day, and they continue to be mainstays of Latin teaching. This proliferation began in 1818 with a grammar by Karl Gottlob Zumpt (no longer in use), which claimed to provide the first systematic overview of syntax. This was followed by the *Antibarbarus* (Against Barbarism) by Johann Philipp Krebs (1843), the Latin-style manual of Carl Friedrich von Nägelsbach (1846), the *Repetitorium der lateinischen Syntax und Stilistik* (Repetition of Latin Syntax and Style) by Herrmann Menge (1873), and finally the Latin grammar of Raphael Kühner (1879), who had published a Greek grammar in 1836. Revised by Carl Stegmann, Kühner's grammar remains one of the most important tools for Latin teachers correcting final German-Latin examinations. None of these works has ever been out of print; Menge's *Repetitorium* was revised in 1999 and again made available. The Latin dictionary by Karl Ernst Georges, which goes back to 1837, is still used. In fact, the 1913 revision is now on CD-ROM and fully searchable.

These grammars were written in large part because people no longer heard, spoke, or wrote Latin as a matter of course. Grammarians become necessary whenever a language ceases to be in active use, as we saw earlier during the crisis at the end of antiquity. People who do not actually speak a language regularly need reference works. At the same time, these particular grammars were characterized by the same scientific vision that we see in all fields at the time, whether languages or the natural sciences, and the authors themselves understood their works as part of this trend. In method, the grammars they wrote are quite different from grammars of earlier times.[24] Not only did they seek to classify usages as precisely as possible, but they also tried to derive inductively a system that would clarify the internal coherence and logic of the Latin language. In other words, in addition to indicating which verbs took the *accusativus cum infinitivo,* this advice was grounded in theory such that the user could, given any instance, also derive what was not explicitly described. The description merely showed that the conjunction *cum* could follow both the conjunctive and the indicative; then, however, the grammars formulated principles that could be used in concrete, and especially in borderline, instances to determine which of the possible constructions to use. Our image of Latin as a logical language that sharpens thinking reflects precisely the analytical perspectives that went into writing these grammars. In the final analysis, it is this same methodological approach that proved so fruitful when applied to the comparative linguistics of the time and the natural sciences. In this respect, there is not much difference between the formulation of the periodic tables in chemistry (1869) and the formulation of laws for indirect speech in Latin. This was also when systematic harmonics was developed in music, first in the form of "terraced harmony," later the "functional harmony" of Hugo Riemann (which introduced the terms *tonic, dominant, and subdominant*). Significantly, Riemann's most important publication was titled *Musikalische Syntax* (Musical Syntax) (1877). Mozart and Schumann managed quite well without it.

The philologists mentioned earlier differed from those who were studying the comparative linguistics of the same period in that they largely neglected the historical dimension. They never asked why a certain usage changed between, say, the time of Plautus and that of Pliny; they merely stated the particular author's preferences. The types of questions that linguists resolved so beautifully when they delineated the sound changes and word formations in the Indo-European languages were largely absent. This is unsurprising in the works of Krebs and Nägelsbach, who wrote explicitly to help students with their exercises in style. But even Kühner's grammar was firmly centered on the classical authors. These grammars are not greatly reflective of the linguistic methods of the time; rather, they are "author grammars." In other words, they do not document the natural laws or regularities of the language but the language usage of particular authors and their internal consistency. Although they pretend to aim at nothing more than neutral description, we discern a normative core. This is why even Kühner's grammar, which is a work of the highest intellectual achievement, has never gained much respect from linguists, who prefer the later grammar by Leumann and Hofmann, which is much closer to their historical approach to languages. However, as learned as it is, this grammar has yet to find a place in modern university classes. That said, the older grammars admirably fulfill their role of imparting a systematic approach to Latin style exercises.

The scientific penetration of the Latin language—that was essentially how educators viewed the changes that Latin teaching and Latin style exercises underwent at the time. Among other things, it armed teachers for educational controversies during the second half of the nineteenth century, especially in their battle against the rising tide of *Realbildung,* which emphasized the natural sciences and the teaching of modern languages. What has become clear—the exact details deserve further study—is that the restructuring of Latin exercises into a logical science shaped the idea of formal education in a particular way and gave Latin a new role. From then on, Latin was no longer beholden to humanist ideas of human development; it was now free to prepare future scientists in logical thinking. In this respect, Latin was on a footing with mathematics, which in the nineteenth century began to assume its function as a basic body of knowledge having special educational properties.[25] This notion of an internal relatedness between Latin and mathematics is common even today. There is no real basis for it in the long history of the Latin language; it came into being during this brief period in the nineteenth century.

What must have seemed especially compelling about this type of introduction to formal logic was the fact that it fit well with the historical tendencies of the times more generally. Let us assume that the proponents of a modern *Realbildung* had been victorious in the middle of the nineteenth century and that the educational system had been reformed along their lines, with drastic reductions in Latin and an increased emphasis on the natural sciences. Let us further assume that this occurred not during the twentieth century (which is what happened) but a hundred years earlier. This would have represented a total break with people's traditional understanding of education.

At the time, churches were being built in the Romanesque or Gothic style, opera houses and schools in the style of the neo-Renaissance or any mixture of styles. As a result, citizens were surrounded by interiors and exteriors of all sorts drawn from historical models, and so it is understandable that people would have wanted to avoid such a break. The perfect compromise was found: Latin teaching was restructured to promote the learning of logic or language. The claim could then be made that it embodied the formal educational values needed for the modern world, not to mention future engineers. Externally at least, the claim could continue to be made that the humanist secondary schools were continuing in the tradition of the Latin schools of the Renaissance. This historicism was a powerful force both in the construction of school buildings and in the curriculum itself. The comparison with architectural history, whose heuristic value for the history of Latin instruction was discussed in an earlier chapter, is equally valid here. In the decades when the houses of Parliament in London (1840–1870) or Saint Paul's Cathedral in New York (1858–1888) were erected in the Gothic style, or when H. H. Richardson (1838–1886) developed his Romanesque architecture, one would not expect that school curricula would give up their historical roots. Some will argue that the design of school entrances in, say, the Renaissance style merely reflected taste and not function, while the secondary-school curriculum was not arbitrary in that sense. However, the adaptation of historical modes of culture to contemporary needs is evident in architecture as well. One should note, however, that the buildings of the nineteenth century that were based on historical antecedents were constructed using state-of-the-art building techniques. Steel beams and poured concrete are often concealed behind stylized external skins regardless of their apparent period. The Neuschwanstein castle, built by King Ludwig II of Bavaria, is a good example. Despite appearances, these buildings all reflect the building techniques and functional requirements of their times. Similarly, we must peer behind the historical façade of nineteenth-century Latin instruction. That is not to say that all Latin instruction was reduced to preparation for the natural sciences; reading the classics remained central to Latin instruction even in a more technical age. But when explaining the importance of a classical education over such a prolonged period of time, we also need to examine these hidden changes in the way Latin was taught.

5

Latin Today

W E HAVE GOOD REASON to believe that Latin is currently at a watershed moment, the implications of which may be comparable
to that reached around 1800. That was when Latin largely ceased to be
a language in active use, although it continued to be taught because it
was viewed as crucial to the education and cultivation of the individual.
Wherever the European tradition of education was valued, Latin continued to hold pride of place in the schools. The question today is whether
learning Latin is of benefit to anyone outside the guild of historians and
those who prefer to spend their lives in the past rather than in our modern world.

This new situation developed over a long period of time. If we examine the history of Latin instruction from the early nineteenth century up to the present day, we find that, since the mid-nineteenth century at the very latest, new trends have been vying for attention in the
public arena. Increasingly, educators have come to view modern foreign
languages, mathematics, the natural sciences, and history as a much
more suitable foundation than Latin for a "useful" public education.
These trends occurred differently in different countries, and exactly
how this new approach came to be accepted and implemented over
time has not yet been adequately researched. It is clear, however, that
this movement went through various stages and that the fortunes of
Latin instruction have waxed and waned inconsistently. In Germany,
in any case, Latin retains a certain cachet; in Italy, where Latin is an
important part of the national identity, it continues to be taught routinely.
Even in Eastern Europe before 1990, where one might have thought that

the remnants of bourgeois education would have been suppressed in favor of a socialist future, Latin was never completely expelled from the curriculum. Nonetheless, the significance of the Latin tradition has decreased continuously over the past 150 years. The real turning point occurred when so few people learned the language well that it achieved the status of a historical language that was needed at most by a few specialists. For many who felt forced to learn the language in school, the exercise was about as pleasurable as going to the dentist.

The fortunes of Latin in the schools may already have bottomed out. In any case, we see increasing signs that knowledge of Latin is rapidly achieving a collective state of cultural forgetting even where it is still taught. A cultural historian looking back from the vantage point of several hundred years would note that the titles of Latin books in university catalogs are full of errors and that the catalogs of antiquarian book dealers selling volumes for the price of a luxury car are not any better. Gross misunderstandings are frequent even in scholarly works underwritten by public research grants. In addition, our understanding of the past is increasingly determined by whether Latin source texts are available in translation. If so, they may be read; if not, they might as well never have been written. In newspapers and periodicals aimed at the general public, Latin quotations (if used at all) are often mangled. Overall, not only are we in danger of losing a broad-based humanist education, but Latin itself may be buried as well. Latin may succumb in the same way as Greek during the Middle Ages in western Europe, when only the bare rudiments of Greek literature were kept alive in Latin translation. Back then, a reader stumbling upon a Greek quotation might simply read past it—much as we do today with Latin. *Latina sunt, non leguntur* (It's Latin; skip it).

It should be noted that Latin is not alone. Scholarship and the educational system in general have tended to disdain "old" languages and literatures, that is, the languages of ancient cultures like Egyptian or Babylonian and non-European historical culture languages like Sanskrit or classical Chinese or even the precursors of European languages like Old High German or Old English. In the nineteenth-century university, all of these languages were subjected to the model of classical philology, which meant a major concentration on their older, "classical" literatures. Their rediscovery, leading in part to their inclusion in the Western cultural tradition, occurred, as we have seen, largely during the nineteenth century and was predicated on a very changed understanding of history. But now, with our more modern cast of mind, the historical languages are again being slighted. After World War II, specialists in the Germanic, Romance, Arabic, and Chinese languages still studied the historical stages of the language and the great historical texts (large numbers of which were rediscovered during the nineteenth century). The language and literature of the present barely merited scholarly treatment. Today the situation has changed almost completely. European and non-European language courses and scholarship now center primarily on the present. The expectation is that the language being imparted will be useful outside one's country of origin and give the learner a certain cultural competence. Historical details, included mainly to give the learner some appreciation of cultural background, are of generally marginal importance.

In subjects like Romance or English literature, which lend themselves to such a present-oriented approach, this change occurs gradually, largely by changing the focus of research and teaching. In Europe, the extent to which the stages of historical language and literatures are still emphasized differs from university to university. Increasingly, however, the student of Romance, German, or English literature is exposed to very little literature from the Middle Ages or the early modern era. This trend is even more pronounced in Sinology or Tibetan and Japanese studies and in the Asian languages generally. In these disciplines, the historical dimension has been largely lost over time and been replaced by the social sciences and economics.

But languages that are exclusively historical and are therefore immune to modernization (e.g., Sumerian, Acadian, Egyptian, Coptic, Old Ethiopian, Syriac, Aramaic, Old Irish, and many others) are facing oblivion. The competence and resources available to study and teach these languages are in steady decline. Some old languages such as those of the Christian Orient can be studied at only a few institutions, and in the case of ancient Oriental studies and Egyptology, which have greater institutional support, research and public interest are, for obvious reasons, focused more on archaeological discoveries. Lavish exhibitions and TV specials satisfy the need for spectacle—and may ensure funding for that reason alone. Latin is very much affected by this trend; at German universities in the past several years, Latin studies has lost more professorships than any of the other arts and sciences.

The End of an Epoch

The approach taken by this volume, which examines the history of the Latin language in order to answer questions about the human culture of language, makes it clear that even dedicated Latinists would do well to set aside the critiques of contemporary culture that they might feel moved to make. Instead of setting up profit-and-loss columns and taking the many losses too personally (not easy to do as a classical scholar), the point is to view the societal loss of Latin in the context of larger processes. This is because, from the perspective of cultural studies, it is clear that Latin is not the only victim. What has happened to Latin has occurred simply because the fundamental beliefs and convictions that reanchored Latin in the early nineteenth century no longer exist. The past few decades have seen the final demise of historicism, the demise of the classical canon, and the replacement of philology as a key area of scholarship.

Let us begin with historicism, not the tradition in and of itself but the entire historicist outlook on the world, which came into being around 1800. As things stand now, we are not far removed from the premodern era up to 1800, when no attention was paid to any of the historical languages. Nor was Latin learned as a historical language but as a timeless and useful world language and as an equally timeless model for how the various vernaculars should be learned. The historical dimension of the Latin literary tradition in a narrower sense played a marginal role. It was not until the nineteenth century that scholars began taking this history seriously. Entering the consciousness of the public as well, an entirely new historical stance toward architecture and art came to the fore. City planners and architects consciously adopted historical models and often clothed technological progress in older, historical forms. And even as the interiors of private homes reflected this new consciousness of the past, so did the way in which people dressed. These were nineteenth-century developments that would not have occurred in this form in earlier times. Even in the Renaissance this narrow predilection for the past had not been as overt. In the nineteenth century, *modern* was a technical term that was applied primarily to technology; it was not, however, an aesthetic concept. One way to conceive of this split between progress and self-stylization might be to consider what might have happened had the computer been invented in the nineteenth century. People would have been more than enthusiastic about the technological possibilities, but laptops might well have been housed in baroque wooden cases. The sleek aesthetic of, say, a Steve Jobs would have been completely out of place. The twentieth century seems largely to have reversed this relationship; one of the attributes of the modern era is that everything old has been stripped away. Twentieth-century modern architecture, for example, speaks in a completely new language, one that is devoid of clear references to historical precedents. The design of computers, automobiles, and even furniture must now embody the aesthetic of an imagined future.

This self-definition by reference to the historical was undoubtedly a major reason that the educational system continued to focus on the literary products of previous centuries. In the case of Latin, this meant retaining it as a tool for disciplining the intellect even though it had lost its function as a means of communication. And of course it is only logical that when people consciously turned away from the past, Latin instruction would come to symbolize the fustiness of days gone by.

Second, in the past several decades, the literary and artistic canon of the educated middle classes, which developed over the course of the eighteenth and nineteenth centuries in Europe and the United States, began to falter. Classical authors from Homer to Cicero, who had played such a central role in the educational system, were dislodged. But large numbers of their more modern national and international counterparts have also been demoted, including Dante and Petrarch, Shakespeare and Milton, Goethe and Schiller, Corneille and Racine, Dickens and Poe. Art and music have experienced a similar shift. Raphael, Rubens, Titian, Turner, Spitzweg, and van Gogh are no longer standard setters, and even Picasso is viewed more in classical than in modern terms. The paradigm shift is even more pronounced in music. The "classical" music of the nineteenth century, from Mozart to Beethoven to Richard Strauss, is having an increasingly difficult time asserting itself in the face of a multiplicity of other musical cultures. In Europe, the middle-class canon of arts and literature has been devalued since World War II, especially in the former Eastern bloc countries, which attempted to free themselves of what they viewed as bourgeois educational traditions. This trend has accelerated since the 1960s, especially in the former West Germany, France, and other European countries. Of course, school curricula are very different in the different countries. But in terms of general education, the "classics," and with them the ancient classics, play at best a subsidiary role.

Third, philology as a scholarly discipline no longer occupies the same position it did in the nineteenth century. Historicist philologists achieved their preeminence at the universities because they were scholarly researchers, not language teachers. The endeavor they were engaged in was a marvelous innovation. They unearthed documents at archaeological sites or by tirelessly digging through the stacks in manuscript libraries. They then deciphered and transcribed, reconstructed the meanings of words and their syntactic relationships, and finally edited and translated entire texts in critical editions. The objects of their attention were old; their techniques and the knowledge they produced were new. They managed to bring back to life languages and language stages that had been completely buried. The historicist philologists of the nineteenth century achieved their preeminence largely because the new philological and linguistic techniques of analysis that they developed were scientifically innovative. Even the classical philologists who studied Latin and Greek were completely won over to these new "scientific" methods. Wilhelm von Humboldt, probably the most important precursor of neohumanist education in Germany, recommended studying Greek and Latin precisely because they were now fixed, that is, no longer in active use. This made them especially suitable for dissection, thereby enabling the student to understand the general structure of language. However, this was clearly no longer the old humanist educational model, which aimed at precise and nuanced expression, always the result of intense practice; a new theoretical understanding of language now formed the basis for comparative linguistics and for the inclusion of Sanskrit as a scholarly discipline as well.

But then one day these new methods were no longer new. The languages of ancient cultures had been discovered, their grammars more or less satisfactorily described, and the classical Greek and Latin texts made available in new critical editions. Philology had more or less reached the stage at which engineering, for example, cedes the methods that it has developed to industry, which exploits them for profitable ends. As a consequence, modern linguistics has been engaged in very different endeavors since the beginning of the twentieth century, mainly studying language production empirically in the present, using mathematical rather than philological methods. Thus the old languages are again falling into neglect as a result of the modernist, scientific paradigm, which places progress at its center and views the constant expansion of what is known as the main task of the university. The mere acquisition of already known knowledge ("prior art," to borrow a phrase from patent law) is most decidedly not what the modern research university is about, and to that extent the mere learning of Latin and Greek has become a dead weight even in classical studies. One of the legacies of historicist philology may well be that it never conclusively settled the question of where scholarship begins and language instruction ends, and the issue remains unresolved to this day.

The decline of philology and historical linguistics has also had an effect on the educational system as a whole. In the nineteenth and early twentieth centuries, language acquisition was theory based, especially at the higher levels, and emphasized grammar. There is evidence that German high schools before 1900 (and perhaps in other countries as well) taught English and French not primarily to enable students to make themselves understood in England or France but to gain insight into the language and an appreciation of the "classical" literary works of those countries. The twentieth century witnessed a clear movement in the opposite direction. Today the goal of foreign-language instruction is to enable students to communicate (especially orally) as quickly as possible; the niceties of grammar are given short shrift and may even be dispensed with altogether. How babies learn their mother tongue is now the guiding model for language acquisition and has been expanded to include the learning of foreign languages.[1] However, Latin did not take part in this shift, although it very well could have because, as we have seen, the humanists aimed to make Latin their students' second mother tongue by constant conversational practice without teaching them grammar. Unfortunately, Latin came to epitomize grammar instruction. Moreover, because grammar was no longer valued, Latin instruction came to be viewed as a bad and an outmoded approach to language.

The Future of Latin

Nonetheless, the expectation that Latin would be expelled from school curricula by the end of the twentieth century, finally achieving the status of ancient Egyptian or Babylonian, useful only to specialists doing arcane historical research, has not come to pass. After decades of heated debate that was critical of traditional education, we seem to have passed into a more reflective phase. This change may be connected with the fact that the final collapse of traditional education has freed Latin, and ancient history generally, from the bothersome role of standard bearer for our cultural heritage. Proclamations of duty and self-declared indispensability always engender rebellion. But as a purely elective subject, Latin has the potential to awaken curiosity in far more students than it would if it were mandatory. For the moment, Latin seems to have found a rather modest place in schools internationally. Rather astonishingly, over the past fifteen years the number of students studying Latin in Germany has risen by more than 10 percent without any intervention by school authorities. And in private schools in the United States, Latin appears to be maintaining itself nicely. Overall, public sentiment toward Latin, which had for decades been roiled by acrimonious arguments between traditionalists and modernists, appears to have become less charged.

Moreover, Latin is cropping up in the most unexpected places. For example, when the American actress Angelina Jolie had the Latin phrase *quod me nutrit me destruit* (What nourishes me also destroys me) tattooed provocatively on her lower abdomen, more than a few young Germans felt inspired to have their own Latin tattoos. Each year I get numerous inquiries asking me to proofread Latin texts before they are immortalized in ink on skin. If only the model Danielle Lloyd had asked, I could have spared her the permanent embarrassment of bad shoulder Latin. Be that as it may, it seems that Latin specialists are no longer viewed simply as hoary emissaries from an ossified, conservative, and elitist discipline but as scholars of an interesting, if perhaps exotic, tradition that might be worth looking into.

It is much too early to speculate on whether this new, more relaxed atmosphere might create the conditions for a new Latin renaissance. Still, I cannot resist venturing some thoughts about the future of Latin in society.

The first and most important one derives basically from the accounts presented in this book. The reason that so many students continue to learn Latin today even though it is unnecessary for communication has less to do with the educational value of the Latin classics than with its two-thousand-year-old history as a world language. That it was the language of the Romans is less important than that Latin, like no other language, makes the history of Europe accessible. Latin classes that focus exclusively on the educational value of reading Cicero, Tacitus, Virgil, and Ovid in the original make an exaggerated claim that does not tally with the historical reality. As I demonstrated at the outset, ancient Latin literature comprises less than 0.01 percent of all extant Latin texts. The other 99.99 percent is the real reason that a broad-based knowledge of Latin still makes sense. Everyone who learns Latin must recognize that it is not the language of the Romans; of all of the ancient languages, it alone may be compared to English today in its role as world language. In addition, those who undertake to learn Latin should have the experience of reading a modern Latin text at least once, whether it is a work of science like Newton's *Principia mathematica,* a piece of neo-Latin literature, or a selection of the millions of Latin inscriptions that dot the European landscape. Without a knowledge of Latin, much of European history must remain opaque.

However, placing Latin as a world language at the center of Latin instruction does not mean that the Roman classics should be excluded. On the contrary, they have always been central to the teaching of Latin, and it is hard to imagine a Latin class to which Cicero would be a stranger. But Cicero can be read in translation. Where knowledge of Latin is more indispensable in a very practical sense is in coming to terms with the countless texts that constitute the two-thousand-year-old tradition. They, along with the myriad texts of other historical cultures, are the written cultural heritage of humanity.

If no one has the skills necessary to read and interpret these texts, this cultural heritage is at risk. If three or four scholars are designated to administer the hundreds of thousands and even millions of pages of poorly legible documents in some far-distant historical language, they are at best archivists who may bring some order to their archives but cannot contribute to bringing this history to life. A document in another language, whether in a modern edition of a manuscript or in the form of inscribed clay tablets or palm leaves is a mute object if no one can read it. The objects unearthed by archaeologists can at least give us a sense of how a palace would have looked three thousand years ago in that particular place or whether a statue of the goddess Venus possessed an erotic aura. But for those who have not mastered the script and the language, written documents are as melodious as musical scores to someone who cannot read them. This is clear and will be admitted by most; however, the consequences for our written cultural heritage usually go unappreciated. There are two reasons for this.

The first is the belief that the most important historical texts have already been deciphered and interpreted. Only the details of textual criticism or the treatment of unimportant texts that for good reason did not make the first cut—that is philology's sole remaining task. This belief, however, is completely erroneous. For example, mountains of cuneiform texts from ancient oriental cultures have been unearthed but have been neither edited nor even read in the most cursory manner. We have no idea how many unknown fragments of the Gilgamesh epic, the oldest epic that we know of, are lying about in museum archives. Fresh excavations continue to add new texts, and no one knows what sensational discoveries the earth still conceals. Other ancient cultures fare no better. The notion persists that the work of philology has largely been completed because in many instances a small corpus of "classical" writings, which cannot be increased by further research in libraries, has been well and thoroughly explored. On the contrary, the vast majority of texts remain unplumbed because they were relegated to the back shelves during the nineteenth century. This is what happened to Latin as well. The canonical Roman writers from Plautus to Cicero to Tacitus have long been accessible in excellently edited volumes and in translation, and the copious literature of late antiquity is largely known and available, although there are still gaps to be closed. But as I have pointed out, the vast majority of Latin texts were written after antiquity came to a close, at a time when Latin was no longer the language of the Romans but was a world language that developed and evolved freely. We do not even have a complete list of existing texts. Even omitting Latin archival material and purely technical texts such as the formulas for concocting drugs—although these might give us valuable insight into the life of apothecaries—it may still be said that 90 percent of all Latin texts are either completely unknown or known only by their title and that 99 percent of all texts are unavailable in modern editions and 99.9 percent of these texts have never been translated. Some aspects of our cultural heritage are about as well understood as ancient Egypt before Jean-François Champollion cracked the hieroglyphic code in 1822. As long as this is the case, people who have mastered Latin will remain indispensable.

The second error is that we vastly underestimate the level of competence needed to engage with historical documents. Our everyday experience with foreign languages gives us the sense that, with a modicum
of effort, we can at least get along in that language. This is especially
the case with passive mastery. After a few weeks of intensive study and
listening, people are generally able to follow a simple conversation or
have a bare-bones understanding of a movie plot. A foreign worker who
is unable to form a correct sentence in German or English will nonetheless be able to follow the supervisor's instructions. And leaving aside issues of style, many researchers in a particular discipline are able to
write intelligible papers in that field in a language they have not completely mastered. But this is possible only because researchers in that
discipline have a communicative context in common and because they
use only a narrow bandwidth of the language. This means that a great
deal can be left unsaid. If you understand that people are talking about
getting together for lunch, all you need to know is the time and place.
Someone who is reading a research paper knows to look only for what
is personally of interest—even if the author may have considered those
particular details to be of lesser importance.

When it comes to historical Latin texts, we often find ourselves in a
similar situation; we can understand the basic drift with only limited
knowledge of the language. For instance, a linguist can evaluate the use
of Latin tenses without having completely mastered the language. Historians with some degree of knowledge of a language can approach
source texts with specific questions as long as they are clear about the
hermeneutics of those texts and know when to consult a language expert. In philosophy and theology, an understanding of the details is
largely dependent on our systematic understanding of the text as a
whole. These sorts of experiences quickly lead us to deny the fundamental hermeneutic difficulties that must be overcome if we are to
understand what a text has to say. In general, however, text documents
in historical languages have no common communicative context. The
languages in which they are written are usually structured very differently from our own, and the texts themselves derive from a completely
different experiential world. Editing, translating, and even understanding such texts all require a very high level of competence in the language, and this in turn is acquired only through intensive study. In the
absence of experts with this competence, not only is it impossible to

make new and unknown texts accessible, but the hermeneutic foundation for understanding known texts such as the ancient Latin classics is
pulled out from under our feet. This leaves us in much the same position as scholars in the Middle Ages struggling with foreign texts. We
are really at a crossroads when it comes to our written cultural heritage. We need many more people than we now have with the kind of
broad-based knowledge of Latin that will enable them to extract meaning, put it in perspective, and make it accessible to the public.

Then there is the matter of how Latin should be learned. Over the
course of the nineteenth century, Latin came to epitomize language as
the sum of its grammatical rules. No thought was given to the development of the kind of spontaneous language competence that enables one
to read longer texts without translating them or that is manifested
throughout the day as people simply go about their lives and talk to
each other.

This is not acceptable because, among the historical languages, Latin
occupies a special place. If we estimate the total number of Latin texts
to be ten thousand times the number of ancient Latin texts, this means
that no other historical language, neither classical Chinese nor classical
Arabic, has left behind a comparable corpus. This fact—even more than
the high quality of a tiny number of texts in the ancient literary canon—is
what cements the importance of Latin. However, dealing with libraries
of Latin texts requires more than the ability to translate a page or two.
It requires real language competence. Because of this, the Latin whose
development as a "fixed" language we have followed is more like modern languages than are other historical languages. When we ask why
and how we should learn Latin as a real language and not merely as a
hermeneutic prerequisite for the interpretation of literature, this is the
perspective from which we must ask that question.

This does not mean that all Latin teaching should aim only at perfect
mastery of the language. Of course, as is the case with all other language
teaching, different levels suffice for different purposes. The existence
of so much Latin in the world today means that most Europeans and
people from countries that have a cultural affinity with Europe will
come into contact with Latin at some time. For this reason alone, there
is utility in having at least the rudiments of the language under one's
belt. With a basic vocabulary of a few hundred words, the ability to

distinguish the nominative case from the accusative, and some feel for constantly recurring structural elements, a person should be able to make sense of the Latin encountered in the course of a day, whether a motto on a university seal or a stray citation in a newspaper or magazine. It is clear that most people who have taken Latin never really go beyond that basic level. Still, it is not nothing; with that much knowledge of a modern language, a person should be able to get to the train station or take the right exit off the highway. Elementary classes in Latin can also impart more than a little about language in general because the structure of Latin differs more from the modern European languages than they differ among themselves and because learning a historical language encourages people to think about linguistic issues. All Latin teachers should bear in mind that there is nothing shameful in an elementary knowledge of Latin. It can be quite useful.

Few students will achieve the ability to understand and translate shorter Latin texts. Where students succeed in mastering the language to that extent, they now have access to the most copious written cultural heritage in the world and are able to make some sense of the innumerable documents from the second century BCE to the nineteenth century CE. Even if they read only excerpts from the Roman classics, they will still get a sense of the fascination that these works have held for readers for two thousand years.

Even such a limited application of Latin is of little consequence, however, in the absence of a group of people who have a deep understanding of the language. The core of any ongoing tradition of Latin must involve a group of people—whether small or large is unimportant—who have internalized Latin as a "normal" language. The cultural heritage of Latin further requires competent Latinists who are able to skim a thousand-page manuscript and quickly separate the gold from the dross. This requires deep competence and experience in writing, reflecting in, and speaking the Latin language. Only people with that kind of training and those skills can appreciate the aesthetic qualities of texts and can understand how a fixed language evolved over time, how other languages affected Latin, and how problems of communication are resolved once the instruction contained in Latin textbooks no longer suffices. The now customary overly scientific approach to Latin instruction that never gets beyond grammatical rules and tedious translation exercises will never get us closer to an understanding of how people spoke and wrote Latin over the centuries or how Latin could have become a world language.

Speaking or writing Latin is a useful historical exercise that can help us to understand the Latin tradition. But the most important aspect of it is not the reconstruction of antiquity along the lines of, say, wearing Roman or medieval clothing to ascertain whether they would have kept people sufficiently warm. The crucial point is more general: speaking Latin is a timeless experiment in how a fixed language is used and adapted to the ever-changing demands of communication. By doing so we may find fresh solutions, as did our forebears in medieval and Renaissance times. We may come to understand what they did, and what the difference is between a "dead language" and a "fixed language."

This is not, I should add, a plea for making a real place in society for Latin or for a rebirth of Latin as a world language. Whether, for example, Latin ever achieves a certain official function within the European Union, as is hoped in some circles, or Latin is given a role in other areas of communication will be decided by history. Since I cannot foretell the future, I cannot render judgment. The new use to which I wish to put Latin is very different. I am suggesting the establishment of a historical cultural practice that is aware of its exclusively historical point of reference, but does not retreat into a purely observational and analytical "scientific" approach, which is what Latin teaching at schools and Latin philology at universities have done for 200 years. Rather, Latin must become a cultural instrument in the elaboration of our history.

Reservations about the spontaneous use of Latin as a cultural instrument are far fewer at present than just a few years ago. The extreme theoretical approach to Latin and mathematics, which reached a high point in the nineteenth century, is slowly giving way to a rediscovery of Latin as a real language. There seems to be a certain curiosity about the language that is manifested when events at which Latin is spoken are commented on in the press, generally without the slightest tone of dismissiveness. Twenty years ago, when the Latinist Wilfried Stroh organized Latin festivals called the LVDI LATINI (which I was very involved in), we were all surprised at the extraordinarily positive public response. Wherever Latin is already being learned, people are increasingly interested in experiencing it as a living language. School and university Latin classes in Germany are increasingly experimenting with spontaneous speech, and when these efforts fail, it is usually because the teachers have not been trained in this aspect of the language, not because the students lack interest. Just a few years ago, classical philologists voiced their concern that speaking Latin was an outdated, prescientific approach to the language. These apprehensions have largely evaporated, and although the practice of speaking is not yet universally recommended, it is now at least deemed worth discussing.

The renewed interest in the active use of Latin also reflects a basic societal change in how history is viewed. A new approach to history is gaining ground on the nineteenth-century model, which favored theory and was an innovative scientific approach at the time. Although that method is still valid, we are now increasingly preoccupied with how people actually lived and with depicting their lives on film, with computer animation, and at historical reenactments. Historical exhibits, which now draw a wide audience, are less concerned with the presentation of high culture than with reconstructing how people spent their time and interacted in the world. Entire villages, including homes and workplaces that can be entered, are reconstructed in accordance with the historical evidence. Historical films have recently experienced an unanticipated popularity, and although historians may quibble about certain questionable portrayals and even approaches, the fact remains that historical events from Troy to the Roman emperors to medieval marketplaces have unexpectedly been turned into public events on a large scale. At least in Europe, these events have been very successful, although they occasionally satisfy a sentimental urge to experience history while turning a blind eye to the ways in which those who lived that past actually experienced it.

On the other hand, a new approach to history based on scholarship is also coming to the fore. The most important example is the performance of "old music," with its detailed reconstruction of historical techniques and instruments. With only the bare notes that have come down to us, medieval, Renaissance, and baroque pieces are performed, taking into account playing habits that would at the time have been so self-evident as not to require notation. The overall effect is heightened by the use of baroque organs, harpsichords, and other instruments, often built for the purpose using the old techniques and materials.

The historical layout of cities is being revived by city planners throughout Europe. This involves a return not only to historical building materials but also to the reconstruction of buildings that have been lost. Examples include the reconstruction of the Frauenkirche in Dresden and the butchers' guild hall in Hildesheim, as well as the plans to reconstruct the Stadtschloss in Berlin and parts of the inner city of Frankfurt. Even modern technologies are adopting the conservator's touch. Many towns now have historic trains pulled by steam locomotives that have been lovingly restored and maintained. Automobile, airplane, and sailboat enthusiasts are no longer limited to viewing the objects of their enthusiasm in museums. They can now build and operate historically accurate models.

The acquisition of "correct" Latin and the living use of the Latin language should undoubtedly be viewed in the context of these retro or throwback cultures. However, there is one big difference. If historians or others dress as Romans or medieval knights, or if musicians use reconstructed baroque violins rather than modern ones in baroque operas, they are imitating a culture of times past. Experiments in conversation and essay writing in Latin are something different. As we have seen, the Latin cultures of the Middle Ages and of the Renaissance started with such restorations of language based not on oral tradition but on grammar books and literature. It is the nature of world languages that nonnative speakers have the same rights in them as native speakers have in their own language. Treating Latin as if it were a living language is therefore not a sentimental step into the past but rather the best way to understand what Latin was as a world language and how it worked. In this sense, the history of Latin is neither special nor exceptional but has much more in common with the linguistic realities of the present day than might at first glance seem apparent.

NOTES

REFERENCES

INDEX

Notes

1. Latin as a World Language

1. Christian Sigmund kindly helped me to calculate the scope of Latin literature.
2. Skutsch (1912, 561).
3. "Prose della volgar lingua," in Pozzi (1978, 78); see also Mayer (1997, 145–147).
4. See Crystal (2007, 141).
5. Lüdtke (2001).
6. Sallaberger (2004); Volk (2000, 2011).
7. Jursa (2008); Soden (1995); Streck (2005).
8. Junge (1984, 1999).
9. Dihle (1992); Schmitz (1997); Hose (2002).
10. Ferguson (1959, 1991); Coulmas 1994; Koch (2008); for Greek, see Niehoff-Panagiotidis (1994).
11. Diem (1974); Fischer (1982); Versteegh (1997).
12. Bartsch (1987); Dissanayake (1989).
13. Koch (1997); Greive (2001).
14. Schlegel (1989, 424); Bär (2000, 214).
15. Zydenbos (2004); Houben (1996); Bhate (1996); Pollock (2001, 2011).
16. See Pollock (2011).

2. The Language of the Empire

1. Compare Gradly (2000), esp. 203–217; Cornell (1995); Adams (2002, 2003, 2007); Baldi (2002).
2. Cornell (1995); Adams (2003); Altheim (1951).
3. Pliny the Elder, *Natural History*, 3.39.
4. See Suerbaum (2003, 83–87); Habinek (1998, 34–68).
5. Varro, ling. Lat. 5; Bernstein (1998, 123).

6. Andreae (2008).

7. Quoted in Meiser (1998, 4); *Corpus inscriptionum Latinarum* I^2 no. 4;

8. Quoted in Meiser (1998, 6); *Corpus inscriptionum Latinarum* I^2 no. 581.

9. Vogt-Spira (2007); Schmidt (1987, 253–254; 2003); Pöschl (1979, 93).

10. See, for example, Neumann and Untermann (1980); Neumann (1977); Kramer (1997); Corradetti (1997).

11. Stroh (2007, 109–112).

12. See Fishman (1993); compare also Janich and Greule (2002).

13. See Pocetti, Poli, and Santini (2005, 93).

14. Funaioli (1907). fr. 15.

15. Michalopoulos (2001).

16. Pöschl (1979); Vogt-Spira (2007). See also Bloomer (1997); Flashar (1979a, 38–41); Habinek (1998) 94–98.

17. Stroh (1983).

18. Zecchini (1998).

19. Epist. to Atticus 4.13.2.

20. Cicero (1967).

21. *Ille se profecisse sciat cui Cicero valde placebit.* Quint. 10.1.112.

22. Quint. 1.6.45.

23. See, in general, Lüdtke (2009); Banniard (1992); Koch (2008).

24. Cowley (1934 [1951], 28).

25. *Cum iumentum, Corpus inscriptionum Latinarum* IV, 8976; *cum soldales,* ibid., 221. Väänänen (1966, 121).

26. *Corpus inscriptionum Latinarum* III, 12700.

27. Kramer (1997, 146).

28. Koch and Österricher (1985).

29. Fuhrmann (1967).

30. Ibid., 62s.

31. Kramer (1983).

32. Kaimio (1979, 239–249).

33. Sidonius, epist. 1.1.2.

34. Norden (1909, vol. 1, 361–367).

35. Schindel (1994).

36. Vössing (1997, 469–476).

37. Herzog (1989, 12, 16, 22).

38. See, for example, McArthur (1998, "World Standard English"); Görlach (1990, "International English"; 2000a, "Englisch als neuer Typ," 1117–1122); Jenkins (2007, 17–30); Grzega (2006b, 2008); Brutt-Griffler (2002, 174–178).

39. Crystal (2007, 185–189).

40. Phillipson (1999).

41. For the grammarians of late antiquity, see in general Peter Lebrecht Schmidt, "Grammatik und Rhetorik," in Herzog (1989, 101–158); Kaster (1997); Holtz (1981).

42. For the educational system see Marrou (1948); Christes, Klein, and Lüth (2006); Vössing (2003); Uhl (1998).
43. Keil (1857).
44. Modern editions: Holtz (1981); Schönberger (2008).
45. Gregor, Epist. 5, 53a (Monumenta Germaniae Historica Epist. I, 2, Berlin 1891, 357): . . . *quia indignum vehementer existimo, ut verba caelestis oraculi restringam sub regulis Donati.*
46. For the innovative character of Donatus's works, see Holtz (1981) and Leonhardt (1989).
47. Text: Keil (1857, vol. 6, 435–442).
48. For this, see also the reference to the Strasbourg oaths in Figure 10.
49. Text: Keil (1857, vol. 4, 355–366); Holtz (1981); Schönberger (2008).
50. Keil (1857, vol. 5, 359, 10–11): Haec sunt declinationis discrimina in numero singulari, quae nos via quadam ad ablativum ducunt, qui declinationem rursum numeri pluralis informat. See also 353, 30ff, 357, 24ff, and 380, 32 *(emendatio loquendi)*. Fögen (1997) does not discuss this sentence.
51. Text: Foca (1974).
52. For Plautus as a model of good Latin, see Deufert (2002).
53. See Göbel (2005).
54. Assmann (1992, 119); Eigler (2003); for Virgil, see Lim (2004).
55. Codex Vaticanus Latinus 3868, fol. 2r (ninth century); illustration, for examaple, in Morello (1997, 76) or Dodwell (2000, plate IIb).
56. Compare Wright (2001, 52).
57. See http://www.fordham.edu/halsall/source/perpetua-excerp.asp.
58. Augustine (1957, 11).

3. Europe's Latin Millennium

1. Poppe (1996).
2. Gneuss (1972); Kelly (1990); Ruhe and Spieß (2000); Burke (2004).
3. Einhard, *Vita Karoli Magni,* ch. 29.
4. Versteegh (1997).
5. Gŭlŭbov (1973); Keipert (1987).
6. Erasmus, *Ciceronianus* xxx.
7. Valla, *De reciprocatione sui et suus libellus,* appeared as an appendix to his *Elegantiae linguae Latini.*
8. Paulsen (1919, vol. 1, 53–70, esp. 65–70).
9. Paulsen (1921, vol. 2, 223).
10. Petrarch, *Epistulae familiares* XIII,5; compare XIV, 1.
11. Beneke (1991, 54–66). Compare McArthur (2002); Crystal (2007).
12. See, for example, Crystal (2007, 59–71). Since 2007, the percentage of non-native speakers of English may have become even larger.
13. See, for example, Brumfit (2001, 116); Jenkins (2007); Seidlhofer (2005a); Brutt-Griffler (2002, 179–181).

14. For the didactic consequences see, for example, Widdowson (2003); Kohn (2007); Seidlhofer (2005b).
15. Lüdtke (2001).
16. See Melchers and Shaw (2003). For the development of a "lingua franca core," see Jenkins (2000): a critical view of Jenkins in Dziubalska-Kołaczyk and Przedlacka (2005).
17. Facsimile with introduction by Bischoff (1973).
18. Pegis (1945).
19. For connections between the history of architecture and the history of language, see Crossley and Clarke (2000); Panofsky (1951). An epilogue concerning the somewhat controversial reception of Panofsky's book is also contained in the 1989 German translation.
20. Versteegh (1997, 121).
21. Abelard (1922, 18).
22. Schneidmüller and Weinfurter (2006).
23. Valla, Lorenzo, *In Pogium libellus primus in dialogo conscriptus*, in Laurentii Vallae opera, Basel 1540, 369–370.
24. For the Italian proto-Renaissance see, for example, Witt (2008).
25. For *grammatica* and *volgare*, see Tavoni (1984) and Ernst et al. (2006, 1563–1581).
26. See Fryde (2000), who unfortunately does not discuss the diglossia situation or the teaching of ancient Greek; Rosenqvist (2007, 151–184).
27. For the "crisi del volgare," see Formentin (1996) and Trabant (2008).
28. For the development of the European national languages, see in general Janich and Greule (2002) and, especially for English, Crystal (1995) and Görlach (1990, 2000a, 2000b). Honey's (1997) focus is on the role of modern standard English. For the Romance languages, see Lebsanft (2000) and Schmitt (2000), and in general compare Holtus, Metzeltin, and Schmitt (1988–2005, vols. 3–7).
29. The best bibliographical information is in Ijesewijn and Sacre (1990, 1998).
30. See especially Knape (2000) and Hirschi (2006).
31. See Böhmer (1897); Fritsch (1990); Kraus (2010). For dialogue books in other European languages, see Ruijsendaal (2002).
32. See, for example, Stotz (2010) and Haye (2005).
33. See Ludwig (1999) for a good example.
34. Assmann (1992, 267).
35. For the development from literary languages to languages for daily conversation, see Haarmann (1993, 210–215, 244–259); Giesecke (1998, 74–77); Burke (2004); Albrecht (1997); Trabant (1983). Bluhm-Faust (2005) gives a detailed analysis of the development in a particular German region.
36. There is no complete analysis of this development; for details and shorter surveys see, for example, Burke (2004); Chartier and Corsi (1996); Blair (1996); Fritsch (1990); Guthmüller (1998); Kühlmann (1980, 1989); Ludwig (2003); Maass (2005); Ostler (2007); Schiewe (1996, 1998); Seidel (2003);

Pörksen (1983). Waquet (2001) provides much interesting information about France.

37. Norden (1909, vol. 2, 767).
38. Stroh (2007, 309).
39. Crystal (2007, 189).
40. See Leonhardt (2010).
41. Johann Amos Comenius, *Lexicon atriale latino-latinum*, Amsterdam 1657, fol. *3v.
42. See http://www.nytimes.com/2012/01/06/opinion/the-new-universal-language-of-plants.html.
43. See http://www.uah.edu/society/readings/1999/fall/Week12.html.

4. World Language without a World

1. Goethe, *Dichtung und Wahrheit* XI; compare Grumach (1949, vol. 1, 80).
2. *Miscellanea Berolinensia ad incrementum scientiarum, ex scriptis Societati Regiae Scientiarum exhibitis edita*, 7 vols. and supplement, Berlin 1710–1744.
3. *Histoire de l'Académie Royale des Sciences et des Belles-Lettres de Berlin*, Berlin 1745.
4. "On a substitué le François au Latin, pour rendre l'usage du Païs Latin se resserent à vuë d'œil, au lieu que la Langue Françoise est à peuprés aujourdhui dans le cas où etoit la Langue Greque du tems de Ciceron . . ." In ibid., préface, 3.
5. Commentarii Societatis Regiae Scientiarum Gottingensis, Tomus I ad annum MDCCLI, Göttingen 1752, XV.
6. For the circumstances of Bach's appointment in Leipzig, see Spitta (1899), Wolff (2001), and especially Siegele (1983–1986, 1999, 2004).
7. See Ruhnke (1966, 178).
8. All documents of the city council's deliberations in *Bach-Dokumente*, edited by the Bach-Archiv, Leipzig, vol. 2, Kassel, 1969.
9. D. Michael Henrici Reinhardi. "De officiis scholarum adversus impietatem seculi," in *Miscellanea Lipsiensia*, vol. 12, Leipzig 1723, 350.
10. Ibid.
11. Io. Matthiae Gesneri Anspacensis institutiones rei scholasticae, Jena 1715, 77.
12. Ibid., caput II, sectio VI, 101–110.
13. Johann Matthias Gersner, Primae lineae isagoges, in Eruditionem universialem, Leipzig 1784, 114–115.
14. Ibid., 100.
15. Spitta (1899, 83).
16. Johann August Ernesti, *Initia doctrinae solidioris*, 3rd ed., Leipzig 1750, fol. *5v.
17. Texts in Johann August Ernesti, Opuscula oratorio-philologica, Leipzig 1794.

18. *Commentarii academiae scientiarum imperialis petropolitanae,* Saint Petersburg 1728–1751.
19. In Leo M. Kaiser (1984, 258–259).
20. See, for example, Meyer Reinhold (1984), Winterer (2002); for a detailed analysis of public speeches, see Hannemann (2008).
21. Nippel (2005).
22. The fact that the years around 1840 marked a break in the development of classical studies was recognized by Paulsen (1919, vol. 2, 445–455) and Landfester (1988, 71).
23. Teuffel (1873, 1).
24. For the role of natural sciences in the first half of the nineteenth century, see, for example, Rusinek (2005).
25. See Landfester (1988, 101).

5. Latin Today

1. For critical overviews, see Rollason (2001) and Mulroy (2003).

References

Abelard, Peter. 1922. *The Story of My Misfortunes*. Translated by Henry Adams Bellows. St. Paul, Minn.: Thomas A. Boyd.

Adams, James N., ed. 2002. *Bilingualism in Ancient Society: Language Contact and the Written Text*. Oxford: Oxford University Press.

———, ed. 2003. *Bilingualism and the Latin Language*. Cambridge: Cambridge University Press.

———. 2007. *The Regional Diversification of Latin 200 BC–AD 600*. Cambridge: Cambridge University Press.

———, Mark Janse, and Simon Swain, eds. 2002. *Bilingualism in Ancient Society: Language Contact and the Written Text*. Oxford: Oxford University Press.

Adrados, Francisco R. 2002. *Geschichte der griechischen Sprache: Von den Anfängen bis heute*. Tübingen: Franke.

Albrecht, Jörn. 1997. "Literatursprache, Schriftsprache (Schreibsprache), Hochsprache, Gemeinsprache: Historische Stadien der Ausprägung der kanonischen Form von Einzelsprachen." In *Kunst und Kommunikation: Betrachtungen zum Medium Sprache in der Romania: Festschrift zum 60. Geburtstag von Richard Baum,* edited by Maria Lieber and Willi Hirdt, 3–12. Tübingen: Stauffenberg.

———. 2003. "Die Standardsprache innerhalb der Architektur europäischer Einzelsprachen." In *Sprachstandards*, vol. 17, *Sociolinguistica,* edited by Ulrich Ammon, Klaus J. Mattheier, and Peter H. Nelde, 11–30. Tübingen: Niemeyer.

Altheim, Franz. 1951. *Geschichte der lateinischen Sprache von den Anfängen bis zum Beginn der Literatur*. Frankfurt: Vittorio Klostermann.

Ammon, Ulrich, Klaus J. Mattheier, and Peter Nelde, eds. 2003. *Sprachstandards,* vol. 17, *Sociolinguistica*. Tübingen: Niemeyer.

Andreae, Bernhard. 2008. *Malerei für die Ewigkeit—die Gräber von Paestum: Eine Ausstellung des Bucerius Kunst Forums 13. Oktober 2007 bis 20. Januar 2008.* Munich: Hirmer.

Aris, Marc-Aeilko, and Hartmut Broszinski. 1996. *Die Glossen zum Jakobusbrief aus dem Viktor-Codex (Bonifatianus 1) in der Hessischen Landesbibliothek zu Fulda.* Fulda: Parzeller.

Assman, Jan. 1992. *Das kulturelle Gedächtnis: Schrift, Erinnerung, und politische Identität in frühen Hochkulturen.* Munich: C. H. Beck.

Auernheimer, Birgit. 2003. *Die Sprachplanung der karolingischen Bildungsreform im Spiegel von Heiligenviten.* Munich: K. G. Saur.

Augustine. 1957. *The City of God against the Pagans.* Translated by George E. McCracken. Loeb Classic Library. Cambridge, Mass.: Harvard University Press.

Ax, Wolfram, ed. 2001. *Von Eleganz und Barbarei: Lateinische Grammatik und Stilistik in Renaissance und Barock.* Wolfenbüttel Forschungen 95. Wiesbaden: Harassowitz.

———, ed. 2005. *Lateinische Lehrer Europas: Fünfzehn Portraits von Varro bis Erasmus von Rotterdam.* Cologne: Böhlau.

Baggioni, Daniel. 1997. *Langues et nations en Europe.* Paris: Payot.

Baldi, Philip. 2002. *Foundations of Latin.* Berlin: de Gruyter.

Banniard, Michel. 1992. *VIVA VOCE: Communication écrite et communication orale du IVe au IXe siècle en Occident latin.* Collection des études augustiniennes: Série Moyen-Âge et temps modernes 25. Paris: Institut des études augustiniennes.

Bär, Jochen A. 2000. "Nation und Sprache in der Sicht romanischer Schriftsteller und Sprachtheoretiker." In *Nation und Sprache: Die Diskussion ihres Verhältnisses in Geschichte und Gegenwart,* edited by Andreas Gardt, 199–228. Berlin: de Gruyter.

Bartsch, Renate, ed. 1987. *Sprachnormen: Theorie und Praxis.* Konzepte der Sprach- und Literaturwissenschaft 38. Tübingen: Max Niemaeyer.

Bauer, Barbara. 1986. *Jesuitische "ars rhetorica" im Zeitalter der Glaubenskämpfe.* Frankfurt: Peter Lang.

Baum, Richard. 1987. *Hochsprache, Literatursprache, Schriftsprache: Materialien zur Charakteristik von Kultursprachen.* Darmstadt: Wissenschaftliche Buchgesellschaft.

Beneke, Jürgen. 1991. "Englisch als lingua franca oder als Medium interkultureller Kommunikation." In *Grenzenloses Sprachenlernen,* edited by Renate Grebing, 54–66. Berlin: Cornelsen.

Bernstein, Frank. 1998. *Ludi publici: Untersuchungen zur Entstehung und Entwicklung der öffentlichen Spiele im republikanischen Rom.* Stuttgart: Franz Steiner.

Besch, Werner, Anne Betten, Oskar Reichmann, and Stefan Sonderegger, eds. 1998–2004. *Sprachgeschichte: Ein Handbuch zur Geschichte der deutschen Sprache,* 4 vols., 2nd ed., rev. and exp. Handbücher zur Sprach- und Kommunikationswissenschaft 2.1–4. Berlin: de Gruyter.

Bhate, Saroja. 1996. "Position of Sanskrit in Public Education and Scientific Research in Modern India." In *Ideology and Status of Sanskrit: Contributions* to the History of the Sanskrit Language, edited by Jan E. M. Houben, 383–400. Leiden: Brill Academic Publishers.

Bischoff, Bernhard. 1973. *Sammelhandschrift Diez B Sant. 66. Grammatici Latini et Catalogus librorum. Vollständige Faksimile-Ausgabe.* Graz: Akademische Druck- und Verlagsanstalt.

Black, Robert. 2001. *Humanism and Education in Medieval and Renaissance Italy: Tradition and Innovation in Latin Schools from the Twelfth to the Fifteenth Century.* Cambridge: Cambridge University Press.

Blair, Ann. 1996. "La persistance du latin comme langue de science à la fin de la Renaissance." In *Sciences et langues en Europe,* edited by Roger Chartier and Pietro Corsi, 21–42. Paris: École des Hautes Études en Sciences Sociales.

Bloomer, W. Martin. 1997. *Latinity and Literary Society at Rome.* Philadelphia: University of Pennsylvania Press.

Bluhm-Faust, Claudia. 2005. *Die Pädagogisierung der deutschen Standardsprache im 19. Jahrhundert am Beispiel Badens.* Variolingua 25. Frankfurt: Peter Lang.

Bömer, Aloys. 1897. *Die lateinischen Schülergespräche der Humanisten: Auszüge mit Einleitungen, Anmerkungen, und Namen- und Sachregister. Quellen für die Schul- und Universitätsgeschichte des 15. und 16. Jahrhunderts.* Berlin: J. Harrwitz Nachfolger.

Briesemeister, Dietrich. 1996. "Mittellatein und Neulatein." In *Lexikon der romanistischen Linguistik,* vol. 2.1, edited by Günther Holtus, 113–120. Tübingen: Max Niemeyer.

Brumfit, Christopher. 2001. *Individual Freedom in Language Teaching.* Oxford: Oxford University Press.

Brutt-Griffler, Janina. 2002. *World English: A Study of Its Development.* Clevedon: Multilingual Matters.

Buck, August. 1987. *Humanismus: Seine europäische Entwicklung in Dokumenten und Darstellungen.* Freiburg: Karl Alber.

Buck, Carl Darling. 1904. *A Grammar of Oscan and Umbrian, with a Collection of Inscriptions and a Glossary.* Boston: Ginn.

Burkard, Thorsten. 2003. "Die lateinische Grammatik im 18. und frühen 19. Jahrhundert: Von einer Wortarten- zu einer Satzgliedgrammatik. Ellipsentheorie, Kasuslehre, Satzglieder." In *Germania latina—Latinitas teutonica: Politik, Wissenschaft, humanistische Kultur vom späten Mittelalter bis in unsere Zeit,* edited by Eckhard Keßler and Heinrich C. Kuhn, 781–830. Munich: Fink.

Burke, Peter. 1993. *The Art of Conversation.* Cambridge: Cambridge University Press.

———. 2004. *Languages and Communities in Early Modern Europe.* Cambridge: Cambridge University Press.

Celenza, Christopher S. 2004. *The Lost Italian Renaissance: Humanists, Historians, and Latin's Legacy.* Baltimore: Johns Hopkins University Press.

Chartier, Roger, and Pietro Corsi, eds. 1996. *Sciences et langues en Europe*. Paris: École des Hautes Études en Sciences Sociales.

Christes, Johannes, Richard Klein, and Christoph Lüth, eds. 2006. *Handbuch der Bildung und Erziehung in der Antike*. Darmstadt: Wissenschaftliche Buchgesellschaft.

Cicero. 1967. *De Oratore*, books I and II, translated by E. W. Sutton. Loeb Classic Library. Cambridge, Mass.: Harvard University Press.

Classen, Carl Joachim. 2003. *Antike Rhetorik im Zeitalter des Humanismus*. Munich: K. G. Saur.

Cornell, Tim J. 1995. *The Beginnings of Rome: Italy and Rome from the Bronze Age to the Punic Wars (c. 1000–264 BC)*. London: Routledge.

Corradetti, Cristina. 1997. "Zur Standardisierung der lateinischen Sprache." In *Standardisierung und Destandardisierung europäischer Nationalsprachen*, edited by Klaus J. Mattheier and Edgar Radtke, 34–40. Frankfurt: Peter Lang.

Coulmas, Florian. 1994. "Schriftlichkeit und Diglossie." *Schrift und Schriftlichkeit: Writing and Its Use. Ein interdisziplinäres Handbuch internationaler Forschung*, vol. 1, edited by Hartmut Günther and Otto Ludwig, 739–745. Berlin: de Gruyter.

Cowley, Malcolm. (1934) 1951. *The Exile's Return*. New York: Viking. Citation refers to the 1951 edition.

Crafton, Anthony. 1997. *Commerce with the Classics: Ancient Books and Renaissance Readers*. Ann Arbor: University of Michigan Press.

Crossley, Paul, and Georgia Clarke, eds. 2000. *Architecture and Language: Constructing Identity in European Architecture, c. 1000–c. 1650*. Cambridge: Cambridge University Press.

Crystal, David. 1995. *The Cambridge Encyclopaedia of the English Language*. Cambridge: Cambridge University Press.

———. 2007. *English as a Global Language*, 2nd ed. Cambridge: Cambridge University Press.

Demandt, Alexander. 2007. *Die Spätantike: Römische Geschichte von Diocletian bis Justinian 284–565 n. Chr.*, 2nd ed., rev. and exp. Handbuch der Altertumswissenschaft III, 6. Munich: C. H. Beck.

Deufert, Marcus. 2002. *Textgeschichte und Rezeption der plautinischen Komödien im Altertum*. Berlin: de Gruyter.

Devoto, Giacomo, ed. 1940. *Tabulae Iguvinae*, 2nd ed. Rome: Publica officinal polygraphica.

———. 1968. *Geschichte der Sprache Roms*. Translated by Ilona Opelt. Heidelberg: Winter.

Diem, Werner. 1974. *Hochsprache und Dialekt im Arabischen: Untersuchungen zur heutigen arabischen Zweisprachigkeit*. Wiesbaden: Harrassowitz.

Dihle, Albrecht. 1977. "Der Beginn des Attizismus." *Antike und Abendland* 23: 162–177.

————. 1989. *Die griechische und lateinische Literatur der Kaiserzeit: Von Augustus bis Justinian.* Munich: C. H. Beck.

————. 1992. "Attizismus." In *Historisches Wörterbuch der Rhetorik,* vol. 1, edited by Gert Ueding, 1163–1176. Tübingen: Niemeyer.

Dissanayake, Wimal. 1989. "Purism, Language, and Creativity: The Sri Lankan Experience." In *The Politics of Language Purism,* edited by Björn H. Jernudd and Michael J. Shapiro, 185–196. Contributions to the Sociology of Language 54. Berlin: de Gruyter.

Dodwell, Charles Reginald. 2000. *Anglo-Saxon Gestures and the Roman Stage.* Cambridge: Cambridge University Press.

Dziubalska-Kołaczyk, Katarzyna, and Joanna Przedlacka, eds. 2005. *English Pronunciation Models: A Changing Scene.* Bern: Peter Lang.

Eck, Werner. 2000. "Latein als Sprache politischer Kommunikation in Städten der östlichen Provinzen." *Chiron* 30: 641–660.

Eckstein, Friedrich August. 1887. *Lateinischer und griechischer Unterricht,* edited by Heinrich Heyden. Leipzig: Fues's Verlag.

Ehlich, Konrad, ed. 2001. *Hochsprachen in Europa: Entstehung, Geltung, Zukunft: Akten zweier Tagungen in München, 2./3. Dezember 1998 und Bad Homburg v.d.H., 18.–20. November 1999.* Freiburg: Fillibach.

Eigler, Ulrich. 2003. *Lectiones vetustatis: Römische Literatur und Geschichte in der lateinischen Literatur der Spätantike.* Zetemata 115. Munich: C. H. Beck.

Elmentaler, Michael. 2003. *Struktur und Wandel vormoderner Schreibsprachen.* Studia linguistica 71. Berlin: de Gruyter.

Ernst, Gerhard, M.-D. Gleßgen, C. Schmitt, and W. Schweickard, eds. 2006. *Romanische Sprachgeschichte.* Handbücher zur Sprach- und Kommunikationswissenschaft 23, 2. Berlin: de Gruyter.

Farrell, Joseph. 2001. *Latin Language and Latin Culture from Ancient to Modern Times.* Cambridge: Cambridge University Press.

Ferguson, Charles A. 1959. "Diglossia." *Word* 15: 325–340.

————. 1991. "Diglossia Revisited." *Southwest Journal of Linguistics* 10: 214–234.

Fischer, Wolfdietrich, ed. 1982. *Grundriß der arabischen Philologie.* Vol. 1, *Sprachwissenschaft.* Wiesbaden: Reichert.

Fishman, Joshua A., ed. 1993. *The Earliest Stage of Language Planning: The "First Congress" Phenomenon.* Berlin: de Gruyter.

Flashar, Hellmut, ed. 1979a. *Le classicisme à Rome aux 1ers siècles avant et après J.-C.* Entretiens sur l'Antiquité 25. Vandœuvres-Genève: Librairie Droz.

————, ed. 1979b, 1983. *Philologie und Hermeneutik im 19. Jahrhundert: Zur Geschichte und Methodologie der Geisteswissenschaften.* 2 vols. Göttingen: Vandenhoeck und Ruprecht.

Foca. 1974. *Ars de nomine et verbo.* Preface, Latin text, and notes by F. Casaceli. Naples: Libreria Scientifica.

Fögen, Thorsten. 1997. "Der Grammatiker Consentius." *Glotta* 74: 164–192.

———. 1998. "Bezüge zwischen antiker und moderner Sprachnormentheorie." *Listy filosophicki* 121: 199–219.

———. 2000. *Patrii sermonis egestas. Einstellungen lateinischer Autoren zu ihrer Muttersprache: Ein Beitrag zum Sprachbewußtsein in der römischen Antike.* Munich: Saur.

Formentin, Vittortio. 1996. "La 'crisi' del volgare nel primo quattrocento." In *Storia della letteratura italiana,* vol. 3, edited by Enrico Malato, 159–210. Rome: Salerno.

Fritsch, Andreas. 1990. *Lateinsprechen im Unterricht: Geschichte—Probleme—Möglichkeiten.* Auxilia 22. Bamberg: C. C. Buchner.

Frühwald, Wolfgang. 2005. "Eine Kultur—viele Sprachen: Zur Identität Europas." In *Europa denkt mehrsprachig. Exemplarisch: Deutsche und französische Kulturwissenschaften,* edited by Fritz Nies, 33–46. Tübingen: Gunter Narr.

Fryde, Edmund. 2000. *The Early Palaeologan Renaissance (1261–1360).* Leiden: Brill Academic Publishers.

Fuhrmann, Horst. 2003. *Cicero und das Seelenheil oder, Wie kam die heidnische Antike durch das christliche Mittelalter?* Munich: K. G. Saur.

Fuhrmann, Manfred. 1967. "Die lateinische Literatur der Spätantike: Ein Betrag zum Kontinuitätsproblem." *Antike und Abendland* 13: 56–79 (also in Manfred Fuhrmann, *Brechungen: Wirkungsgeschichtliche Studien zur antik-europäischen Bildungstradition,* Stuttgart: Klett-Cotta, 1982).

———. 1994. *Rom in der Spätantike: Porträt einer Epoche.* Zurich: Artemis.

———. 2001. *Latein und Europa: Geschichte des gelehrten Unterrichts in Deutschland. Von Karl dem Großen bis Wilhelm II.* Cologne: DuMont.

Funaioli, Gino. 1907. *Grammaticae romanae fragmenta.* Stuttgart: In aedibus B. G. Teubner.

Garber, Klaus, ed. 1989. *Nation und Literatur im Europa der frühen Neuzeit: Akten des 1. Internationalen Osnabrücker Kongresses zur Kulturgeschichte der frühen Neuzeit.* Tübingen: Niemeyer.

———. 2004. "Zur Archäologie nationalliterarischer Diskurse in der frühen Neuzeit." *Neulateinisches Jahrbuch* 6: 51–67.

Gardt, Andreas, ed. 2000. *Nation und Sprache: Die Diskussion ihres Verhältnisses in Geschichte und Gegenwart.* Berlin: de Gruyter.

———, Ulrike Haß-Zumkehr, and Thorsten Roelcke, eds. 1999. *Sprachgeschichte als Kulturgeschichte.* Studia Linguistica Germanica 54. Berlin: de Gruyter.

Giesecke, Michael. 1998. *Sinnenwandel, Sprachwandel, Kulturwandel: Studien zur Vorgeschichte der Informationsgesellschaft.* 2nd rev. ed. Frankfurt: Suhrkamp.

Gneuss, Helmut. 1972. "The Origin of Standard Old English and Æthelwold's School at Winchester." *Anglo-Saxon England* 1: 63–83.

Göbel, Johannes. 2005. "Beobachtungen zum Umgang mit Vergil in den Juvenalscholien." *Philologus* 145: 110–132.

Görlach, Manfred. 1990. *Studies in the History of the English Language.* Heidelberg: Winter.

———. 1999. *English in Nineteenth-Century England: An Introduction.* Cambridge: Cambridge University Press.

———. 2000a. "Englisch als neuer Typ von Weltsprache und europäische Nationalsprachen." In *Sprachgeschichte: Ein Handbuch zur Geschichte der deutschen Sprache,* 4 vols., 2nd ed., rev. and exp., edited by Werner Besch, Anne Betten, Oskar Reichmann, and Stefan Sonderegger. Handbücher zur Sprach- und Kommunikationswissenschaft 2.1–4, vol. 2, 1117–1122. Berlin: de Gruyter.

———. 2000b. "Nation und Sprache: Das Englische." In *Nation und Sprache: Die Diskussion ihres Verhältnisses in Geschichte und Gegenwart,* edited by Andreas Gardt, 613–642. Berlin: de Gruyter.

Goyens, Michèle, and Werner Verbeke, eds. 2003. *The Dawn of the Written Vernacular in Western Europe.* Leuven: Leuven University Press.

Graddol, David. 2000. *The Future of English: A Guide to Forecasting the Popularity of the English Language in the 21st Century.* London: British Council.

Gradley, Guy. 2000. *Ancient Umbria: State, Culture, and Identity in Central Italy from the Iron Age to the Augustan Era.* Oxford: Oxford University Press.

Greive, Artur. 2001. "Sprachbewertung in frühen französischen Grammatiken: Zur Wortgeschichte in der Diskurstradition." In *Gebrauchsgrammatik und Gelehrte Grammatik: Französische Sprachlehrer und Grammatikographie zwischen Maas und Rhein vom 16. bis zum 19. Jahrhundert,* edited by Wolfgang Dahmen, Günter Holtus, and Johannes Kramer, 3–27. Tübingen: Gunter Narr Verlag.

Grendler, Paul F. 1989. *Schooling in Renaissance Italy: Literacy and Learning, 1300–1600.* Baltimore: Johns Hopkins University Press.

Grumach, Ernst. 1949. *Goethe und die Antike,* 2 vols. Potsdam: Eduard Stichnote.

Grzega, Joachim. 2006a. *EuroLinguistischer Parcours: Kernwissen zur europäischen Sprachkultur.* Frankfurt: Verlag für Interkulturelle Kommunikation.

———. 2006b. "Globish and Basic Global English (BGE): Two Alternatives for a Rapid Acquisition of Communicative Competence in a Globalized World?" *Journal for EuroLinguistiX* 3: 1–13.

———. 2008. "Lingua Franca English as a Way to Intercultural and Transcultural Competence: Basic Global English (BGE) and Other Concepts of English as a Lingua Franca." *Journal for EuroLinguistiX* 5: 134–161.

Gŭlŭbov, Ivan. 1973. *Das Altbulgarische und das Latein im europäischen Mittelalter: Zur Problematik der übernationalen Kultursprachen.* Salzburg: Pustet.

Günther, Hartmut, and Otto Ludwig. 1994, 1996. *Schrift und Schriftlichkeit. Writing and Its Use: Ein interdisziplinäres Handbuch internationaler Forschung.*

2 vols. Handbücher zur Sprach- und Kommunikationswissenschaft 10.1–2. Berlin: de Gruyter.

Guthmüller, Bodo, ed. 1998. *Latein und Nationalsprachen in der Renaissance.* Wolfenbütteler Abhandlungen zur Renaissanceforschung 17. Wiesbaden: Harrassowitz.

———, and Wolfgang Müller, eds. 2004. *Dialog und Gesprächskultur in der Renaissance.* Wolfenbütteler Abhandlungen zur Renaissanceforschung 22. Wiesbaden: Harrassowitz.

Haarmann, Harald.1993. *Die Sprachenwelt Europas: Geschichte und Zukunft der Sprachnationen zwischen Atlantik und Ural.* Frankfurt: Campus.

———. 2002. *Lexikon der untergegangenen Sprachen.* Munich: C. H. Beck.

Haase, Wolfgang, and Hildegard Temporini. 1983. *Aufstieg und Niedergang der Römischen Welt,* II 29, vols. 1–2. Sprachen und Schriften. Berlin: de Gruyter.

Habinek, Thomas N. 1998. *The Politics of Latin Literature: Writing, Identity, and Empire in Ancient Rome.* Princeton, N.J.: Princeton University Press.

———, and Alessandro Schiesaro, eds. 1997. *The Roman Cultural Revolution.* Cambridge: Cambridge University Press.

Hagendahl, Harald. 1958. *Latin Fathers and the Classics: A Study on the Apologists, Jerome, and Other Christian Writers.* Gothenburg: University of Gothenburg Press.

Hallet, Judith P. 2009. *British Classics outside England: The Academy and Beyond.* Waco, Tex.: Baylor University Press.

Hammerstein, Notker, ed. 1996. *Handbuch der deutschen Bildungsgeschichte.* Vol. 1, *15. bis 17. Jahrhundert: Von der Renaissance und der Reformation bis zum Ende der Glaubenskämpfe.* Munich: C. H. Beck.

———, ed. 2005. *Handbuch der deutschen Bildungsgeschichte.* Vol. 2, *18. Jahrhundert: Vom späten 17. Jahrhundert bis zur Neuordnung Deutschlands um 1800.* Munich: C. H. Beck.

Hannemann, Denis. 2008. *Klassische Antike und amerikanische Identitätskonstruktion: Untersuchungenzu Festreden der Revolutionszeit und der frühen Republik 1770–1815.* Beiträge zur englischen und amerikanischen Literatur 27. Munich: Ferdinand Schöningh.

Haye, Thomas. 2005. *Lateinische Oralität: Gelehrte Sprache in der mündlichen Kommunikation des hohen und späten Mittelalters.* Berlin: de Gruyter.

Helmchen, Annette. 2005. *Die Entstehung der Nationen im Europa der frühen Neuzeit: Ein integraler Ansatz aus humanistischer Sicht.* Bern: Peter Lang.

Herzog, Reinhart, ed. 1989. *Restauration und Erneuerung.* Vol. 5 of *Handbuch der lateinischen Literatur der Antike.* Munich: C. H. Beck, 1989–.

Hingley, Richard. 2005. *Globalizing Roman Culture: Unity, Diversity, and Empire.* London: Taylor and Francis Group.

Hirschi, Caspar. 2006. "Vorwärts in neue Vergangenheiten: Funktionen des humanistischen Nationalismus in Deutschland." In *Funktionen des Humanismus: Studien zum Nutzen des Neuen in der humanistischen Kultur,* edited by Thomas Maissen and Gerrit Walther, 362–395. Göttingen: Wallstein.

Holtus, Günter, Michael Metzeltin, and Christian Schmitt, eds. 1988–2005. *Lexikon der romanistischen Linguistik.* 12 vols. Tübingen: Max Niemeyer.

Holtz, Louis. 1981, 2010. *Donat et la tradition de l'enseignement grammatical: Étude sur l'Ars Donati et sa diffusion (IVe–IXe siècle) et édition critique.* Paris: Centre national de la recherche scientifique.

Holtz, Sabine, ed. 2002. *Bildung und Herrschaft: Zur Verwissenschaftlichung politischer Führungsschichten im 17. Jahrhundert.* Leinfelden-Echterdingen: DRW-Verlag.

Honey, John. 1997. *Language Is Power: The Story of Standard English and Its Enemies.* London: Faber and Faber.

Hose, Martin. 1999. "Die zweite Begegnung Roms mit den Griechen, oder: Zu den politischen Ursachen des Attizismus." In *Rezeption und Identität: Die kulturelle Auseinandersetzung Roms mit Griechenland als europäisches Paradigma,* edited by Gregor Vogt-Spira and Bettina Rommel, 274–288. Stuttgart: Franz Steiner.

———. 2002. "Die Kehrseite der Memoria, oder über die Notwendigkeit des Vergessens von Literatur." *Antike und Abendland* 48: 1–17.

Houben, Jan E. M., ed. 1996. *Ideology and Status of Sanskrit: Contributions to the History of the Sanskrit Language.* Leiden: Brill Academic Publishers.

Hüllen, Werner, and Friederike Klippel, eds. 2002. *Heilige und profane Sprachen: Die Anfänge des Fremdsprachenunterrichts im westlichen Europa.* Wiesbaden: Harrassowitz.

———, eds. 2005. *Sprachen der Bildung—Bildung durch Sprachen im Deutschland des 18. und 19. Jahrhunderts.* Wiesbaden: Harrassowitz.

Ijsewijn, Jozef, and Dirk Sacré. 1990, 1998. *Companion to Neo-Latin Studies.* 2 vols. Leuven: Leuven University Press.

Janich, Nina, and Albrecht Greule, eds. 2002. *Sprachkulturen in Europa: Ein internationales Handbuch.* Tübingen: Gunter Narr.

Janson, Tore. 2006. *Latein: Die Erfolgsgeschichte einer Sprache* (A Natural History of Latin). Hamburg: Buske.

Jenkins, Jennifer. 2000. *The Phonology of English as an International Language.* Oxford: Oxford University Press.

———. 2003. *World Englishes: A Resource Book for Students.* London: Taylor and Francis Group.

———. 2007. *English as a Lingua Franca: Attitude and Identity.* Oxford: Oxford University Press.

Jernudd, Björn H., and Michael J. Shapiro, eds. 1989. *The Politics of Language Purism.* Contributions to the Sociology of Language 54. Berlin: de Gruyter.

Jones-Davies, Marie-Thérèse, ed. 1991. *Langues et nations au temps de la Renaissance.* Paris: Librairie Klincksieck.

Junge, Friedrich. 1984. "Sprache." In *Lexikon der Ägyptologie*. Vol. 5, *Pyramidenbau–Steingefäße*, edited by Wolfgang Helck, Eberhard Otto, and Wolfhart Westendorf, 1179–1211. Wiesbaden: Harrassowitz.

———. 1999. *Einführung in die Grammatik des Neuägyptischen*, 2nd rev. ed. Wiesbaden: Harrassowitz.

Jursa, Michael. 2008. *Die Babylonier: Geschichte, Gesellschaft, Kultur*, 2nd ed. Munich: C. H. Beck.

Kabatek, Johannes. 2004. *Die bolognesische Renaissance und der Ausbau romanischer Sprachen*. Beihefte zur Zeitschrift für romanische Philologie 321. Tübingen: de Gruyter.

Kaimio, Jorma. 1979. *The Romans and the Greek Language*. Helsinki: Societas Scientiarum Fennica.

Kaiser, Leo M. 1984. *Early American Latin Verse 1625–1825: An Anthology*. Chicago: Bolchazy-Carducci.

Kaster, Robert A. 1997. *Guardians of Language: The Grammarian and Society in Late Antiquity*. Berkeley: University of California Press.

Keil, Heinrich. 1855–1868. *Grammatici latini*, vols. 1–7. Leipzig: B. G. Teubner.

Keipert, Helmut. 1987. "Kirchenslavisch und Latein: Über die Vergleichbarkeit zweier mittelalterlicher Kultursprachen." In *Sprache und Literatur Altrußlands*, edited by G. Birkfellner, 71–109. Münster: Aschendorff.

Kelly, Susan. 1990. "Anglo-Saxon Lay Society and the Written Word." In *The Uses of Literacy in Early Medieval Europe*, edited by Rosamond Kitterick, 39–62. Cambridge: Cambridge University Press.

Keßler, Eckhard, and Heinrich C. Kuhn, eds. 2003. *Germania latina—Latinitas teutonica: Politik, Wissenschaft, humanistische Kultur vom späten Mittelalter bis in unsere Zeit*. Munich: Wilhelm Fink.

Kipf, Stefan. 2006. *Altsprachlicher Unterricht in der Bundesrepublik Deutschland: Historische Entwicklung, didaktische Konzepte, und methodische Grundfragen von der Nachkriegszeit bis zum Ende des 20. Jahrhunderts*. Bamberg: Buchner.

Knape, Joachim. 2000. "Humanismus, Reformation, deutsche Sprache und Nation." In *Nation und Sprache: Die Diskussion ihres Verhältnisses in Geschichte und Gegenwart*, edited by Andreas Gardt, 103–138. Berlin: de Gruyter.

Koch, Peter. 1997. "Diglossie in Frankreich?" In *Frankreich an der Freien Universität*, edited by Winfried Engler, 219–249. Stuttgart: Franz Steiner.

———. 2008. "Le Latin—langue diglossique?" In *Zwischen Babel und Pfingsten: Sprachdifferenzen und Gesprächsverständigung in der Vormoderne (8.-16. Jh.)*, edited by Peter von Moos, 287–316. Vienna: Lit.

———, and Wulf Österreicher. 1985. "Sprache der Nähe—Sprache der Distanz: Mündlichkeit und Schriftlichkeit im Spannungsfeld von Sprachtheorie und Sprachgeschichte." *Romanistisches Jahrbuch* 36: 15–43. Also appears as "Language of Immediacy—Language of Distance: Orality and Literacy from the Perspective of Language Theory and Linguistic

History." In *Communicative Spaces: Variation, Contact, and Change: Papers in Honour of Ursula Schaefer*, edited by Claudia Lange, Beatrix Weber, and Göran Wolf, 441–473. Frankfurt: Peter Lang, 2012.

Kohn, Kurt. 2007. "Englisch als globale Lingua Franca: Eine Herausforderung für die Schule." In *Mehrsprachigkeit bei Kindern und Erwachsenen*, edited by Tanja Anstatt, 207–222. Tübingen: Attempto.

Korenjak, Martin, and Florian Schaffenrath, eds. 2010. *PONTES VI: Der altsprachliche Unterricht in der frühen Neuzeit*. Vienna: Studien Verlag Comparanda.

Kornexl, Lucia. 2000. "Concordes equali consuetudinis usu—Monastische Normierungsbestrebungen und sprachliche Standardisierung in spätenglischer Zeit." In *Prozesse der Normbildung und Normveränderung im mittelalterlichen Europa*, edited by Doris Ruhe and Karl-Heinz Spieß, 237–273. Stuttgart: Franz Steiner.

Kramer, Johannes. 1983. "Der kaiserzeitliche griechisch-lateinische Sprachbund." In *Ziele und Wege der Balkanlinguistik*, edited by Norbert Reiter, 115–131. Balkanologische Veröffentlichungen 8. Wiesbaden: Harrassowitz.

———. 1997. "Geschichte der lateinischen Sprache." In *Einleitung in die lateinische Philologie*, edited by Fritz Graf, 115–162. Stuttgart: B. G. Teubner.

Kraus, Manfred. 2010. "Zwischen ars und usus—Schülergespräche im Lateinunterricht des Humanismus." In *PONTES VI: Der altsprachliche Unterricht in der frühen Neuzeit*, edited by Martin Korenjak and Florian Schaffenrath, 105–118. Vienna: Studien Verlag Comparanda.

Kühlmann, Wilhelm. 1980. "Apologie und Kritik des Lateins im Schrifttum des deutschen Späthumanismus." *Daphnis* 9: 33–63.

———. 1989. "Nationalliteratur und Latinität: Zum Problem der Zweisprachigkeit in der frühneuzeitlichen Literaturbewegung Deutschlands." In *Nation und Literatur im Europa der frühen Neuzeit: Akten des 1. Internationalen Osnabrücker Kongresses zur Kulturgeschichte der frühen Neuzeit*, edited by Klaus Garber, 164–206. Tübingen: Max Niemeyer.

Landfester, Manfred. 1988. *Humanismus und Gesellschaft im 19. Jahrhundert: Untersuchungen zur politischen und gesellschaftlichen Bedeutung der humanistischen Bildung in Deutschland*. Darmstadt: Wissenschaftliche Buchgesellschaft.

Law, Vivien. 1982. *The Insular Latin Grammarians*. Woodbridge, Suffolk: Boydell.

Lebek, Wolfgang Dieter. 1970. *Verba prisca: Die Anfänge des Archaisierens in der lateinischen Beredsamkeit und Geschichtsschreibung*. Hypomnemata 25. Göttingen: Vandenhoeck and Ruprecht.

Lebsanft, Franz. 2000. "Nation und Sprache: das Spanische." In *Nation und Sprache: Die Diskussion ihres Verhältnisses in Geschichte und Gegenwart*, edited by Andreas Gardt, 643–671. Berlin: de Gruyter.

Leonhardt, Jürgen. 1989. *Dimensio syllabarum: Studien zur lateinischen Prosodie-und Verslehre von der Spätantike bis zur frühen Renaissance.* Göttingen: Vandenhoeck and Ruprecht.

———. 2010. "Latein als Weltsprache und als Bildungssprache—Stationen eines Konflikts." In *PONTES VI: Der altsprachliche Unterricht in der frühen Neuzeit,* edited by Martin Korenjak and Florian Schaffenrath, 247–258. Vienna: Studien Verlag Comparanda.

Lim, Richard. 2004. "Augustine, the Grammarians, and the Cultural Authority of Vergil." In *Romane memento: Vergil in the Fourth Century,* edited by Roger Rees, 112–127. London: Duckworth.

Limbach, Jutta. 2008. *Hat Deutsch eine Zukunft? Unsere Sprache in der globalisierten Welt.* Munich: C. H. Beck.

Lüdtke, Helmut. 2001. " 'Tote' Sprachen." In *Language Typology and Language Universals: An International Handbook,* vol. 2, edited by Martin Haspelmath, Ekkehard König, Wulf Österreicher, and Wolfgang Raible, 1678–1691. Berlin: de Gruyter.

———. 2009. *Der Ursprung der romanischen Sprachen: Eine Geschichte der sprachlichen Kommunikation.* Kiel: Westensee-Verlag.

Ludwig, Walther. 1997. "Die neuzeitliche lateinische Literatur seit der Renaissance." In *Einleitung in die lateinische Philologie,* edited by Fritz Graf, 323–356. Stuttgart: B. G. Teubner.

———. 1999. *Vater und Sohn im 16. Jahrhundert: Der Briefwechsel des Wolfgang Reichart genannt Rychardus mit seinem Sohn Zeno (1520–1543).* Hildesheim: Weidmann.

———. 2003. "De linguae Latinae in Germania fatis: Jacob Burckhard und der neuzeitliche Gebrauch der lateinischen Sprache." *Neulateinisches Jahrbuch* 5: 171–185.

———. 2004. *Miscella Latina,* edited by Astrid Steiner-Weber. Hildesheim: Georg Olms.

———. 2008. *Supplementa neolatina: Ausgewählte Aufsätze 2003–2008,* edited by Astrid Steiner-Weber. Hildesheim: Georg Olms.

Maass, Christiane, and Annett Volmer, eds. 2005. *Mehrsprachigkeit in der Renaissance.* Heidelberg: Winter.

Marrou, Henri Irénée. 1948. *Histoire de l'éducation dans l'antiquité.* Paris: Éditions du Seuil.

Mattheier, Klaus J. 2000. "Die Herausbildung neuzeitlicher Schriftsprachen." In *Sprachgeschichte: Ein Handbuch zur Geschichte der deutschen Sprache,* 4 vols., 2nd ed., rev. and exp., edited by Werner Besch, Anne Betten, Oskar Reichmann, and Stefan Sonderegger. Handbücher zur Sprach- und Kommunikationswissenschaft 2.1–4, vol. 2, 1117–1122. Berlin: de Gruyter.

———, and Edgar Radtke, eds. 1997. *Standardisierung und Destandardisierung europäischer Nationalsprachen.* Frankfurt: Peter Lang.

Mayer, Kathrin. 1997. "Die *questione della lingua:* Auf der Suche nach der einen Sprache für die Nation." In *Was heißt hier "fremd"? Studien zu Sprache und Fremdheit,* edited by Dirk Naguschewski and Jürgen Trabant, 137–149. Berlin: Akademie Verlag.

McArthur, Tom. 1998. *The English Languages.* Cambridge: Cambridge University Press.

———. 2002. *The Oxford Guide to World English.* Oxford: Oxford University Press.

McKitterick, Rosamond, ed. 1990. *The Uses of Literacy in Early Medieval Europe.* Cambridge: Cambridge University Press.

Meiser, Gerhard. 1998. *Historische Laut- und Formenlehre der lateinischen Sprache.* Darmstadt: Wissenschaftliche Buchgesellschaft.

Melchers, Gunnel, and Philip Shaw, eds. 2003. *World Englishes.* London: Taylor and Francis.

Meyer, Reinhold. 1984. *Classica Americana: The Greek and Roman Heritage in the United States.* Detroit: Wayne State University Press.

Michalopoulos, Andreas. 2001. *Ancient Etymologies in Ovid's Metamorphoses: A Commented Lexicon.* Leeds: Francis Cairns.

Moos, Peter von, ed. 2008. *Zwischen Babel und Pfingsten: Sprachdifferenzen und Gesprächsverständigung in der Vormoderne (8.-16. Jh.).* Vienna: Lit.

Morello, Giovanni, ed. 1997. *Kostbarkeiten der Buchkunst: Illuminationen klassischer Werke von Archimedes bis Vergil.* Stuttgart: Belser.

Moss, Ann. 2003. *Renaissance Truth and the Latin Language Turn.* Oxford: Oxford University Press.

Muhlack, Ulrich, ed. 2003. *Historisierung und gesellschaftlicher Wandel in Deutschland im 19. Jahrhundert.* Berlin: Akademie Verlag.

Müller, Gernot Michael. 2003. "Auf der Suche nach der rechten Latinität: Sprachreflexion und akademisches Selbstverständnis in den Dialogen Giovanni Pontanos." *Neulateinisches Jahrbuch* 5: 219–244.

Müller, Jan-Dirk, and Jörg Robert, eds. 2007. *Maske und Mosaik: Poetik, Sprache, Wissen im 16. Jahrhundert.* Vienna: Lit.

Müller, Roman. 2001. *Sprachbewußtsein und Sprachvariation im lateinischen Schrifttum der Antike.* Munich: C. H. Beck.

———. 2003. "Konzeptionen des Sprachwandels in der Antike." *Hermes* 131: 196–221.

Mulroy, David. 2003. *The War against Grammar.* Portsmouth, N.H.: Boynton-Cook.

Münkler, Herfried. 2005. *Imperien: Die Logik der Weltherrschaft—vom alten Rom bis zu den Vereinigten Staaten.* Berlin: Rowohlt Taschenbuch.

Neumann, Günter. 1977. "Die Normierung des Lateinischen." *Gymnasium* 84: 199–212.

———, and Jürgen Untermann, eds. 1980. "Die Sprachen im römischen Reich der Kaiserzeit." Colloquium, April 8–10, 1974. Bonn: Habelt in Komm.

Niehoff-Panagiotidis, Johannes. 1994. *Koine und Diglossie*. Wiesbaden: Harrassowitz.

Nies, Fritz, ed. 2005. *Europa denkt mehrsprachig. Exemplarisch: Deutsche und französische Kulturwissenschaften*. Tübingen: Gunter Narr.

Nippel, Winfried. 2005. "Die Antike in der amerikanischen und französischen Revolution." In *Popolo e potere nel mondo antico: Atti del convegno internazionale Cividale del Friuli, 23–25 settembre 2004*, edited by G. Urso, 259–269. Pisa: Editioni ETS.

Norden, Eduard. 1909. *Die antike Kunstprosa*, 2nd ed., 2 vols. Leipzig: B. G. Teubner.

Österreicher, Wulf. 2005. "Mehrsprachigkeit als Bedingung geisteswissenschaftlicher Produktivität und die Aufgabe einer Hierarchisierung der europäischen Sprachen." In *Sprache, Bewußtsein, Stil: Theoretische und historische Perspektiven*, edited by Daniel Jacob and Thomas Krefeld, 97–112. Tübingen: Narr Francke Attempto.

Ostler, Nicholas. 2005. *Empires of the Word: A Language History of the World*. London: HarperCollins.

———. 2007. *Ad Infinitum: A Biography of Latin*. London: HarperCollins.

Overhoff, Jürgen. 2004. *Die Frühgeschichte des Philanthropismus (1715–1771): Konstitutionsbedingungen, Praxisfelder, und Wirkung eines pädagogischen Reformprogramms im Zeitalter der Aufklärung*. Tübingen: Max Niemeyer.

Palmer, Leonard R. 1954. *The Latin Language*. Norman: University of Oklahoma Press.

Panofsky, Erwin. 1951. *Gothic Architecture and Scholasticism*. Latrobe, Penn.: Archabbey. Also appears as *Gotische Architektur und Scholastik: Zur Analogie von Kunst, Philosophie und Theologie im Mittelalter*, edited and with a preface by Thomas Frangenberg; translated by Helga Willinghöfer. Cologne: Dumont, 1989.

Paulsen, Friedrich. 1919, 1921. *Geschichte des gelehrten Unterrichts auf den deutschen Schulen und Universitäten vom Ausgang des Mittelalters bis zur Gegenwart: Mit besonderer Rücksicht auf den klassischen Unterricht*, 3rd exp. ed., 2 vols. Leipzig: Veit.

Pegis, Anton C., ed. 1945. *Basic Writings of Saint Thomas Aquinas*, vol. 2. New York: Random House.

Perini, Giorgio Bernardi, ed. 2004. *Il Latino nell'età dell'umanesimo: Atti del convegno Mantova, 26–27 ottobre 2001*. Florence: Leo S. Olschki.

Petersmann, Hubert. 1989. "Die Urbanisierung des römischen Reiches im Lichte der lateinischen Sprache." *Gymnasium* 96: 406–428.

———, and Astrid Petersmann. 2004. "Standardisierung und Destandardisierung der lateinischen Sprache." In *Studia Humanitatis ac Litterarum Trifolio Heidelbergensi dedicata: Festschrift für Eckhard Christmann, Wilfried Edelmaier, und Rudolf Kettemann*, edited by Angela Hornung, Christian Jäkel, and Werner Schubert, 235–254. Frankfurt: Peter Lang.

Petzold, Martin. 1998. "Bachs Prüfung vor dem kurfürstlichen Konsistorium in Leipzig." *Bach-Jahrbuch* 84: 19–30.

Phillipson, Robert. 1999. "Voice in Global English: Unheard Chords in Crystal Loud and Clear." *Applied Linguistics* 20(2): 265–276.

Pocetti, Paolo, Diego Poli, and Carlo Santini, eds. 2005. *Eine Geschichte der lateinischen Sprache: Ausformung, Sprachgebrauch, Kommunikation.* Tübingen: Francke.

Pollock, Sheldon. 2001. "The Death of Sanskrit." *Comparative Studies in History and Society* 43(2): 392–426.

———. 2011. "Crisis in the Classics." *Social Research* 78: 21–48.

Polomé, Edgar C. 1983. "The Linguistic Situation in the Western Provinces of the Roman Empire." In *Aufstieg und Niedergang der Römischen Welt,* II 29, vols. 1–2, edited by Wolfgang Haase and Hildegard Temporini, 509–553. Sprachen und Schriften. Berlin: de Gruyter.

Poppe, Erich. 1996. "Die mittelalterliche irische Abhandlung Auraicept na n-Éces und ihr geistesgeschichtlicher Standort." In *Theorie und Rekonstruktion: Trierer Studien zur Geschichte der Linguistik,* edited by Klaus D. Dutz and Hans J. Niederehe, 55–74. Münster: Nodus.

Pörksen, Uwe. 1983. "Der Übergang vom Gelehrtenlatein zur deutschen Wissenschaftssprache: Zur frühen deutschen Fachliteratur und Fachsprache in den naturwissenschaftlichen und mathematischen Fächern (ca. 1500–1800)." *Zeitschrift für Literaturwissenschaft und Linguistik* 51/52: 227–258.

Pöschl, Viktor. 1979. "Grundzüge der augusteischen Klassik." In *Kunst und Wirklichkeitserfahrung in der Dichtung, Abhandlungen, und Aufsätze zur römischen Poesie,* edited by Wolf Lüder Liebermann, 21–34. Heidelberg: Winter.

Poultney, James Wilson. 1959. *The Bronze Tables of Iguvium.* Baltimore: American Philological Association.

Pozzi, Mario, ed. 1978. *Trattatisti del cinquecento.* Naples: R. Ricciardi.

Rädle, Fidel. 1988. "Lateinisches Theater fürs Volk: Zum Problem der frühen Jesuitendramas." In *Zwischen Festtag und Alltag,* edited by Wolfgang Raible, 133–147. Tübingen: Gunter Narr.

Raible, Wolfgang. 1996. "Relatinisierungstendenzen." In *Lexikon der Romanistischen Linguistik,* vol. 2, 1, edited by Günter Holtus, Michael Metzeltin, and Christian Schmitt, 120–134. Tübingen: Max Niemeyer.

Reynolds, Leighton D., and Nigel G. Wilson, eds. 1991. *Scribes and Scholars: A Guide to the Transmission of Greek and Latin Literature.* Oxford: Oxford University Press.

Rollason, Christopher. 2001. "The Question of Standard English: Some Considerations on John Honey's *Language Is Power.*" *Terminologie et Traduction. Terminology and Translation: A Journal of the Language Services of the European Institutions* 3: 30–60.

Rosenqvist, Jan Olof. 2007. *Die byzantinische Literatur vom 6. Jahrhundert bis zum Fall Konstantinopels 1453.* Berlin: de Gruyter.

Ruhe, Doris, and Karl-Heinz Spieß, eds. 2000. *Prozesse der Normbildung und Normveränderung im mittelalterlichen Europa.* Stuttgart: Franz Steiner.

Ruhnke, Martin. 1966. "Georg Philipp Telemann." In *Die Musik in Geschichte und Gegenwart,* vol. 13, edited by Friedrich Blume, 175–211. Kassel: Bärenreiter.

Ruijsendaal, Els. 2002. "Mehrsprachige Gesprächsbüchlein und Fremdsprachengrammatiken: Vom Niederländischen zum Italienischen und das Französische in der Mitte." In *Heilige und profane Sprachen: Die Anfänge des Fremdsprachenunterrichts im westlichen Europa,* edited by Werner Hüllen and Friederike Klippel, 199–209. Wiesbaden: Harrassowitz.

Rusinek, Bernd-A. 2005. " 'Bildung' als Kampfplatz: Zur Auseinandersetzung zwischen Geistes- und Naturwissenschaften im 19 Jahrhundert." *Jahrbuch für Historische Bildungsforschung* 11: 315–350.

Sabbadini, Remigio. 1886. *Storia del ciceronianismo e di altre questioni letterarie nell'età della rinascenza.* Turin: Ermanno Loescher.

Sáenz-Badillos, Angel. 1993. *A History of the Hebrew Language.* Translated by John Elwolde. Cambridge: Cambridge University Press.

Sallaberger, Walther. 2004. "Das Ende des Sumerischen: Tod und Nachleben einer altmesopotamischen Sprache." In *Sprachtod und Sprachgeburt,* edited by Peter Schrijver and Peter-Arnold Mumm, 108–140. Münchner Forschungen zur historischen Sprachwissenschaft 2. Bremen: Hempen.

Sallmann, Klaus, ed. 1997. *Die Literatur des Umbruchs.* Vol. 4 of *Handbuch der lateinischen Literatur der Antike.* Munichi: C. H. Beck, 1989–.

Schiewe, Jürgen. 1996. *Sprachenwechsel—Funktionswandel—Austausch der Denkstile: Die Universität Freiburg zwischen Latein und Deutsch.* Tübingen: Max Niemeyer.

———. 1998. *Die Macht der Sprache: Eine Geschichte der Sprachkritik von der Antike bis zur Gegenwart.* Munich: C. H. Beck.

———. 2003. "Über die Ausgliederung der Sprachwissenschaft aus der Sprachkritik: Wissenschaftsgeschichtliche Überlegungen zum Verhältnis von Normsetzung, Normreflexion, und Normverzicht. In *Sprache und mehr: Ansichten einer Linguistik der sprachlichen Praxis,* edited by Angelika Linke, 401–416. Tübingen: Max Niemeyer.

Schindel, Ulrich. 1994. "Archaismus als Epochenbegriff: Zum Selbstverständnis des 2. Jahrhunderts." *Hermes* 122: 327–341.

Schindling, Anton. 1977. *Humanistische Hochschule und freie Reichsstadt: Gymnasium und Akademie in Straßburg 1538–1621.* Wiesbaden: Steiner.

Schlegel, August Wilhelm. 1989. *Vorlesungen über schöne Literatur und Kunst, 1798–1803.* Vol. 1 of *Kritische Ausgabe der Vorlesungen,* ed. with commentary and epilogue by Ernst Behler. Paderborn: Ferdinand Schöningh.

Schmidt, Ernst August. 1987. "Historische Typlogie: Orientierungsfunktionen von Kanon in der griechischen und römischen Literatur." In *Kanon und Zensur: Archäologie der literarischen Kommunikation,* vol. 2, edited by Jan Assmann and Aleida Assmann, 247–258. Munich: Fink.

————. 2003. *Augusteische Literatur: System in Bewegung.* Heidelberg: Winter.

Schmitt, Christian. 2000. "Sprach- und Nationenbildung in Westeuropa (bis zur Jahrtausendwende)." In *Sprachgeschichte: Ein Handbuch zur Geschichte der deutschen Sprache,* 4 vols., 2nd ed., rev. and exp., edited by Werner Besch, Anne Betten, Oskar Reichmann, and Stefan Sonderegger. Handbücher zur Sprach- und Kommunikationswissenschaft 2.1–4, vol. 2, 1015–1029. Berlin: de Gruyter.

Schmitt, Rüdiger. 1983. "Die Sprachverhältnisse in den östlichen Provinzen des römischen Reiches." In *Aufstieg und Niedergang der Römischen Welt,* II 29, vol. 2, edited by Wolfgang Haase and Hildegard Temporini, 554–586. Sprachen und Schriften. Berlin: de Gruyter.

Schmitz, Thomas. 1997. *Bildung und Macht: Zur sozialen und politischen Funktion der zweiten Sophistik in der griechischen Welt der Kaiserzeit.* Munich: C. H. Beck.

Schneidmüller, Bernd, and Stefan Weinfurter, eds. 2006. *Ordnungskonfigurationen im hohen Mittelalter.* Ostfildern: Thorbecke.

Schönberger, Axel, ed. 2008. *Die Ars minor des Aelius Donatus: Lateinischer Text und kommentierte deutsche Übersetzung einer antiken Elementargrammatik aus dem 4. Jahrhundert nach Christus.* Frankfurt: Valentia-Verlag.

Schrijver, Peter, and Peter-Arnold Mumm, eds. 2004. *Sprachtod und Sprachgeburt.* Münchner Forschungen zur historischen Sprachwissenschaft 2. Bremen: Hempen.

Seidel, Robert. 2003. "Die 'tote Sprache' und das Originalgenie: Poetologische und literatursoziologische Transformationsprozesse in der Geschichte." In *Lateinische Lyrik der frühen Neuzeit,* edited by Beate Czapla, Ralf Georg Czapla, and Robert Seidel, 422–448. Tübingen: Max Niemeyer.

Seidensticker, Bernd, ed. 2006. *Altertumswissenschaften in Berlin um 1800 an Akademie, Schule, und Universität.* Hannover: Wehrhahn.

Seidlhofer, Barbara. 2005a. "Language Variation and Change: The Case of English as a Lingua Franca." In *English Pronunciation Models: A Changing Scene,* edited by Katarzyna Dziubalska-Kołaczyk and Joanna Przedlacka, 59–75. Bern: Peter Lang.

————. 2005b. "Standard Future or Half-Baked Quackery? Descriptive and Pedagogic Bearings on the Globalisation of English." In *The Globalisation of English and the English Language Classroom,* edited by Claus Gnutzmann and Frauke Intemann, 155–169. Tübingen: Gunter Narr.

Siebenborn, Elmar. 1976. *Die Lehre von der Sprachrichtigkeit und ihren Kriterien: Studien zur antiken normativen Grammatik.* Amsterdam: B. R. Grüner.

Siegele, Ulrich. 1983–1986. "Bachs Stellung in der Leipziger Kulturpolitik seiner Zeit." *Bach-Jahrbuch* 69 (1983): 7–50; 70 (1984): 7–43; 72 (1986): 33–67.

————. 1999. "Bachs politisches Profil, oder Wo bleibt die Musik?" In *Bach-Handbuch,* edited by Konrad Küster, 6–30. Kassel: Bärenreiter.

————. 2004. "Im Blick von Bach auf Telemann: Arten, ein Leben zu betrachten." In *Biographie und Kunst als historiographisches Problem,* edited by Joachim Kremer, Wolf Hobohm, and Wolfgang Ruf, 49–89. Hildesheim: Olms.

Skutsch, Franz. 1912. "Die lateinische Sprache." In *Die Kultur der Gegenwart.* Vol. 1, sec. 8, *Die griechische und lateinische Literatur und Sprache,* 3rd ed., rev. and exp., edited by Paul Hinneberg, 512–565. Leipzig: B. G. Teubner.

Soden, Wolfram v. 1995. *Grundriß der akkadischen Grammatik,* 3rd rev. ed. Analecta Orientalia 33. Rome: Editrice Pontificio Istituto Biblico.

Spitta, Philipp. 1899. *Johann Sebastian Bach,* 2 vols. Translated by Clara Bell and J. A. Fuller Maitland. London: Novello.

Stotz, Peter. 1996–2004. *Handbuch zur lateinischen Sprache des Mittelalters,* 5 vols. Handbuch der Altertumswissenschaft II, 5. Munich: C. H. Beck.

———. 2003. "Normgebundenheit, Normen-Entfaltung, und Spontaneität im mittelalterlichen Latein." In *The Dawn of the Written Vernacular in Western Europe,* edited by Michèle Goyens and Werner Verbeke, 39–50. Leuven: Leuven University Press.

———. 2010. "Miteinander reden lernen in der Sprache Roms—Lateinische Gesprächsszenen aus dem hochmittelalterlichen England." In *PONTES VI: Der altsprachliche Unterricht in der frühen Neuzeit,* edited by Martin Korenjak and Florian Schaffenrath, 11–22. Vienna: Studien Verlag Comparanda.

Streck, Michael P. 2005. "Akkadisch." In *Sprachen des alten Orients,* ed. Michael P. Streck, 44–79. Darmstadt: Wissenschaftliche Buchgesellschaft.

Stroh, Wilfried. 1983. "Ciceros demosthenische Redezyklen." *Museum Helveticum* 40: 35–50.

———, ed. 1994. "Latein sprechen." *Der altsprachliche Unterricht* 37(5).

———. 2004. Ein unsterbliches Gespenst: Latein. In *Sprachtod und Sprachgeburt,* edited by Peter Schrijver and Peter-Arnold Mumm, 77–107. Münchner Forschungen zur historischen Sprachwissenschaft 2. Bremen: Hempen.

———. 2007. *Latein ist tot, es lebe Latein! Kleine Geschichte einer großen Sprache.* Berlin: List.

Suerbaum, Werner, ed. 2003. *Die archaische Literatur.* Vol. 1 of *Handbuch der lateinischen Literatur der Antike.* Munich: C. H. Beck, 1989–.

Swain, Simon. 2002. *Hellenism and Empire: Language Classicism and Power in the Greek World, AD 50–250.* Oxford: Oxford University Press.

Tavoni, Mirko. 1984. *Latino, grammatica, volgare: Storia di una questione umanistica.* Padua: Editrice Antenore.

Teuffel, W. S. 1873. *A History of Roman Literature.* Translated by Wilhelm Wagner. London: George Bell and Sons.

Trabant, Jürgen. 1983. "Das Andere der Fachsprache: Die Emanzipation der Sprache von der Fachsprache im neuzeitlichen europäischen Sprachdenken." *Zeitschrift für Literaturwissenschaft und Linguistik* 51/52: 27–47.

———. 2003. *Mithridates im Paradies: Kleine Geschichte des Sprachdenkens.* Munich: C. H. Beck.

———. 2008. *Was ist Sprache?* Munich: C. H. Beck.

Treadgold, Warren, ed. *Renaissances before the Renaissance: Cultural Revivals of Late Antiquity and the Middle Ages.* Stanford, Calif.: Stanford University Press.

Uhl, Anne. 1998. *Servius als Sprachlehrer: Zur Sprachrichtigkeit in der exegetischen Praxis des spätantiken Grammatikerunterrichts.* Göttingen: Vandenhoeck and Ruprecht.

Väänänen, Veiko. 1966. *Le Latin vulgaire des inscriptions pompéiennes,* 3rd ed. Berlin: Akademie Verlag.

Verbaal, Wim, Yanick Maes, and Jan Papy, eds. 2007, 2009. *Latinitas perennis.* Vol. 1, *The Continuity of Latin Literature.* Vol. 2, *Appropriation and Latin Literature.* Leiden: Brill Academic Publishers.

Versteegh, Kees. 1986. "Latinitas, Hellenismos, 'Arabiyya.'" *Historiographia Linguistica* 13(2–3): 425–448.

———. 1997. *The Arabic Language.* Edinburgh: Edinburgh University Press.

———. 2002. "Dead or Alive? The Status of the Standard Language." In *Bilingualism in Ancient Society: Language Contact and the Written Text,* edited by James N. Adams, Mark Janse, and Simon Swain, 52–74. Oxford: Oxford University Press.

Vogt-Spira, Gregor. 2007, 2009. "'The Classics' as Potential for the Future." In *Latinitas perennis,* edited by Wim Verbaal, Yanick Maes, and Jan Papy, 64–92. Leiden: Brill Academic Publishers.

———, and Bettina Rommel, eds. 1999. *Rezeption und Identität: Die kulturelle Auseinandersetzung Roms mit Griechenland als europäisches Paradigma.* Stuttgart: Franz Steiner.

Volk, Konrad. 2000. "Edubba'a und Edubba'a-Literatur: Rätsel und Lösungen." *Zeitschrift für Assyriologie und Vorderasiatische Archäologie* 90: 1–30.

———. 2012. "Über Bildung und Ausbildung in Babylonien am Anfang des 2. Jahrtausends v. Chr." *Orientalia Nova Series* 80, 269–299.

Vössing, Konrad. 1997. *Schule und Bildung im Nordafrika der römischen Kaiserzeit.* Brussels: Latomus.

———. 2003. "Die Geschichte der römischen Schule: Ein Abriß vor dem Hintergrund der neueren Forschung." *Gymnasium* 110: 455–497.

Waquet, Françoise. 2001. *Latin, or the Empire of a Sign: From the Sixteenth to the Twentieth Centuries.* Translated by John Howe. London: Verso.

Whitmarsh, Tim. 2001. *Greek Literature and the Roman Empire: The Politics of Imitation.* Oxford: Oxford University Press.

Widdowson, Henry. 2003. *Defining Issues in English Language Teaching.* Oxford: Oxford University Press.

Wiersing, Erhard, ed. 2001. *Humanismus und Menschenbildung: Zur Geschichte, Gegenwart, und Zukunft der bildenden Begegnung der Europäer mit der Kultur der Griechen und Römer.* Essen: Blaue Eule.

Winterer, Caroline. 2002. *The Culture of Classicism: Ancient Greece and Rome in American Intellectual Life, 1780–1910.* Baltimore: Johns Hopkins University Press.

Witt, Ronald G. 2008. "The Early Communal Historians, Forerunners of the Italian Humanists." In *The Renaissance in the Streets, Schools, and Studies: Essays in Honour of Paul F. Grendler,* edited by Konrad Eisenbichler and Nicholas Terpstra, 103–124. Toronto: CRRS Publications.

———. 2012. *The Two Latin Cultures and the Foundation of Renaissance Humanism in Medieval Italy.* Cambridge: Cambridge University Press.

Wolff, Christopher. 2001. *Johann Sebastian Bach: The Learned Musician.* Oxford: Oxford University Press.

Woodard, Roger, ed. 2004. *The Cambridge Encyclopedia of the World's Ancient Languages.* Cambridge: Cambridge University Press.

Wright, David H. 2001. *Der Vergilius Romanus und die Ursprünge des mittelalterlichen Buches.* Stuttgart: Belser.

Yaron, R. 1995. "The Competitive Coexistence of Latin and Greek in the Roman Empire." In *Collatio Iuris Romani: Études dédiées à Hans Ankum à l'occasion de son 65e anniversaire,* vol. 2, edited by Robert Feenstra et al., 657–664. Amsterdam: J. C. Gieben.

Zanker, Paul. 1987. *Augustus und die Macht der Bilder (The Power of Images in the Age of Augustus).* Munich: C. H. Beck.

Zecchini, Giuseppe. 1998. "Die staatstheoretische Debatte der caesarischen Zeit." In *Politische Theorie und Praxis im Altertum,* edited by Wolfang Schuller, 149–165. Darmstadt: Wissenschaftliche Buchgesellschaft.

Zilliacus, Henrik. 1935. *Zum Kampf der Weltsprachen im oströmischen Reich.* Helsingfors: Universität Helsingfors.

Ziolkowski, Jan. 1991. "Cultural Diglossia and the Nature of Medieval Latin Literature." In *The Ballad and Oral Literature,* edited by Joseph Harris, 193–213. Cambridge, Mass.: Harvard University Press.

———. 1997. "Die mittellateinische Literatur." In *Einleitung in die Lateinische Philologie,* edited by Fritz Graf, 297–322. Stuttgart: B. G. Teubner.

Zydenbos, Robert. 2004. "Sanskrit: Ewige Sprache der Götter, wiedergeboren und noch immer da." In *Schrijver and Mumm,* edited by P. Schrijver and P. Mumm, 278–300. Bremen: Hempen.

Index